The Market Approach to Valuing Businesses

Second Edition

The Market Approach to Valuing Businesses

Second Edition

Shannon P. Pratt, CFA, FASA, MCBA, MCBC, CM&A

JOHN WILEY & SONS, INC.

Library of Congress Cataloging-in-Publication Data

Pratt, Shannon P.
  The market approach to valuing businesses / Shannon P. Pratt.—2nd ed.
    p. cm.
  Includes bibliographical references and index.
  ISBN-13: 978-0-471-69654-4 (cloth)
  ISBN-10: 0-471-69654-4 (cloth)
  1. Corporations—Valuation.   2. Corporations—Valuation—Law and legislation—United States.   I. Title
  HG4028.V3P69 2005
  658.15—dc22   2005050193

Printed in the United States of America.

10 9 8 7 6 5 4 3 2 1

To Ray Miles
the pioneer of private company transaction databases

About the Authors

Shannon P. Pratt is chairman and CEO of Shannon Pratt Valuations, LLC, a business valuation firm headquartered in Portland, Oregon. He is also a member of the board of directors of Paulson Capital Corporation, an investment banking firm.

Over the last 35 years, he has performed valuation engagements for mergers and acquisitions, employee stock ownership plants (ESOPs), fairness opinions, gift and estate taxes, incentive stock options, buy-sell agreements, corporate and partnership dissolutions, dissenting stockholder actions, damages, marital dissolutions, and many other business valuation purposes. He has testified in a wide variety of federal and state courts across the country and frequently participates in arbitration and mediation proceedings.

He holds an undergraduate degree in business administration from the University of Washington and a doctorate in business administration, majoring in finance, from Indiana University. He is a Fellow of the American Society of Appraisers, a Master Certified Business Appraiser, a Chartered Financial Analyst, a Master Certified Business Counselor, and is certified in mergers and acquisitions.

Dr. Pratt's professional recognitions include being designated a life member of the Business Valuation Committee of the American Society of Appraisers, a life member of the American Society of Appraisers, past chairman and a life member of the ESOP Association Advisory Committee on Valuation, a life member of the Institute of Business Appraisers, the Magna Cum Laude in Business Appraisal award from the National Association of Certified Valuation Analysts, and the distinguished service award of the Portland Society of Financial Analysts. He recently completed two three-year terms as trustee-at-large of the Appraisal Foundation.

Dr. Pratt is the author of *Business Valuation Body of Knowledge, Cost of Capital: Estimation and Application, Business Valuation Discounts and Premiums*, and coauthor with the Honorable David Laro of *Business Valuation and Taxes: Procedure, Law and Perspective,* all published by John Wiley & Sons, Inc.

He is publisher emeritus of a monthly newsletter, *Shannon Pratt's Business Valuation Update* (primarily for the professional appraisal community).

Dr. Pratt develops and teaches business valuation courses for the American Society of Appraisers and the American Institute of Certified Public Accountants, and frequently speaks on business valuation at national legal, professional, and trade association meetings. He also developed and often teaches a full-day seminar (sometimes divided into two partial days) on business valuation for judges and lawyers.

Noah Gordon, Esquire updated the court cases and wrote several case abstracts for this book. He also serves as in-house counsel for Shannon Pratt Valuations, LLC. Prior to joining Business Valuation Resources, LLC, Mr. Gordon was an executive editor with Aspen Publishers and a managing editor with Prentice Hall. He has served as a contributing author and editor of several legal treatises and publications, and currently maintains a freelance editorial business. Mr. Gordon is admitted to the state bars of Oregon, New York, New Jersey, and the District of Columbia. He holds a BA in Political Science and a BA in French Literature from Haverford College and a JD from the Benjamin N. Cardozo School of Law.

Doug Twitchell wrote Chapters 8 and 9 on comparative financial analysis and compiling useful market value tables. Mr. Twitchell holds a bachelor of science in mechanical and industrial engineering from Clarkson University, a master's in business administration from Portland State University, and a certificate of advanced graduate studies in computational finance from the Oregon Graduate Institute of Science and Technology. He is comanager of *Pratt's Stats*™, the official completed business sale transaction database of the International Business Brokers Association, published by Business Valuation Resources, LLC.

Chad Phillips prepared the two sample cases presented as Chapters 13 and 14. Mr. Phillips holds a bachelor of science degree in finance from Portland State University. He is a business valuation analyst with Moss Adams, LLP.

Alina Niculita prepared Appendixes A and B: "Bibliography" and "Data Resources." Ms. Niculita holds two masters in business administration degrees from the CMC Graduate School of Business (Czech Republic) and the Joseph M. Katz Graduate School of Business at the University of Pittsburgh, and is a Chartered Financial Analyst (CFA). She is president and chief operating officer of Shannon Pratt Valuations, LLC.

Z. Christopher Mercer is founder and CEO of Mercer Capital, one of the leading independent business appraisal firms in the country. He is an Accredited Senior Member (ASA) of the American Society of Appraisers and holds the Chartered Financial Analyst (CFA) professional designation. In addition, Mr. Mercer is a member of the Editorial Advisory Board of *Valuation Strategies,* a national magazine published by the RIA Group, and a member of the Editorial Review Board of the *Business Valuation Review,* a quarterly journal published by the American Society of Appraisers. Mr. Mercer is also the author of three textbooks, *Quantifying Marketability Discounts, Valuing Financial Institutions,* and *Valuing Enterprise and Shareholder Cash Flows: The Integrated Theory of Business Valuation.*

Contents

Contents

List of Exhibits

Foreword

I no longer remember when I purchased my copy of the first edition of Shannon Pratt's *Valuing a Business* (published in 1981), but it was sometime in the early 1980s. However, I do remember what the book did for me: It provided an organized basis to begin what has been a career-long study of the how and the whys of valuing businesses. And I acknowledge Shannon Pratt's important role in sharing his vision of the business of business valuation with me, and challenging me to be the best that I could be.

Shannon continues to play the role of challenger for us all with the second edition of *The Market Approach to Valuing Businesses*. The market approach, which generally relates to the application of guideline company methods in business valuation, is undoubtedly one of the two most challenging approaches in our field. The income approach has its own challenges, particularly with the development of the cost of capital. However, the challenges of the market approach remain daunting for appraisers.

In *The Market Approach to Valuing Businesses,* we have the most comprehensive discussion of guideline company methods written to date. The book focuses on the *guideline public company method,* where valuation multiples are developed by comparisons of a subject company with publicly traded comparables. Often, there is so much data, and so little usable pricing information. This method is difficult to employ in many circumstances, ranging from unprofitable subject companies to unprofitable public guideline companies, to the inability to find even reasonably comparable guideline companies.

The book also focuses on what Shannon terms the *guideline merged and acquired company method.* Here, valuation multiples are developed based on change-of-control transactions involving companies similar to a subject company being valued. Often, there is so little data and so little usable pricing information! This method is also difficult to employ in many circumstances.

Look to *The Market Approach to Valuing Businesses* for guidance and ideas for how to address important issues ranging from the identification of guideline companies, availability of data, to adjusting financial statements, to when to apply valuation premiums and discounts, to reconciling indications of value using the market value methods with indications under the income and asset approaches.

As with his first book written in 1981, *Market Approach* provides a roadmap to begin a serious study of the market approach to business valuation. I am often asked in litigated matters if I consider one or more of Shannon's books to be "authoritative references" in the business valuation field. And I always answer, "Of course!"

Do Shannon and I always agree on every point of valuation theory and practice? Of course not! But I have enjoyed our many debates and look forward to many more. It is through the process of debate and publication that we grow as a profession. No other single individual has done more for the business appraisal profession in these regards than Shannon Pratt, and he continues with *The Market Approach to Valuing Businesses!*

Z. Christopher Mercer, ASA, CFA
Chief Executive Officer
Mercer Capital
Memphis, Tennessee

Preface

The market approach is a pragmatic way to value businesses, essentially by comparison to the prices at which other similar businesses or business interests changed hands in arm's-length transactions. It is favored by the Internal Revenue Service in Revenue Ruling 59-60 and is widely used by buyers, sellers, investment bankers, business brokers, and business appraisers.

The market approach has a high degree of acceptance in the courts, but courts also often reject it when it is not well implemented. It is an arduous method to complete, and many appraisers do not have the hands-on training to do it as thoroughly as is necessary to stand up in court. Guideline company and transaction methods are often critically attacked by opposing witnesses, who are often successful in their attacks. There are a vast areas that can be questioned with the intent to undermine the methodology. Hopefully, this book and the accompanying workbook will help appraisers to implement the market approach more thoroughly and appropriately so that their market approach methodology will be accepted in court.

This book provides a primer for both the neophyte and the experienced buyer or seller, intermediary, appraiser, lawyer, or judge in understanding and applying the market approach to valuing businesses, business interests, and professional practices. It covers all the basics, including all the latest available data, and also many nuances that may not be encountered frequently but can be extremely important.

This book addresses the market approach for valuing

- Businesses, from sole proprietorships through multibillion-dollar enterprises
- Professional practices
- Partial (usually minority) interests in businesses and professional practices

It addresses using the market approach for valuation in many applications, including but not limited to

- Pricing for purchases and sales
- Marital dissolution property valuation
- Valuation for gift and estate taxes
- Shareholder matters, such as dissenting stockholder suits, minority oppression actions, and resolutions of value under buy-sell agreements

The book is fully indexed and is designed to be both a straightforward tutorial and a handy desk reference for

- Business valuation analysts
- Acquirers and sellers
- Investment bankers, business brokers, and other intermediaries
- Investors and lenders
- CPAs
- Judges and lawyers
- Academicians and students

The book lays out the basic market approach methods and data sources, so that anyone can use it immediately either to carry out a market approach valuation or to review someone else's market approach valuation. It covers

- Definitions, especially of the various market value multiples that may be used
- Market approach valuation methods
- Finding data
- Analyzing and adjusting financial statements
- Comparative financial analysis
- Presenting comparative market value tables
- Selecting and weighting market value multiples and methods
- Discounts and premiums
- Reconciling market approach results with results of other approaches

The book also presents

- Two sample cases
  - Sole proprietorship
  - Midmarket commercial company
- A critique of U.S. acquisitions over the last 20 years
- An analysis of the effect of size on value
- Common errors in applying the market approach
- Court reactions to the market approach
- A bibliography
- An extensive appendix on data resources

The power of the market approach for valuing midmarket and small companies has been greatly enhanced in recent years by several developments:

- Emergence of thousands of relatively small public companies
- Securities and Exchange Commission's EDGAR (Electronic Data Gathering and Retrieval) system
- Expansion of old and the development of new and more detailed databases on sales of private companies

Each of these types of data is covered in detail.

My goal has been to make this book a state-of-the-art treatise on the market approach, while still making it understandable to the nonprofessional. To this end, it starts with the basic concepts and moves on through implementation. The market approach to valuation of the mom-and-pop business is presented along with the market approach to valuing middle-market companies because while the comparative market data are quite different, the principles are the same. The presentation is generously supplemented with illustrative examples.

The market approach is dynamic. This is especially true in terms of data sources and also in terms of the ways courts accept, reject, or modify market approach valuations presented to them.

In addition to updated data sources and other data, this edition has benefited from Noah Gordon's extensive additions to Chapter 19, "The Market Approach in the Courts." In addition, it has benefited from the insights of many astute reviewers, especially Steve Bravo, Poonam Vaidya, Gil Matthews, and Rob Schlegel, whose company affiliations are listed in the acknowledgements. Readers can stay current on data developments through the monthly "Data and Publications" section in *Shannon Pratt's Business Valuation Update* and on court cases through the monthly "Legal and Court Case Update" sections of that newsletter and its Web site, *www.BVResources.com.*

Please contact us with any questions or comments on the book. For a complimentary copy of the newsletter or for a catalog of current books on business valuation, please contact Business Valuation Resources at 888 BUS-VALU [(888) 287-8258], or fax (503) 291-7955.

Shannon P. Pratt
Shannon Pratt Valuations, LLC
7412 S.W. Beaverton-Hillsdale Hwy.
Suite 111
Portland, Oregon 97225
email: shannonp@shannonpratt.com

Acknowledgments

This book has benefited immensely from review by many people with a high level of knowledge and experience in business valuation. The following people reviewed most or all of the entire manuscript, and the book reflects their unstinting efforts and legion constructive suggestions:

Jim Alerding
Clifton Gunderson
Indianapolis, IN

Steve Bravo
Apogee Business Valuations
Framington, MA

John Emory, Sr.
Emory Business Valuations
Milwaukee, WI

Jay Fishman
Financial Research Associates
Philadelphia, PA

Bruce Johnson
Munroe Park & Johnson
San Antonio, TX

Gil Matthews
Sutter Secrities
San Franciso, CA

Michele Miles
Institute of Business Appraisers
Plantation, FL

Rob Schlegel
Houlihan Valulation Advisors
Indianapolis, IN

Poonam Vaidya
Morrison Brown Argiz
Miami, FL

Butch Williams
Dixon Odom, PLLC
Birmingham, AL

In addition, I thank Kathryn Aschwald of Columbia Financial Advisors in Portland, Oregon, for her review of Chapters 6, 10, and 16; Cary Carruthers of Corporate Valuations in Portland, Oregon, for reviewing Chapters 13 and 14, and David King of PricewaterhouseCoopers in Chicago, Illinois, for his work in reviewing Chapter 16. I also very much appreciate the help of Jack Sanders of BIZCOMPS® in San Diego, California, for his review of Chapter 13, and David Schue of Corporate Valuations in Portland, Oregon, for his review of Chapter 14.

Melanie Walker of Business Valuation Resources provided much assistance with this project and was responsible for obtaining permissions to reprint material from other sources. For these permissions, I thank:

Administrative Science Quarterly
American Society of Appraisers
BIZCOMPS®
Mr. Warren Buffett
Financial Research Associates
Mr. Glenn Desmond, MAI, ASA
Ibbotson Associates
Institute of Business Appraisers
John Wiley & Sons, Inc.
Marshall & Swift, LP
Mergerstat® LP
National Restaurant Association
Partnership Profiles, Inc.
Peabody Publishing
Practitioners Publishing Company
Prentice-Hall
PricewaterhouseCoopers
Robert Morris Associates
Simon & Schuster
Thompson Financial Securities
Time-Life Syndication
University of Chicago Press
World M&A Group

Noah Gordon wrote Chapter 19, "The Market Approach in the Courts," and updated many court cases throughout the book; Chris Mercer wrote Appendix D, "The Quantitative Marketability Discount Model"; Paul Heidt updated the broker list in Appendix E; Angelina McKedy updated data resources; and Adam Manson updated many of the tables and exhibits.

I greatly appreciate the enthusiastic cooperation of the professionals at John Wiley & Sons, John DeRegemis, executive editor, and Judy Howarth, associate editor.

The second edition manuscript was compiled by Melanie Walker, an editor at Business Valuation Resources.

Shannon Pratt
Portland, Oregon

Notation System Used in This Book

A source of confusion for those trying to understand financial theory and methods is the fact that financial writers have not adopted a standard system of notation. The following notation system is used throughout the book.

VALUE AT A POINT IN TIME

PV   = Present value

FV   = Future value

MVIC = Market value of invested capital

COST OF CAPITAL AND RATE OF RETURN VARIABLES

k = Discount rate (generalized)

k_e = Discount rate for common equity capital (cost of common equity capital). Unless otherwise stated, it generally is assumed that this discount rate is applicable to net cash flow available to common equity.

$k_{e(pt)}$ = Cost of equity prior to tax effect

k_p = Discount rate for preferred equity capital

k_d = Discount rate for debt (net of tax effect, if any)

(*Note*: For complex capital structures, there could be more than one class of capital in any of the preceding categories, requiring expanded subscripts.)

$k_{d(pt)}$ = Cost of debt prior to tax effect

k_{ni} = Discount rate for equity capital when net income rather than net cash flow is the measure of economic income being discounted

c = Capitalization rate

c_e = Capitalization rate for common equity capital. Unless otherwise stated, it generally is assumed that this capitalization rate is applicable to net cash flow available to common equity.

c_{ni} = Capitalization rate for net income

c_p = Capitalization rate for preferred equity capital

c_d = Capitalization rate for debt

(*Note:* For complex capital structures, there could be more than one class of capital in any of the preceding categories, requiring expanded subscripts.)

t = Tax rate (expressed as a percentage of pretax income)

R = Rate of return

R_f = Rate of return on a risk-free security

$E(R)$ = Expected rate of return

$E(R_m)$ = Expected rate of return on the "market" (usually used in the context of a market for equity securities, such as the NYSE or S&P 500)

$E(R_i)$ = Expected rate of return on security i

B = Beta (a coefficient, usually used to modify a rate of return variable)

B_L = Levered beta

B_U = Unlevered beta

RP = Risk premium

RP_m = Risk premium for the "market" (usually used in the context of a market for equity securities, such as the NYSE or S&P 500)

RP_s = Risk premium for "small" stocks (usually average size of lowest quintile or decile of NYSE as measured by market value of common equity) over and above RP_m

RP_u = Risk premium for unsystematic risk attributable to the specific company

RP_i = Risk premium for the ith security

$K_1 \ldots K_n$ = Risk premium associated with risk factor 1 through n for the average asset in the market (used in conjunction with Arbitrage Pricing Theory)

WACC   = Weighted average cost of capital

INCOME VARIABLES

E = Expected economic income (in a generalized sense; i.e., could be dividends, any of several possible definitions of cash flows, net income, and so on)

NI = Net income (after entity-level taxes)

NCF_e = Net cash flow to equity

NCF_f = Net cash flow to the firm (to overall invested capital, or entire capital structure, including all equity and long-term debt)

PMT = Payment (interest and principal payment on debt security)

D	= Dividends
T	= Tax (in dollars)
GCF	= Gross cash flow (usually net income plus non-cash charges)
EBT	= Earnings before taxes
EBIT	= Earnings before interest and taxes
EBDIT	= Earnings before depreciation, interest, and taxes ("Depreciation" in this context usually includes amortization. Some writers use EBITDA to specifically indicate that amortization is included.)

PERIODS OR VARIABLES IN A SERIES

i	= The ith period or the ith variable in a series (may be extended to the jth variable, the kth variable, and so on)
n	= The number of periods or variables in a series, or the last number in a series
∞	= Infinity
o	= Period$_o$, the base period, usually the latest year immediately preceding the valuation date

WEIGHTINGS

W	= Weight
W_e	= Weight of common equity in capital structure
W_p	= Weight of preferred equity in capital structure
W_d	= Weight of debt in capital structure

(*Note:* For purposes of computing a weighted average cost of capital [WACC], it is assumed that preceding weightings are at market value.)

GROWTH

g	= Rate of growth in a variable (e.g., net cash flow)

MATHEMATICAL FUNCTIONS

Σ	= Sum of (add all the variables that follow)
Π	= Product of (multiply together all the variables that follow)

$\bar{x}$ = Mean average (the sum of the values of the variables divided by the number of variables)

G = Geometric mean (the product of the values of the variables taken to the root of the number of variables)

ADDITIONAL ABBREVIATIONS USED IN THIS BOOK

$MM   = Million dollars

CAGR   = Compound annual growth rate

CV   = Coefficient of variation

DE   = Discretionary earnings

DFCF   = Debt free cash flow

DFNI   = Debt free net income

EDGAR   = Electronic Data Gathering and Retrieval (SEC system)

FF&E   = Furniture, fixtures and equipment

FIFO   = First in, first out

FYE   = Fiscal year-end

IBD   = Interest-bearing debt

LIFO   = Last in, first out

LTD   = Long-term debt

LTM   = Last twelve months

NAICS   = North American Industrial Classification System

OCF   = Owner's cash flow (same as discretionary earnings)

P/E   = Price/earnings ratio

SDCF   = Seller's discretionary cash flow (same as discretionary earnings)

SIC   = Standard Industrial Classification

TBVIC   = Tangible book value of invested capital

Introduction

Theory and Relevance of the Market Approach

PURPOSE AND OBJECTIVE OF THIS BOOK

The purpose of this book is to present both the theoretical development of estimating value by the market approach and, especially, its practical application in buying, selling, and estimating value for other purposes. It is intended both as a learning text for those who want to study the subject and as a handy reference for those who are interested in background or who seek direction on some specific aspect of the market approach.

OVERVIEW

The reader can expect these discussions:

- Finding the data
- Analyzing and adjusting the data
- Presenting the data

- Applying discounts and premiums
  - When appropriate
  - How to quantify
- Reaching the conclusion
- Using the market data in
  - Deal making
  - Valuation
- Understanding the terminology
- Using market data in court

The objective is to serve five primary categories of users:

1. Corporate finance and corporate development officers
2. Business intermediaries
   - Investment bankers
   - Merger and acquisition specialists
   - Business brokers
3. Buyers and sellers of businesses
4. Business appraisers
5. Professional advisors
   - Attorneys
   - CPAs
   - Financial planners

THEORY OF THE MARKET APPROACH

The theory of the market approach to valuation is the economic principle of substitution: One would not pay more than one would have to pay for an equally desirable alternative. Therefore, we seek valuation guidance from the prices of other similar companies (or interests in companies) that have sold.

RELEVANCE OF THE MARKET APPROACH

The market approach to valuation is relevant because it uses observable factual evidence of actual sales of other properties to derive indications of value. It is, of course, important to insure that the transactions used for guidance are sales on an arm's-length basis, assuming that the buyers and sellers were each acting in their own self-interests.

The market approach is especially relevant if the standard of value is fair market value. The classic definition of *fair market value* is

> The price at which the property would change hands between a willing buyer and a willing seller, neither being under any compulsion to buy or sell, and both having reasonable knowledge of relevant facts.[1]

Revenue Ruling 59-60 strongly advocates the guideline public company method within the market approach. Section 3.03 reads:

> .03 Valuation of securities is, in essence, a prophecy as to the future and must be based on facts available at the required date of appraisal. As a generalization, the prices of stocks that are traded in volume in a free and active market by informed persons best reflect the consensus of the investing public as to what the future holds for the corporations and industries represented. When a stock is closely held, is traded infrequently, or is traded in an erratic market, some other measure of value must be used. In many instances, the next best measure may be found in the prices at which the stocks of companies engaged in the same or a similar line of business are selling in a free and open market.[2]

Section 4.02(h) reads:

> (h) Section 2031 (b) of the Code states, in effect, that in valuing unlisted securities the value of stock or securities of corporations engaged in the same or a similar line of business which are listed on an exchange should be taken into consideration along with all other factors. An important consideration is that the corporations to be used for comparisons have capital stocks, which are actively traded by the public. In accordance with section 2031(b) of the Code, stocks listed on an exchange are to be considered first. However, if sufficient comparable companies whose stocks are listed on an exchange cannot be found, other comparable companies that have stocks actively traded in on the over-the-counter market also may be used. The essential factor is that whether the stocks are sold on an exchange or over-the-counter there is evidence of an active, free public market for the stock as of the valuation date. In selecting corporations for comparative purposes, care should be taken to use only comparable companies. Although the only restrictive requirement as to comparable corporations specified in the statute is that their lines of business be the same or similar, yet it is obvious that consideration must be given to other relevant factors in order that the most valid comparison possible will be obtained. For illustration, . . . a company with a declining business and decreasing markets is not comparable to one with a record of current progress and market expansion.

When Revenue Ruling 59-60 was written in 1959, none of the private company transaction databases that we use today existed. The emergence of these private company transaction databases in recent years makes the use of sales data for entire companies, including many very small companies, a viable method within the market approach. While no company is exactly comparable to another, a thorough appraisal requires seeking out the best of the extensive guidance that the market can provide. The company need not be in exactly the kind of business as the subject, but should be impacted by the same economic influences. For example, when I was valuing a company that manufactured electronic controls for the forest products industry, I used guideline companies that manufactured various kinds of capital equipment for the forest products industry, not necessarily electronic controls. In the same vein, there can be wide size differences between the subject and guideline companies, which differences can be adjusted for, as discussed in one of the chapters.

PRACTICAL IMPORTANCE OF THE MARKET APPROACH

Good market comparisons can provide the most compelling evidence of the value of a business or a business interest. These comparisons allow us to make informed pricing decisions for purchases and sales and to present convincing empirical evidence of value for other purposes.

In the marketplace, more comprehensive market data and incisive analysis of the data will improve literally billions of dollars' worth of merger, acquisition, and sales decisions every day. In other valuation situations, a strong market approach can carry the day, while a weak or nonexistent market approach can leave the client poorly served and vulnerable. Analysis of market data can help to identify differences in prices paid by "financial" buyers versus "strategic" buyers in various industries and can be used to compare multiples paid for companies of varying size.

SOUND MARKET DATA ESSENTIAL IN THE COURTROOM

In the courts, billions of dollars turn on the strength or weakness of the market approach in many litigation contexts:

- Gift, estate, and income tax disputes[3]
- Marital property settlements
- Dissenting stockholder and minority oppression suits
- Corporate and partnership dissolutions and resolution of buy-sell agreement prices
- Bankruptcy reorganizations
- Employee stock ownership plans (ESOPs)

Courts are becoming more sophisticated and increasingly able to evaluate market approach testimony. Many case decisions ultimately depend on the relative quality of respective experts' market approach presentations. While the market approach can provide an excellent indication of value, it can be one of the easiest approaches to poke holes in during cross-examination, so careful selection and analysis of market data is critical to the success of the approach in the courtroom. The appraiser needs to know as much as possible about the companies selected, such as where they operate, size, etc.

ORGANIZATION OF THIS BOOK

Part I: Defining Market Multiples and Market Approach Methods

The market approach primarily uses *multiples*. These multiples are factors by which we multiply some fundamental financial variable to get an indication of value. For example, a price/earnings multiple would be the factor by which we would multiply a measure of earnings to derive an indication of value for a stock or for a company. The inverse of the price/earnings multiple (or earnings/price) can be shown as a capitalization factor applied to earnings.

Part I describes the many different multiples that are generally used in the market approach to valuation. It also describes the methods that are in commonly accepted use within the broad umbrella of the market approach.

Part II: Finding and Analyzing Comparative Market Transaction Data

The data fall largely into three categories:

1. Publicly traded company daily market transactions
2. Sales of entire companies
   - Privately held companies
   - Publicly held companies
3. Other market evidence that may be relevant
   - Past transactions in the subject company
   - Offers to buy
   - Buy-sell agreements
   - Rules of thumb

Public company market data can be compiled directly from the Securities and Exchange Commission (SEC) filings or from secondary sources. There are a wide variety of sources for merger and acquisition data. In recent years there have been new and expanded sources for data on sales of small and medium-size private companies.

Analysis and possible adjustments to financial statements is an important step in the market approach. Sometimes adjustments are appropriate not only for the subject company's statements but also for the guideline companies' statements.

Comparative analysis may involve any or all of three aspects:

1. Comparing the subject company's statements over time
2. Comparing the subject company's statements to industry averages
3. Comparing the subject company's statements to specific companies selected, for market multiple guidance.

Part III: Compiling Market Value Tables and Reaching a Value Conclusion

Once a potential list of guideline companies has been selected and analyzed, the useful market valuation data need to be compiled into one or a group of tables showing relevant valuation multiples for each company. The table or tables could include

- Guideline public companies
- Acquisitions of public companies
- Acquisitions of private companies
- Past subject company transactions

The appraiser usually compiles all the tables on the same basis, by use of either

- Market value of invested capital (MVIC) multiples and/or
- Common equity valuation multiples

In some instances, some tables may be compiled on an MVIC basis and others on an equity basis.

Often the first draft of the market value tables will contain a wide variety of market valuation multiples. The appraiser then usually narrows down the number of relevant valuation multiples, depending on factors such as the quantity of available data for each multiple and the relative dispersion of the values for each multiple. After deciding which multiples to use, the appraiser must decide the relative weight to be accorded to each.

To reach a final estimate of value, the appraiser must decide whether indications of value for each method need to be adjusted for relative ownership attributes. These usually involve the relative minority or control attributes and degree of marketability of the subject interest compared with the guideline market transactions used. In some cases, other discount or premium adjustments may be considered.

Part IV: Sample Market Approach Cases

Sample market approach valuations are presented for two types of entities:

1. Small sole proprietorship
2. Midsize software company

Part V: Important Aspects of Using the Market Approach

This part contains chapters on a variety of subjects that are important to users of the market approach. The first is how the market approach relates to the two other primary approaches to business and professional practice valuation: the income approach and the asset approach.

We then show market evidence about the impact of company size in various industries on the magnitudes of market multiples. This is followed by a chapter on reviewing a market approach presentation, including common errors. This list of errors raises many potential cross-examination questions for litigated cases.

Another chapter shows the widespread tendency to overpay in U.S. company acquisitions. Finally, we discuss the acceptance—and reasons for rejection—of the market approach in the courts, including

- The U.S. Tax Court
- Family law courts
- Courts adjudicating dissenting stockholder, minority oppression, and other shareholder valuation disputes

Finally, several useful appendixes contain reference materials, such as a bibliography, data resources, glossary of definitions, the Quantitative Marketability Discount Model, and a list of business brokers and their specialties.

SUMMARY

This book takes the reader all the way through the market approach, from theory to implementation and critique. It provides an introduction, a road map, and a reference guide to one of the essential approaches to valuing a business, a practice, or an interest in one.

Notes

1. Sec. 20-2031(b), Estate Tax Regs; see also sec. 25-2512-1, Gift Tax Regs.
2. Rev. Rul. 59-60, 1959-1 C.B. 237
3. Hon. David Laro, judge, U.S. Tax Court, estimates that the annual impact of valuation disputes before the Tax Court exceeds $60 billion (*Shannon Pratt's Business Valuation Update,* February 2000, 1).

PART I

Defining Market Multiples and Market Approach Methods

Chapter 1

Defining Market Value Multiples and Market Approach Methods

Common Equity Only versus Total Invested Capital Multiples
> Defining Common Equity
> Defining Invested Capital
> Guideline Company Equity and Invested Capital Price Data Must Be at Market Price
> Handling the Subject Company That Has No Senior Securities

Computing Market Value of Equity Multiples

Commonly Used Market Value of Equity Multiples
> Equity Price
> Price/Earnings
> Price/Gross Cash Flow
> Price/"Cash Earnings"
> Price/Pretax Earnings
> Price/Book Value (or Price/Adjusted Net Asset Value)
>> Price/Adjusted Net Asset Value
>> Tangible versus Total Book Value or Adjusted Net Asset Value
> Price/Dividends (or Partnership Withdrawals)
> Price/Net Cash Flow to Equity

Computing Market Value of Invested Capital (MVIC) Multiples
> Only Long-term Debt versus All Interest-bearing Debt
> Include or Subtract Cash and Cash Equivalents
> Calculating Fully Diluted Shares

Commonly Used MVIC Multiples
> MVIC/Sales
> MVIC/Discretionary Earnings
> MVIC/EBITDA
> MVIC/EBIT
> MVIC/Debt-free Gross Cash Flow
> MVIC/Debt-free Net Income
> MVIC/TBVIC
> MVIC/Physical Activity or Capacity
> MVIC/Net Cash Flow to Invested Capital

A *market value multiple* is the result of dividing a numerator, which represents dollars of price or value, by a denominator, which usually represents dollars of a financial variable of a company. The most familiar market value multiple is the *price/earnings (P/E) multiple*:

$$\frac{\text{Price of stock per share}}{\text{Latest 12 months earnings per share}} \qquad \frac{\$15.00}{\$1.00} = 15\times$$

In a few cases, the denominator may be some physical fundamental of a company measured other than in dollar terms. For example, denominators could include

- For a tavern: monthly barrels of beer sold
- For a manufacturing plant: units of annual production capacity, such as thousands of board feet of plywood
- For a funeral home: annual number of full-service funerals
- For cable TV: number of subscribers
- For a gas station: number of gallons sold per month
- For a child care center, number of children, licensed and registered

The market value multiples are computed from transactions actually observed in the marketplace. The multiples so computed are then applied to the same financial variable for the subject company to derive an indication of value. *It is critical that the computation of the multiple for the market transactions be done on a basis that is consistent with the way the multiple is applied to data for the subject company.*
There are two basic categories of multiples used in the market approach:

1. Equity multiples
2. Invested capital multiples

The next section defines the concepts of equity and invested capital as the terms are used in valuation. Following sections will define and show sample computations of equity valuation multiples and invested capital valuation multiples.

COMMON EQUITY ONLY VERSUS TOTAL INVESTED CAPITAL MULTIPLES

The market value multiples are computed on one of two bases:

1. Amounts attributable to *common equity*
2. Amounts attributable to the company's *total invested capital*

If the company has preferred stock and/or other classes of senior equity, they conventionally are included with total invested capital, not with common equity.

Either the equity or the invested capital procedure can be used for valuing either controlling or minority interests. However, the invested capital procedure is sometimes preferable for valuing controlling interests, and the direct valuation of equity is often preferable for valuing minority interests. The reason is because a controlling interest holder can change the capital structure if that may enhance the value of the equity, while the minority interest owner does not have that option. However, if the subject and guideline companies have very different capital structures, eliminating the potential effects of that difference sometimes is a reason (sometimes a compelling reason) to use the invested capital procedure even when valuing minority interests.

The attitude toward using invested capital procedures for valuing minority interest varies among appraisers. One reviewer of the manuscript opined that we should "boldly note as a primary principle" that invested capital procedure is preferred for valuing controlling interests and direct valuation of equity preferred for minority interests. Another well-known reviewer said, "There is no reason that MVIC multiples are not just as appropriate when valuing minority interests. These multiples are readily observable in public markets." In any case, there is general agreement that if using an invested capital method to value on a minority interest basis, no adjustment should be made to the subject company's actual capital structure, since a minority stockholder could not force such an adjustment.

Defining Common Equity

Common equity is the lowest (or residual) class of ownership. If preferred shares are outstanding, they are *not* part of common equity. However, more than one class of common equity may exist. For example, there may be both voting and nonvoting stock with equivalent rights to distributions. Similarly, there may be both general and limited partnership interests.

For valuation purposes, the number of units of common equity usually should be computed on a *fully diluted* basis. In other words, if there are options, warrants, or convertible securities outstanding, the number of equity units should be

Exhibit 1.1   Guideline Company A—Balance Sheet

ASSETS:		
Current Assets:		
Cash and Cash Equivalents		$ 200,000
Accounts Receivable		300,000
Inventory		400,000
Total Current Assets		$ 900,000
Plant and Equipment		
At Cost	$4,200,000	
Less Depreciation	1,200,000	3,000,000
Operating Patent		
At Cost	$ 650,000	
Less Amortization	50,000	600,000
Total Assets		**$ 4,500,000**
LIABILITIES & EQUITY:		
Liabilities:		
Accounts Payable		$ 800,000
Notes Payable		600,000
Current Portion of Long-term Debt		400,000
Long-term Debt		2,000,000
Total Liabilities		$ 3,800,000
Stockholders Equity:		
Class A voting common (400,000 shares		
authorized, 320,000 outstanding @ 12/31/xx)$	80,000	
Class B nonvoting common (800,000 shares		
authorized, 400,000 outstanding @ 12/31/xx)	100,000	
Retained Earnings	$ 520,000	$ 700,000
Total Liabilities & Equity		**$ 4,500,000**

Note: Classes A and B are both traded on NASDAQ and both closed at $10 per share on the effective valuation date.

computed as if the conversion rights were exercised, assuming it would be to the financial advantage of the holders.[1]

The number of equity units is based on the number *outstanding* (after allowing for dilution). There may be more units *authorized* but the additional units authorized do not count if they are not outstanding.

If companies repurchase shares, some states still require such stock to be shown on the balance sheet as *treasury stock*. These shares should *not* be included in shares outstanding.

Exhibit 1.1 shows two classes of common stock, but no treasury stock, senior equity, warrants, options, or convertible securities. In this simple example, a total of 720,000 shares of common stock are outstanding.[2]

Exhibit 1.2 shows a simplified income statement from which multiples of performance results can be computed. Multiples of book value can be computed from Exhibit 1.1. We will assume that these exhibits represent Guideline Company A

Exhibit 1.2 Guideline Company A—Income Statement

Sales	$10,000,000
Cost of Goods Sold	6,000,000
Gross Margin	$ 4,000,000
General & Administrative Expense[a]	2,500,000
Operating Income	$ 1,500,000
Interest Expense	300,000
Pretax Income	$ 1,200,000
Income Taxes (20%)	240,000
Net Income	$ 960,000

Note: The Company pays dividends of $.50 per share.

[a] Includes depreciation of $400,000 patent amortization of $50,000, and compensation and benefits of $500,000 to the chief executive officer (who is also the controlling owner).

and that similar statements are available for each guideline company. For the purpose of the definitions of multiples in this chapter, it makes no difference whether the guideline companies are public stock market transactions or public or private merged or acquired companies. In other words, the market multiples defined in this chapter are equally applicable whether using the publicly traded guideline company method or the guideline transaction method.

Defining Invested Capital

Technically, *invested capital* includes all common and preferred equity plus long-term debt, including the current portion of long-term debt. In Exhibit 1.3, the book value of invested capital defined this way is $3,100,000.

Some computations of invested capital include all interest-bearing debt. In Exhibit 1.3, the book value of invested capital defined in this alternative way is $3,700,000. One reason to include all interest-bearing debt is because it may not be possible to determine how much interest is attributable to short-term versus long-term debt. Another reason, for some companies, is that many small companies use short-term debt as if it were long-term debt. The analyst should be consistent with regard to treatment of LTD with subject and guideline companies.

Other computations of invested capital subtract cash and cash equivalents. If the company owns marketable securities, they usually are included with the cash equivalents. This computation tends to be preferred by investment bankers.[2] The advantage of this computation is to make the market value multiples using invested capital more comparable among various companies with differing percentages of cash and cash equivalents in their asset mix.

Exhibit 1.3 Composition of Equity and Invested Capital

LIABILITIES & EQUITY:

Liabilities:

Accounts Payable		$ 800,000
Notes Payable		600,000
Current Portion of Long-term Debt		400,000
Long-term Debt		2,000,000
Total Liabilities		$3,800,000

Stockholders Equity:

Class **A** voting common (400,000 shares authorized 320,000 outstanding @ 12/31/xx)	$ 80,000	
Class **B** nonvoting common (800,000 shares authorized, 400,000 outstanding @ 12/31/xx)	100,000	
Retained Earnings	520,000	$ 700,000
Total Liabilities & Equity		**$4,500,000**

Book value of common equity = $700,000

Book value of invested capital including only long-term debt $3,100,000

Alternative computation: Book value of invested capital including all interest bearing debt $3,700,000

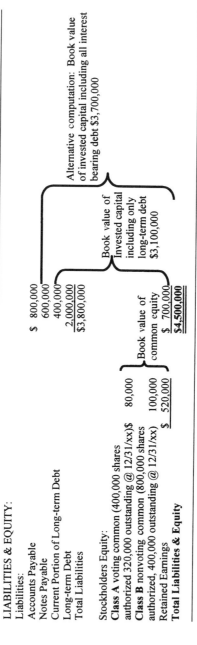

Note: Classes A and B are both traded on NASDAQ and both closed at $10 per share on the effective valuation date.

If cash and cash equivalents were subtracted, the book value of invested capi-tal for Guideline Company A would be $2,900,000, including only long-term debt, and $3,500,000 including all interest-bearing debt.

If cash and cash equivalents are subtracted in computing the value of invested capital for the guideline companies, then the valuation multiples derived do not reflect the value of cash and cash equivalents. If the subject company has cash and cash equivalents, they must be added back to the values indicated by the valuation multiples that were computed after subtracting cash and cash equivalents.

Guideline Company Equity and Invested Capital Price Data Must Be at Market Price

In this section, we have defined the components of equity and invested capital only in terms of book value. To get the numerators of the equations to compute market valuation multiples, it is necessary to find, for each guideline company, the *market price* of each component of capital being used, that is, the market price of common equity for equity multiples, and market price of common equity plus mar-ket value of preferred equity and debt for invested capital multiples.

Handling the Subject Company That Has No Senior Securities

If the company being valued has no senior securities (preferred stock or interest-bearing debt) in its capital structure, then the common equity is equal to the entire invested capital. Any or all of the multiples can be presented in a single table because there is no senior security value (i.e., no obligations that take prece-dence over the common equity) to be subtracted from the market value of invested capital.

Especially when valuing small companies, it is quite typical that neither the subject nor the guideline companies have any senior securities. In such a case there is no meaningful distinction between equity multiples and invested capital multiples.

However, it is also often the case that the guideline companies have senior securities, even if our subject company does not. When this is the situation, the sub-ject company should be valued using invested capital multiples from the guideline companies, not on an equity basis.

COMPUTING MARKET VALUE OF EQUITY MULTIPLES

Market value of equity multiples can be computed either on a per-share basis or on a total equity basis. On a per-share basis, the multiple is simply the price per share divided by the company fundamental per share, as shown in the earlier price/earnings multiple. Alternatively, equity multiples can be computed using the total value of the company's common equity divided by the total amount of the company's fundamental, for example, total net income. By *fundamental,* we mean an income statement or balance sheet financial value, such as an income variable or a balance sheet value, or a book value of equity.

It is important that the denominator include *only* those returns available to common equity. For example, any interest on debt or any dividends to preferred stock would not be included in computing the denominator of the market value of equity value multiple.

COMMONLY USED MARKET VALUE OF EQUITY MULTIPLES

The most commonly used market value of equity valuation multiples are:

- Price/earnings (price/net income after taxes)
- Price/gross cash flow
- Price/"cash earnings"
- Price/pretax earnings
- Price/book value (or price/net asset value)
- Price/dividends (or partnership withdrawals)

For the purpose of the equity multiples in this illustration, we will do computations on a per-share basis. The multiple would come out the same if computed on an aggregate basis. To follow the convention, we will round multiples to one decimal place. Valuation is not an exact science, and many analysts feel that carrying multiples to more decimal places conveys a specious sense of precision.

Equity Price

Equity price in the context of valuation multiples usually means only *common* equity, and may be expressed on either a per-share or an aggregate basis. If using public companies to compute market multiples per share, information usually is available. If using acquisitions of private companies to compute market multiples, usually only the aggregate price paid for all the equity is available.

As noted in Exhibit 1.1, the stock of Guideline Company A closed on the NASDAQ stock market at $10 per share on our valuation date.

The definitions of the market valuation multiples and computations thereof are the same if using mergers and acquisitions of acquired companies. We would compute the amount received per common share and divide that by each of the merged or acquired company's fundamental financial data per share (e.g., gross cash flow, pretax earnings, net income, book value) to derive valuation multiples for each fundamental. Again, the resulting multiples would be the same if computed on an aggregate rather than on a per-share basis.

Of course, in the case of merged and acquired companies, the transactions would not fall on our valuation date. For that reason, the multiples may have to be adjusted for timing differences, but that is covered in a later chapter.

Price/Earnings

Assuming that there are taxes, the term *earnings,* although used ambiguously in many cases, is generally considered to mean earnings *after* corporate-level taxes, or, in accounting terminology, net income.

Net income for Guideline Company A, $960,000, can be taken directly from the income statement shown in Exhibit 1.2. On a per-share basis, this is

$$\frac{\text{Net income}}{\text{Number of shares}} \quad \frac{\$960,000}{720,000} = \$1.33 \text{ per share}$$

The multiple is computed as

$$\frac{\text{Price per share}}{\text{Earnings per share (net income per share)}} \quad \frac{\$10.00}{\$1.33} = 7.5\times$$

Price/Gross Cash Flow

Gross cash flow is defined here as net income plus all noncash charges (e.g., depreciation, amortization, depletion, deferred revenue). In Guideline Company A, this is

Net income	$ 960,000
plus Depreciation and amortization	1,250,000
Gross cash flow	$2,210,000
	÷ 720,000 shares
Gross cash flow per share	$ 1.96

The multiple is computed as

$$\frac{\text{Price per share}}{\text{Gross cash flow per share}} \quad \frac{\$10.00}{\$1.96} = 3.3\times$$

Price/"Cash Earnings"

Cash earnings equals net income plus amortization, but not other traditional noncash charges, such as depreciation. This is a measure developed by investment bankers in recent years for pricing mergers and acquisitions as an attempt to even out the effects of very disparate accounting for intangibles. In Guideline Company A, this is

Net income	$ 960,000
plus Amortization	50,000
Cash earnings	$1,010,000
	÷ 720,000 shares
Cash earnings per share	$ 1.40

The multiple is computed as

$$\frac{\text{Price per share}}{\text{Cash earnings per share}} \quad \frac{\$10.00}{\$1.40} = 7.1\times$$

However, recent FASB for financial reporting of goodwill and other intangibles may minimize the relevance of "cash earnings."

Price/Pretax Earnings

Pretax income for Guideline Company A, $1,200,000, can be taken directly from the income statement shown in Exhibit 1.2. On a per-share basis, this is

$$\frac{\text{Pretax income}}{\text{Number of shares}} \quad \frac{\$1,200,000}{720,000} = \$1.67 \text{ per share}$$

The multiple is computed as

$$\frac{\text{Price per share}}{\text{Pretax income per share}} \quad \frac{\$10.00}{\$1.67} = 6.0\times$$

Price/Book Value (or Price/Adjusted Net Asset Value)

Book value includes the amount of par or stated value for shares outstanding plus retained earnings. Book value for Guideline Company A, from Exhibit 1.1, is computed as

Class A stated value	$ 80,000
Class B stated value	100,000
Retained earnings	520,000
Book value of common equity	$ 700,000

On a per-share basis, this is

$$\frac{\text{Book value of common equity}}{\text{Number of shares}} = \frac{\$700,000}{720,000} = \$0.97 \text{ per share}$$

The multiple is computed as

$$\frac{\text{Price per share}}{\text{Book value per share}} = \frac{\$10.00}{\$0.97} = 10.3\times$$

Price/Adjusted Net Asset Value.   Sometimes it is possible to estimate adjusted net asset values for the guideline and subject companies, reflecting adjustments to current values for all or some of the assets and, in some cases, liabilities. In the limited situations where such data are available, a price to adjusted net asset value generally is a more meaningful indication of value than price/book value. Examples could include real estate holding companies where real estate values are available or forest products companies for which estimates of timber values are available. This procedure can be particularly useful for family limited partnerships.

Generally, if the assets are written up, an offsetting liability for the trapped-in capital gains tax should be added. Some courts, however, especially family law courts, decline to recognize the trapped-in capital gains tax liability unless a sale is imminent.

Tangible versus Total Book Value or Adjusted Net Asset Value.   If the guideline and/or subject companies have intangible assets on their balance sheets, analysts generally prefer to subtract them out and use only price/tangible book value or price/tangible net asset value as the valuation multiple.

This is to avoid the valuation distortions that could be caused because of accounting rules. On one hand, if a company purchases intangible assets, the item becomes part of the assets on the balance sheet. If, on the other hand, a company creates the same intangible asset internally, it usually is expensed and never appears on the balance sheet. Because of this difference, tangible book value or tangible net asset value may present a more meaningful direct comparison among companies that may have some purchased and some internally created intangible assets.

Price/Dividends (or Partnership Withdrawals)

If the company being valued pays dividends or partnership withdrawals, the multiple of such amounts can be an important valuation parameter. This variable can be especially important when valuing minority interests, since the minority owner normally has no control over payout policy, no matter how great the company's capacity to pay dividends or withdrawals.

As noted in Exhibit 1.2, Guideline Company A pays dividends of $.50 per share. The market multiple is computed as

$$\frac{\text{Price per share}}{\text{Dividend per share}} \quad \frac{\$10.00}{\$0.50} = 20\times$$

This is one market multiple that is more often quoted as the reciprocal of the multiple, that is, the capitalization rate (also called the *yield*). The yield is computed as

$$\frac{\text{Dividend per share}}{\text{Price per share}} \quad \frac{\$0.50}{\$10.00} = 5.0\% \text{ yield}$$

Price/Net Cash Flow to Equity

The net cash flow to equity measure of investment returns is widely used in the income approach, but is used very little in the market approach. Net cash flow to equity is defined as follows

	Net income (after taxes)
+	Noncash charges
−	Net capital expenditures (the net change in fixed and other noncurrent assets)*
±	Changes in working capital*
±	Changes in long-term debt*
=	Net cash flow to equity

Of course, if there are payments to preferred shareholders, these would need to be deducted to arrive at net cash flow to common equity.

The main reason that net cash flow is not typically used in the market approach is the difficulty in getting normalized capital expenditures and normalized changes in working capital for the guideline companies. If one is willing to do the work, using the statement of cash flows, along with the income statements and balance sheets, one can compute net cash flow for most public companies for each year. However, if data such as capital expenditures and changes in net working capital have been subject to wide variations, as they frequently are, these data generally are harder to

---

*Assumes that these amounts are those necessary to support projected business operations.

adjust objectively for abnormal or nonrecurring items than for most other data. Thus, gross cash flow is used more frequently than net cash flow in the market approach because it is straightforward, easier to compute, and simple to explain.

COMPUTING MARKET VALUE OF INVESTED CAPITAL (MVIC) MULTIPLES

Market value of invested capital multiples should be computed on a total company rather than on a per-share basis. This avoids the problem of getting multiples that really are not comparable because of differing capital structures.

The basic computation of the numerator is to add the total market value of common equity to the total market value of preferred stock (if any) plus the market value of long-term debt (or, alternatively, interest-bearing debt). Cash and equivalents may be subtracted.

The denominator is computed to include the returns available to all classes of capital. This means that the denominator would include all returns to common equity plus dividends on preferred stock plus interest (either on long-term debt or on all interest-bearing debt, depending on which is used in the numerator).

If cash and equivalents are deducted from the numerator, then interest earned on cash and equivalents should be subtracted from the denominator.

The critical thing is that the numerator and denominator be consistent: Returns included in the denominator should be those that are available to the components of the capital structure that are included in the numerator.

Market value of invested capital includes the values of all equity and the senior securities included in the capital structure. As with equity multiples, the definitions of the MVIC multiples and computations thereof are the same whether using guideline publicly traded companies or guideline merged and acquired companies.

Several options exist regarding how to compute market value of invested capital. In particular, the choices include whether to

- Include only long-term debt or all interest-bearing debt
- Deduct cash and cash equivalents

Because of these alternative acceptable procedures, it is essential that the analyst define how MVIC is computed in each report. Many analysts do not automatically use the same definition of MVIC in each case, but select the definition that best fits the facts, circumstances, and available data.

Caution: If you or your valuation firm does not necessarily use the same definition of MVIC in each case, be careful about boilerplate definitions in your reports. Be sure to check the MVIC definition in each report to be sure that it accurately describes the computations that actually were made.

Only Long-term Debt versus All Interest-bearing Debt

From a conceptual viewpoint, only long-term debt (but including the current portion) is really part of a company's capital structure. Also, short-term debt may have significant seasonal fluctuations. These factors favor using only long-term debt (including current portion) in computing MVIC.

However, as a practical matter, it may not be possible to determine from the guideline companies' financial statements how much interest expense is attributable to short-term versus long-term debt. To exclude short-term debt in the MVIC numerator but include the interest on it in the denominator of the MVIC valuation multiple would create a distorted multiple.

Also, many companies, especially smaller companies, use short-term debt *as if* it were long-term debt, that is, perhaps never paying it down. These factors favor using *all* interest-bearing debt in computing MVIC.

We suggest that, however MVIC is calculated, this decision should be made on the basis of the facts and circumstances on a case-by-case basis and disclosed in the definitions and/or footnotes in the report.

Include or Subtract Cash and Cash Equivalents

The main reason to subtract cash and cash equivalents is to even out differences among guideline companies and between guideline companies and the subject company where they may have excesses or shortages of cash and equivalents relative to their respective needs. Of course, if the cash equivalents are subtracted out of the MVIC, any return on such securities should be subtracted out of the denominator of the MVIC multiples. Again, this is a decision that can be made on a case-by-case basis and the procedure chosen should be fully disclosed.

For simplicity, for the illustrative multiples in this chapter, we will define MVIC to include *all* interest-bearing debt, and we will *not* subtract out cash and cash equivalents. We will assume that the book value of debt equals the market value of debt. Therefore, the computation of MVIC for Guideline Company A that we will use to compute the multiples in this chapter is

Common stock	
720,000 shares @ $10 (NASDAQ closing	
price on valuation date)	$ 7,200,000
Long-term debt (including current portion)	2,400,000
Notes payable	600,000
Market value of invested capital	$10,200,000

Calculating Fully Diluted Shares

The calculation of fully diluted shares for valuation purposes is fairly straight-forward, but the analyst should use a method appropriate to the valuation being conducted. Under GAAP, public companies use the "treasury stock" method to report the number of diluted shares. This method assumes that the proceeds from exercise of options and warrants that are "in-the-money" are used to buy shares in the market. Thus, this is the method used by publicly traded guideline companies.

For the subject company, the analyst should consider whether to use the treasury stock method or to calculate the maximum dilutive effect, assuming that the incremental shares are added to outstanding shares with no repurchase. If the maximum dilutive effect is used, the incremental cash to be received upon the stock option exercise must be added to cash, thereby reducing net debt. The analyst should also consider whether it is appropriate to discount the cash to be received to present value.

The analyst should be sure not to double-count "in-the-money" convertible securities. Because the calculation of diluted earnings per share assumes conversion of these securities, dilutive convertible debt and preferred stock should be excluded in the MVIC calculation, and related interest on convertible debt and dividends on convertible preferred stock should be appropriately adjusted for.

COMMONLY USED MVIC MULTIPLES

The most commonly used MVIC valuation multiples are

- MVIC/sales
- MVIC/discretionary earnings (also called seller's discretionary cash flow [SDCF] or owner's cash flow [OCF])
- MVIC/EBITDA (earnings before interest, taxes, depreciation, and amortization)
- MVIC/EBIT (earnings before interest and taxes)
- MVIC/TBVIC (tangible book value of invested capital)

Some other measures include

- MVIC/some physical measure of activity or capacity
- MVIC/debt-free net cash flow to invested capital
- MVIC/debt-free net income
- MVIC/net cash flow to invested capital

Invested capital multiples must be computed on an aggregate rather than on a per-share basis. It is totally meaningless, for example, to divide aggregate equity and debt value by number of shares of equity, which would produce the per-share values combining equity and debt, a number that would be more nonsensical than a combined value of each piece of fruit in a crate of oranges and watermelons.

As with equity multiples, we will round to one decimal place, except MVIC/sales, where two decimals usually are significant because the multiples are likely to be less than 1.0.

MVIC/Sales

The figure for sales for Guideline Company A, $100,000, is taken directly from the income statement, Exhibit 1.2. The multiple is computed as

$$\frac{\text{MVIC}}{\text{Sales}} \quad \frac{\$10,200,000}{\$10,000,000} = 1.02$$

Analysts generally prefer MVIC/sales rather than equity/sales because the sales are attributable to the resources provided by the entire capital structure. Equity/sales can give a distorted picture if there are substantial differences in the capital structures of the guideline and subject companies.

Revenue multiples are better used in select industries, such as mature industries with fairly homogenous operations, and widely published and available data on income and expenses. E.g. Retail Auto Dealerships. If a Honda store makes $X in revenues, one can expect a certain percentage of profits with some degree of certainty.

MVIC/Discretionary Earnings

The International Business Brokers Association defines *discretionary earnings* (or SDCF or OCF) as pretax income (after adjustments for non-operational elements and nonrecurring activities) plus interest plus all noncash charges plus all compensation prerequisites and benefits to one owner/operator. Discretionary earnings for Guideline Company A are

Pretax income	$1,200,000
plus Interest expense	300,000
plus Depreciation and amortization	450,000
plus Owner's compensation	500,000
Discretionary earnings	$2,450,000

The multiple is computed as

$$\frac{\text{MVIC}}{\text{Discretionary earnings}} \quad \frac{\$10,200,000}{\$2,450,000} = 4.2\times$$

The multiple of discretionary earnings is used primarily for smaller businesses and professional practices where the involvement of the key owner/operator is an important component of the business or practice. For such businesses or practices, meaningful multiples generally fall between 1.5 and 3.5, although some fall outside that range.

MVIC/EBITDA

Earnings before interest, taxes, depreciation, and amortization for Guideline Company A are

	Pretax income	$1,200,000
plus	Interest expense	300,000
plus	Depreciation and amortization	450,000
	EBITDA	$1,950,000

The multiple is computed as

$$\frac{\text{MVIC}}{\text{EBITDA}} \quad \frac{\$10,200,000}{\$1,950,000} = 5.2\times$$

EBITDA multiples are particularly favored to eliminate differences in depreciation policies.

MVIC/EBIT

Earnings before interest and taxes for Guideline Company A are

Pretax income	$1,200,000
plus Interest expense	300,000
EBIT	$1,500,000

The multiple is computed as

$$\frac{\text{MVIC}}{\text{EBIT}} \quad \frac{\$10,200,000}{\$1,500,000} = 6.8\times$$

EBIT multiples are good where differences in accounting for noncash charges are not significant.

MVIC/Debt-free Gross Cash Flow

Debt-free gross cash flow is the gross cash flow that the company *would have* if it had no debt; it is a hypothetical number, computed by adding the interest expense, net of the tax effect, to the gross cash flow.

For Guideline Company A, the gross cash flow was computed to be $1,410,000 ($960,000 net income plus $400,000 depreciation and $50,000 amortization). Interest expense was $300,000, and the tax rate 20%. If there were no debt, gross cash flow would be $240,000 higher ($300,000 × [1 − 0.20]) = $240,000. Therefore, debt-free gross cash flow for Guideline Company A is

	Gross cash flow	$1,410,000
plus	Interest expense, net of tax effect	240,000
	Debt-free gross cash flow	$1,650,000

The multiple is computed as

$$\frac{\text{MVIC}}{\text{Debt-free gross cash flow}} \quad \frac{\$10,200,000}{\$1,650,000} = 6.2\times$$

MVIC/Debt-free Net Income

Debt-free net income is the net income that the company *would have* if it had no debt. As such, it is a hypothetical number, computed by adding the interest expense, net of the tax effect, to the net income.

For Guideline Company A, net income was $960,000. If there were no debt, net income would be $240,000 higher ($300,000 [1 − .20]) = $240,000. Therefore, debt-free net income for Guideline Company A is

	Net income	$ 960,000
plus	Interest expense, net of tax effect	240,000
	Debt-free net income	$1,200,000

The multiple is computed as

$$\frac{\text{MVIC}}{\text{Debt-free net income}} \quad \frac{\$10,200,000}{\$1,200,000} = 8.5\times$$

Debt-free gross cash flow and debt-free net income are used to put companies with very divergent capital structures on a more comparable basis. However, since they are hypothetical numbers, they are not widely used. Most analysts prefer multiples of EBITDA and EBIT.

MVIC/TBVIC

Tangible book value of invested capital for Guideline Company A is

	Book value of common stock	$ 700,000
plus	Long-term debt (including current portion)	2,400,000
plus	Notes payable	600,000
less	Operating patent	(600,000)
	TBVIC	$3,100,000

The multiple is computed as

$$\frac{\text{MVIC}}{\text{TBVIC}} \quad \frac{\$10,200,000}{\$3,100,000} = 3.3\times$$

As discussed in the section on equity multiples, this MVIC multiple can be used on TBVIC and also with adjusted net asset value instead of book value if data are available.

MVIC/Physical Activity or Capacity

The denominator in a market value multiple may be some measure of a company's units of sales or capacity to produce. Analysts generally prefer that the numerator in such a multiple be MVIC rather than equity for the same reasons as the sales multiple—that is, the units sold or units of capacity are attributable to the resources provided by all components of the capital structure, not just the equity.

MVIC/Net Cash Flow to Invested Capital

For the same reasons as when valuing equity directly, net cash flow to invested capital tends to be the earnings variable of choice in the context of the income approach, but is not widely used as the basis for a multiple in the market approach. Net cash flow to invested capital is computed as

	Net income (after taxes)
+	Noncash charges
−	Net capital expenditures (the net change in fixed and other noncurrent assets)*
−	Changes in working capital*

---

*Assumes that these amounts are those necessary to support projected business operations.

+   Interest expense, net of the income tax effect (i.e., interest expense ×
     [1 – tax rate])
+   Preferred dividends, if any
=   Net cash flow to overall invested capital

TIME PERIODS TO MEASURE FINANCIAL VARIABLES

It is critical that the time period or periods for which the financial variables are measured are the same (or close to the same) for the guideline companies as for the subject company.

Sometimes the time period may be suggested by comparative facts and circumstances of the guideline and subject companies or by industry conditions. In many cases, selection of time periods from which to calculate market valuation multiples may be limited by the availability of comparative data.

Matching Times for Income Variables

There are many choices of time periods for measuring income variables derived from the guideline and subject companies, such as (but not limited to)

- Latest 12 months
- Latest fiscal year
- Average of some number of past years
- Weighted average of some number of past years
- Expected results for the year ahead, either the current or following fiscal year, or next 12 months (generally available only for guideline public companies, not for merged and acquired companies)

The choice of comparative time periods is an important analytical judgment. Conceptually, we are interested in the future. However, the use of expected results is dependent on having both credible projections for the subject company and estimates of future performance for guideline companies.

Use of the latest year can be good, if it is a normal period, to use as a base year, or if it is influenced by industry or economic factors to an extent similar to the guideline companies. If considering a series of past years, the analyst should compare the patterns of results between the subject and guideline companies. Sometimes, when using an average of past years, it is appropriate to rely most heavily on a subset of the guideline companies that have patterns of results most similar to the subject company.

Matching Times for Asset Variables

For financial variables derived from the guideline and subject companies' balance sheets, the general rule is to select the balance sheet data as close as possible to the valuation date. Unlike income data, averages of past asset data are meaningless for valuation purposes in most cases.

RELATIONSHIP BETWEEN MARKET MULTIPLES AND CAPITALIZATION RATES

Market multiples and capitalization rates are the inverse of each other. For example, if the P/E ratio is 20 times last year's earnings, then last year's earnings are capitalized at 5%:

$$\frac{1}{20} = .05 = 5\%$$

Conversely, if the capitalization rate is 5%, then the market multiple for that variable is 20:

$$\frac{1}{5\%} = \frac{1}{.05} = 20\times$$

Any market multiple can be converted to a capitalization rate, and vice versa. The capitalization rate form of presentation is commonly used in the income approach to valuation. It is more common to use the market multiple form of presentation in the market approach. For consistency, we will use the market multiple form of presentation throughout this book, with the exception of dividend yields, which we will present as a yield or capitalization rate.

A word of caution: Published P/E ratios of public guideline companies have high growth rates embedded in them. If your subject company does not even pretend to have similar growth, be sure to add back the growth rate expectations of the analyst, before you develop a capitalization rate.

SUMMARY

The market approach is based on observing actual market transaction prices relative to companies' fundamental financial data. Multiples of the observed prices to the respective companies financial data are computed to create observed market valuation multiples.

The market multiples are grouped into two categories:

1. *Equity multiples*—prices for equity (common stock or partnership interests) relative to observed returns available to the companies' equity owners
2. *Invested capital multiples*—market values of companies' total invested capital relative to observed returns available to all owners of components of the companies' respective capital structures

Either category of multiple can be used to value either minority or controlling interests. Analysts often tend to prefer equity multiples for valuing minority interests and invested capital multiples for valuing controlling interests, because a minority owner cannot change the existing capital structure and a control owner generally can. However, invested capital multiples often are used to minimize potentially distorting effects of disparate capital structures among companies. If invested capital multiples are used, then the value of senior securities in the subject company's capital structure needs to be subtracted from the indicated value of invested capital to arrive at an estimate of common equity value.

Subject to availability of data, all the same market multiples may be used with the guideline public company method, the guideline merger and acquisition method, or other market methods (see subsequent chapters).

Balance sheet multiples generally are based on balance sheet figures as of a date as near as possible to the valuation date. Income multiples may be based on many different time periods (as long as they are comparable between guideline and subject companies), such as

- Latest 12 months
- Latest fiscal year
- Straight average of several years
- Weighted average of several years
- Expected results for next 12 months, current fiscal year, or following fiscal year

Notes

1. Rules for computing dilution are beyond the scope of this text. See Doug R. Carmichael, Steven B. Lillien, and Martin Mellman, *Accountant's Handbook,* 9th ed. (Hoboken: John Wiley & Sons, 1999), 7.10(c).
2. Gilbert Matthews, "Fairness Opinions: Common Errors and Omissions," in *The Handbook of Business Valuation and Intellectual Property Analysis,* Robert F. Reilly and Robert P. Schweihs, eds. (McGraw Hill, 2004), 213.

The Guideline Public Company Method

By *guideline public companies*, we mean companies similar to the subject company with stocks that trade freely in the public markets on a daily basis. The primary strengths of using these daily stock transaction prices in the market approach to valuing businesses are because of

- Securities and Exchange Commission (SEC) filing requirements: There is a great deal of information available for each company, and that information is verifiable and generally very reliable.
- Active trading: The market price represents informed investors' consensus of value on an arm's-length basis.
- Daily trading: Market prices can be observed as of the actual effective valuation date.
- Investment interest: There is a great deal of analytical information published on most public companies, including projected earnings.

This chapter presents the basic methodology; subsequent chapters provide details of implementation.

SCOPE OF MARKET

Companies filing with the SEC include over 12,550 companies. In addition, there are another 15,000 or so companies that are public, but do not have to file with the SEC because they are below either the number of stockholders or the asset value thresholds that require filing.

While the guideline public company method has always been good for valuing larger businesses, in the last 20 years the number of medium-size and small businesses in the public market has increased. There are several reasons for this:

1. To allow smaller companies better access to the capital markets, Congress has encouraged regulations allowing less onerous initial SEC filing requirements for smaller companies. For example, there are forms SB-1 for offerings under $10 million and SB-2 for offerings under $25 million, each requiring less information than the full S-1 registration form.
2. Public investors have become increasingly willing to invest in such smaller initial public offerings (IPOs), although these offerings suffered a drought in 2001 and 2002.
3. A substantial number of underwriting firms that specialize in smaller IPOs have sprung up around the country, thus facilitating smaller company offerings.

When a company first goes public, it is not necessary to list on an exchange or other listed trading market. The company can simply trade in the over-the-counter (OTC) market. However, listing requirements for major exchanges and the National Association of Security Dealers Automated Quotations (NASDAQ) market are far lower than many people realize. Initial market capitalization (share price times number of shares publicly traded) requirements are

New York Stock Exchange (NYSE)	$60,000,000
American Stock Exchange (ASE)	$ 3,000,000
NASDAQ	$ 8,000,000
NASDAQ "Small Cap Market"	$ 5,000,000

Once these initial market capitilization requirements have been met, a company's market capitalization subsequently can fall considerably lower, but it can still maintain its listing.

AVAILABILITY OF PUBLIC COMPANY DATA

Many print and online sources summarize public company data. They are generally convenient to use. They are not inexpensive (some are very expensive), but most major city public libraries carry one or more of such sources. A listing of the most widely used of such sources is contained in the Guideline Public Company Data Sources in Chapter 5 on gathering guideline public company data and in Appendix B, "Data Resources."

The print and online sources almost universally derive their data from SEC filings. The various line items or variables may be summarized or defined differently from one source to another. Although they are generally accurate, they cannot guarantee accuracy and occasionally contain mistakes. If one wants to verify the definitions of line items or variables, to read and interpret the explanatory footnotes firsthand, or have access to the complete information as supplied by the company and ensure complete accuracy, then it is best to go to the actual SEC filings.

As shown in Exhibit 2.1, the number of public companies listed on the New York Stock Exchange, American Stock Exchange, and NASDAQ has been declining in recent years, from a peak of 9,305 in 1997 to 6,614 at the end of 2004 (a decline of almost 30%). This decline is attributable to three primary reasons:

1. Consolidation in many industries resulted in many public companies being acquired.
2. The dot-com boom and bust and other economic factors caused many public companies to drop below listing maintenance requirements.
3. Lack of market receptiveness to IPOs, especially in 2001 and 2002, although a pickup in IPOs started in 2003 and accelerated in 2004 and 2005.

This decline in the number of public guideline companies has reduced usefulness of the guideline public company method, although it is still a viable method for some industries. In the meantime, the data available for the transaction method have burgeoned (see Chapters 3 and 6).

SEC Filings and EDGAR

Although there are a wide variety of forms filed with the SEC, the most important are

- 10-K annual report
- 10-Q quarterly report
- 8-K special events filing (e.g., a significant acquisition)

Since mid-1996, all companies required to file with the SEC must do so electronically. The data are gathered and stored by the Electronic Data Gathering and Retrieval (EDGAR) system. All such data are available on the Internet, and access to the data is *free*.

Exhibit 2.1   Number of Listed Companies Yearly
Comparison of NASDAQ, NYSE, and AMEX

Year	NASDAQ	NYSE	Amex	Total
1975	2,467	1,557	1,215	5,239
1976	2,456	1,576	1,161	5,193
1977	2,456	1,575	1,098	5,129
1978	2,475	1,581	1,004	5,060
1979	2,543	1,565	931	5,039
1980	2,894	1,570	892	5,356
1981	3,353	1,565	867	5,785
1982	3,264	1,526	834	5,624
1983	3,901	1,550	822	6,273
1984	4,097	1,543	792	6,432
1985	4,136	1,541	783	6,460
1986	4,417	1,575	796	6,788
1987	4,706	1,647	869	7,222
1988	4,451	1,681	896	7,028
1989	4,293	1,720	859	6,872
1990	4,132	1,774	859	6,765
1991	4,094	1,885	860	6,839
1992	4,113	2,089	814	7,016
1993	4,611	2,361	869	7,841
1994	4,902	2,570	824	8,296
1995	5,122	2,675	791	8,588
1996	5,556	2,907	751	9,214
1997	5,487	3,047	771	9,305
1998	5,068	3,114	770	8,952
1999	4,829	3,025	769	8,623
2000	4,734	2,862	765	8,361
2001	4,109	2,798	691	7,598
2002	3,765	2,783	678	7,226
2003	3,335	2,750	700	6,785
2004	3,271	2,768	575	6,614
2004 vs. peak	**58.9%**	**88.9%**	**47.3%**	**71.1%**

Source: all of 1999 data was missing in original document but was provided by Tim McCormick (Academic Liason) of NASDAQ.

2003 and 2004 data provided by Tim McCormick (Academic Liason) of NASDAQ.

Source document was corrected with NYSE data from:

Nasdaq: http://www.nasdaq.com/investorrelations/10k.pdf

NYSE: http://www.nysedata.com/factbook/viewer_edition.asp?mode=table&key=76&category=4

AMEX: Sean Jenkins (Director-Equity Research)

Analysts can access the data free of charge from both the SEC and the New York University (NYU) Stern School of Business Internet home pages. The formatting is virtually impossible to work with, but this problem is easily solved with readily available freeware.

Several commercial services provide EDGAR data for a low fee, with some value-added features. For example, Global Securities Information's (GSI) online *LIVEDGAR* costs $10 to access and $2 per minute to retrieve documents. Disclosure's *Global Access* indexes EDGAR to allow a variety of searches and downloading of selected portions of documents as desired. The various services are listed in Appendix B. Of course, the more refinements, the greater the cost of the service. 10kWizard (10kwizard.com) costs a nominal fixed fee for unlimited access and retrieval and is easy to search.

Secondary Sources for Public Company Data

As noted earlier, there is a wide variety of print and electronic sources for public company data. These are described in some detail in Appendix B.

One of the advantages of the guideline public company method is that balance sheet and income statement data are available for most companies for five years or more, whether collected from original or secondary sources. Therefore, trends over time in growth and various financial ratios can be compared between the subject company and each of the guideline public companies. An example of the comparative analysis between the subject (Colossal Software) and guideline companies is shown as Exhibit 2.2. Comparative financial analysis is the subject of Chapter 8.

ANALYTICAL DATA FOR PUBLIC COMPANIES

One of the advantages of the guideline public company method is the plethora of analytical data available for most of the companies. Because of public investor interest on the parts of both individual and institutional investors, there are hundreds of sources providing investment outlook information for thousands of companies and hundreds of industries. Although the classifications are arbitrary and not totally discrete nor exhaustive, these sources can be identified by three categories:

1. Investor publications
2. Brokerage house reports
3. Consensus earnings forecasts

Investor publications range from popular individual investor sources such as Value Line to greatly detailed institutional services published by companies such

Exhibit 2.2 Guideline Public Company Common Size Comparison

Fiscal Year Ended	Best Software 12/31/98 (%)	IDX Systems 12/31/98 (%)	Symix Systems 6/30/98 (%)	Median (%)	Colossal Software 12/31/98 (%)
Size					
Assets ($MM)	75	284	66	75	57
Revenues ($MM)	69	322	98	98	69
Balance Sheets					
ASSETS					
Cash & Equivalents	39.6	3.9	9.2	9.2	16.1
Short-term Investments	22.4	39.9		31.2	12.5
Accounts Receivable, Net	11.0	34.9	49.6	34.9	30.3
Other Current Assets	4.2	3.4	4.3	4.2	9.4
Total Current Assets	77.3	82.2	63.1	77.3	68.4
Fixed Assets, Net	5.8	11.2	9.8	9.8	12.4
Capitalized Software Costs, Net		0.2	16.6	8.4	3.7
Intangible Assets, Net	9.6		7.7	8.6	12.3
Other Assets	7.3	6.4	2.9	6.4	3.2
TOTAL ASSETS	100.0	100.0	100.0	100.0	100.0
LIABILITIES & EQUITY					
Accounts Payable	8.4	5.1	20.0	8.4	7.0
Other Accrued Liabilities	10.7	5.8	2.4	5.8	6.9
Deferred Revenue	25.9	6.4	19.8	19.8	16.4
Current Portion of LTD	0.2	0.0	0.4	0.2	1.5
Total Current Liabilities	45.3	19.3	42.6	42.6	31.7
Deferred Income Taxes		0.0	3.7	1.9	1.8
Long-term Debt	0.2	0.0	3.5	0.2	12.2
Total Liabilities	46.2	22.4	52.8	46.2	45.7
Shareholders' Equity	53.9	77.6	47.2	53.9	54.3
TOTAL LIABILITIES & EQUITY	100.1	100.0	100.0	100.0	100.0
Income Statements					
Net Sales	100.0	100.0	100.0	100.0	100.0
Cost of Sales	19.4	50.7	36.6	36.6	42.6
Gross Profit	80.6	49.3	63.4	63.4	57.4
Depreciation Expense	4.3	3.5	6.4	4.3	3.0
Operating Expenses	70.8	34.7	61.4	61.4	52.2
Operating Profit	9.8	14.7	2.1	9.8	5.3
Interest Expense		0.0		0.0	0.9
Other Income (Expenses), Net	3.4	1.6	(0.2)	1.6	1.2
Pretax Income	13.2	16.3	1.9	13.2	5.5
Income Taxes	(5.0)	6.9	3.3	3.3	2.2
NET INCOME	8.1	9.4	(1.4)	8.1	3.3

as Standard & Poor's. The analyst can compare the outlooks for each of the guideline companies with the outlook for the subject company for guidance as to where the market multiples to be applied to the subject company should fall.

Brokerage house reports similarly give outlook information for thousands of companies, which can be compared to the outlook for the subject company. Brokerage house reports are heavily oriented to the "buy side" and therefore have been known to contain some degree of positive bias. Besides individual reports, there are services that index and abstract brokerage house reports.

Three services present consensus earnings estimates for thousands of public companies (see Appendix B). This makes it possible to have a multiple of next year's expected earnings as one of the market value multiples.

THE GUIDELINE PUBLIC COMPANY BASIC PROCEDURE

As discussed in Chapter 1, valuation multiples can be computed on either an equity basis or an invested capital basis. An example of computing market value of invested capital for guideline public companies is shown in Exhibit 2.3.

The object of the guideline public company method is to derive multiples to apply to the fundamental financial variables of the subject company. These fundamental financial variables may be either balance sheet amounts or, in most cases, operating variables derived from the income statements. Thus, one starts with a description of the subject company, in terms of lines of business, markets served, size, and other criteria, and then uses the information to develop criteria for selection of guideline companies. Based on these criteria, the analyst defines a population of companies (e.g., NYSE, ASE, or NASDAQ) and gets data on the companies meeting the criteria. www.hoovers.com is an excellent starting point to determine which companies are engaged in similar lines of business. Then, one can move the search to an Edgar website or go to Yahoo Profiles and click on SEC Filings. Those filings are formatted and free.

The analyst then analyzes both the subject and guideline companies' financial statements to "normalize" them, eliminating nonrecurring items and putting them on a comparable accounting basis. If a company seems to have unexplained abnormalities, the analyst might decide to exclude it. Using these adjusted statements, the analyst does comparative financial analysis, identifying similarities and relative strengths and weaknesses between the guideline and subject companies.

The analyst also conducts site visits and management interviews with the subject company to better understand the company and its similarities and strengths and weaknesses relative to the guideline companies. In the course of the site visits and interviews, the analyst may glean some ideas as to additional guideline companies or may find reason to reject one or more of the guideline companies originally selected.

At some point in the process, the analyst will also gather relevant industry and economic data. This will help the analyst to understand the nature of and outlook

Exhibit 2.3 Guideline Public Company Market Value of Invested Capital

Company	Mkt./Sym.	FYE[a]	Lat. Qtr. BV IBD ($000)	Lat. Qtr. MV IBD[b] ($000)	As of or for Period Ending	Bid/Close Price per Common Share 3/26/99 ($)	Common Shares Outstanding (000)	MV Common Equity ($000)	MVIC ($000)
Best Software	NASD/BEST	12/31/98	125	125	3/26/99	13.750	11,640	160,050	160,175
IDX Systems	NASD/IDXC	12/31/98	0	0	3/26/99	15.437	26,493	408,972	408,972
Symix Systems	NASD/SYMX	6/30/98	2,305	2,305	3/26/99	16.125	6,711	108,215	110,520
Colossal Software	N/A	12/31/98	6,594	6,594	3/26/99				

[a] FYE = Fiscal year-end.
[b] IBD = Interest-bearing debt.

for the industry, and how the subject company is positioned relative to the industry. The analyst should also consider how economic and industry factors will impact the subject company and, in particular, the extent to which these impacts will be greater or less for the subject company relative to the guideline companies, and the extent to which this analysis should affect the multiples chosen for the subject company relative to the multiples observed for the guideline companies.

Based on the comparative analysis between the guideline and subject companies, as well as site visits and management interviews and the nature of the industry, the analyst chooses what valuation multiple(s) to rely on and the appropriate value for each multiple relative to those observed for the guideline companies. The analyst then weights the indications of value from each multiple, either subjectively or by assigning a mathematical weight to each to get an indication of value. In some cases, it may be appropriate to add values for cash and/or excess assets or subtract for asset deficiencies. This indication of value is often called *value as if publicly traded* or *publicly traded equivalent value.*

PREMIUMS AND DISCOUNTS

The publicly traded equivalent value is a value based on publicly traded minority stocks. Premiums and/or discounts may be applied to this value, depending on the type of value being sought in the assignment (e.g., control value, nonmarketable minority value).

Valuing Controlling Interests

Since the indication of value is based on minority interest transactions, if one is valuing a controlling interest, it may sometimes be necessary to consider applying a premium for control; this is often appropriate. There are two schools of thought on this. (See Chapter 11.)

Quantification of a control premium, however, requires a challenging combination of empirical analysis and analytical judgment. Acquisition premiums observed in the market reflect both elements of control and also synergistic value. This is addressed in more detail in Chapter 11 on premiums and discounts. A discount for lack of marketability may or may not be appropriate, as discussed in Chapter 12.

Valuing Minority Interests

If valuing a minority interest in a privately held company, it is usually appropriate to apply a discount for lack of marketability to the value as if publicly traded. This discount often is substantial, and should be based on the facts and circumstances of each individual case, as discussed in Chapter 12.

SUMMARY

The basic steps in the guideline public company method are as follows (not necessarily in the following order)

- Set criteria for selection of guideline companies.
- Identify the population and source from which the guideline companies will be selected (see Chapter 5).
- List the companies that meet the criteria.
- Obtain financial data on the companies selected.
- Analyze and make adjustments to the subject company financial statements and the guideline company financial statements, if appropriate (see Chapter 7).
- Prepare comparative financial analysis between the guideline companies and the subject company (see Chapter 8).
- Prepare guideline company market value tables, on an equity basis and/or an invested capital basis (see Chapter 9).
- Gather and analyze relevant industry and economic data, and summarize it in terms of its impact on value.
- Visit the subject company facilities and conduct management interviews.
- Choose which multiples to apply to the subject company.
- For each multiple selected, decide on the value of that multiple to be applied to the subject company relative to the range of that multiple observed for the guideline companies.
- Decide on the relative weight to be accorded to the indication of value from each valuation multiple used (total weight must equal 1.00) (see Chapter 10).
- Prepare a publicly traded company method valuation summary table.
- Add any cash or excess assets or subtract asset deficiencies, if appropriate, to reach a publicly traded equivalent value or value as if publicly traded.
- Apply premiums or discounts, if appropriate, to reach the level of value called for in the assignment.

Throughout the process, the analyst may modify guideline selection criteria as necessary to try to obtain the best possible set of guideline companies. Companies often are eliminated for various reasons, such as lack of adequate comparability or lack of adequate data. The analyst should document such changes and additions, so that it is clear that objective selection criteria have been followed and that the analyst has not chosen a biased sample of guideline companies.

Chapter 3

The Guideline Transaction (Merged and Acquired Company) Method

The basic principles of the transaction method are the same as for the guideline publicly traded company method. The differences in implementation are a result of the differences in data available and, in some cases, the structure of the transactions.

One of the biggest differences is that mergers and acquisitions do not conveniently occur on the effective date of our subject company valuation. Thus, the analyst must decide how far back in time to go in collecting transactions. Also, the analyst may need to adjust observed market multiples for differences in economic and industry conditions between the dates of the observed transactions and the effective date of valuation for the subject company.

Because the companies have been bought out and there is no trading of shares, there is no body of analytical data or forecasts such as there are for public companies. Consequently, there will be no publicly available multiple of price to projected earnings. However, if a company was public before being acquired, it is possible to get current EPS estimates from the forecasting services. Also, for small companies and professional practices, usually only the latest year's data are available. In these cases, there will be no price to some average of past years' data.

Advantages of the guideline merged and acquired company method in some circumstances include:

• If valuing a very small business or practice, merged and acquired company transaction data are available for thousands of comparable businesses and practices far below the size for which guideline public company data are available.

• Hundreds of Standard Industrial Classification (SIC) or North American Industrial Classification System (NAICS) codes (industry or practice groups) are available for merged and acquired company or practice data for which there are no guideline public companies.

• The merged and acquired company data are for controlling interest transactions. Therefore, if valuing a controlling interest, it is not necessary to address the question of a control premium. (Of course, if valuing a minority interest, a minority interest discount may be applicable in many cases, and usually a discount for lack of marketability as well.)

Disadvantages include:

• The M&A company data is for successful or desirable businesses.

• The multiples may not apply to similar businesses if they lack the key financial and non-financial characteristics of the M&A company.

• The multiples may not apply if there are no eager or willing buyers on the scene.

There is clearly a great difference between the data available for a sale of a public company and the sale of a private company. The *Pratt's Stats*™ database has completely separate sections for sales of private companies and sales of public companies. However, the principles are the same, so we are treating the entire spectrum of guideline control transactions in a single chapter.

DIFFERENCES IN TRANSACTION STRUCTURE

In order to derive meaningful guidance for pricing or valuation from completed transactions, it is necessary to examine, and often adjust for, differences between the guideline and subject transactions related to what was or was not included in the transaction, and in terms of the transaction.

What Assets and Liabilities Are Included?

An important difference among transactions, particularly for sales of private companies, is the need to understand what was included in the transaction. The guideline public companies are virtually all stock transactions, and all of the companies' assets and liabilities are reflected in the stocks' public market trading prices. Many of the acquisitions, however, are asset sales, especially for smaller private companies. For an asset sale, it is important to know what was transacted, so that the multiples applied reflect the same assets. Many small private company sales include no current assets or liabilities, or in some cases do include inventory but not other current assets. One must carefully ascertain if real estate was included in the price.

Noncompete and Employment Agreements

Private company sales very often also include noncompete agreements and/or employment or consulting agreements that may be nonexistent or not of material amounts in public company transactions. It frequently is necessary to adjust for these factors. Dealing with the question of what may or may not be included in an asset sale is illustrated in Chapter 13, which is a sample valuation of a small sandwich shop.

Transaction Terms

If the standard of value is fair market value, then, by definition, that means a cash or cash-equivalent value. The terms for many transactions are not on a cash or cash-equivalent basis. If that is the case, and fair market value is being sought, then the prices of the guideline transactions might have to be adjusted to a cash-equivalent value before multiples are computed.

Restricted Stock.   Public companies often issue restricted stock for all or a portion of the purchase price of acquisitions. The value of restricted stock usually is somewhat less than its freely traded counterpart (see Chapter 12). If the consideration is restricted stock, the analyst should consider whether the deal value should be adjusted to reflect that difference.

Below Market Financing.   In some transactions, the seller carries back a note at less than an arm's-length market rate of interest. If fair market value is sought, the transaction price should be adjusted to a cash-equivalent value. This is merely a function of discounting the note payments to a cash-equivalent value at what would be a market rate for comparable borrowing.[1]

Earnouts.   An *earnout* means some sort of contingent payment, often contingent on customer retention or realizing certain revenue or profit goals. There necessarily is some subjectivity in adjusting these values to cash equivalences because it is necessary to adjust each payment to the expected value of the amount to be received. Rather than make such estimates, some analysts simply remove transactions involving earnouts from consideration.

SCOPE OF MARKET

The merger and acquisition method can cover businesses and practices of virtually any size, from a few thousand dollars in market value up to billions. It can also cover virtually any type of industry or practice.

In the public company sector, several hundred mergers, acquisitions, and going private transactions are reported each year.

In the private company sector, the number of transactions is substantial. Private company databases are capturing close to 3,000 transactions per year and working toward increasing that number.

In a paper presented to the American Society of Appraisers, veteran business appraiser Mike Hill[2] emphasized the size of the "small" business sector in this way:

- 23.32 million nonfarm businesses of which over 99% were small according to the Small Business Administration (SBA).
- 15 million small businesses *not* counting sole proprietorships.
- 18 million full-time businesses that are family dominated.
- Family-run businesses account for 50% of gross national product (GNP), and also over 50% of employment.
- From 1992 to 1996, all net new jobs were created by companies with under 500 employees.
- Almost 43% of the leadership of family-owned businesses will change hands within the next five years, even not counting sole proprietorships. This is over 1.2 million businesses per year.

AVAILABILITY OF MERGED AND ACQUIRED COMPANY TRANSACTION DATA

Several database providers have made major advances in recent years in capturing prices and other useful data on middle-market and small-company transactions so that they can be used as guidelines for pricing other transactions and for valuing businesses for all purposes. Collectively, these databases are adding several thousand transactions per year, and the number of transactions being captured is growing.

Depending on the status of the public or private acquiree and/or acquirer, varying amounts of detail may be available on each transaction. Although these classifications are not absolute, it is helpful to think of four categories:

1. Public company being acquired or going private
2. Private company acquired by public company, when transaction is significant enough to public company (10% or more of value of public company) to require filing of SEC Form 8-K
3. If a transaction is material, the financial data may be available in the acquieror's next 10-K
4. Private company acquired by public company with no 8-K report required
5. Private company sold to private company or individual

There is no single source of data listing all company sale transactions. Chapter 6 on finding merged and acquired company data addresses available sources.

Public Company Sale

If a public company sells or goes private, it must file a *prospectus* giving details of the sale. In this case, there will be as much information available as for a guideline publicly traded company. The data are a matter of public record and are readily available.

The primary source for such transactions is the *Mergerstat®/Shannon Pratt's Control Premium Study™*, details of which are presented in Chapter 6.

Private Company Sale to Public Company Requiring 8-K Filing

If a public company makes an acquisition of a company worth over 10% of the value of the public company, it must file a special events Form 8-K with the SEC. Form 8-K contains significant information, although not as much as a prospectus for a public company selling out. The data are a matter of public record and readily available through the SEC. Also, if the transaction is material, the data may be available in the acquieror's next 10-K.

Primary sources for such transactions are *Pratt's Stats™*, and *Done Deals*, details of which are presented in Chapter 6.

Private CompanyF Sale to Public Company with No 8-K

If a private company sells out to a public company and an 8-K is not required, then data may or may not be available, depending on the disclosure policy of the public company acquirer. The degree of public access and verifiability varies.

The primary source for such transactions is *Pratt's Stats™*, the details of which are presented in Chapter 6. There are also some industry-specific databases, for example, Kagan's database for cable acquisitions.

Private Company Sale to Private Buyer

If a private company sells to a private party, there is no legal requirement that any information be released. Since it would be helpful to intermediaries, acquirers, and business appraisers to have such data to implement a market approach to valuation, three database providers have worked to compile such data:

1. *IBA Market Data Base* (from the Institute of Business Appraisers)
2. *BIZCOMPS®*
3. *Pratt's Stats™* (the official database of the International Business Brokers Association [IBBA])

The information is provided primarily by intermediaries, that is, those who broker the transactions. In the case of *Pratt's Stats™* and the IBA database, some information comes from certified public accountant (CPA) firms. *Pratt's Stats™* also gathers data from financiers and acquirers.

The financial data are usually limited to the latest year. The *IBA Market Data Base* and *BIZCOMPS®* present only sales and discretionary earnings, while *Pratt's Stats™* presents summarized income statement and balance sheet information.

In most cases, the names of sellers and buyers are omitted, so the information is not verifiable by the end user. However, the databases are compiled by people and organizations that are well regarded for honesty and competence, with much of the data coming from members of the International Business Brokers Association and some from members of the Institute of Certified Business Counselors. There is no reason to consider the data to be biased, and the databases are well accepted by appraisers and the courts. More detail on these databases is presented in Chapter 6.

HOW FAR BACK IN TIME ARE TRANSACTIONS RELEVANT?

Obviously, we would like transactions as close in time to our effective valuation date as possible. We also would like to have enough transactions to have a meaningful sample. As a generality, the more data we have per transaction (to select those comparable to our subject) and the more reliable the data, the fewer transactions we need to have a meaningful sample.

Ray Miles did a study on the *IBA Market Data Base* and concluded that there were no long-term secular changes over time in the multiples of the industries represented in that database, and, therefore, the whole 20 years of data are relevant. One should be wary, however, that the general stability of average multiples over the long term may mask significant differences in multiples for interim periods within the long term. In general, during periods when interest rates are high and financing is difficult to obtain, multiples are lower. Also, the stability or volatility of multiples varies considerably from one industry to another, as some industries become "hot targets," while others fall out of favor. Perhaps due to rapid technological change, an example of what to consider is historic consolidations that push multiples up, but no longer apply. An appraiser would overstate the value if he simply used these historic multiples without considering the industry conditions at the time of the transaction. Much more research on this is necessary.

In the meantime, the analyst should consider relative similarities or differences in economic and industry conditions for some guidance as to how far back to search, as well as the amount and reliability of available data.

THE GUIDELINE MERGER AND ACQUISITION BASIC PROCEDURE

The guideline merger and acquisition basic procedure is essentially the same as for guideline public companies. The valuation analysis can be done on either an invested capital basis or an equity basis or both. Some steps may be omitted because of lack of available data.

One step that may be added is an adjustment to multiples to account for differences in industry and economic conditions from the date of the observed transaction to the date of the subject valuation. Standard & Poor's (S&P) and other services publish statistical series, such as industry average P/E ratios. Multiples may be adjusted by changes in industry average multiples. For example, suppose that the S&P industry average P/E multiple was 15× earnings at the time of the guideline transaction and 18× at the time of the subject company effective valuation date. This would be an increase of 20%, or an index of 1.20. The guideline company multiple could be adjusted by the index multiple. If the guideline company P/E multiple had been 12, it could be adjusted $1.20 \times 12 = 14.4\times$. However, the analyst must be cautious in applying such an adjustment. Private company transaction multiples tend to be less volatile over time than multiples in daily public market trading. Also, some analysts believe that the gap between market and acquired company multiples narrows when the market rises, although we are not aware of any definitive studies on this.

Because the transactions are, by definition, control transactions, the value indicated by the guideline merged and acquired company method is a control value. It is important that the analyst understands whether this control value is the value of all invested capital or only the value of the equity. Of course, in some transactions, especially of smaller companies, there are no senior securities, so the equity value represents the value of all the invested capital. In such a case—in *Pratt's Stats™* for example—the number shown for deal price and equity price is the same.

PREMIUMS AND DISCOUNTS

Because the indicated value is a control value, it normally would not be appropriate to add a control premium. One or more discounts may be appropriate.

Valuing Controlling Interests

If valuing a controlling interest, a discount for lack of marketability *may* be appropriate in limited circumstances. There could be significant time and costs that would need to be incurred in order to make the subject company salable, which could be the basis for a lack of marketability discount. Also, there may be considerable risk as to whether the estimated value can actually be attained. This is discussed further in Chapter 12.

Valuing Minority Interests

If valuing a minority interest in a privately held company, a discount for lack of control usually would be warranted, and frequently a discount for lack of marketability as well. Most analysts (and most courts) prefer to deal with the marketability and minority discounts separately because, although related, they are two separate concepts and lend themselves to being quantified by different types of market evidence and analysis. It is quite common for a minority interest in a closely held company to be worth less than half its proportionate share of the value of a controlling interest. Sometimes we see the minority and marketability factors lumped as a single discount. Minority discounts are discussed in Chapter 11, and discounts for lack of marketability are discussed in Chapter 12. The analyst should carefully evaluating the lack of control elements and how minority and marketability discounts reflect this lack of control.

SUMMARY

The basic steps in the guideline merged and acquired company method are (not necessarily in the following order):

- Set criteria for collection of guideline merged and acquired transactions, including the time frame (e.g., back three years, back five years).
- Identify the population and source or sources from which the guideline transactions will be selected (see Chapter 6).
- List the companies that meet the criteria. (When using multiple sources, be careful not to list the same transaction twice, which could result in giving double weight to a single transaction.)
- Obtain financial data on the companies selected.
- Analyze and make adjustments to the subject company's financial statements and, to the extent that the guideline companies' historical financial statements are available, analyze and adjust those statements, if appropriate (see Chapter 7).

- Prepare comparative financial analysis between the guideline companies and the subject company to the extent that financial information is available for the companies in the guideline company transactions. (Of the databases on private company transactions, *Pratt's Stats*™ is the only one that provides sufficient information for this step, and even then the comparative data are limited to summaries of the latest year's statements (see Chapter 8).

- Prepare guideline merged and acquired company market valuation tables, on an equity basis and/or an invested capital basis (see Chapter 9). If necessary, adjust face values of transactions to a cash equivalent value before calculating multiples.

- Adjust, if appropriate, observed multiples by an index (i.e., an index of S&P industry P/E ratios) to account for changes in industry and economic conditions between the observed guideline transaction and the subject effective valuation date.

- Gather and analyze relevant economic and industry data, and summarize in terms of their impact on value.

- Visit the subject company facilities and conduct management interviews.

- Choose which multiples to apply to the subject company.

- For each multiple selected to be used, decide on the value of that multiple to be applied to the subject company relative to the range of that multiple observed for the guideline companies.

- Decide on the relative weight accorded to the indication of value from each valuation multiple used (total weights must equal 1.00) (see Chapter 10).

- Prepare a merged and acquired company method valuation summary table.

- Adjust for any assets or liabilities included in the subject company valuation but not included in the guideline transactions.

- Apply discounts, if appropriate, to reach the level of value called for in the assignment.

Notes

1. For a detailed explanation of converting a price on terms to a cash equivalent value, see "Trade-off between Cash and Terms," chap. 27, in Shannon P. Pratt, Robert F. Reilly, and Robert P. Schweihs, *Valuing Small Businesses and Professional Practices,* 3rd ed. (New York: McGraw-Hill, 1998), 487–502.

2. J. Michael Hill, "Small Business Valuation Revisited," American Society of Appraisers International Conference, Kaanapali Beach, Hawaii, 1998. Full text available on www.BVLibrary .com.

Chapter 4

Other Market Methods

Besides guideline public companies and guideline independent mergers and acquisitions, there are a few other categories of evidence of value that we can properly consider under the broad umbrella of the market approach:

- Past transactions involving the subject company
- Bona fide offers to buy
- Rules of thumb
- Buy-sell agreements

PAST TRANSACTIONS

One of the most useful but often overlooked market approach methods is analysis of past transactions involving the subject company. These transactions can be classified into three groups:

1. Past changes of control ownership of the subject company
2. Past transactions in minority ownership interests in the subject company
3. Acquisitions made by the subject company

As with other transactions, it is important to determine that they were conducted on an arm's-length basis. The question of whether transactions were on an arm's-length basis is often an issue in this respect; the definitions shown in Exhibit 4.1 may prove helpful.

Past Control Transactions

If the subject company itself has changed hands on an arm's-length basis in the recent past, that transaction might provide a good basis for valuation. The transaction should be handled basically like any other guideline merged and acquired company transaction, that is, multiples derived from the transaction applied to the same financial fundamentals as of the new valuation date, with multiples adjusted for changes in economic and industry conditions, if appropriate. The Standard & Poor's industry price index may be a good source for this adjustment.

Exhibit 4.1   Definitions of Arm's-length Transactions

Black's Law Dictionary

Arm's length transaction. Said of a transaction negotiated by unrelated parties, each acting in his or her own self interest; the basis for a fair market value determination. A transaction in good faith in the ordinary course of business by parties with independent interests. Commonly applied in areas of taxation when there are dealings between related corporations, *e.g.*, parent and subsidiary. Inecto, Inc. v. Higgins, D.C.N.Y., 21 F. Supp. 418. The standard under which unrelated parties, each acting in his or her own best interest, would carry out a particular transaction. For example, if a corporation sells property to its sole shareholder for $10,000, in testing whether $10,000 is an "arm's length" price it must be ascertained for how much the corporation could have sold the property to a disinterested third party in a bargained transaction.[a]

Barron's Dictionary of Finance and Investment Terms

Arm's Length Transaction. Transaction that is conducted as though the parties were unrelated, thus avoiding any semblance of conflict of interest. For example, under current law parents may rent real estate to their children and still claim business deductions such as depreciation as long as the parents charge their children what they would charge if someone who is not a relative were to rent the same property.[b]

---

[a] Henry Campbell Black, Joseph R. Nolan, Jacqueline M. Nolan-Haley, et al., *Black's Law Dictionary* 6th ed. (St. Paul, MN: West Publishing, 1990), 109.

[b] John Downes and Jordan Elliot Goodman, *Barron's Dictionary of Finance and Investment Terms,* 4th ed. (Hauppauge, NY: Barron's Educational Series, 1995), 26.

Past Minority Transactions

If there have been past minority transactions in the subject company's stock or partnership interests, they may provide worthwhile evidence of market value. It is important to know whether they are on an arm's-length basis and between knowledgeable buyers and sellers. These last two points require careful investigation by the analyst to determine whether, or the extent to which, they should be given weight as evidence of value. For example, care should be taken in evaluating prices paid to buy out trouble-making shareholders or partners, as the implied value of 100% interests may be higher than reasonable FMV.

Past Acquisitions

Past acquisitions by the subject company are often a fertile field for very valid guideline market transaction data and are a source often overlooked. We would suggest, "Have you made any acquisitions?" as a standard question in management interviews.

Such acquisitions almost always are in the subject company's line of business. They can be treated just as other guideline merger and acquisition transactions. Particularly in FASB 142 engagements, these are a valuable reference source.

During the management interviews, three questions that the analyst might ask are:

1. Have you made any acquisitions?
2. Have you received any offers to be purchased?
3. Have you made any offers to be acquired?

OFFERS TO BUY

Usually, for offers to buy to be probative evidence of value, they must be firm, arm's length, with sufficient detail of terms to be able to estimate the cash equivalent value, and from a source with the financial ability to consummate the offer. All of these requirements rarely are met.

If the requirements are met, then the offer to buy could be handled in the same way that past transactions were to arrive at one indication of value as of the valuation date. Even so, however, because the offer did not conclude in a consummated transaction, the weight accorded its indication of value may be limited.

RULES OF THUMB

Many industries, especially those characterized by very small businesses, have valuation rules of thumb, some more valid than others. If they exist, they should be considered if they have a wide industry following. However, they should never be relied on as the only valuation method.

Nature of Rules of Thumb

Rules of thumb come in many varieties, but the most common are

- Multiple of sales
- Multiple of some physical measure of activity
- Multiples of discretionary earnings (also called seller's discretionary cash flow [SDCF] or owner's cash flow [OCF])
- Assets plus any of the above

Proper Use of Rules of Thumb

Rules of thumb are best used as a check on the reasonableness of the conclusions reached by other valuation methods, such as capitalization of earnings or a market multiple method. A good source for guidance on when to use rules of thumb is in the American Society of Appraisers Business Valuation Standards:

Rules of thumb may provide insight on the value of a business, business ownership interest, or security. However, value indications derived from the use of rules of thumb should not be given substantial weight unless supported by other valuation methods and it can be established that knowledgeable buyers and sellers place substantial reliance on them.[1]

Problems with Rules of Thumb

One problem with rules of thumb is the lack of knowledge about the derivation of the "rules." Several other problems are discussed next.

Not Knowing What Was Transacted. Most, but not all, rules of thumb presume that the valuation rule applies to an asset sale. Few of them, however, specify what assets are assumed to be transferred. The asset composition may vary substantially from one transaction to another.

It is also important to remember that the rules of thumb almost never specify whether they assume a noncompete agreement or an employment agreement, even though such types of agreements are very common for the kinds of businesses for which rules of thumb exist.

Not Knowing Assumed Terms of the Transactions. Most transactions for which there are rules of thumb are not all-cash transactions, but involve some degree of seller financing. The financing terms vary greatly from one transaction to another and affect both the face value and also the fair market value (which, by definition, assumes a cash or cash-equivalent value).

Not Knowing the Assumed Level of Profitability.   The level of profitability impacts almost all real-world valuations. However, for rules of thumb that are based on either gross revenue or some measure of physical volume, there is no indication of the average level of profitability that the rule of thumb implies.

Uniqueness of Each Entity.   Every business is, to some extent, different from every other business. Rules of thumb give no guidance for taking the unique characteristics of any particular business into account.

Multiples Change over Time.   Rules of thumb are basically timeless, but in the real world, market valuation multiples do change over time. Some industries are more susceptible than others to changes in economic and industry conditions. Changes occur in the supply/demand relationship for valuing various kinds of businesses and professional practices because of many factors, sometimes including legal/regulatory changes. When using market transaction multiples, adjustments can be made for changes in conditions from the time of the guideline transaction to the subject valuation date, but there is no base date for rules of thumb.

Sources for Rules of Thumb

Two popular sources for rules of thumb are Glenn Desmond's *Handbook of Small Business Valuation Formulas and Rules of Thumb*[2] and Tom West's annual *Business Reference Guide.*[3] The rules of thumb section in West's reference guide has expanded every year in recent years. For example, the 2005 Guide contains over 500 pages of rules of thumb, covering a wide variety of industries, including many specific franchises.

For some industries, articles or trade publications may provide some industry rules of thumb. The appraiser may also make some phone calls to people in the industry locally to get a feel for local rules of thumb which, for some businesses, may vary widely from one locale to another. For example, analysts may call local business brokers to help evaluate local rules of thumb.

BUY-SELL AGREEMENTS

Buy-sell agreements are included here as a market approach category on the assumption that they represent parties' agreements on pricing potential subsequent transactions. The pricing mechanism set forth in the buy-sell agreement may be determinative of value in certain circumstances, such as where it is legally binding for the purposes of the valuation. In other cases, the buy-sell agreement price might be one method of estimating value, but not determinative. In still other instances, the buy-sell agreement might be ignored because it does not represent a bona fide arm's-length sale agreement.

For estate tax purposes, for example, a buy-sell agreement price is binding for estate tax determination only if it meets *all* of these conditions:

- The agreement is binding during life as well as at death.
- The agreement creates a determinable value as of a specifically determinable date.
- The agreement has at least some bona fide business purpose (this could include the promotion of orderly family ownership and management succession, so this is an easy test to meet).
- The agreement results in a fair market value for the subject business interest, when executed. Often buy-sell agreement values will generate future date of death or gift date values substantially above or below what the fair market value otherwise would have been for the subject interest—even though the value was reasonable when the agreement was made.
- Its terms are comparable to similar arrangements entered into by persons in arm's-length transactions.[4]

If a buy-sell agreement does not meet these conditions, it is entirely possible to have a buy-sell value that is legally binding on an estate for transaction purposes that does not even provide enough money for the estate taxes on the value of the business or business interest.

Marital dissolution is a valuation context where the applicability of buy-sell agreements as evidence of value often is hotly contested. Analysts who find themselves in that situation should both consult the relevant case law and seek advice of counsel.

SUMMARY

This chapter has briefly discussed four valuation methods that sometimes are classified under the general grouping of the market approach:

- Past subject company transactions
- Bona fide offers to buy
- Rules of thumb
- Buy-sell agreements

Of these, past transactions may be the most useful, yet are often overlooked. Offers to buy rarely reach the point of negotiation or commitment to be considered viable indications of value. Rules of thumb should never be used alone, but may provide a check on valuations reached by other methods. Buy-sell agreements can range all the way from a binding determination of value to no weight at all, depending on the purpose of the valuation and the facts and circumstances surrounding the buy-sell agreement.

Notes

1. American Society of Appraisers, Business Valuation Standards, BVS-V.
2. Glenn Desmond, *Handbook of Small Business Valuation Formulas and Rules of Thumb,* 3rd ed. (Camden, ME: Valuation Press, 1993).
3. Tom West, *The Business Reference Guide* (Concord, MA: Business Brokerage Press), published annually.
4. This requirement was added as part of Section 2703 of Internal Revenue Code Chapter 14 and is mandatory only for buy-sell agreements entered into or amended after October 8, 1990. For an extensive discussion of buy-sell agreements, see "Buy-Sell Agreements" in Shannon P. Pratt, Robert F. Reilly, and Robert P. Schweihs, *Valuing a Business,* 4th ed. (New York: McGraw-Hill, 2000).

PART II

Finding and Analyzing Comparative Market Transaction Data

Chapter 5

Finding Public Company Market Transaction Data

If the public company population is defined to include only those that report to the Securities and Exchange Commission (SEC) (over 12,550 companies), then the population is finite. This population can be searched either through EDGAR or through any of several secondary sources.

The search generally proceeds by industry classification, primarily SIC (Standard Industrial Classification) and, increasingly among some services, by NAICS (North American Industrial Classification System). The various services do not necessarily classify companies by SIC code by the same criteria, so one may uncover more companies by searching two or more sources.

In order to be required to report to the SEC, a publicly traded company must meet *both* of these two criteria:

1. Assets over $1 million
2. Over 300 stockholders (over 500 stockholders to start with, but, once reporting, can avoid reporting only if the number of stockholders falls below 300)

Businesses assign their own SIC codes, and secondary sources sometimes accept the SIC code assigned. One might start with an online service like One-Source and type in various words that describe the businesses. This can identify multiple SICs from which guideline public companies might be selected. Another good starting point to identify companies engaged in similar businesses could be hoovers.com.

EDGAR

Starting in May 1996, all companies required to report to the SEC are required to report electronically. The system is called the Electronic Data Gathering and Retrieval System (EDGAR).

The system collects all major filings, particularly including

- 10-Ks (annual reports)
- 10-Qs (quarterly reports)
- 8-Ks (special events reports)
- All other required or voluntary public disclosures

Access to EDGAR is free at www.sec.gov. It is also available free from the New York University Stern School of Business, www.edgar.stern-nyu.edu. However, the format is difficult to use. This problem is easily corrected with a free-ware program, available from both the foregoing URLs.

EDGAR Online Pro provides data from SEC filings of over 15,000 companies, including some no longer active. Filings are updated daily as they are filed with the SEC. Some of the features of EDGAR Online Pro are: alerts can be set for new filings; filings can be formatted in HTML, Word, Excel, or Adobe Acrobat; and data can be pulled to conduct peer comparisons with up to five years of annual or five quarterly filings. The comparisons contain more than 75 data elements. 10k Wizard is also a useful source.

Additional detail on these services is contained in Appendix B.

SECONDARY SOURCES FOR SEC REPORTING COMPANIES

It often is most expedient to do SIC code searches from secondary sources, especially electronic sources. The electronic sources are available in two forms: CD-ROM and online.

CD-ROM Public Company Sources

Two convenient CD-ROM sources are *Standard & Poor's Corporations* and *Compact D/SEC* from Primark. Both are updated monthly and come out about the middle of the month with stock prices as of the close of the last trading day of the previous month. These two products use different criteria for assigning SIC codes.

Another possibility is *Dialog on Disc* from Knight Ridder Information.

Online Services

Compustat is available online, and is a good source for detailed financial statements. The most cost-effective way to get detailed financial statements (with all the original detail) is to use EDGAR data. EDGAR Online is a popular source for complete SEC filings.

Print Sources

Many print sources for public company data are available as well. The two most comprehensive sources are *Standard & Poor's Corporation Records* and *Moody's Manuals.* Each of these is comprised of several volumes, and both are available in many public libraries. The Government Printing Office publishes a single-volume work entitled *Directory of Companies Required to File Annual Reports with the SEC,* and it is updated annually.

PUBLICLY REGISTERED LIMITED PARTNERSHIP DATA

Starting in the late 1970s, thousands of limited partnerships were syndicated to raise money for cable companies, real estate, equipment leasing, and mortgage investment ventures. In the late 1980s, these partnerships began trading through a small number of brokerage firms. Because the limited partnerships are publicly traded, there is a significant amount of information available about the interests to be used when valuing privately held family limited partnerships. The primary reporting source for publicly registered partnerships is Partnership Profiles, Inc. The data are available in print through an online database at www .partnershipprofiles.com. However, the number of such partnerships has been reduced in recent years due to liquidations. As the partnerships mature and approach liquidation, discounts from pro-rata net asset value tend to diminish. The volume of partnership equity being exchanged has fallen from about $600 million per year in the mid 1990's to about $60 million per year in the mid 2000's.

Nevertheless, these data have taken on increased importance in recent years as the scrutiny of the IRS has increased regarding valuation of family limited partnerships. Also, many of the valuation dates are as of prior years when the volume of trading in these instruments was more active.

SOURCES FOR NONREPORTING COMPANIES

Thousands of companies that are publicly traded do not have to report to the SEC because of their number of stockholders or their total value of assets.

The most comprehensive way to find nonreporting public companies is somewhat cumbersome. *Standard & Poor's Corporation Records* contains many such companies, but they are not identified as public or private. One can find the companies from *S&P Corporation Records* under the desired SIC code, and then turn to the *National Monthly Stock Summary*. If they are listed there, one or more market makers will quote them.

One other source is the Walker's manuals. These include the *Walker's Manual of Penny Stocks* and the *Walker's Manual of Unlisted Stocks*. Each of these is published annually in June, and includes about 500 nonreporting companies. Other sources could include regional brokerage houses that quote small stocks, usually local or regional in nature.

One drawback to the nonreporting companies is that most do not have as much volume of active trading as the reporting companies. The extent to which their trading prices provide arm's-length evidence of value becomes a matter of judgment in each case. Sometimes they are the only arm's-length evidence of value available. A few years ago, the author was valuing a ski resort and found four public, but nonreporting, ski resort companies when there were no public ski resort companies reporting to the SEC (and the expert on the other side made a flat statement in his report that he had made a thorough search and there were no public ski resort companies). This additional evidence made a strong contribution toward settling the case favorably for our client.

SUMMARY

About 12,550 companies are required to report to the SEC. All are required to report electronically through the system called EDGAR. Access is free through the SEC or at a reasonable cost through vendors that provide features such as enhanced searching and sorting.

Having identified potentially relevant guideline companies through searches by industry (usually SIC or NAICS codes), one then obtains company financial documents and reviews them to further define the search to reflect those public companies that have the greatest degree of comparability with the subject. Company financial statements may be obtained through EDGAR or through any of several commercial CD-ROM, online, or print sources. Many of these were mentioned in this chapter, and access information for all of them is covered in Appendix B. Updates of existing data sources and newly developed data sources are reported monthly in the Data and Publications department of *Shannon Pratt's Business Valuation Update*® and summarized regularly in the *Business Valuation Data Publications, and Internet Directory*™ supplement to that newsletter. There are also thousands of nonreporting public companies, for which several sources were listed in this chapter.

Finding Merger and Acquisition Market Data

Finding merger and acquisition (M&A) market data is a good deal more complicated than finding guideline public company data, although it has become easier in the last few years now that we have several databases that specialize in reporting transactions. There is a wide variety of sources, but no single comprehensive source. In almost all cases, it is necessary to consult two or more sources in order to conduct a comprehensive search.

The searches generally proceed by industry classification, which is typically identified by either an SIC (Standard Industrial Classification) or a NAICS (North American Industrial Classification System) code. Different services have different criteria for classifying companies in terms of these codes, which is one of the reasons several sources are necessary. Another reason for needing several sources is that services have very different criteria for defining the population of transactions that they report.

For convenience, we will organize this chapter into three sections, in terms of the transaction size, usually defined by market value of invested capital:

1. Large transactions
2. Middle-market and small transactions
3. Very small transactions

LARGE TRANSACTIONS

The search for large transactions sometimes can include two steps—identifying the transaction and gathering data on the transaction or background company data.

Securities Data Publishing Inquiry Service

Securities Data Corporation (SDC) is one of the most comprehensive sources of large transactions, and actually includes some transactions as small as $10 million deal value (MVIC). The data go back to 1982. Although SDC includes primarily sales of public companies, it also includes some acquisitions of private companies by public companies. The SDC service also posts foreign transactions and has the most data points per transaction of any of the services.

The search can be started with SDC by providing the search parameters. These need to include at least the four-digit SIC code(s) and the range of transaction dates desired. Other criteria can be specified, such as size in terms of revenue, assets, EBIT (earnings before interest and taxes), or EBITDA (earnings before interest, taxes, depreciation, and amortization).

The cost is determined by the number of companies that the search produces and the number of data fields requested per company. An inquiry can be made as to the number of companies produced by the initial parameters, and then the search criteria can be narrowed or broadened before the printout of the data fields is requested.

The data fields available include

*   Announcement date
*   Transaction date
*   Target name
*   Target SIC
*   Target description
*   Acquirer name
*   Total assets
*   Total revenue
*   EBIT
*   EBITDA
*   A synopsis of the transaction, including

- ◆ Percent of target company acquired
- ◆ Whether a stock or an asset deal
- ◆ Number of shares
- ◆ Debt assumed
- ◆ Whether registered or restricted stock, if a stock deal

The Securities Data Corporation also has many other data fields, but these are usually the ones of greatest interest. An example of an SDC printout is shown as Exhibit 6.1.

Exhibit 6.1 Example of Data Contained in Report from Securities Data Publishing's SDC Platinum Mergers and Acquisitions Database

Date Announced	Date Effective	Target Primary SIC Code	Target Name	Target Business Description	Acquirer Name
01/23/1997	01/16/1997	5944	Barry's Jewelers Inc.	Operate retail jewelry stores	Investor

Equity Value ($mil)	Target Net Sales LTM ($mil)	Target Operating Income LTM ($mil)	Target Total Assets ($mil)	Target Cash Flow ($mil)	Synopsis	Value of Transaction ($mil)
9.559	155.1	5.410	151.1	21.8	An investor Gary Gelman raised his stake to 11.42% from 4.25% in Barry's Jewelers by acquiring 286,700 common shares in open market for an indicated value of up to $0.685 mil in cash. The shares were purchased from Nov 21, 96 to Jan 16, 97 at prices ranging from $1.16 to $2.38 per share with the valued (SIC) based on the high price in the range.	0.7

Date Announced	Date Effective	Target Primary SIC Code	Target Name	Target Business Description	Acquirer Name
05/06/1997	05/06/1997	5944	Little Switzerland Inc.	Own and operate jewelry store	Investor Group

Equity Value ($mil)	Target Net Sales LTM ($mil)	Target Operating Income LTM ($mil)	Target Total Assets ($mil)	Target Cash Flow ($mil)	Synopsis	Value of Transaction ($mil)
44.310	84.3	7.554	84.8	10.6	An investor group comprised of ValueVest Partners and Mr. Donald Sfurm acquired a 9.89% stake, or 837,400 common shares, in Little Switzerland between Jan 8 and May 2 for between $4.700 and $5.237 per share, for a total of approximately $4.38 mil in cash.	4.4

Source: Thomson Financial Securities Data (973/622-5200). Used with permission.

After receiving the printout, the analyst needs to decide which transactions appear to meet the desired criteria. At this point the criteria could again be modified, possibly to eliminate transactions with terms that would be difficult to convert to cash equivalent value. If there are not enough transactions to gain meaningful guidance, the analyst may broaden the criteria and go back and ask for more.

Once the population of guideline M&A transactions has been established, the next step is to get historical financial data on the merged and acquired companies. This can be done through any of several electronic or print sources, such as Compustat. If the analyst wishes to examine and possibly adjust the guideline M&A companies' financial statements, then the analyst can go to EDGAR, either directly or through one of the enhanced EDGAR sources such as EDGAR Online.

Alacra.com

Another useful online source for large- and middle-market transaction data is alacra.com, formerly xls.com. It provides extensive detailed company financial information. All the searching is included in a monthly fee, and the desired data can be purchased on the basis of the quoted price.

Mergerstat®/Shannon Pratt's Control Premium Study™

The *Mergerstat®/Shannon Pratt's Control Premium Study™* is available online at BVMarketData.com℠. It contains all transactions in takeovers of public companies resulting in 50.1% ownership or more since the beginning of 1998, more than 4,000 transactions as this edition goes to press.

It is called the "Control Premium Study" because it presents the percentage premium of the takeover relative to public market prices one day, one week, one month, and two months prior to the acquisition date and the "Mergerstat Control Premium," intended to be the premium from when the stock was "at rest," that is, not influenced by the merger rumors. However, it also contains some 60 data fields for each transaction, including five valuation multiples.

A transaction report from the *Mergerstat®/Shannon Pratt's Control Premium Study™* is presented in Exhibit 6.2. If the analysis needs more data, SEC filings are available.

Public Stats™

The Public Stats™ transaction database contains data variously described as guideline company, guideline transaction, comparable sales data, business comparable, and/or market data. This database reports the financial and transactional details of the sales of publicly held companies and currently contains over 1,740

Exhibit 6.2   *Mergerstat®/Shannon Pratt's Control Premium Study™* Transaction Report

Transaction Details

	Acquiror	Target
SIC	7372 Prepackaged Software	7372 Prepackaged Software
NAICS	334611 Software Reproducing	334611 Software Reproducing
Name	Oracle Corp.	PeopleSoft, Inc.
Business Description	Designs, develops, markets, and supports a diversified line of computer software products	Develops and markets business management software
Stock Exchange	Nasdaq	Nasdaq
Nation	United States	United States

Premiums

2 Month	1 Month	1 Week	1 Day	MergerStat Control Premium
0.764	0.606	0.617	0.754	0.754

Target Stock Prices (per share) (Home Currency)

CUSIP	Target Stock Ticker	Unaffected Price	Announce Day Price	1 Day Price	1 Week Price	1 Month Price	2 Month Price
	PSFT	15.110	17.820	15.110	16.390	16.500	15.020

Sale Details

Date Announced	6/6/2003
Date Effective	1/7/2005
Deal Value ($mil-US)	$9,957
Deal Currency	United States Dollar
% of Shares Acquired	100.0
% of Shares Held at Date Announced	N/A
% of Shares Held after Acquisition	100.0
Purchase Price Per Share ($'s-US)	$26.50
Common Shares Acquired (mil)	375.746
Deal Exchange Rate	1.000
Purchase Price/Share (Home currency)	26.50
Consideration	C
Attitude	Friendly
Form	Acq-TO
Transaction Purpose	Horizontal

Target Financial Data ($mil-US)

LTM Net Sales	1,925.937
LTM EBITDA	387.664
LTM EBIT	281.625
LTM Net Income	183.999
BV Target Common Equity	1,980.358
Target Invested Capital	9,957.280
Book Value Per Share	6.255
Common Shares Outstanding (000's)	375.746
Operating Profit Margin	0.146
Net Profit Margin	0.096

Target Pricing Multiples

Implied MVE ($mil-US)	9,957.280
Price/Sales	5.170
Price/Income	
Price/Book Value	5.028
Target Invested Capital/EBIT	
Target Invested Capital/EBITDA	

N/A = Not Available

transactions between 1995 through the present. For an example of a Public Stats™ transaction, see Exhibit 6.3.

Large-Company Print M&A Sources

Analysts on a limited budget may consult several print sources, including the *Mergerstat Transaction Roster* and the *Merger Yearbook,* in order to compile a list

Exhibit 6.3 *Mergerstat® Transaction Roster* M&A Transactions

Seller Industry [Banking & Finance]   Select Seller SIC: [6000 to 6099]

Seller Name: [   ] Buyer Name: [   ] Dates: [2004] Go Reset=

Heartland Bancshares, Inc.

Franklin, IN, US

SIC 6021   Provides commercial and retail banking services through Heartland Community Bank

Acquired by: Blue River Bancshares, Inc.
Shelbyville, IL, US

SIC 6035   Federally chartered savings institution and holding company for Shelby County Bank

Announced	Closed	Base Price	PE Ratio	Pmt Methd
9/1/2004	3/31/2005	$19.1	NEG	Stock

Blue River Bancshares Inc, the holding company for Shelby County Bank, entered a definitive merger agreement with Heartland Bancshares Inc, the holding company of Heartland Community Bank, for about US$19.1 million in stock. BRB's will issue 3,541,196 shares to be exchanged for each outstanding common shares of Heartland Bancshares at an exchange ratio of 2.54. The offer price is US$13.69 based on BRB's August 31, 2004 closing price at US$5.69. The merged entity will be named Heartland Bancshares, and will operate as Heartland Community Bank. Heartland Community Bank will have Jeffrey Joyce as its CFO and will consist of 5 directors, four of which came from BRB. Howe Barnes Investments Inc served as the financial adviser to BRB, and Donnelly Penman & Partners, Grosse Pointe served as Heartland's financial adviser. The transaction is expected to close on the first quarter of 2005.

Redwood Empire Bancorp

Santa Rosa, CA, US

SIC 6021   National commercial bank

Acquired by: Westamerica Bancorporation
San Rafael, CA, US

SIC 6021   National commercial bank

Announced	Closed	Base Price	PE Ratio	Pmt Methd
8/26/2004	3/2/2005	$141.6	NEG	Combo

Westamerica Bancorporation acquired Redwood Empire Bancorp for approximately US$141.6 million in stock and cash. Under the terms of agreement, Empire Bancorp shareholders will receive consideration consisting of US$11.37 in cash and 0.3263 Westamerica shares for each Redwood share. Westamerica Bancorporation through its wholly owned subsidiary, Westamerica Bank, operates 87 branches and two trust offices throughout 22 northern and central California counties.

BankNorth Group, Inc.

Portland, ME, US

SIC 6021   National commercial bank

Acquired by: Toronto Dominion Bank
Toronto, CA

SIC 6081   International commercial bank

Announced	Closed	Base Price	PE Ratio	Pmt Methd
8/26/2004	3/1/2005	$2,089.7	NEG	Combo

Toronto Dominion Bank Financial Group acquired a 51% majority stake in BankNorth Group Inc for US$4 billion in cash and stock. Toronto Dominion Bank agreed to pay US$12.24 per share in cash, plus 0.2351 of its shares plus 0.49 of new BankNorth Group shares for every BankNorth Group share acquired. BankNorth Group Inc will continue to trade on the New York Stock Exchange. Toronto Dominion Bank also has to option to acquire up to 66 2/3% of BankNorth Group. The acquisition allow Toronto Dominion Bank to enter the northeastern United States banking markets. The management team of BankNorth Group will remain with the company. BankNorth Group operates 389 bank branches in six states and had $29.3 billion in assets, as of June 30, 2004.

Ripley National Bank

Ohio, OH, US

SIC 6021   National commercial bank

Acquired by: Oak Hill Financial, Inc.
Jackson, OH, US

SIC 6022   State commercial bank

Announced	Closed	Base Price	PE Ratio	Pmt Methd
7/20/2004	10/1/2004	$5.5		Cash

Oak Hill Finance signed a definitive agreement for the acquisition of Ripley National Bank for $5.5 million in cash. Ripley National had $55.9 million in total assets, $43.5 million in loans, $50.8 million in deposits, and $4.6 million in shareholders equity. The acquiring is expected to be completed by October 1.

Riggs National Corp.

Washington, DC, US

SIC 6021   National commercial bank

Acquired by: PNC Financial Services Group, Inc.
Pittsburgh, PA, US

SIC 6021   National commercial bank

Announced	Closed	Base Price	PE Ratio	Pmt Methd
7/16/2004	5/13/2005	$654.5	NEG	Combo

PNC Financial Group acquired Riggs National Corp for approximately $654.5 million in stock and cash. Under terms of the agreement, shareholders will receive 0.3008 shares of PNC stock and US$3.61 in cash for each Riggs National share. Riggs has about $6 billion in its asset through 50 branches in the metropolitan Washington, D.C. area. The acquisition is expected to support PNC's growth in its banking business.

Source: Mergerstat Online. Used with permission.

of relevant M&A transactions. An example of the *Mergerstat® Transaction Roster* is shown as Exhibit 6.3.

Other possible sources include the *Merger Sourcebook* and *Mergers & Acquisitions.* Descriptions of these sources are included in Appendix B.

It is clear from the sample exhibits and the descriptions in Appendix B that these sources provide limited data. If the seller were a public company, the analyst would need to go to EDGAR or one of the summary sources to obtain background financial data.

MIDDLE-MARKET AND SMALL TRANSACTIONS

Two databases specialize in transactions with a deal value under $1 billion: *Done Deals* and *Pratt's Stats™. Done Deals* includes transactions starting at $1 million. *Pratt's Stats™* also includes smaller transactions, even those under $100,000.

Done Deals

The *Done Deals* database is created from SEC filings, covering partial and 100% transactions with a deal value of $1 million to $500 million. The number of transactions and distribution by size as of March 2004 is shown in Exhibit 6.4.

Done Deals shows five market multiples, but not the underlying data from which they are computed. A sample *Done Deals* printout is shown as Exhibit 6.5.

Exhibit 6.4 *Done Deals* Number of Transactions by Price as of December 20, 2004

Price ($millions)	Number of Transaction	Percent of Database
0–$1	338	5.3%
$1–$5	1,301	20.3%
$5–$10	959	15.0%
$10–$20	1,097	17.1%
$20–$30	636	9.9%
$30–$40	414	6.5%
$40–$50	288	4.5%
$50–$60	218	3.4%
$60–$70	183	2.9%
$70–$80	133	2.1%
$80–$90	116	1.8%
$90–$100	98	1.5%
$100+	632	9.9%
Total	6,413	100.0%

Exhibit 6.5 *Done Deals* Sample Data

DONE DEALS DATA
Search Results

Closing Date: 4/13/98	SIC: 3679 Look up SIC Code	Price: $8 (MM)

Buyer	Seller
Pacific Aerospace & Electronics, Inc. 430 Olds Station Road Wenatchee, WA 98801 Donald A. Wright, President 509-667-9600	Electronic Specialty Corporation (WA), an 82% owned subsidiary of Deltec International, Inc.

Seller Description
Manufacturing and distribution of electromechanical RELAYS AND SOLENOIDS in Clark County, Washington

Seller Type: Subsidiary

Terms
$2MM cash + $6MM in PA&E (PCTH) com. stk. (substantially all assets)

Sale Type: Asset

Seller's Financials & Ratios

Amounts expressed in $MM.MM	Amount	Months	Comments		
Assets:	$9.20	N/A	12/97	P/A:	0.9
Stockholder's Equity	$2.40	N/A	12/97	P/SE:	3.3
Revenue	$8.00	9	end 12/97	P/R:	0.8
Net Income (Loss):	$0.28	9	end 12/97	P/E:	21.1
Cash Flow:	$0.13	9	end 12/97	P/CF:	44.8

Source: Done Deals December 20, 2004 (Fort Worth, TX: Practitioners Publishing Company). Reprinted with permission.

One reviewer, Steve Bravo, wrote the following:

1. For *Done Deals,* read the 8-Ks (each one can be hundreds of pages) in order to know as much as you can about the transaction, especially when you have to test.

2. Verifying the *Done Deals* summary deal information by tracing to the 8-Ks (to make sure the figures used to compute the multiples are correct). A lot of times you have to add and subtract financial information from different reporting periods in order to first determine LTM figures, from which a multiple is derived . . . it can be a lot of work!

Pratt's Stats™

The newest and most detailed of the middle-market and small-company databases is *Pratt's Stats™,* the official completed transaction database of the International Business Brokers Association (IBBA). Data are gathered primarily from business intermediaries such as the IBBA, the Certified Business Counselors, and other business intermediaries.

Pratt's Stats™ is the only private company database that includes balance sheets and income statements for the companies sold. There are a total of 81 data points for each transaction, including

- Both SIC and NAICS codes
- Business description
- Sale data
- Months on market
- Location
- Type of organization (C corp., sole proprietorship, etc.)
- Stock or asset sale
- Asking price
- Selling price
- Lease terms
- Whether noncompete agreement is included, and if so, terms and amount of purchase price allocated
- Whether employment agreement is included, and if so, terms and amount of purchase price allocated
- Terms of sale
  - ◆ Amount of down payment
  - ◆ Terms of balance
  - ◆ If stock, how much and whether freely tradable or restricted
- Number of employees
- Age of company
- Name of intermediary
- Notes giving any unusual details or factors pertinent to the particular industry

A sample data collection form for *Pratt's Stats™* is shown as Exhibit 6.6 and a sample transaction record is shown as Exhibit 6.7.

Pratt's Stats™ computes 10 market value multiples for each transaction (see Chapter 1 for definitions of market multiples):

1. MVIC/sales
2. MVIC/discretionary earnings

Exhibit 6.6 *Pratt's Stats*™ Sample Data Collection Form

Pratt's Stats™ Submittal Form

Broker/Source ID:	Date of Report:
Intermediary Name:	Firm Name:
Product/Service Description:	
SIC Code:	NAICS Code:	Company Name:
Years in Business:	Number of Employees:	City of Sale:	State of Sale:

Income Data	Asset Data	Transaction Data
☐ Data is "Latest Full Year" Reported	☐ Data is "Latest Full Year" Reported	Date Sale Initiated:
☐ Data is Restated (See Notes field for any additional explanation)	☐ Data is "Purchase Price Allocation"	Date of Sale:
Income Statement Date:	Balance Sheet Date:	Asking Price:
Net Sales:	Cash and Equivalents:	Selling Price:
COGS:	Trade Receivables:	Liabilities Assumed:
Gross Profit:	Inventory:	Emplymnt/ConsultAgrmnt:
Yearly Rent:	Other Current Assets:	Noncompete Value:
Owner's Compensation:	Total Current Assets:	Amount of Down Payment:
Other Operating Exp.:	Fixed Assets:	Stock or Asset Sale
Noncash Charges:	Real Estate:	Company Type: (C or S Corp., LLC, LLP, Sole Prop., etc.)
Total Operating Exp.:	Intangibles:	
Operating Profit:	Other Noncurrent Assets:	Was there an Employment/Consulting Agrmnt?
Interest Expense:	Total Assets:	☐ Yes ☐ No
EBT:	Long-term Liabilities:	Was there an Assumed Lease in the sale?
Taxes:	Total Liabilities:	☐ Yes ☐ No
Net Income:	Stockholders' Equity:	Is there a Renewal Option with the Lease? ☐ Yes ☐ No

Additional Transaction Information

Was there a Note in the consideration paid? ☐ Yes ☐ No   Was there a personal guarantee on the Note? ☐ Yes ☐ No

Terms of Loan Balance: (Length, Rate, Payment, Balloon Payment, etc.)

Balance of Assumed Lease: (Months) [ ]   Terms of Lease: [ ]

Noncompete Length: (Months) [ ]   Noncompete Description: (Miles Radius, etc.)

Employment/Consulting Agreement Description: (Obligation, Length of Time, Services Required, etc.)

Additional Notes:

Please send to: Business Valuation Resources, 7412 SW Beaverton Hillsdale Hwy., Suite 106, Portland, OR 97225 or Fax to 503-291-7955
If you have any questions, please call us toll free at 888-BUS-VALU [287-8258]
© Copyright Business Valuation Resources, LLC 2003   Revised 3/2003

Source: Pratt's Stats™, December 2004 (Portland, OR: Business Valuation Resources, LLC). Reprinted with permission.

Exhibit 6.7 *Pratt's Stats™* Sample Completed Transaction Form

Pratt's Stats™ Transaction Report Prepared: 12/21/2004 11:43:45 AM (PST)

Transaction Details

Intermediary Name	Shappee, Mark B.
Firm Name	Venture Management, Inc.
SIC	7373 Computer Integrated Systems Design
NAICS	541512 Computer Systems Design Services
Business Description	Information Technology Services and Consulting

Company Name	N/A
Sale Location	United States
Years in Business	4
Number Employees	16
Report Date	7/15/1998

Income Data

Data is "Latest Full Year" Reported	No
Data is Restated (see Notes for any explanation)	Yes
Income Statement Date	12/31/1996
Net Sales	$3,639,000
COGS	$1,498,000
Gross Profit	$2,141,000
Yearly Rent	$47,000
Owner's Compensation	$160,000
Other Operating Expenses	$942,000
Noncash Charges	$54,000
Total Operating Expenses	$1,203,000
Operating Profit	$938,000
Interest Expenses	$0
EBT	$974,000
Taxes	$391,000
Net Income	$583,000

Asset Data

Data is Latest Reported	Yes
Data is "Purchase Price Allocation agreed upon by Buyer and Seller"	No
Balance Sheet Date	12/31/1996
Cash Equivalents	$204,219
Trade Receivables	$418,066
Inventory	$0
Other Current Assets	$4,297
Total Current Assets	$626,582
Fixed Assets	$60,911
Real Estate	$0
Intangibles	$0
Other Noncurrent Assets	$0
Total Assets	$687,493
Long-term Liabilities	N/A
Total Liabilities	N/A
Stockholder's Equity	N/A

Transaction Data

Date Sale Intiated	7/1/1997
Date of Sale	10/1/1997
Asking Price	N/A
Equity Price*	$10,625,000
Market Value of Invested Capital*	$10,625,000
Liabilities Assumed	$0
Employment Agreement Value	N/A
Noncompete Value	N/A
Amount of Down Payment	$7,968,750
Stock or Asset Sale	Asset
Company Type	S Corporation
Was there an Employment/Consulting Agreement?	Yes
Was there an Assumed Lease in the sale?	Yes
Was there a Renewal Option with the Lease?	No

*Includes noncompete value; excludes real estate and employment/consulting agreement values.

Additional Transaction Information

Was there a Note in the consideration paid?	Yes
Was there a personal guarantee on the Note?	No
Terms	Notes had a stated value of $2,656,250, term of 5 years, interest of 8%. Principal to be paid at time of IPO or at end of term, whichever comes earlier. An additional sum of $297,500 was paid after a hold back period. Consideration paid includes stock of privately held company valued at $4,250,000.
Balance of Assumed Lease (Months)	N/A
Terms of Lease	N/A
Noncompete Length (Months)	36
Noncompete Description	United States
Employment/Consulting Agreement Description	No extraordinary consideration associated with the employment agreement; owner to continue to operate the business for a minimum of 3 years.
Additional Notes	

Valuation Multiples

Equity Price/Net Sales	2.920
Equity Price/Gross Cash Flow	16.680
Equity Price/EBT	10.909
Equity Price/Net Income	18.225
Equity Price/Book Value of Equity	N/A
MVIC/Net Sales	2.920
MVIC/Gross Profit	4.963
MVIC/EBITDA	10.336
MVIC/EBIT	10.909
MVIC/Discretionary Earnings	8.944
MVIC/Book Value of Invested Capital	N/A

Financial Ratios

Net Income/Sales	0.160
EBIT/Sales	0.268
Sales/Total Assets	5.293
Sales/Fixed Assets	59.743
EBIT/Interest Expense	N/A
Long-term Debt/Total Assets	N/A
Return on Assets	0.848
Return on Equity	N/A

N/A = Not Available

Source: Pratt's Stats™ December, 2004 (Portland, OR: Business Valuation Resources, LLC). Reprinted with permission.

3. MVIC/EBITDA
4. MVIC/EBIT
5. MVIC/gross profit
6. Common equity price/sales
7. Common equity price/gross cash flow
8. Common equity price/pretax income
9. Common equity price/net income
10. Common equity/gross profit.

Deal price includes common equity plus preferred equity plus interest-bearing debt. If the transaction did not include any preferred equity or interest-bearing debt, then the common equity price and the deal price are the same. The data included are also sufficient to compute a variety of other market value multiples.

The number and size distribution of *Pratt's Stats*™ transactions as of April 2005 is shown as Exhibit 6.8. Transactions are being added at the rate of 1,800 to 2,500 per year. The *Pratt's Stats*™ transactions go back as far as 1996.

The *Pratt's Stats*™ data are all private companies prior to the transaction. Those that were public companies prior to the transaction are now covered in a separate database, *Public Stats,* described earlier.

Exhibit 6.8   *Pratt's Stats*™ Transaction Data: Number of Transactions by Price as of April 2005

Price ($millions)	Number of Transactions	Percent of Database
0 to 1	2923	45.0%
>1 to 5	1122	17.3%
>5 to 10	593	9.1%
>10 to 20	612	9.4%
>20 to 30	347	5.3%
>30 to 40	214	3.3%
>40 to 50	151	2.3%
>50 to 60	108	1.7%
>60 to 70	95	1.5%
>70 to 80	58	0.9%
>80 to 90	61	0.9%
>90 to 100	48	0.7%
> 100	160	2.5%
Total	**6492**	**100.0%**

Source: Pratt's Stats™ (Portland, OR: Business Valuation Resources, LLC). Reprinted with permission December 2004.

Note: Pratt's Stats™ Sale Price = Equity Price plus Liabilities Assumed = MVIC = Market Value of Invested Capital.

VERY SMALL TRANSACTIONS

Two databases specialize in very small transactions: *BIZCOMPS®* and the *IBA Market Data Base*. Both are primarily transactions under $500,000, although *BIZCOMPS®* has a few hundred between $500,000 and $5,000,000. Also, *Pratt's Stats™* contains transactions under $1,000,000, some under $500,000.

BIZCOMPS®

BIZCOMPS® shows two market value multiples for each company:

1. Price/sales
2. Price/sellers discretionary cash flow (defined identically to *discretionary earnings* used in *Pratt's Stats™*)

BIZCOMPS® also includes

- SIC and NAICS codes
- Date of sale
- Asking price
- Sale price
- Pricing terms
- Location
- Sales
- Seller's discretionary cash flow (discretionary earnings)
- Inventory
- Furniture fixtures and equipment
- Rent as a percent of sales

Exhibit 6.9 is a sample transaction report from *BIZCOMPS®*. Exhibit 6.10 is a breakdown of the number of *BIZCOMPS®* transactions, which cover a span of just under 12 years, by size of transaction.

The *BIZCOMPS®* online database (www.BVMarketData.com) is designed for accountants, business appraisers, business intermediaries, and their clients. The *BIZCOMPS®* database contains transactional information on "Main Street" businesses for the past 10 years. Jack Sanders, who is located in San Diego, California, publishes this study. As of March 2005, *BIZCOMPS®* contained 7,600 total transactions.

The *BIZCOMPS®* Studies (www.BIZCOMPS.com) are a printed resource that are based on small business transaction sale data contained in three databases—Western, Central, and Eastern. They are updated annually with each con-

Exhibit 6.9 *BIZCOMPS® 2005 Central States Edition*, Sample Page

EXHIBIT #13 – All Printing Businesses in Data Base

SIC #	NAICS #	BUS TYPE	ASK PRICE (000)	ANN GROSS (000)	SDE (000)	SDE/GROSS SALES	SALE DATE	SALE PRICE (000)	% DOWN	TERMS	SALE/GROSS SALES	SALE/SDE	INV AMT	FF&E (000)	RENT/SALES	DAYS ON MKT	FRAN ROYALTY	AREA
2752	323114	Printing & Graphics	343	557	107	0.19	10/1/03	194	67%	7 Yrs @ 7%	0.35	1.8	6	100	0.6%	45	No	Dallas, TX
2752	323114	Printing & Graphics	262	338	100	0.30	12/30/02	217	41%	7 Yrs @ 7%	0.64	2.2	3	37	4.6%	150	No	Texas
2752	323114	Print Shop	500	1,310	(95)	-0.07	9/6/01	225	N/A	N/A	0.17	-2.4	7	250	N/A	450	No	Minnesota
2752	323114	Fast Print Shop	40	215	24	0.11	6/1/00	34	76%	2 Mos @ 0%	0.16	1.4	2	32	11.2%	187	No	Dallas/Ft. Worth
2752	323114	Printer-Commercial	193	469	127	0.27	12/31/99	187	26%	5 Yrs @ 10%	0.40	1.5	7	226	10%	300		Texas
2752	323114	Printer-Laminating	1,500	2,136	267	0.12	10/19/99	1,002	80%	5 Yrs @ 10%	0.47	3.8	75	675	N/A	90		Central Kentucky
2752	323114	Printing Shop	480	707	194	0.27	4/1/99	572	100%	N/A	0.81	2.9	0	78	5.7%			Madison, WI
2752	323114	Printer-Commercial	325	1,358	145	0.11	4/21/98	325	100%	N/A	0.24	2.2	25	400	N/A	180		Central Iowa
2752	323114	Printer-Commercial	1,525	3,500	750	0.21	1/31/98	1,525	75%	3 Yrs @ 10%	0.44	2.0	75	1 M	N/A	270		Texas
2752	323114	Printer-Commercial	2,450	3,000	924	0.31	1/31/98	2,160	90%	5 Yrs @ 0%	0.73	2.4	150	1 M	N/A	210		Temple, TX
2752	323114	Print Shop-Franchise	435	386	121	0.31	7/18/97	360	100%	N/A	0.93	3.0	15	260	4%	98	Y-.5%	Louisville, KY
2752	323114	Printer-Commercial	147	262	34	0.13	6/9/97	142	100%	10 Yrs @ 8.5%	0.54	4.2	3	100	6%	349		Grand Rapids, MI
2752	323114	Printing Shop	216	295	110	0.37	5/8/97	178	15% SBA	7 Yrs @ Pr+2.5	0.60	1.6	2	57	5.3%	28		North Texas
2752	323114	Printing Shop	54	92	33	0.36	11/27/96	38	100%	N/A	0.41	1.2	2	18	9%			Southern Iowa
2752	323114	Printer-Commercial	182	214	57	0.27	11/15/96	148	47%	5 Yrs @ 9%	0.69	2.6	3	39	5.5%	50		Knoxville, TN
2752	323114	Printing Shop	216	298	110	0.37	11/8/96	178	100%	N/A	0.60	1.6	2	58	8.5%			Dallas/Ft Worth
2752	323114	Printing Shop	220	200	50	0.25	10/31/96	113	100%	N/A	0.56	2.3	10	30	N/A			Austin, Texas
2752	323114	Printer-Commercial	160	164	60	0.37	2/28/96	155	19%	7 Yrs @ 9%	0.95	2.6	2	100	7.6%			Cincinnati, OH
2752	323114	Printer-Commercial	162	390	30	0.08	4/24/95	102	50%	6 Yrs @ 9%	0.26	3.4	18	105	7%			Madison, WI
2752	323114	Printing Shop	120	136	39	0.29	1/16/95	96	N/A	N/A	0.71	2.5	10	90	N/A	255		Minnesota
2752	323114	Printing Shop	105	360	40	0.11	12/31/94	105	100%	N/A	0.29	2.6	5	50	7%			Minneapolis, MN
2752	323114	Print & Copy Shop	150	320	95	0.30	11/10/94	160	47%	5 Yrs @ 8%	0.50	1.7	2	122	6.4%	44		Texas
2752	323114	Printing Shop	65	120	24	0.20	8/31/94	55	55%	5 Yrs @ 10%	0.46	2.3	1	48	8%			Austin, TX
2752	323114	Printing Shop	81	192	48	0.25	6/30/94	68	100%	N/A	0.35	1.4	3	67	4%			North Illinois
2752	323114	Printer-Commercial	240	306	72	0.24	6/30/94	219	50%	7 Yrs @ 8%	0.72	3.0	10	165	10%			Minneapolis, MN
2752	323114	Printer-Commercial	350	630	188	0.30	2/28/94	340	26%	10 Yr @ 10%	0.54	1.8	15	385	1.9%			Houston, TX
2752	323114	Printer-Commercial	121	249	47	0.19	12/31/93	102	92%	6 Mo @ 0%	0.41	2.2	4	50	3.4%			Cincinnati, OH
2752	323114	Printing Shop	30	85	40	0.47	9/30/93	30	100%	N/A	0.35	0.8	2	14	8%			Baton Rouge, LA
2752	323114	Printing Shop	70	225	33	0.15	5/28/93	65	100%	N/A	0.29	2.0	2	25	1%			Austin, TX
2752	323114	Printer-Commercial	68	225	32	0.14	4/30/93	63	50%	3 Yrs @ 8%	0.28	2.0	2	25	3%			Austin, TX
2752	323114	Litho Printing Shop	4,400	6,900	1,087	0.16	2/28/93	4,400	30%	7 Yr @ Pr+1	0.64	4.0	100	1.8M	1.5%			Dallas, TX
2752	323114	Printer-Commercial	183	235	78	0.33	12/31/92	148	60%	5 Yrs	0.63	1.9	2	135	5%			Verona, WI
2752	323114	Printing Shop	77	132	61	0.46	10/31/92	70	56%	2 Yrs @ 10%	0.53	1.1	2	57	4%			Houston, TX
2752	323114	Printing Shop	98	323	60	0.19	10/31/92	95	31%	5 Yrs @ 10%	0.29	1.6	2	70	7%			No Ft. Worth
2752	323114	Printer-Franchise	115	300	60	0.20	3/31/92	105	63%	3 Yrs @ 9%	0.35	1.8	5	50	6%			New Orleans, LA
2752	323114	Printing Shop	76	220	46	0.21	1/1/92	71	25%	5 Yrs @ 10%	0.32	1.5	4	60	4%			Midwest
2752	323114	Printing Shop	330	637	164	0.26	1/1/92	330	82%	N/A	0.52	2.0	N/A	N/A	N/A			Illinois
2752	323114	Printer-Commercial	2,900	3,800	725	0.19	1/1/92	2,900	50%	10 Yrs @ 10%	0.76	5.3	N/A	N/A	2.5%			Cincinnati, OH

All Printing Businesses
In Data Base Sold For An
Average of 91.1% of Asking Price.

Average Sale Price Divided By
Gross Sales = .50 (ie: Sale Price
Was 50% of Gross Sales)
Median = .49

Average Sale Price Divided By
SDE = 2.2 (ie: Sale Price Was
2.2 Times SDE)
Median = 2.0

Source: BIZCOMPS® 2005 Central States Edition (San Diego: Bizcomps, 2005), 109. Reprinted with permission.

Exhibit 6.10 *BIZCOMPS*® Number of Transactions by Price as of December 2004

Price ($millions)	Number of Transactions	Percent of Database
0 to 1	7101	95.33%
>1 to 5	316	4.24%
>5 to 10	21	0.28%
>10 to 20	8	0.11%
> 20	3	0.04%
Total	7449	**100.0%**

Source: Bizcomps (San Diego: BIZCOMPS®, 2004). Reprinted with permission.

Note: Bizcomps Sale Price = Actual Sale Price plus transferred inventory.

taining sale data over the last 10 years. Each study currently contains 1,500 to 3,060 transactions. In addition, a National Industrial edition contains data only on Manufacturing, Wholesale/Distribution, and Business to Business Service Businesses. This study has 1,025 of these unique businesses with sales prices averaging over $1,000,000.

The following was submitted by reviewer Robert Schlegel:

BIZCOMPS® reports sales data for fixed assets and goodwill only, and separately reports fixed assets data. While some appraisers (and taxing authorities) have subtracted reported net fixed assets from the sales price and recalculated goodwill multiples alone, imprecision with the fixed assets entries and deal terms may lead to spurious results. Jack Sanders of *BIZCOMPS*® has indicated that he will share the names and phone numbers of submitting brokers to business appraisers desiring to further investigate the transaction evidence.

The *IBA Market Data Base*

The pioneer of the small business and professional practice databases is the *IBA* (Institute of Business Appraisers) *Market Data Base,* including transactions going back over 20 years.

Data in the IBA database include

- SIC code
- Brief company description
- Month and year of sale
- Sales
- Annual earnings (defined as "reported annual earnings before owner's compensation, interest, and taxes")
- Sale price
- Price/sales

- Price/earnings
- Location

Access to the *IBA Market Data Base* is free to IBA members. At press time, membership is $300 the first year and $250 per year thereafter. Access is achieved by submitting the request by SIC code, and the printout is returned by fax or e-mail. A sample of an IBA database printout is shown as Exhibit 6.11. A distribution of *IBA Market Data Base* transactions by transaction size is shown as Exhibit 6.12.

Using *Pratt's Stats™*, *BIZCOMPS®*, and the *IBA Market Data Base* Together for Small Company Transactions

Transactions for many industries and size ranges can be found in *Pratt's Stats™*, *BIZCOMPS®*, and the *IBA Market Data Base*. An example of this is shown in Chapter 13, which examines a sample market approach valuation of a submarine sandwich shop.

One way to use these databases together is to make a separate market value table for each database. Alternatively, one may combine the data from the three databases into a single table. If the latter procedure is followed, the analyst must be aware of and make certain adjustments to reflect that the three databases do not define the underlying financial variables in exactly the same way. The two differences are

1. Inclusion or exclusion of inventory in the market value multiples
2. Definition of earnings

Differences in Treating Inventory. *Pratt's Stats™* assumes that inventory is included in what is being transferred, but shows the amount of inventory so that the multiples can be recomputed without inventory if desired. *BIZCOMPS® National Industrial Edition* (transactions averaging an $850,000 sale price) assumes inventory is included, and also shows how much inventory. Otherwise, *BIZCOMPS®* assumes that inventory is *not* included in the market multiples. *BIZCOMPS®* shows the amount of inventory. The *IBA Market Data Base* assumes that inventory is included, but does not indicate how much.

If using *BIZCOMPS®*, and if inventory is included in the subject valuation, it must be added back to the indication of value after applying the market valuation multiples to the subject company. If all three databases or *Pratt's Stats™* and the *IBA Market Data Base* are used together, inventory must be subtracted from the *Pratt's Stats™* and *IBA Market Data Base* sale price, the multiples recomputed, and any inventory included in the subject company valuation added back after applying the market valuation multiples to the subject company.

If *Pratt's Stats™* and *BIZCOMPS®* are used together, there are two choices:

Exhibit 6.11   Market Comparison Data

SIC CODE: 5812

The information below is supplied in response to your request for data to be used in applying the "Market Data Approach" to business appraisal. Because of the nature of sources from which the information is obtained, we are not able to guarantee its accuracy. Neither do we make any representation as to the applicability of the information to any specific appraisal situation.

The following is an explanation of the entries in the data table:

Business Type	Principal line of business.
SIC CODE	Principal Standard Industrial Classification number applicable to the business sold.
Annual Gross	Reported annual sales volume of business sold.
Discretionary Earnings	Reported annual earnings, excluding owner's compensation and before interest and taxes.
Owner's Comp.	Reported owner's compensation.
Sale Price	Total reported consideration; i.e. cash, liabilities assumed, etc. excluding real estate.
Price/Gross	Ratio of total consideration to reported annual gross.
Price/Earnings	Ratio of total consideration to reported discretionary earnings.
Yr/Mo of Sale	Year and month during which transaction was consummated.

Business Type	Annual Gross $000's	Discret. Earnings $000's	Owner's Comp. $000's	Sale Price $000's	Price/ Gross	Price/ Earnings	Geographic	Yr/Mo of Sale
Bagel Restaurant	13000	300	300	500	0.04	1.67	FL	03/08
Food services	8481	127	115	2000	0.24	15.75	IN	95/05
Fast Food 13 Locations	8123	1500		3900	0.48	2.6	NC	88/03
Restaurant	4244	290	160	2108	0.5	7.27	FL	91/11
Restaurant	4193			1700	0.41		CA	87/05
Restaurant, mexican	3600	461		2766	0.77	6	TX	92/08
Fast Food 3 Locations	3311	489		940	0.28	1.92	NC	89/10
Restaurant/bakery	3167	375		900	0.28	2.4	WA	89/01
Deli Restaurant	3100	350		800	0.26	2.29	FL	
Pizza rest.	2403			20	0.01		UT	93/01
Catering	2250	250		365	0.16	1.46	FL	93/02
Restaurant-Dinnerhouse	2200	234		741	0.34	3.17	NY	92/11
Restr Family	2100	222		875	0.42	3.94	TN	90/11
Seafood Restaurant	2097	167	53	1900	0.91	11.38	FL	01/12
Restaurant-Dinnerhouse	2000	289		742	0.37	2.57	NY	92/11
Own,op restaurants	1900			300	0.16		KS	93/03
Restr W/Cocktails	1750			295	0.17		WA	94/05
Restr Dinner	1700	165		70	0.04	0.42	MA	92/05
Fast Food-Hamburgers	1668	273		1319	0.79	4.83	NV	90/04
Family Restaurant	1640	1122		1350	0.82	1.2	MA	01/04
Restr-Dinner W/Cocktails	1491	87		117	0.08	1.34	NC	93/02
Restr Dinner House	1480	112		140	0.09	1.25	ME	92/06
Restr-Dinnerhouse	1416	173		1100	0.78	6.36	FL	97/10
Bagel restaurant	1400	330		590	0.42	1.79	FL	04/02
Restaurant-Seafood	1400	163		610	0.44	3.74	FL	93/06
Restaurant	1386	230		350	0.25	1.52	FL	03/12
Restaurant, family	1350	223	50	1075	0.8	4.82	VT	90/08

Source: IBA Market Data Base Market Analysis Portfolio Report (Plantation, FL: The Institute of Business Appraisers, December 2004). Reprinted with permission.

1.   Subtract inventory from the *Pratt's Stats*™ sale price, recompute the multiples, and add back any inventory included in the subject company valuation after applying the multiples.
2.   Add inventory to the *BIZCOMPS*® sale price, recompute the multiples, and apply them to the subject company without further adjustment.

Exhibit 6.12   *IBA Market Database:* Number of Transactions by Price as of
              December 27, 2004

Price (in $ millions)	Number of Transactions	Percent of Database
0 to 1	19611	93.591
>1 to 5	871	4.157
>5 to 10	233	1.112
>10 to 20	56	0.267
>20 to 30	19	0.091
>30 to 40	17	0.081
>40 to 50	12	0.057
>50 to 60	9	0.043
>60 to 70	8	0.038
>70 to 80	16	0.076
>80 to 90	6	0.029
>90 to 100	2	0.010
>100	58	0.277
No price stated	36	0.172
Total	**20954**	**100.000**

Source: IBA Market Data Base (Plantation, FL: The Institute of Business Appraisers, 2004). Reprinted with permission.

Differences in Defining Earnings.   *Pratt's Stats™* and *BIZCOMPS®* define *discretionary earnings* and *seller's discretionary cash flow* identically, that is, earnings before interest, taxes, all noncash charges, and all compensation to one owner. The *IBA Market Data Base* defines earnings the same way except that it is not before noncash charges. If one believes the IBA definition literally, then separate computations and adjustments to the results need to be made for the IBA database. However, many believe that the brokers actually report earnings to the *IBA Market Data Base* before noncash charges. If one believes this, then the multiples of discretionary earnings for *Pratt's Stats™,* seller's discretionary cash flow for *BIZCOMPS®,* and earnings for the *IBA Market Data Base* may be used interchangeably.

SUMMARY

A wide variety of sources are available to identify and obtain information for merger and acquisition transactions. For companies that were public prior to the transaction, it often is most efficient to use one, or preferably several, source(s) to identify the transaction and determine the transaction price and terms, and then either SEC filings or secondary sources to obtain company background financial data.

If the company was private before the transaction, the available background financial data usually are limited to the latest year, and are included in the same source that provides the financial details of the transaction.

In recent years, the availability of financial data for sales of private companies has greatly increased. If using two or more private company transaction databases together, one must be careful because definitions of market value multiples, items transferred, and underlying financial variables are not consistent from one database to another.

Adjusting Financial Statements

If using public guideline companies, we usually collect five years' worth of annual statements plus whatever interim statements are available for the subject and/or guidelines companies between their respective latest fiscal years and the valuation date. If using the private guideline companies in the transaction method, usually only the latest year's statements are available.

While five years' statements are the typical time period, there is nothing magic about five years. In a highly cyclical industry, one might want statements for a full cycle, which could be as long as 10 years. On the other hand, if the subject company is only three years old, or if there was a major change in the industry or subject company operations three years ago, it may be relevant to analyze and compare only three years' statements. The main criterion is to compare the subject and guideline company statements for a *relevant* time period.

For the purpose of this chapter, we will generally assume that we have five years of statements for both our subject and guideline companies, plus, in some cases, latest partial-year interim statements.

CHOOSING THE TIME PERIODS FOR COMPARATIVE STATEMENTS

One of the most crucial decisions is getting the best match of time periods between the subject and guideline companies that will produce the most meaningful market approach estimate of value. There are almost an infinite number of possible scenarios. We will examine a few of the most common, and hope that the principles suggested will help the reader to make good decisions for other scenarios.

Valuation Date at Fiscal Year-end

The simplest scenario usually is when the valuation date is at the subject company's fiscal year-end. The general rule is to use fiscal year-end financial statements. A few analysts would say that they should not be used because they were not compiled as of the valuation date. However, the rule is to use information that was "known or reasonably knowable" as of the valuation date. Most agree that year-end financial information meets this criterion, even if it were not yet compiled. In the world of transactions, many take place as of fiscal year-ends. Almost always, the final price is subject to adjustment if the final statements show results significantly different from expectations.

Guideline companies in the same industry often do have the same fiscal years as the subject, and the general rule is to use matching year-end statements for the guideline companies. If the guideline companies' fiscal years end one month following or one or two months before the subject company's fiscal year, the closest matching year-end statements usually are used. This presumes, of course, that results do not deviate significantly from what would have been predicted at the valuation date.

Valuation Date Removed from Fiscal Year-end

If the valuation date does not coincide with the subject company's fiscal year-end, then the analyst is faced with making a judgment concerning what statements to rely on. This judgment involves assessing several factors:

- How far removed the valuation date is from the fiscal period
- What interim statements are available, and how complete and reliable they are
- The extent to which operations have varied or significant events have occurred since the latest available statements

- If the guideline company's financial statements are as of a single month after the subject company valuation date, then most analysts use the post valuation date statements of the guideline companies. This seems to be consistent with the "known or knowable" rule, in that in most cases, company officials would have a pretty good idea of the expected results for the coming month, and, for most public companies analysts forecasts would be available.

If the valuation date is within a month before the fiscal year-end, the general rule is to use the latest fiscal year data. Exceptions would be if

- Waiting for the year-end data would unduly delay completion of the valuation
- The company had unusually complete and reliable monthly statements
- Significant events occurred between the valuation date and the fiscal year-end that should not be reflected in the valuation

If the valuation date is removed three months or more from the fiscal year-end, then the most meaningful comparison usually is created using interim statements. For example, a September 30 year can be created by using the first nine months of the latest year combined with the last quarter of the previous year. The feasibility of this procedure depends on the availability of adequate interim data.

The procedure could be carried back for five or more years of financial data. However, this is cumbersome. Usually analysts use the reconstructed year for the latest 12 months and actual fiscal years prior to that. Note that this procedure results in double counting the last quarter of the previous full year. That generally is not a serious problem unless that particular quarter was abnormal for some reason, which would have the undesirable result of double-counting an abnormal quarter.

Whatever periods are chosen for the subject company, the same should be chosen for the guideline companies, or as close a time period as fiscal periods are available. It is essential that the subject and guideline company financial statement periods match as closely as possible, or a meaningless or misleading comparison could result.

OBJECTIVES OF FINANCIAL STATEMENT ADJUSTMENTS

The objectives of financial statement adjustments in the context of the market approach to valuation is to put them on a comparable basis to assess the relative strengths and weaknesses of the subject versus the guideline companies.

Assess Relative Growth Prospects

Growth prospects are a major factor in estimating appropriate market multiples. Whatever growth is reflected in projections in the discounted cash flow method in the income approach should also be reflected in the market value multiples in the market approach (described in some detail in Chapter 15).

One should carefully compare the growth trends between the subject company and the guideline companies. At the same time, it is not appropriate to blindly assume that the past relative growth trends will continue. The analyst's reading about the guideline companies, site visits, and interviews with management should provide insight about the extent to which the future growth will parallel, exceed, or underperform that of the guideline companies. This comparison will impact valuation multiples neutrally, positively, or negatively relative to the guideline companies' observed market multiples.

Assess Relative Risk

Another important factor that affects the levels of market multiples chosen is the relative degree of risk. The extent to which the subject companies' operating results have equal, greater, or less volatility than the guideline companies is an important indication of similar, greater, or less risk inherent in the subject company relative to the guideline companies. It is important to have the financial statements on a comparable basis for this comparison to be meaningful. To the extent that volatility of the subject company's operating results (e.g., operating margin, return on sales) are about equal, greater, or less than the guideline companies, this risk comparison would lead to a similar, lower, or higher market value multiple. Thus, the assessment of risk will lead to adjustments to the observed market multiples. In this sense, the risk that is reflected in the discount rate in the income approach is reflected in the market value multiple in the market approach.

ADJUSTMENTS FOR NONOPERATING OR EXCESS ASSETS

Unless the subject is an asset holding company, the usual objective of guideline company analysis is to compare operating companies. Therefore, at least for valuations of controlling interests, the subject and guideline company statements should be adjusted to remove nonoperating items.

Process for Handling Nonoperating Items

At least for valuations of controlling interests, nonoperating assets should be removed from the balance sheet. Frequently this also involves removing related income or expenses from the income statement. If income or expenses are removed from the income statement, the items should be adjusted net of their tax effect.

Let us suppose that most companies of the same size in the same industry do not use corporate planes, but our subject company has one. Although it survived an

Internal Revenue Service (IRS) audit, no buyer of the company would buy the plane, much less pay the operating expenses. The balance sheet is adjusted to remove the cost of the plane and the related depreciation. The income statement is adjusted for the cost of operation of the plane net of the tax effect, often adding whatever commercial airline costs that would be incurred if the company did not have the plane. At the end of the valuation procedure, the liquidation value of the aircraft would be added back to the indicated value of the company on an operating basis.

When valuing a minority interest, minority stockholders generally do not ascribe very much value to nonoperating assets. Therefore, for a minority interest valuation, the amount added back usually should be net of a minority interest discount.

Controversies over Nonoperating Assets

Whether to classify certain assets as operating or nonoperating often is a major controversy that affects the value. If the asset produces little or no revenue, classifying it as nonoperating and adding its value to the value of the operating company would tend to result in a higher value. Leaving it as an operating asset would tend to result in a lower value.

A parking lot would be a good example. Those seeking a low value would argue that it is a necessary operating asset because the employees need parking. Those seeking a high value would argue that its value as a parking lot is nowhere near the highest and best use of the land, and the land's value should be added to the operating company's value.

There are no hard and fast rules governing these controversies, and the analyst must use the most objective possible judgment in deciding how to treat each item. However, the question of whether the value is on a controlling or minority basis may determine the treatment. A control owner has the power to redeploy the nonoperating assets, while a minority owner does not. Therefore, the nonoperating assets are more likely to be treated as an add-on to value in a control valuation. The public markets often give little value to nonproducing assets. In a minority valuation, they may be ignored or reflected by a slight increase in the market value multiple to reflect the strength of extra assets.

Excess Assets or Asset Deficiencies

A similar controversy may surround the question of the adequacy of assets to support the company's operations. The most common example of this controversy is the proper level of net working capital.

In the market approach to valuation, the analyst has the advantage of observing the amount of working capital as a percentage of sales for each of the guideline companies. If the subject company's net working capital is out of line as a percentage of sales compared with the guideline companies from which market multiples are derived, then it often is appropriate to adjust for excess or deficient working capital.

Again, the question of a control or minority valuation may come into play. The control owner has the power to change the working capital policy, while the minority owner does not. Some managements may observe a conservative fiscal policy that includes what many analysts may regard as more than adequate working capital. If doing a minority valuation of an interest in such a company on a going concern basis, no adjustment may be appropriate because no change will be made.

NONRECURRING ITEMS

It is preferred that the statements of both the subject and guideline companies represent ongoing operations. Therefore, the analyst should consider removing nonrecurring items on the income statements of the subject and/or the guideline companies.

It is important for the person adjusting the statements to realize that many items that could be considered nonrecurring from a financial analysis point of view are not necessarily "extraordinary" from a GAAP (generally accepted accounting principles) point of view. A good example would be gains and losses on the sale of assets. For example, if a company sells its only corporate plane, the gain or loss is ordinary income from a GAAP viewpoint, but nonrecurring from a financial analysis viewpoint. This is one reason to use original financial statements rather than secondary sources if one wishes to be totally accurate. Secondary sources usually report on a GAAP basis, and there usually would be no way to know about an item that was nonrecurring but not extraordinary.

Other common nonrecurring items could include

- Costs of strikes
- Costs of other business interruptions
- Recovery of insurance proceeds
- Gains or losses from discontinued operations or closing of facilities
- Write-downs in connection with acquisitions
- Costs, recoveries, and losses from lawsuits
- Costs associated with environmental problems
- Payments on covenants not to compete and employment contracts
- Effects of abnormal market conditions (occasionally)
- Abandonment losses

ADJUSTMENTS FOR ACCOUNTING COMPARABILITY

For the market value multiples to be meaningful, they should be computed from financial figures that are compiled on a comparable basis. Because GAAP allows a wide latitude of accounting treatments and measurements of amounts, it often is necessary to make adjustments to achieve comparability of accounting treatment. There are many examples, but we will discuss just four:

1. Cash versus accrual accounting
2. Inventory accounting
3. Depreciation accounting
4. Intangibles accounting

Cash versus Accrual Accounting

Cash basis accounting means that revenues are recorded on the financial statements when they are received, and expenses are recorded when they are paid. Accrual basis accounting means that revenues are recorded when they are earned and expenses are matched to the time period in which they are used to create revenue; that is, they are recorded when the item of expense (e.g., rent, insurance) is used in the course of the company's operations.

Absent some agreement to the contrary, valuation usually is based on accrual accounting. Therefore, if a company's financial statements are on a cash basis, they usually need to be adjusted to an accrual basis for the comparison with the guideline companies to proceed.

Using accounts receivable as an example, the adjustment from cash to accrual accounting would involve bringing the accounts receivable onto the balance sheet as of the end of each fiscal year (or other fiscal period). Then the income statement for each period would have to be adjusted for the difference between products or services billed and accounts receivable collected. Income taxes applicable, if any, should also be reflected in both the balance sheet and income statement adjustments.

Inventory Accounting

There are many ways to account for inventory, but the only "common denominator" for comparative financial purposes is first in, first out (FIFO). Therefore, if there is any difference in inventory accounting between the subject and any of the guideline companies, it may be appropriate to adjust all to a FIFO basis.

Depreciation Accounting

Companies have wide discretion in both methods of depreciation accounting and the length of the estimated useful lives over which they depreciate some assets.

If there is a difference in the depreciation method between the subject company and any of the guideline companies, the most expeditious procedure is to adjust all the companies' statements to the depreciation method most commonly used. However, this can be a cumbersome and time-consuming process, so it usually is undertaken only when the differences are significant.

Occasionally, depreciation lives are a factor. For example, the author encountered a company that used an eight-year life for a major asset class when the industry standard was six years. Even though the actual useful life probably was eight years, I adjusted the company statements to a six-year life. Of course, this lowered both the book value of equity on the balance sheet and the earnings on the income statement. However, as we were deriving market value multiples from companies that depreciated over six years, we had to use the six-year basis for comparability. Otherwise, we would be applying the multiples of book value and earnings from the guideline companies to subject company figures that were compiled to get a higher base, thus inflating the indicated values.

Intangibles Accounting

If a company purchases an intangible asset, it places the asset on its balance sheet at cost and amortizes it over time. If the company develops the intangible asset internally, then the cost usually is expensed as incurred.

Therefore, if either the subject company or the guideline companies have intangible assets, they usually are removed from the balance sheet so that the asset multiple relating to book value will be comparable between the subject and the guideline companies, either

- MVIC/TBVIC (tangible book value of invested capital)
- Price/TBV (tangible book value) of equity

It would also be ideal if the income statements were adjusted to remove the amortization for those companies with purchased intangibles so that market value multiples such as price/earnings can be calculated on a comparable basis. If there is not sufficient information to make this adjustment but the analyst believes that it would be significant, then the solution might rely more heavily, or even exclusively, on cash flow rather than earnings-based market multiples (e.g., MVIC/EBITDA versus MVIC/EBIT or price/gross cash flow versus price/earnings).

ADJUSTMENTS FOR "INSIDER" ANOMALIES

Many private companies have expenses that would not be typical of the guideline companies in the industry. That is, the controlling stockholders cause or allow expenditures that deviate from the norm that one would find in most guideline companies. Examples of such items would be

- Excess compensation and other perquisites
- Lease or other special transactions with company principals or relatives
- Entertainment expenses for employees or customers
- Charitable contributions to company principals' favorite charities

If valuing a controlling interest, these items normally would be adjusted to conform to the policies of the industry, often as evidenced by the guideline companies.

If valuing a minority interest by the market approach, there are two schools of thought. The most typical is to not adjust for such items, because they are going to continue in any case. The second procedure would be to make the adjustments to put the subject and guideline companies on a comparable basis for the purpose of calculating and applying market value multiples, and then take the anomalies into consideration through some amount of lack of marketability and/or minority interest discount from the value indicated by applying the market value multiples from the guideline companies.

An alternative, of course, to making detailed adjustments is to use a pricing multiple such as price to revenue where one does not have to contend with deciding if adjustments are appropriate.

ADJUSTMENTS FOR INCOME TAXES IN PASS-THROUGH ENTITIES AND S CORPORATIONS

Valuation of Subchapter S corporations and other pass-through entities is a controversial issue that has been very difficult to resolve, as divergent, complex, and competing financial theories have been formulated to attempt to address this issue. For the valuation practitioner, the application of reasoned financial theory has proven to be an extremely difficult undertaking, given the multitude of viewpoints and uncertainties of the IRS audit process.

There are four key Tax Court opinions, one of which was affirmed on appeal by Court of Appeals, that suggest S corporation earnings should not be tax-affected for valuation purposes:

1. *Walter L. Gross, Jr. et ux, et al. v. Commissioner*[1]
2. *Estate of John E. Wall v. Commissioner*[2]
3. *Estate of William G. Adams, Jr. v. Commissioner*[3]
4. *Estate of Richie C. Heck v. Commissioner*[4]

Each of these opinions is a "T.C. Memo." Such opinions are case-fact specific and do not necesssarily reflect the opinion of the Tax Court as a whole on a particular topic.

The more general, traditional approach is to fully tax-affect the S corporation's earnings as if it were a C corporation. Prior to *Gross,* the IRS had supported the traditional approach it opposed in *Gross.* These rejections of the traditional valuation approaches have left business valuation analysts searching for an acceptable method. The cases point to a rejection of the traditional valuation practice of automatically income tax-affecting S corporation pretax income when valuing an interest in an S corporation or other pass-through entity. Instead, what is indicated is a wholly fact-driven inquiry when valuing minority interests, taking into consideration the facts and circumstances in each case. Under this imprecise standard, the choice between methods thus remains with the analyst, who must be guided by the facts of the case and perceived appropriateness of each model. The subject is beyond the scope of this text, but an excellent and extensive discussion by leading analysts is found in Laro and Pratt's *Business Valuation and Taxes: Procedure, Law and Perspective.*[5]

See the discussion of these cases in Chapter 8 in the context of calculating the return on equity ratio, and whether the analyst should impute entity-level taxes.

SUMMARY

The market approach to valuing businesses or interests in businesses uses market value multiples derived from the prices of actual observed transactions relative to underlying financial fundamentals of the companies in those transactions. To make the market valuation multiples meaningful, the underlying financial variables must be compiled on a basis that is comparable from one to another. It is also important that the statements' time periods be comparable between the subject and the guideline companies.

For various reasons, it is often necessary to make certain adjustments to the financial statements of the subject or guideline companies to achieve this comparability. Although analysts routinely adjust the subject company statements, they frequently overlook adjustments to the guideline company statements that would be necessary to put them on a comparable basis.

Once the statements are on a comparable basis, the analyst can compare them in various respects to assist in choosing market value multiples to apply to the subject company. If the subject company appears to have higher growth potential than the guideline companies, that would tend to raise the multiples relative to the guideline companies, and vice versa.[6] To the extent that the subject company appears to have more risk than the guideline companies (as evidenced by higher volatility of margins, for example), that would tend to lower the multiples relative to the guideline companies, and vice versa.

The subject company may have various financial characteristics that differ from the guideline companies that augur for adjustments other than to the choice of multiples, such as treating nonoperating or excess assets or asset deficiencies.

Some of the most common adjustments could be for

- Nonrecurring items
- Differences in accounting policies
- Insider factors (e.g., excess compensation)

Financial statement adjustments take many forms, and this chapter has presented a few of the most common for purposes of valuation within the market approach.

Notes

1. T. C. Memo. 1999-254, No. 4460-97 (July 29, 1999), *aff'd*. 272 F. 3d 333 (6th Cir., November 19, 2001).
2. T. C. Memo. 2001-75, 2001 Tax Ct. Memo LEXIS 97 (U.S. Tax Ct., March 27, 2001).
3. T. C. Memo. 2002-80, 2002 Tax Ct. Memo LEXIS 84 (U.S. Tax Ct., March 28, 2002).
4. T. C. Memo. 2002-34, 2002 Tax Ct. Memo LEXIS 38 (U.S. Tax Ct., February 5, 2002).
5. David Laro and Shannon P. Pratt, *Business Valuation and Taxes: Procedure, Law and Perspective* (Hoboken, NJ: John Wiley & Sons, 2005).
6. Adjusting from public company multiples for differences in risk and growth is addressed by Richard W. Goeldner in "Bridging the Gap Between Public and Private Market Multiples," *Business Valuation Review* (September 1998): 95–101.

Chapter 8

Comparative Financial Analysis

The objective of comparative financial analysis, in the context of the market approach, is to provide guidance in deciding what level of multiples to apply to the subject company's financial data relative to the multiples for the guideline public or merged and acquired companies. When a thorough analysis is performed, it can help identify and quantify some of the company's strengths and weaknesses, both on an absolute basis and relative to other companies. With this information, the analyst will be better able to make a projection about the financial future activity of the subject company—which is one of the key analyses underlying the selection of multiples based on the range observed in the market approach to valuing a business.

The most common method of incorporating the results of ratio analysis of financial statements in the final valuation is to make appropriate adjustments to the selection of various fundamental financial multiples (e.g., price/earnings [P/E] multiple). If the ratios indicate sustainable growth, the business should be worth a higher multiple than if they did not indicate growth. Conversely, the higher degree of risk factors the ratios reveal, the lower should be the business's worth relative to earnings, book value, and other fundamental financial variables.

TYPES OF COMPARATIVE FINANCIAL ANALYSIS

In this chapter, we will discuss three types of comparative financial analysis: (1) trend analysis, (2) comparison with industry averages, and (3) comparison with guideline companies (both public and privately held companies).

Trend Analysis

One commonly employed comparison technique is to compare a company's figures over time; this method is often called *trend analysis*. By viewing the trends of various financial variables, an analyst is able to identify:

- Trends over time with a particular variable
- The high and low point of each analyzed variable
- Whether a variable is deteriorating or improving over time
- Whether a variable is consistent over time

Comparisons with Industry Averages and Guideline Companies

Another often-used comparison technique is to compare the subject company with other companies. This comparison can be made with either specific comparable companies or industry averages derived from various sources. If the subject company exhibits a pattern of strength in a particular financial variable or multiple, this would tend to support the selection of a multiple in the high end of the industry range. If the exhibited pattern is one of weakness, this would encourage the selection of a multiple in the low end of the industry range.

Common-size financial statements are the last comparison technique that we will discuss. To "common size" a company's financial statements, the analyst converts the dollar figures on the balance sheet and income statement to percentage figures. In doing so, the subject company's statements are more easily compared with other guideline companies or with published industry figures. The balance sheet figures are divided by the total assets figure to convert them to a percent of total assets. The income statement figures are divided by the total sales figure to convert them to a percent of total sales.

How does an analyst decide whether to make adjustments prior to the analysis? First, if the ratios are to be compared with those of similar publicly traded companies, the analyst should make the same adjustments to the statements of both the subject company and the guideline company. Second, if the computed ratios are to be compared with industry norms, the analyst should make only those adjustments that are likely to put the subject company on a basis comparable with other companies in the industry. In most cases, however, ratios calculated on adjusted statements will reveal a more accurate picture of the company's financial health.

The analyst should be cognizant of the analyzed variables and the impact they may have on the valuation result. Certain ratios will have greater significance for value in particular industries. If a ratio significantly departs from industry norms, it may also hold some great significance to the valuation. The analyst must carefully select and evaluate the significance of figures as they apply to the particular situation.

A good practice for the analyst is to perform a financial statement analysis prior to a site visit with the company. This analysis will invariably reveal several areas of concern that can be raised and clarified during the site visit.

Throughout this chapter we will refer to the Colossal Software Corporation as our primary example. For certain examples, companies in other industries are used. Exhibit 8.1 presents the balance sheet of Colossal Software and Exhibit 8.2 presents its income statement. For illustrative purposes, we will use the data shown in the 1998 and 1997 income statement and balance sheet. For the examples in this chapter, we will also assume that all appropriate adjustments have been made to the income statements and balance sheets.

SOURCES OF COMPARATIVE FINANCIAL ANALYSIS

There are three key types of comparative financial data: (1) industry average performance information, (2) guideline merged and acquired company data on privately held company sales, and (3) guideline publicly traded company data.

Exhibit 8.1 Colossal Software Balance Sheets

		December		
		2004		2003
		($000)		($000)
Current Assets				
Cash and Cash Equivalents	$	9,209	$	9,962
Short-term Investments		7,135		6,180
Accounts Receivable, Net		17,296		13,963
Other Current Assets		5,365		4,948
Total Current Assets	$	39,005	$	35,053
Equipment, Furniture and Fixtures, Net		7,092		6,535
Capitalized Software Costs, Net		2,103		2,217
Intangible Assets, Net		7,041		6,100
Other Assets		1,812		1,360
Total Assets	$	57,053	$	51,265
Current Liabilities				
Accounts Payable		4,001		3,589
Other Accrued Liabilities		3,909		3,159
Deferred Revenue		9,335		7,969
Current Portion of Long-term Liabilities		856		787
Total Current Liabilities	$	18,101	$	15,504
Deferred Income Taxes		1,014		816
Long-term Liabilities		6,967		7,824
Total Liabilities	$	26,082	$	24,144
Shareholders' Equity				
Common Stock		22,181		20,625
Retained Earnings		8,790		6,496
Total Shareholders' Equity	$	30,971	$	27,121
Total Liabilities and Shareholders' Equity	$	57,053	$	51,265

Industry Average Performance Information

The six key sources on industry average performance are

1. Risk Management Association's (formerly Robert Morris Associates) *Annual Statement Studies*[1]
2. Financial Research Associates' *Financial Studies of the Small Business*[2]
3. Schonfeld & Associates' *IRS Corporate Financial Ratios*[3]
4. *Almanac of Business and Industrial Financial Ratios*[4]
5. John Wiley & Sons' *IRS Corporate Ratios*[5]
6. Warren Gorham and Lamont's *Financial Ratio Analyst*[6]

Exhibit 8.2 Colossal Software Income Statement

	December 2004 ($000)
Revenues	
Software Licenses	$ 35,209
Support & Other Services	34,272
Total Revenues	$ 69,481
Cost of Revenues	
Software Licenses	6,750
Support & Other Services	22,848
Total Cost of Revenues	29,598
Gross Profit	$ 39,883
Operating Expenses	
Sales and Marketing	16,642
Research and Development	9,673
General and Administrative	7,352
Depreciation and Amortization	2,086
Acquisition Related Costs	482
Total Operating Expenses	36,235
Income (Loss) from Operations	$ 3,648
Interest Expense	638
Other Income (Expense), Net	814
Income (Loss) before Income Taxes	$ 3,824
Provision (Benefit) for Income Taxes	1,530
Income before Extraordinary Item	$ 2,294
Extraordinary Item, Net of Taxes	0
Net Income	$ 2,294
Income (Loss) before Extraordinary Gain per Common Share—Basic	$ 2.29
Common shares outstanding (000)	1,000
Income (Loss) before Extraordinary Gain per Common Share—Diluted	$ 2.29
Common shares outstanding assuming dilution (000)	1,000

Risk Management Association's *Annual Statement Studies* collects data from over 3,000 commercial banks and thrift institutions on companies representing close to 500 SIC (Standard Industrial Classification) codes with the presentation of the data sorted by both asset size and sale size. Common-size financial statements and a selection of widely used ratios are provided and organized in various sizes based on the companies' total assets and sales.

Exhibit 8.3 compares Colossal Software and *Annual Statement Studies* common-size statements for five years.

Exhibit 8.4 compares our subject company to a select group of other computer programming companies that are publicly traded on either the New York Stock Exchange or the NASDAQ.

Exhibit 8.3 Colossal Software: Risk Management Association Common Size Comparison

	2004		2003		2002		2001		2000	
	Subject	RMA	Subject	RMA	Subject	RMA	Subject	RMA	Subject	RMA
Number of Observations	1	54	1	59	1	39	1	25	1	26
Average Asset Size ($MM)	57	62	51	57	43	56	40	53	29	49
Average Sales Volume ($MM)	69	117	58	83	40	91	30	89	22	88
	%	%	%	%	%	%	%	%	%	%
Common Size Balance Sheets										
Current Assets:										
Cash & Equivalents	28.6	22.1	31.5	23.9	40.1	19.7	42.4	17.3	39.0	17.7
Accts. & Notes Receivable (Trade)	30.3	41.2	27.2	38.1	24.4	40.1	24.2	39.2	23.8	45.9
Inventory		1.5		3.9		2.7		3.4		3.2
All Other Current Assets	9.4	5.8	9.7	5.8	7.0	5.5	8.2	6.0	5.5	4.0
Total Current Assets	68.4	70.5	68.4	71.7	71.5	67.9	74.8	65.9	68.3	70.8
Net Fixed Assets	12.4	15.5	12.7	14.4	12.2	16.2	9.7	18.7	11.1	14.1
Net Intangible Assets	12.3	7.5	11.9	4.8	6.8	5.8	6.9	7.7	9.9	8.0
Net Other Assets	6.9	6.6	7.0	9.1	9.6	10.1	8.6	7.7	10.7	7.1
TOTAL ASSETS	100.0	100.0	100.0	100.0	100.0	100.0	100.0	100.0	100.0	100.0

Liabilities:										
Current Liabilities:										
Notes Payable	1.5	8.7	1.5	4.9	1.7	7.4	1.7	5.1	0.0	4.2
Current Mat. LTD	1.0	1.0	1.5	3.7	3.3	1.1	3.7	1.6	5.4	2.2
Accounts & Notes Payable (Trade)	7.0	9.9	7.0	11.7	11.2	12.3	5.6	11.2		11.3
Income Taxes Payable		0.9		1.5		0.8		1.4		2.3
All Other Current Liabilities	23.2	18.9	21.7	21.7	13.4	22.4	17.1	17.0	15.0	20.9
Total Current Liabilities	31.7	39.4	30.2	43.4	18.4	43.9	24.3	36.3	20.4	40.9
Total Long-term Debt	12.2	3.3	15.3	4.3	23.5	6.0	19.9	3.2	0.0	5.4
Total Other Noncurrent Debt	1.8	4.0	1.6	0.9	1.0	0.9	1.2	0.6	0.7	0.7
Total Liabilities	45.7	46.7	47.1	53.1	42.9	56.2	45.4	45.2	21.1	52.3
Total Equity	54.3	53.3	52.9	46.9	57.1	43.8	54.6	54.8	78.9	47.7
Total Liabilities and Equity	100.0	100.0	100.0	100.0	100.0	100.0	100.0	100.0	100.0	100.0
Common Size Income Statements										
Net Sales	100.0	100.0	100.0	100.0	100.0	100.0	100.0	100.0	100.0	100.0
Cost of Goods Sold	42.6				42.8		40.7	45.6		50.9
Gross Profit	57.4				57.2		59.3	54.4		49.1
Operating Expenses	52.2	93.2	93.5	94.3	50.1	92.8	50.8	47.7	91.6	44.9
Operating Income	5.3	6.8	6.5	5.7	7.1	7.2	8.5	6.7	8.4	5.6
Other Income (Expense), Net	0.3	0.7	0.0	(0.2)	(1.0)	0.4	(3.5)	(4.8)	(1.2)	(1.5)
Pretax Profit	5.5	7.5	6.5	5.5	6.1	7.6	5.0	1.9	7.2	4.1

Source: Data from RMA Annual Statement Studies, 1999. Used with permission of Risk Management Association.

Exhibit 8.4 Colossal Software: Guideline Public Company Common Size Comparison

	Ardent Software 12/31/04 (%)	Best Software 12/31/04 (%)	Cadence Design 1/2/05 (%)	Centura Software 12/31/04 (%)	Sterling Software 9/30/04 (%)	Symix Systems 6/30/04 (%)	Median (%)	Subject 12/31/04 (%)
Size								
Assets ($MM)	83	75	1406	29	1189	66	79	57
Revenues ($MM)	119	69	1216	53	720	98	108	69
Balance Sheet								
Assets								
Cash & Equivalents	29.2	39.6	13.0	21.8	33.4	9.2	25.5	16.1
Short-term Investments		22.4	1.9		26.1		22.4	12.5
Accounts Receivable, Net	25.6	11.0	19.7	44.2	16.9	49.6	22.7	30.3
Other Current Assets	8.1	4.2	6.6	12.3	2.7	4.3	5.4	9.4
Total Current Assets	62.9	77.3	41.2	78.4	79.1	63.1	70.2	68.4
Fixed Assets, Net	8.0	5.8	18.7	9.8	5.6	9.8	8.9	12.4
Capitalized Software Costs, Net			0.9		6.9	16.6	6.1	3.7
Intangible Assets, Net	13.2	9.6	20.1	5.2	6.4	7.7	9.6	12.3
Other Assets	15.9	7.3	19.1	6.5	2.0	2.9	6.9	3.2
Total Assets	100.0	100.0	100.0	100.0	100.0	100.0	100.0	100.0

Liabilities and Equities								
Accounts Payable	6.6	8.4	15.0	9.5	13.6	20.0	11.6	7.0
Other Accrued Liabilities	23.6	10.7	1.4	11.3		2.4	10.7	6.9
Deferred Revenue	17.0	25.9	6.8	45.2	8.9	19.8	18.4	16.4
Current Portion of LTD		0.2	0.1			0.4	0.2	1.5
Total Current Liabilities	47.1	45.3	23.3	75.1	22.5	42.6	43.9	31.7
Deferred Income Taxes						3.7	3.7	1.8
Long-term Debt	0.2	0.2	9.7			3.5	3.5	12.2
Total Liabilities	47.1	46.2	39.0	75.2	27.5	52.8	46.7	45.7
Shareholders' Equity	52.9	53.8	61.0	24.8	72.5	47.2	53.3	54.3
Total Liabilities and Equities	100.0	100.0	100.0	100.0	100.0	100.0	100.0	100.0

Income Statements								
Net Sales	100.0	100.0	100.0	100.0	100.0	100.0	100.0	100.0
Cost of Sales	25.5	19.4	23.1	16.9	40.0	36.6	24.3	42.6
Gross Profit	74.5	80.6	76.9	83.1	60.0	63.4	75.7	57.4
Operating Expenses	70.6	70.8	68.3	75.8	88.0	61.4	70.7	52.2
Depreciation Expense		1.3	1.4				1.4	3.0
Operating Profit	3.8	9.8	8.6	7.3	12.0	2.1	8.0	5.2
Interest Expense	0.3	3.4	0.6	0.9	0.1		0.3	0.9
Other Income (Expenses), Net	0.5			(1.9)	4.1	(0.2)	0.6	1.2
Pretax Income	4.0	13.2	9.3	4.5	16.6	1.9	6.9	5.5
Income Taxes	2.6	(5.0)	6.6	0.5	6.1	3.3	3.0	2.2
Net Income	1.4	18.2	2.6	4.0	10.6	(1.4)	3.3	3.3

Exhibit 8.5 includes a comparative ratio analysis for our subject company, Colossal Software, and industry average performance data for a period of five years for SIC 7371 (computer programming) as published in *RMA Annual Statement Studies*. In this case, the median figures for the public guideline companies and the *Annual Statement Studies* companies are quite similar, but that would not necessarily be so for all industries.

Financial Research Associates' *Financial Studies of the Small Business* contains many industries that are not included in any of the other data sources and includes details on only those companies with total capitalization of less than $1,000,000—an area that is often neglected by the other data sources. Data from over 30,000 financial statements and over 1,500 independent CPA firms have been included in this study. To illustrate the type of information the *Financial Studies of the Small Business* collects, we will review the reported information for retail, nursery/garden supply firms as it relates to a subject company. The *Financial Studies of the Small Business* differs from the *Almanac of Business and Industrial Financial Ratios* because it reports the median, upper, and lower quartile of the financial ratios. See Exhibit 8.6 for a sample table using the information provided by the *Financial Studies of the Small Business*.

Sources 3 through 6, inclusive, are all based on the most recently available income statement and balance sheet data compiled by the Internal Revenue Service. Each of these sources transforms the raw data from the IRS into usable data. The benefits to using these data are that (1) the data are based on uniform accounting standards, (2) it is fairly comprehensive in nature, and (3) the data are separated into two reports—one based on companies with and without net income and one based on companies with net income. The drawbacks to the data contained in these sources are that the data are typically three to four years old and are slightly biased because they tend to underestimate profitability because of the companies' planned tax avoidance. John Wiley & Sons' current *IRS Corporate Ratios* is delivered only in electronic format.

The *Almanac of Business and Industrial Financial Ratios* contains information on many industries and is organized by SIC codes. Each covered SIC code is grouped into 13 categories by size of assets and ranges from zero assets to assets of $250,000,000 or more. There are two tables for each SIC code. One is labeled "Corporations with and without Net Income" and the other "Corporations with Net Income." In our example in Exhibit 8.7, our subject company is one with net income, so we will compare our subject to the asset size of "Corporations with Net Income."

For our example, we will look at a restaurant and compare it to Table II (Corporations with Net Income) in the *Almanac of Business and Industrial Financial Ratios*. The subject restaurant has total assets of $94,000, so we will focus on the column of data in the almanac labeled "Under $100K" (signifying total assets under $100,000). One of the almanac's benefits is its historical data content in selected ratios and factors. These can be very helpful in the analysis of the subject company and the industry in which it operates.

Exhibit 8.5 Colossal Software: Comparative Ratio Analysis with Data from Risk Management Association

		2004		2003		2002		2001		2000	
		Subject	RMA	Subject	RMA	Subject	RMA	Subject	RMA	Subject	RMA
Number of Observations		1	54	1	59	1	39	1	25	1	26
Average Asset Size ($MM)		57	62	51	57	43	56	40	53	29	49
Average Sales Volume ($MM)		69	117	58	83	40	91	30	89	22	88
Liquidity Ratios											
Current Ratio	High		3.5		2.9		3.3		3.1		3.1
	Median	2.2	1.9	2.3	1.6	2.9	1.6	4.1	1.8	3.3	2.0
	Low		1.3		1.1		1.2		1.3		1.2
Quick Ratio	High		2.9		2.7		2.7		2.9		2.6
	Median	1.9	1.7	1.9	1.5	2.6	1.3	3.6	1.5	3.1	1.6
	Low		1.2		1.1		0.9		1.0		1.1
Sales/Receivables	High		7.0		6.5		6.8		7.3		6.3
	Median	4.0	4.8	4.2	5.2	3.8	5.2	3.1	5.5	3.1	5.2
	Low		3.7		3.7		3.7		3.8		3.3
Sales/Working Capital	High		3.0		2.9		3.7		3.7		4.3
	Median	3.3	8.3	3.0	7.1	2.0	9.8	1.3	6.6	1.6	7.1
	Low		21.4		32.3		34.3		17.0		22.0
Coverage Ratios											
EBIT/Annual Int. Expense	High		60.7		31.5		22.4		31.3		58.4
	Median	5.7	16.1	5.9	9.9	4.4	10.4	2.4	9.8	N/A	14.7
	Low		3.0		2.3		2.1		4.2		7.7
Net Profit + Depr. and	High		44.5		38.9		12.0				
Amort./Cur. Mat. LTD	Median	5.1	7.7	4.9	7.3	3.0	4.6	0.5		N/A	
	Low		3.4		1.2		3.1				

(continued)

Exhibit 8.5 Colossal Software: Comparative Ratio Analysis with Data from Risk Management Association (*continued*)

	2004		2003		2002		2001		2000	
	Subject	RMA	Subject	RMA	Subject	RMA	Subject	RMA	Subject	RMA
Leverage Ratios										
Fixed Assets/Net Worth — High	0.2		0.1		0.2		0.1		0.2	
Fixed Assets/Net Worth — Median	0.3	0.2	0.3	0.2	0.4	0.2	0.2	0.2	0.4	0.1
Fixed Assets/Net Worth — Low	0.8		0.7		1.1		0.8		0.8	
Debt/Net Worth — High	0.4		0.5		0.4		0.6		0.6	
Debt/Net Worth — Median	1.0	0.8	0.9	0.9	1.3	0.8	0.9	0.8	1.4	0.3
Debt/Net Worth — Low	3.2		4.7		5.0		1.5		3.3	
Operating Ratios										
% Profit Before Taxes/Tangible Net Worth — High	54.8		51.6		81.5		56.3		60.4	
% Profit Before Taxes/Tangible Net Worth — Median	34.9	12.3	28.0	13.2	35.6	8.5	30.8	2.5	39.9	3.9
% Profit Before Taxes/Tangible Net Worth — Low	8.9		11.1		16.6		11.8		22.5	
% Profit Before Taxes/Total Assets — High	28.0		20.9		26.5		26.0		25.9	
% Profit Before Taxes/Total Assets — Median	14.0	6.7	11.7	7.0	11.4	4.6	12.7	1.4	16.8	3.1
% Profit Before Taxes/Total Assets — Low	3.7		1.2		3.4		5.2		8.7	
Sales/Net Fixed Assets — High	36.3		25.9		22.4		54.4		29.9	
Sales/Net Fixed Assets — Median	15.8	9.8	15.8	8.9	16.6	7.6	15.6	7.8	13.8	6.7
Sales/Net Fixed Assets — Low	8.5		8.2		8.0		7.5		9.4	
Sales/Total Assets — High	3.5		2.6		2.5		2.8		2.8	
Sales/Total Assets — Median	1.8	1.2	1.6	1.1	2.1	0.9	2.0	0.8	2.3	0.7
Sales/Total Assets — Low	1.1		1.0		1.1		1.6		1.4	
Expense to Sales Ratios										
% Depr. and Amort./Sales — High	0.8		1.3		1.2		0.9		1.1	
% Depr. and Amort./Sales — Median	1.9	3.0	2.8	3.0	2.3	2.9	2.5	2.8	3.5	2.5
% Depr. and Amort./Sales — Low	3.8		5.2		4.0		3.6		4.9	

Source: Data from *RMA Annual Statement Studies*, 1999. Used with permission of Robert Morris Associates.

Exhibit 8.6 Subject Nursery Compared with Data from the *Financial Studies of the Small Business*

	Subject Company[a]	Financial Studies Data[b] Median	Financial Studies Data[b] Upper Quartile	Financial Studies Data[b] Lower Quartile
Number of Enterprises	1	49	49	49
Selected Financial Ratios				
Current Ratio (times)	2.50	2.00	4.20	1.10
Quick Ratio (times)	1.00	0.80	2.10	0.40
Current Assets / Total Assets	58.00%	53.70%	70.50%	23.10%
Short-term Debt / Total Debt	47.00%	45.60%	87.70%	18.60%
Short-term Debt / Total Assets	18.20%	20.50%	36.90%	6.60%
Long-term Debt / Total Assets	24.30%	21.10%	46.70%	0.50%
Sales / Receivables (times)	18.00	14.30	62.40	0.00
Average Collection period (days)	7.00	3.00	21.00	0.00
Sales / Inventory (times)	12.30	7.60	18.30	1.00
Sales / Total Assets (times)	3.00	2.10	4.10	1.70
Profit (pretax) / Total Assets	6.50%	4.60%	27.30%	-1.10%
Profit (pretax) / Net Worth	12.00%	9.10%	34.80%	-2.30%

Source: Karen Goodman and Grant Lacerte, *Financial Studies of the Small Business*, 22nd ed. (Winter Haven, FL: Financial Research Associates, 1999). Reprinted with permission of Financial Research Associates, PO Box 7708, Winter Haven, FL 33883-7708.

[a] Subject company data is fictitious and for this exhibit only.

[b] *Financial Studies of the Small Business* includes companies with total assets from $10,000 to $1,000,000.

Exhibit 8.7   Subject Restaurant Compared with Data from the *Almanac of Business and Industrial Financial Ratios*

	Subject Company[a] 1999	Almanac Data[b] 1999
Total Assets	$94,000	Under $100K
Number of Enterprises	1	53,548
Selected Financial Ratios		
Current Ratio	0.54	1.40
Quick Ratio	0.20	1.00
Total Asset Turnover	1.90	6.60
Inventory Turnover	26.80	N/A[c]
Total Liabilities to Net Worth	0.91	4.80
Selected Financial Factors		
Return on Assets	36.30%	N/A
Return on Equity	66.90%	N/A
Profit Margin, before Income Tax	19.50%	6.20%
Profit Margin, after Income Tax	19.50%	6.00%

Source: From the *Almanac of Business and Industrial Financial Ratios* by Leo Troy. Copyright © 1999. Reprinted with permission of Prentice Hall Direct.

Note: Almanac data are specifically for restaurants with a total assets range that includes the subject company.

[a] Subject company is the same as used in the restaurant case found in Chapter 13.
[b] 1999 *Almanac of Business and Industrial Financial Ratios* are from Table II, Corporations with Net Income.
[c] Not available.

    Exhibit 8.7 illustrates a select number of financial ratios and financial factors, as defined by the *Almanac of Business and Industrial Financial Ratios*. In this example, we do not demonstrate the comparison of the trends in selected ratios and factors as provided in the almanac. However, analysts may want to include information from the trends section and compare this to the subject company. In addition to the general sources listed above, there are many industry-specific sources. Many of these are listed in the *Business Valuation Data, Publications, and Internet Directory*™, published annually by Business Valuation Resources, LLC.

Guideline Merged and Acquired Company Data on Privately Held Company Sales

    Four databases contain various financial information on sales of privately held companies:

1. *BIZCOMPS*®[7]
2. *Done Deals*[8]

3. *Pratt's Stats*™[9]
4. *IBA Market Data Base*[10]

Each of these databases contains financial information on the sales of privately held companies, including the selling price and various valuation multiples. If using guideline mergers and acquisitions from the databases on private company transactions, the analyst must use year-end data instead of average data, because these sources only provide data for the latest year. Detailed contact information for all of the above sources can be found in Appendix B.

Guideline Publicly Traded Company Data

Once the subject company's industry is defined by a specific SIC code, publicly traded companies within that SIC code can be obtained by going to www. FreeEdgar.com on the Internet, clicking on "Search Filings," entering an SIC code in the appropriate box, and clicking on "Search." A list of publicly traded companies operating in that SIC code will be listed. The analyst can then view the filings for each of the reported companies. Income statements and balance sheets for these companies are available in the companies' annual 10K filings. Depending on the length of time the companies have been public, several years of filings are available at this site. From these filings, trend analysis and comparative analysis can be performed. There are many sources of publicly traded company data. The most widely used of these are listed in Appendix B.

TYPES OF RATIOS

This section demonstrates the computation of four categories of financial ratios:

1. Short-term liquidity measures
2. Activity ratios
3. Balance sheet leverage ratios
4. Profitability ratios

The ratios shown in this section may not all be calculated in every case, and in some cases additional ratios may be calculated.

A five-year summary of Colossal's ratios is shown in Exhibit 8.8. For the most part, they have been improving over time. The analyst generally will discuss the outlook for such ratios in the future during management interviews. Colossal's ratios are compared with the medians of the guideline company ratios in Exhibit 8.9. Comparable ratios for merged and acquired companies are shown in

Exhibit 8.8   Colossal Software: Summary of Ratio Analysis

	Fiscal Years Ended December				
	2004	2003	2002	2001	2000
Liquidity Ratios					
Current Ratio	2.2	2.3	2.9	4.1	3.3
Quick Ratio	1.9	1.9	2.6	3.6	3.1
Working Capital ($MM)	20.9	19.5	20.4	22.4	13.9
Activity Ratios					
Accounts Receivable Turnover	4.4	4.8	4.0	3.6	N/A[a]
Average Collection Period	82.1	76.6	92.1	100.9	N/A
Fixed Asset Turnover	10.2	9.9	8.8	8.5	N/A
Asset Turnover	1.3	1.2	1.0	0.9	N/A
Working Capital Turnover	3.4	2.9	1.9	1.6	N/A
Coverage/Leverage Ratios					
Total Debt to Total Assets (%)	45.7	47.1	45.4	42.9	21.1
Long-term Debt to Equity (%)	22.5	28.8	36.4	41.2	N/A
Times Interest Earned	5.7	5.9	4.4	2.4	N/A
Fixed-charges Coverage Ratio	3.0	3.3	2.8	1.8	N/A
Profitability Ratios (%)					
Gross Profit Margin	57.4	57.2	59.3	54.4	49.1
Operating Profit Margin	5.3	7.1	8.5	6.7	5.6
Net Profit Margin	3.3	3.7	2.5	(1.7)	0.6
Cash Flow to Sales[b]	6.3	6.6	5.4	1.1	3.1
Return on Total Assets[c]	4.9	5.4	3.5	0.0	N/A
Return on Equity	7.4	7.9	4.2	(2.2)	0.6

[a] Not available.
[b] Cash flow = net income plus depreciation and amortization expense.
[c] Tax rate of 40% used in return on assets calculation.

Chapter 14 in Exhibit 14.6B. The ratios are computed and discussed in the following sections.

Short-term Liquidity Measures

The liquidity measures give us an idea of the company's ability to pay its bills on time. They also provide a measure as to how easily the company can meet a need for unexpected cash. When analyzing the subject company and its operating needs, liquidity measures can help resolve one of the common business valuation-related questions: Are the company's assets in excess of those required, or do they fall short, and what impact will these answers have on the valuation? That is, does

Exhibit 8.9 Colossal Software: Comparative Ratio Analysis with Guideline Public Companies

	Ardent Software 12/31/04	Best Software 12/31/04	Cadence Design 1/2/05	Centaur Software 12/31/04	Sterling Software 9/30/04	Semi Systems 6/30/04	Median	Colossal 12/31/04
Liquidity Ratios								
Current Ratio	1.3	1.7	1.8	1.0	3.5	1.5	1.6	2.2
Quick Ratio	1.2	1.6	1.5	0.9	3.4	1.4	1.4	1.9
Working Capital ($MM)	13.1	23.9	251.8	1.0	673.3	13.6	18.7	20.9
Activity Ratios								
Accounts Receivable Turnover	5.6	10.8	5.0	4.3	3.9	3.6	4.7	4.4
Average Collection Perio	64.9	33.8	72.4	84.4	93.2	102.1	78.4	82.1
Fixed Asset Turnover	10.6	21.3	5.3	16.7	12.1	16.0	14.0	10.2
Asset Turnover	1.3	1.1	1.0	1.9	0.6	1.8	1.2	1.3
Working Capital Turnover	9.3	2.8	4.1	-6.2	1.2	9.1	3.4	3.4
Coverage/Leverage Ratios								
Total Debt to Total Assets (%)	47.1	46.2	39.0	75.2	27.5	52.8	46.7	45.7
Long-term Debt to Equity (%)		0.3	15.9			7.4	7.4	22.5
Times Interest Earned	11.8	75.6	34.6	7.7	204.0	5.4	23.2	5.7
Fixed-Charges Coverage Ratio	11.8	30.3	24.7	7.7	204.0	3.5	18.2	3.0
Profitability Ratios (%)								
Gross Profit Margin (%)	74.5	80.6	76.9	83.1	60.0	63.4	75.7	57.4
Operating Profit Margin (%)	3.8	9.8	8.6	7.3	12.0	2.1	8.0	5.3
Net Profit Margin (%)	1.4	8.1	2.6	4.0	10.6	-1.4	3.3	3.3
Cash Flow to Sales (%)[a]	8.4	12.4	11.1	10.8	16.8	5.0	10.9	6.3
Return on Total Assets (%)[b]	15.9	8.6	2.8	8.4	6.7	-2.0	7.5	4.9
Return on Equity (%)	3.7	14.0	439.7	29.1	8.8	-4.3	11.4	7.9

[a] Cash flow = net income plus depreciation and amortization expense.

[b] Tax rate of 40% used in return on assets calculation.

Note: This exhibit is for illustration only. The numbers in the table do not represent actual numbers for the years indicated.

the company have excess working capital, a working capital deficit, or about the right amount of working capital?

If valuing a controlling interest, an amount of excess working capital may be added on to an indication of value derived from applying market multiples to company fundamental variables. Conversely, a working capital deficit could result in a deduction from values indicated by market multiples, because a buyer may have to invest more money in the business to bring it to normal financial strength.

If, however, we are valuing a minority interest, we usually would not make an addition or deduction for excess or deficient working capital, because the minority owner does not have any power to cause changes in working capital. Instead, in a minority interest valuation, excess or deficient working capital may be regarded as a relative strength or weakness of the company, which may be a reason to vary upward or downward from valuation multiples found in the guideline public or guideline merged and acquired companies.

Current Ratio.   The current ratio is the most commonly used short-term liquidity measure. The current ratio provides information to the analyst with respect to the subject company's ability to pay for their current liabilities. If the calculated ratio is significantly lower than the industry norm, in the near term, the company is more likely to find itself in murky financial straits than if the calculated ratio was greater than the industry norm. The current ratio is defined as the current assets divided by the current liabilities.

Formula 8.1

$$\text{Current Ratio} = \frac{\text{Current Assets}}{\text{Current Liabilities}}$$

Referring to Colossal Software's balance sheet (Exhibit 8.1), the current ratio for 2004 is

Formula 8.2

$$\text{Current Ratio} = \frac{\$39,005}{\$18,101} = 2.2$$

Note that current assets include inventory. Inventory will take longer to convert to cash (it is less liquid) than other current assets.

It is important to compare the calculated ratio for the subject company to the industry norm (or to selected guideline companies) and then arrive at some conclusion as to the company's relative strength or weakness based on this comparison.

Quick (Acid-test) Ratio.   The next most commonly used short-term liquidity ratio is the quick ratio, also referred to as the *acid-test* ratio. The quick ratio differs from the current ratio in that the quick ratio does not include the inventory and is therefore a measure of the ability of the company to meet current liabilities with its most liquid resources. This ratio tends to be a preferred and more conservative measure than the current ratio because of its focus on the company's liquid assets to pay current liabilities.

The quick ratio is defined as the sum of the cash and cash equivalents plus receivables (usually all current assets above the inventory on the balance sheet) divided by the current liabilities.

Formula 8.3

$$\text{Quick Ratio} = \frac{(\text{Cash} + \text{Cash Equivalents} + \text{Investments} + \text{Receivables})}{\text{Current Liabilities}}$$

Referring to Colossal Software's balance sheet, the quick ratio for 2004 is

Formula 8.4

$$\text{Quick Ratio} = \frac{(\$9{,}209 + \$7{,}135 + \$17{,}296)}{\$18{,}101} = 1.9$$

In the equation, investments generally relate to marketable securities—to be most meaningful, the investments that qualify as current assets should be computed at market values. Because we are using the company's balance sheet, it is important to realize that the two ratios that we have discussed so far measure liquidity at a point in time and may not reflect a company's use of short-term credit to finance its short-term liquidity needs. If the subject company's quick ratio and current ratio are suspiciously outside of the industry norms, the site visit is an excellent time to gather additional information that may be beneficial in the overall analysis. Colossal's liquidity ratios are slightly above the guideline companies' average, suggesting slightly less risk in this category.

Activity Ratios

Activity ratios generally measure how efficiently a company uses its assets. The denominator for all of the activity ratios (except average collection period) consists of an average figure—adding the data for the current and past year and then dividing by 2. If comparing with publicly traded guideline companies, the denominator can be computed in this preferred manner for both the subject and guideline companies. However, as noted in the next paragraph, some data sources have only year-end figures for comparison. The key is that it is important to be consistent—that is, using "apples to apples" comparisons.

The definitions of the activity ratios vary in the six main data sources of industry average performance. The analyst should take particular note of the ratio definitions in each of the various sources. When calculating the ratios of the subject company and comparing them to the published data on industry average performance, the analyst must use the ratio definitions as defined by the published source. All six industry sources use year-end data rather than average data.

Accounts Receivable Turnover. The accounts receivable turnover indicates how efficiently a company is using one of its current assets—accounts receivable. The accounts receivable turnover is typically calculated by dividing the net credit sales (or total revenues) by the average accounts receivable.

Formula 8.5

$$\text{Accounts Receivable Turnover} = \frac{\text{Net Credit Sales}}{\text{Average Accounts Receivable}}$$

$$= \text{Number of Times Turned Over}$$

Referring to Colossal Software's balance sheet and income statement (Exhibits 8.1 and 8.2), the accounts receivable turnover for 2004 is

Formula 8.6

$$\text{Accounts Receivable Turnover} = \frac{\$69,481}{(\$17,296 + \$13,963)/2} = 4.4\times$$

Note that the net sales figure was used for the numerator—the net credit sales was unavailable.

The reason we prefer to use net credit sales, as opposed to net sales, in the numerator is because the net credit sales is a comparable variable to the accounts receivable account. An increase in the accounts receivable line item in the balance sheet only occurs when there is a credit sale—it does not occur on a cash sale. For a more accurate depiction of the company's financial ratios, it is always better to compare like variables. We discuss the numerator and the denominator separately.

The numerator—net credit sales—does not include the cash sales; we include only sales where credit was used. It may be quite difficult to obtain the net credit sales data for the subject company, the industry norm, or the selected guideline companies. If the cash sales are insignificant, or if the analyst cannot differentiate between cash and credit sales, the total sales figures may be used in the computation.

The denominator—average accounts receivable—may be calculated using the average of the receivables at the beginning and end of the year. A more timely measure would result if the analyst used either the most recent quarterly average or the most recent monthly average. This procedure will give a more accurate picture, especially when there are seasonal fluctuations. It is paramount that whatever time period is used for the subject company, the same timeline must be used for the selected comparative ratios.

Note that the accounts receivable turnover calculation provides the analyst with the number of times the accounts receivable account has turned over in a one-year period. The higher the number, the shorter the time period between the credit sale and the receipt of the accounts receivable. As an illustration, if Example.com (turnover = 4) has an accounts receivable turnover that is lower than the industry norm (turnover = 8), this indicates that Example.com has a slower accounts receivable collection process than does the industry. The analyst may want to investigate the collection process during the site visit.

The accounts receivable turnover can be expressed as the average number of days that accounts are outstanding. To determine the average number of days, we take 365 days per year and divide it by the number of times that accounts receivable turned over. This exercise is demonstrated later in a section on average collection period.

Inventory Turnover. The inventory turnover calculation provides a similar measure as the accounts receivable calculation—how many times does the inventory turn over in one year? The calculation is defined as

Formula 8.7

$$\text{Inventory Turnover} = \frac{\text{Cost of Goods Sold}}{\text{Average Inventory}}$$

Colossal Software shows no inventory on its balance sheet, so this ratio will not be calculated. Similar to the accounts receivable turnover, for this ratio it is preferable to use the most recent available inventory figures when calculating the average inventory level (i.e., monthly or quarterly).

When analyzing the results, if the subject company's inventory turnover calculation results in a small number when compared with a larger industry norm, we know that the inventory in the subject company is being carried in inventory longer than it is at its peer companies. This may signify an aging inventory that may become obsolete or otherwise undesirable. Conversely, the subject company may have a large inventory turnover number when compared to a smaller industry norm, indicating a more rapid turnover of inventory. One interpretation of this situation is that the company may be losing sales due to insufficient on-hand inventory.

Also, as with the accounts receivable turnover, the inventory turnover can be expressed as the average number of days in inventory. To determine the average number of days in inventory, we take 365 days per year and divide it by the number of times the inventory has turned over.

The analyst should be duly cautioned: All six data sources on industry average performance use the inventory figure as of the end of the year, not the average over a period of time. If the analyst will be using these data sources, the ratio for the subject company must be computed in the same fashion as the ratio in the data source.

Caution: Some analysts use sales instead of cost of goods sold in the numerator for the inventory turnover. This makes the turnover look better (faster). However, it is misleading analytically because it overstates the actual physical turnover. It is important, if comparing inventory turnover figures with industry averages or guideline companies, to be sure that the ratio is computed the same way for both to make a valid comparison. Financial Research Associates' *Financial Studies of the Small Business* uses sales in the numerator of the inventory turnover calculation; the other industry-average performance sources that calculate this ratio use the cost of goods sold in the numerator.

For companies with large seasonal variations in inventory, such as retailers before Christmas (high) or ski manufacturers in March (low) it may be necessary to use monthly averages of inventory to get an accurate picture of inventory turnover.

Average Collection Period. To determine the average collection period, we take 365 days per year and divide it by the number of times the accounts receivables have turned over.

Formula 8.8

$$\text{Average Collection Period} = \frac{365 \text{ Days per Year}}{\text{Accounts Receivable Turnover per Year}}$$

$$= \text{Number of Days}$$

Referring to our earlier accounts receivable calculation, the average collection period for 2004 is

Formula 8.9

$$\text{Average Collection Period} = \frac{365}{4.4} = 82.1 \text{ days}$$

This calculation results in the average collection period in days. The greater this number, the more likely the accounts receivable will become unpaid. The analyst will want to compare the terms that the subject company affords its customers versus the terms the industry in general offers its customers. To continue our Example.com scenario, Example.com has an average collection period of 365/4 = 91 days whereas the industry has an average collection period of 365/8 = 46 days.

We see that Example.com requires approximately double the amount of time to collect its accounts receivables than does the industry.

Again, the analyst should be cautioned: The six data sources on industry average performance use the accounts receivable figure as of the end of the year, not the average over a period of time. The ratio for the subject company must be computed in the same fashion as the ratio in the data source. The analyst should also be cautioned that the end-of-year (or latest quarter) figures are also the ones available from the *Pratt's Stats*™ database on sales of privately held companies; the two years of data required to calculate the average is unavailable.

Fixed Asset Turnover and Total Asset Turnover. Both of these ratios indicate how efficiently the company's net fixed assets are producing sales. They are both measures of asset productivity. The fixed asset turnover ratio is also known as the sales to fixed asset ratio and is calculated as

Formula 8.10

$$\text{Fixed Asset Turnover} = \frac{\text{Sales}}{\text{Average Fixed Assets}}$$

Using Formula 8.10 and referring to Colossal Software's balance sheet and income statement, the fixed asset turnover ratio for 2004 is

Formula 8.11

$$\text{Fixed Asset Turnover} = \frac{\$69,481}{[(\$7,092 + \$6,535)/2]} = 10.2\times$$

The total asset turnover ratio is also known as the sales to total assets ratio and is calculated as:

Formula 8.12

$$\text{Total Asset Turnover} = \frac{\text{Sales}}{\text{Average Total Assets}}$$

Using Formula 8.12 and referring to Colossal Software's balance sheet and income statement, the total asset turnover ratio for 2004 is

Formula 8.13

$$\text{Total Asset Turnover} = \frac{\$69,481}{[(\$57,053 + \$51,265)/2]} = 1.3\times$$

This ratio can be calculated using the year-ending asset levels or an average of the asset levels over the last two years.

The calculation results in a figure that indicates the amount of sales per either the company's fixed assets or the company's total assets. Performing this analysis over a several-year time period may enlighten the analyst about positive or negative trends when compared with either the industry or the guideline company(s).

Caution: The age and, thus, the depreciated book value of the assets used in these calculations should be considered, particularly when comparing them with those of other, similar companies.

Working Capital Turnover. This ratio is also known as the sales to net working capital ratio. Net working capital is defined as current assets minus current liabilities and is widely used as a measure of the ability of a company to finance its current operations. It is also used to indicate the efficiency of current asset usage. This ratio is calculated as

Formula 8.14

$$\text{Working Capital Turnover} = \frac{\text{Sales}}{\text{Current Assets} - \text{Current Liabilities}}$$

Typically, fiscal year-end figures are used for this equation. Another more reasonable method to compute this ratio is to use the average net working capital rather than the ending net working capital as the denominator. This equation is

Formula 8.15

$$\text{Working Capital Turnover} = \frac{\text{Sales}}{[(\text{Current Assets} - \text{Current Liabilities})_{2004} + (\text{Current Assets} - \text{Current Liabilities})_{2003}]/2}$$

Note in the denominator that we are adding the two years of year-end working capital and dividing the result by 2. Using Formula 8.15 and referring to Colossal Software's balance sheet and income statement, the working capital turnover ratio for 2004 is

Formula 8.16

$$\text{Working Capital Turnover} = \frac{\$69,481}{[(\$39,005 - \$18,101) + (\$35,053 - \$15,504)]/2}$$
$$= 3.4\times$$

When comparing a calculated turnover ratio with a guideline company or industry average, a high ratio of sales to net working capital may indicate either

- Efficient use of current assets resulting from a favorable turnover of accounts receivable and inventory
- Risk arising from possibly inadequate short-term liquidity

In order to more accurately assess the subject company's ability to meet peak needs, the analyst may want to perform a worst-case analysis. To do this, one will want to consider the highest reasonable level of anticipated sales coupled with the lowest accounts receivable turnover and slowest inventory turnover that might occur. Under this worst-case scenario, one analyzes the adequacy of the working capital. Colossal's activity ratios indicate no significant departures from industry norms as exhibited by the guideline companies.

Balance Sheet Leverage Ratios

Balance sheet leverage ratios are used to analyze the long-term solvency of the subject company. They help determine the company's ability to take advantage of opportunities when they arise or its ability to financially weather a storm if one ensues. As with the other ratios, the analyst will want to compare the subject company's current ratios with those of the industry and any guideline companies, as well as ratios over time within the subject company.

Total Debt to Total Assets.   The total debt (liabilities) to total assets ratio is one of the more popular leverage ratios. It places a measure on the subject company's total funding as a percentage of the company's total assets.

Formula 8.17

$$\text{Total Debt to Total Assets Ratio} = \frac{\text{Total Liabilities}}{\text{Total Assets}}$$

Using Formula 8.17 and referring to Colossal Software's balance sheet, the total debt to total assets ratio for 2004 is

Formula 8.18

$$\text{Total Debt to Total Assets Ratio} = \frac{\$26,082}{\$57,053} = 0.457 \text{ or } 45.7\%$$

Long-term Debt to Equity.   The long-term debt to equity ratio (also known as the interest-bearing debt to equity ratio) provides the analyst with information regarding the extent to which long-term debt financing was used to fund the company's assets. The formula for this ratio is

Formula 8.19

$$\text{Long-term Debt to Equity} = \frac{\text{Long-term Debt}}{\text{Total Equity}}$$

Using Formula 8.19 and referring to Colossal Software's balance sheet, the long-term debt to equity ratio for 2004 is

Formula 8.20

$$\text{Long-term Debt to Equity} = \frac{\$6,967}{\$30,971} = 0.225 \text{ or } 22.5\%$$

The *RMA Annual Statement Studies* ratio definition varies from Formula 8.19 because it uses total debt, not just long-term debt, and only tangible equities, not total equities. Risk Management Association's debt to equity ratio is computed as:

$$\text{RMA Debt to Equity} = \frac{\text{Total Liabilities}}{(\text{Total Equity} - \text{Intangible Assets})}$$

When comparing ratios with *RMA Annual Statement Studies,* the analyst needs to remember this difference and make any appropriate adjustments.

Times Interest Earned.   The times interest earned ratio provides an indication as to the ability of the company operations to cover its interest expense. It is also known as the interest coverage ratio. The formula for this ratio is

Formula 8.21

$$\text{Times Interest Earned} = \frac{\text{Earnings before Interest and Taxes}}{\text{Interest Expense}}$$

Using Formula 8.21 and referring to Colossal Software's income statement, the times interest earned ratio for 2004 is

Formula 8.22

$$\text{Times Interest Earned} = \frac{\$3,648}{\$638} = 5.7\times$$

Fixed-charges Coverage. Analysis of the fixed-charges coverage ratio signifies the ability of the subject company to pay its fixed charges, such as lease payments and the current portion of long-term debt. The subject company will have its unique set of fixed charges, which may include more than these two items. This ratio is more inclusive than the times interest earned ratio because it includes coverage of items in addition to interest.

Formula 8.23

$$\text{Fixed-charges Coverage Ratio} = \frac{\text{EBIT} + \text{Fixed Charges}}{\text{Interest Expense} + \text{Fixed Charges}}$$

Using Formula 8.23 and referring to Colossal Software's income statement and balance sheet, the fixed-charges coverage ratio for 2004 is

Formula 8.24

$$\text{Fixed-Charges Coverage Ratio} = \frac{\$3,648 + \$856}{\$638 + \$856} = 3.0$$

Note that the $856 fixed charges appears on Colossal Software's balance sheet listed as "Current Portion of Long-term Liabilities."

The financial coverage ratios for the guideline companies as shown in Exhibit 8.9 are so widely scattered that any comparison with Colossal is not very meaningful.

Profitability Ratios

The profitability ratios are in two categories:

1. The income statement profitability ratios, which relate to sales
2. The balance sheet profitability ratios, which relate to returns on book values carried on the balance sheet

Higher-than-average ratios suggest higher price or MVIC ratios to sales, and vice versa. Furthermore, a low operating margin is an indication of higher risk, and vice versa. Higher-than-average returns relative to balance sheet variables suggest higher price/book value of equity or MVIC/book value of invested capital ratios.

Apart from the *levels* of these ratios relative to those of other companies, it is also significant to look at the *stability* of these ratios over time as an important indicator of risk. Studies by Roger Grabowski and David King of Pricewaterhouse-

Coopers show that high coefficients of variation of both operating margin and return on book value of equity are important measures of risk.[11]

Gross Profit Margin.   The gross profit margin provides the analyst the percentage remaining for all other expenses after the direct cost of purchasing or manufacturing is deducted. When this ratio is analyzed over time and compared to an industry average, we can obtain a trend of the company's relative cost to price standing in the industry. Gross profit is defined to be net sales minus the cost of goods sold.

Formula 8.25

$$\text{Gross Profit Margin} = \frac{\text{Gross Profit}}{\text{Sales}}$$

Using Formula 8.25 and referring to Colossal Software's income statement, the gross profit margin ratio for 2004 is

Formula 8.26

$$\text{Gross Profit Margin} = \frac{\$39,883}{\$69,481} = 0.574 \text{ or } 57.4\%$$

Operating Profit Margin.   Operating profit margin provides a measure of profitability based on an income statement line item farther down the income statement from the gross profit margin. Operating profit margin is a measure of the firm's or industry's profitability based on its operations and is often used as a measure of creditworthiness. Here we measure the profitability based on the operating profit, which is defined as the gross profit minus total operating expenses including both fixed and variable costs. We have not deducted the interest or taxes from this figure. The higher the operating profit margin of a subject company with respect to the industry average, the greater is the subject company's productivity and the better prepared they are to withstand a downturn in the economy. The operating profit is also known as EBIT—earnings before interest and taxes.

Formula 8.27

$$\text{Operating Profit Margin} = \frac{\text{Operating Profit}}{\text{Sales}}$$

Using Formula 8.27 and referring to Colossal Software's income statement, the operating profit margin for 2004 is

Formula 8.28

$$\text{Operating Profit Margin} = \frac{\$3,648}{\$69,481} = 0.053 \text{ or } 5.3\%$$

Net Profit Margin. The net profit margin is based on the net income of the firm in relation to the sales. The definition for this ratio and two following ratios (return on total assets and return on equity) uses the net income after taxes—entity taxes, not personal taxes—but before dividends on preferred and common stock. For many small companies, the pretax net income is the same as the after-tax net income because they do not pay entity taxes. The reader should also note that for non-tax-paying S corporations and limited liability companies, there is an ongoing controversy about whether to include a tax amount in calculating the net income after taxes, a controversy that is beyond the scope of this book.

We also use the net income as a result of the continuing operations—adjusting the net income figure for any discontinued operations or gains or losses from the sale of operations. Our objective is to derive a ratio based on the future expectations of the subject firm—discontinued operations and the sale of operations are usually not a recurring item. The net profit margin equation is

Formula 8.29

$$\text{Net Profit Margin} = \frac{\text{Net Income}}{\text{Sales}}$$

Using Formula 8.29 and referring to Colossal Software's income statement, the net margin ratio for 2004 is

Formula 8.30

$$\text{Net Profit Margin} = \frac{\$2,294}{\$69,481} = 0.033 \text{ or } 3.3\%$$

Cash Flow to Sales. Cash flow to sales measures the relative amount of funds generated by the subject company. We define cash flow as net income plus all non-cash charges (depreciation and amortization). This measure of cash flow is on the gross basis, and does not deduct outlays such as capital expenditures and debt principal repayment. This measure is one of the most critical measures of a company's productivity and creditworthiness. If the calculated measure is low relative to industry averages or guideline companies, any plans for increased sales or company expansion may be difficult to complete because the firm may not generate the necessary cash to meet these goals. If the calculated measure is high, the opportunity for increased sales or expansion will be greater.

Formula 8.31

$$\text{Cash Flow to Sales} = \frac{\text{Cash Flow}}{\text{Sales}}$$

Using Formula 8.31 and referring to Colossal Software's income statement, the cash flow to sales ratio for 2004 is

Formula 8.32

$$\text{Cash Flow to Sales} = \frac{(\$2,294 + \$2,086)}{\$69,481} = 0.063 \text{ or } 6.3\%$$

These returns relative to sales are generally lower than those of the guideline companies, suggesting a lower price/sales or MVIC/sales valuation multiple.

Return on Total Assets.   The return on total assets ratio gives us a measure of the amount of income that is generated per the subject company's total assets. The analyst needs to be aware of the definition used by publishers of industry information; we are using the average total assets in our definition, not the year-end total assets, and we tax-effect the interest, which they do not.

Formula 8.33

$$\text{Return on Total Assets} = \frac{\text{Net Income} + \text{Interest } (1 - \text{Tax Rate})}{\text{Average Total Assets}}$$

Using Formula 8.33 and referring to Colossal Software's income statement and balance sheet, the return on total assets ratio for 2004 is

Formula 8.34

$$\text{Return on Total Assets} = \frac{\$2,294 + \$638 \ (1 - 0.40)}{[(\$57,053 + \$51,265)/2]} = 0.049 \text{ or } 4.9\%$$

Return on Equity.   When we calculate the return on equity ratio, we are using it as an after-tax ratio, not before taxes. We are also computing the return on equity based on the common equity capital. Some companies have issued preferred stock. In this case, the analyst may want to compute the return on the total equity and the return on the common equity. In doing so, there will be two measures of return on equity to which a subject company may be compared. The analyst should exercise a high degree of caution when comparing the subject company with other guideline companies that also issue preferred stock. As in all ratio comparisons, the ratios to be compared should be calculated on the same basis.

In the definition of return on equity, net income available to common stockholders refers to the after-tax net income. When we refer to after-tax, we are referring to entity-level taxes, not personal taxes. In other words, we are generally referring to the income taxes that would be paid by a regular C corporation.

If valuing an S corporation or a partnership, there is some controversy as to whether the analyst should impute entity-level taxes that would be paid if it were a C corporation. The answer to this may depend on the purpose of the valuation and the standard of value. For fair market value, the *IRS Valuation Training for Appeals Officers Coursebook*[12] recommends that corporate taxes be imputed for S corporations and partnerships. However, a 1999 U.S. Tax Court decision, *Gross v. Commissioner,*[13] denied the tax adjustment for an S corporation and was affirmed on appeal. *Gross* was followed by the *Estate of Wall* in which both the Internal Revenue Service expert and the taxpayer's expert tax-affected the S corporation earning and the court rejected this approach.[14] Next came the *Estate of Heck* in which neither expert tax-affected the earnings.[15] Then in *Estate of Adams*[16] the court ruled that the capitalization rate did not need to be adjusted for lack of income taxes because the income was after income taxes, albeit at a 0% tax rate.[17]

There are some circumstances where the pretax income may be used. In these cases, it should be defined as a pretax return on equity and described as a departure from the conventional use of the definition in the accompanying text of the report.

Formula 8.35

$$\text{Return on Equity} = \frac{\text{Net Income}}{\text{Average Equity}}$$

Using Formula 8.35 and referring to Colossal Software's income statement and balance sheet, the return on equity ratio for 2004 is

Formula 8.36

$$\text{Return on Equity} = \frac{\$2,294}{(\$30,971 + \$27,121)/2} = 0.079 \text{ or } 7.9\%$$

As with the returns on sales, returns on book values tend to be in the low range of the guideline companies, suggesting below-median price/equity or MVIC/book value of invested capital valuation multiples.

SUMMARY

In this chapter, we have reviewed the most commonly used comparative financial ratios used in the market approach. Many other ratios may or may not be appropriate for a particular engagement. It is important to remember that before a valuation conclusion is made, the overall analysis of a subject company includes a comparison of these ratios with both the industry averages and the selected guideline companies, as well as for the company itself over time. When comparing the subject company to industry averages, it is also important to identify the definition of terms used by the source information of the industry averages—and to make any necessary adjustments. If the analyst has performed a thorough investigation of these data, a better conclusion will be reached.

For review, all of the ratios we have discussed are presented in summary form.

Short-term Liquidity Measures

Current Ratio = Current Assets/Current Liabilities

Quick Ratio = (Cash + Cash Equivalents + Investments + Receivables)/ Current Liabilities

Activity Ratios

Accounts Receivable Turnover = Net Credit Sales/Average Accounts Receivable

Inventory Turnover = Cost of Goods Sold/Average Inventory

Average Collection Period = 365 Days per Year/Accounts Receivable Turnover per Year

Fixed Asset Turnover = Sales/Average Fixed Assets

Total Asset Turnover = Sales/Average Total Assets

Working Capital Turnover = Sales/Average Net Working Capital

Balance Sheet Leverage Ratios

Total Debt to Total Assets = Total Liabilities/Total Assets

Long-term Debt to Equity = Long-term Debt/Total Equity

Times Interest Earned = Earnings Before Interest and Taxes/Interest Expense

Fixed-charges Coverage = (EBIT + Fixed Charges)/(Interest Expense + Fixed Charges)

Profitability Ratios

Gross Profit Margin = Gross Profit/Sales

Operating Profit Margin = Operating Profit/Sales

Net Profit Margin = Net Income/Sales

Cash Flow to Sales = Cash Flow/Sales

Return on Total Assets = (Net Income + Interest [1 – Tax Rate])/Average Total Assets

Return on Equity = Net Income/Average Equity

Notes

1. *RMA Annual Statement Studies* (Philadelphia: Rick Management Association 2004), published annually.
2. Karen Goodman and Grant Lacerte, *Financial Studies of the Small Business*, 22nd ed. (Winter Haven, FL: Financial Research Associates 2004), published annually.
3. *IRS Corporate Financial Ratios*, 14th ed. (Riverwoods, IL: Schonfeld & Associates), published annually.
4. Leo Troy, *Almanac of Business and Industrial Financial Ratios* (New Jersey: Prentice-Hall), published annually.
5. *IRS Corporate Ratios* (Hoboken, NJ: John Wiley & Sons), published annually.
6. James R. Hickman and E. W. Bud Lester, *Financial Ratio Analyst* (New York: Warren Gorham & Lamont), published annually.
7. *BIZCOMPS®* (San Diego: Bizcomps 2004), available at BVMarketData.com.
8. *Done Deals* (Fort Worth, TX: Practitioners Publishing Co. 2004).
9. *Pratt's Stats* (Portland, OR: Business Valuation Resources, LLC 2004), available at BVMarket-Data.com.
10. *IBA Market Data Base* (Plantation, FL: The Institute of Business Appraisers 2004).
11. Roger Grabowski and David King, "New Measures of Risk That Really Work!" *Shannon Pratt's Business Valuation Update* (December 1999): 1, 3–4. See also Grabowski and King, "New Evidence on Equity Returns and Company Risk," *Business Valuation Review* (September 1999). Details of these and other related Standard & Poor's Corporate Value Consulting studies are updated on the Ibbotson Cost of Capital Web site, www.valuation.ibbotson.com.
12. *IRS Valuation Training for Appeals Officers Coursebook,* chap. 7 (Chicago: Commerce Clearing House, 1998), 12.
13. *Gross v. Commissioner,* T.C. Memo 1999-254, 78 T. C. M. (CCH) 201 (July 29, 1999), *aff'd,* 272 F.3d 333, 2001 U.S. App. LEXIS 24803 (6th Cir., November 19, 2001).
14. *Wall v. Commissioner,* T.C. Memo 2001-75, 2001 Tax Ct. Memo Lexis 97 (U.S. Tax Ct., March 27, 2001)
15. *Estate of Heck v. Commissioner,* T.C. Memo 2002-34, 2002 Tax Ct. Memo Lexis 38 (U.S. Tax Ct., February 5, 2002)
16. *Estate of Adams v. Commissioner,* T.C. Memo 2002-80, 2002 Tax Ct. Memo Lexis 84 (U.S. Tax Ct., March 28, 2002)
17. The cases cited were all very fact-specific. For an excellent discussion by several analysts who have made a study of S corp. valuations, see Chapter 8 in David Laro and Shannon P. Pratt, *Business Valuation and Taxes: Procedure, Law and Perspective* (Hoboken, NJ: John Wiley & Sons, 2005).

PART III

Compiling Market Value Tables and Reaching a Value Conclusion

Chapter 9

Compiling Useful Market Value Tables

Two Distinct Alternatives in Market Multiples
> Direct Valuation of Equity
> Valuing Total Invested Capital

Examples of Market Value Tables
> Subject Company to Guideline Publicly Traded Companies
> Subject Company to Comparative Transactions in *Pratt's Stats*™

Summary

The purpose of gathering data on guideline companies is to derive some benchmarks by which to value the subject privately held company. We start by gathering a group of companies that will be used for comparison; those companies may be public companies used in the guideline public company method or either public or privately held companies used in the comparative transaction method (also know as the mergers and acquisitions method). We then construct tables presenting the financial fundamentals and the resulting valuation multiples for each company. Market value tables, for presentation in a valuation report, can take several forms. In this chapter we will review the subject company to guideline companies:

- Subject company to guideline publicly traded companies
- Subject company to other comparative private transactions

Presenting market value tables in a valuation report provides the reader with a visual means of comparison. We will review several illustrations of valuation tables that the analyst may include in the final valuation report. In an actual report, the analyst would discuss these tables, including a listing of the assumptions, a written discussion of the results of each of the tables, and details on how they relate to the final valuation. This narrative is not included in this chapter—we concentrate on the presentation of tables. The reader is directed to the sample valuation reports found in Chapters 13 and 14 in this text for a narrative discussion relating to the valuation tables.

TWO DISTINCT ALTERNATIVES IN MARKET MULTIPLES

As discussed in Chapter 1, there are two different types of valuation multiples: the equity-based and the invested capital valuation multiples. When valuing the total invested capital of a firm, the analyst considers the equity and the interest-bearing debt of the subject companies. When valuing the equity of a firm, the analyst considers only the common equity of the firm.

Direct Valuation of Equity

The direct valuation of equity is typically used by some appraisers when valuing minority interests: those interests that do not have the ability to change the capital structure of the company. In this procedure, the analyst uses market multiples of various levels of income available to equity owners. Some of these include

- Price/sales (generally not preferred if there are senior securities because the sales are the result of the resources of the entire capital structure)
- Price/gross cash flow (gross cash flow = net income + noncash charges)
- Price/earnings before taxes (EBT)
- Price/discretionary earnings (discretionary earnings = net income + taxes + interest + noncash charges + compensation to one owner manager)
- Price/dividends or withdrawals
- Price/book value of equity (most often tangible book value, but may be total book value)
- Price/adjusted book value (sometimes referred to as price/net asset value)

Valuing Total Invested Capital

Invested capital includes the total value of all components of the capital structure and is defined as the sum of the market values of common and preferred stock plus the market value of the interest-bearing debt. The invested capital valuation procedure is sometimes preferred over the equity method for valuing controlling interests—mainly because of the ability of the controlling party to directly impact the overall capital structure (debt versus equity) of the company.

Many appraisers consider the invested capital procedure as the preferred way to value any company. Subtracting the debt from the results of the indicated market value of invested capital (MVIC) to get the indicated value of equity permits the appraiser to see the company for what it is without the debt creating a blurring effect.

In the invested capital procedure, the denominator of the equation used to compute the valuation multiples needs to include all of the returns available to all the invested capital. Usually this means adding all of the interest paid in addition to all the returns available to common equity. If there is preferred stock, the dividends on the preferred stock must also be included. Some of the more commonly used invested capital multiples are

- MVIC/sales
- MVIC/EBITDA (earnings before interest, taxes, depreciation and amortization)
- MVIC/EBIT (earnings before interest and taxes)
- MVIC/DFNI (debt-free net income—based on an estimation of what net income would be if there were no interest-bearing debt)
- MVIC/DFCF (debt-free cash flow—based on an estimation of what gross cash flow [debt free net income + noncash charges] would be if there were no interest-bearing debt)
- MVIC/book value of invested capital (most often only tangible book value, although the analyst might consider both tangible and total book value)
- MVIC/adjusted book value of invested capital (where major assets for subject and guideline companies are adjusted to market values)

The most widely used invested capital valuation multiple is the MVIC/ EBITDA multiple, because it eliminates the possible distortion in differing depreciation policies among companies. The second most frequently used invested capital multiple is the MVIC/EBIT multiple. For smaller companies where less complete data may be available, MVIC/sales and MVIC/discretionary earnings are often used. When invested capital multiples are used, the market value of the senior securities (debt and preferred stock) must then be subtracted from the indicated value of MVIC to arrive at the value of common equity.

EXAMPLES OF MARKET VALUE TABLES

The examples include various valuation tables that an analyst typically may include in the final valuation report. ClearSkies is a privately held company, which we will use to illustrate the direct valuation of equity and total invested capital methods. Exhibit 9.1 shows the balance sheet of ClearSkies, and Exhibit 9.2 shows the income statement.

Subject Company to Guideline Publicly Traded Companies

Exhibit 9.3 includes a line-by-line comparison of the income statement and balance sheet for the subject company and the five publicly traded guideline companies. Exhibit 9.4 shows the calculations of market value of equity and market value of invested capital for the five guideline public companies selected.

For illustrative purposes, detailed calculations for the equity valuation multiples of one of the public guideline companies (Nimbus Corporation) are found in Exhibit 9.5 and include

Exhibit 9.1   ClearSkies Corporation Balance Sheet

Assets		
Current Assets		
Cash		$ 1,750,000
Accounts Receivable		2,750,000
Inventory		4,000,000
Total Current Assets		$ 8,500,000
Plant & Equipment		
At Cost	$45,000,000	
Less: Accumulated Depreciation	37,500,000	
Net Plant & Equipment		$ 7,500,000
Total Assets		$16,000,000

Liabilities and Equity		
Current Liabilities		
Accounts Payable		$ 3,500,000
Long-term Debt		7,500,000
Total Liabilities		$11,000,000
Common Equity (2,500,000 share outstanding)		$ 5,000,000
Total Liabilities and Equity		$16,000,000

Exhibit 9.2   ClearSkies Corporation Income Statement

Sales	$48,000,000
Cost of Goods Sold	28,000,000
Gross Margin	$20,000,000
Noncash Charges	1,200,000
Selling General and Administrative Expenses	14,200,000
Operating Income, before taxes (EBIT)	$ 4,600,000
Interest Expense	525,000
Income before Taxes	$ 4,075,000
Income Taxes	1,426,250
Net Income	$ 2,648,750

Note: The data have been condensed from various sources, including the statement of cash flows, footnotes to financial statements, and other sources: (1) long-term debt instruments bear an interest rate of 7%, (2) market value of the debt is approximately the same as the book value of the debt, and (3) effective tax rate equates to 35%.

Exhibit 9.3 Comparative Income Statement and Balance Sheets

Income Statement

	ClearSkies	Cumulus	Nimbus	Cirrus	Stratus	Stormy
Sales	$48,000,000	$5,200,000	$35,000,000	$66,000,000	$58,000,000	$96,500,000
Cost of Goods Sold	28,000,000	2,700,000	21,000,000	36,300,000	33,060,000	49,250,000
Gross Margin	$20,000,000	$2,500,000	$14,000,000	$29,700,000	$24,940,000	$47,250,000
Noncash Charges	1,200,000	200,000	800,000	1,500,000	685,000	4,825,000
Selling General and Administrative Expenses	14,200,000	1,700,000	11,800,000	17,820,000	19,980,000	32,810,000
Operating Income, before taxes (EBIT)	$4,600,000	$600,000	$1,400,000	$10,380,000	$4,275,000	$9,615,000
Interest Expense	525,000	350,000	525,000	988,000	32,500	1,365,000
Income before Taxes	$4,075,000	$250,000	$875,000	$9,392,000	$4,242,500	$8,250,000
Income taxes	1,426,250	100,000	288,750	3,756,800	1,590,938	3,465,000
Net Income	$2,648,750	$150,000	$586,250	$5,635,200	$2,651,562	$4,785,000

Balance Sheet

	ClearSkies	Cumulus	Nimbus	Cirrus	Stratus	Stormy
Assets						
Current Assets						
Cash	$1,750,000	$556,000	$2,275,000	$1,485,000	$2,250,000	$5,200,000
Accounts Receivable	2,750,000	810,000	2,450,000	1,875,000	2,250,000	3,750,000
Inventory	4,000,000	1,535,000	3,500,000	3,250,000	4,500,000	6,250,000
Total Current Assets	$8,500,000	$2,901,000	$8,225,000	$6,610,000	$9,000,000	$15,200,000

(*continued*)

127

Exhibit 9.3 Comparative Income Statement and Balance Sheets *(continued)*

	ClearSkies	Cumulus	Nimbus	Cirrus	Stratus	Stormy
Plant & Equipment						
At Cost	45,000,000	10,000,000	35,000,000	62,000,000	42,000,000	83,500,000
Less: Accumulated Depreciation	37,500,000	3,700,000	31,500,000	48,000,000	37,500,000	52,000,000
Net Plant & Equipment	$7,500,000	$6,300,000	$3,500,000	$14,000,000	$4,500,000	$31,500,000
Total Assets	$16,000,000	$9,201,000	$11,725,000	$20,610,000	$13,500,000	$46,700,000
Liabilities and Equity						
Current Liabilities						
Accounts Payable	3,500,000	624,000	3,350,000	3,410,000	2,500,000	3,250,000
Long-term Debt	7,500,000	5,000,000	7,000,000	15,200,000	500,000	21,000,000
Total Liabilities	$11,000,000	$5,624,000	$10,350,000	$18,610,000	$3,000,000	$24,250,000
Stockholders' Equity	5,000,000	3,577,000	1,375,000	2,000,000	10,500,000	22,450,000
Shares Outstanding	2,500,000	3,577,000	275,000	200,000	525,000	4,490,000
Market Price of Stock on Valuation Date	$2.50	$2.50	$22.50	$65.00	$80.00	$7.50
Total Liabilities and Equity	$16,000,000	$9,201,000	$11,725,000	$20,610,000	$13,500,000	$46,700,000

Note: Figures represent year-end 1999.

Exhibit 9.4 Guideline Companies Market Value of Invested Capital

Company	Market Value per Share	Number of Shares	Long-term Debt[a]	Market Value of Equity	Market Value of Invested Capital
Cumulus	$2.50	3,577,000	$5,000,000	$8,942,500	$13,942,500
Nimbus	$22.50	275,000	$7,000,000	$6,187,500	$13,187,500
Cirrus	$65.00	200,000	$15,200,000	$13,000,000	$28,200,000
Stratus	$80.00	525,000	$500,000	$42,000,000	$42,500,000
Stormy	$7.50	4,490,000	$21,000,000	$33,675,000	$54,675,000

Note: Long-term debt in Exhibit 9.3 was used to create this table, assuming that market value of long-term debt approximates book value of long-term debt.

[a] None of these companies has issued preferred stock; if any had, we would include another column showing the value of the preferred stock and add this value to the market value of invested capital column.

Exhibit 9.5 Nimbus Corporation Equity Valuation Multiples

Market Value of Equity = Number of shares X Market Value per share[a]

= 275,000 shares X $22.50 per share = $6,187,500

Market Value of Equity / Sales

Market Value of Equity / Sales = $6,187,500 / $35,000,000 = 0.18

Market Value of Equity / Gross Cash Flow

Net Income	$ 586,250
Plus Noncash charges	800,000
Gross Cash Flow	$1,386,250

Market Value of Equity / Gross Cash Flow = $6,187,500/ $1,386,250 = 4.5

Market Value of Equity / Earnings (Net Income after taxes)

Market Value of Equity / Earnings = $6,187,500 / $586,250 = 10.6

Market Value of Equity / Book Value

Market Value of Equity / Book Value = $6,187,500 / $1,375,000 = 4.5

Note: When valuing equity directly, these multiples often are presented on a per-share basis. The multiple should be exactly the same whether computed on a per-share or aggregate common equity basis.

[a] Market value per share from Exhibit 9.4.

- Price/sales
- Price/gross cash flow
- Price/earnings (net income after taxes)
- Price/book value

Detailed calculations for the invested capital valuation multiples of one of the public guideline companies (Nimbus Corporation) are found in Exhibit 9.6 and include

- MVIC/sales
- MVIC/EBITDA

Exhibit 9.6   Nimbus Corporation Invested Capital Valuation Multiples

Market Value of Invested Capital (MVIC)			
	Long-term Debt	53%	$ 7,000,000
	Equity: (275,000 shares at $22.50)	47%	6,187,500
	Market Value of Invested Capital[a]	100%	$13,187,500
MVIC / Sales			
	MVIC / Sales = $13,187,500 / $35,000,000 = 0.38		
MVIC / EBITDA			
	Net Income		$ 586,250
	Plus Taxes		288,750
	Plus Interest		525,000
	Plus Noncash Charges		800,000
	EBITDA		$2,200,000
	MVIC / EBITDA = $13,187,500 / $2,200,000 = 6.0		
MVIC / EBIT			
	Net Income		$ 586,250
	Plus Taxes		288,750
	Plus Interest		525,000
	EBIT		$1,400,000
	MVIC / EBIT = $13,187,500 / $1,400,000 = 9.4		
MVIC / Book Value of Invested Capital			
	Book Value of Long-term Debt		$7,000,000
	Book Value of Equity		1,375,000
	Book Value of Invested Capital		$8,375,000
	MVIC / BV of Invested Capital = $13,187,500 / $8,375,000 = 1.6		

[a]Market value of invested capital from Exhibit 9.4.

- MVIC/EBIT
- MVIC/book value of invested capital

Exhibit 9.7 illustrates the guideline companies' equity multiples. The top half of the exhibit includes four calculated equity multiples. Take particular note of the values for the four calculated multiples for the Cumulus Company. The majority of the multiples are drastically different from those of the other four guideline companies.

The bottom half of Exhibit 9.7 communicates the summary statistical analysis of the four invested capital valuation multiples and includes the mean, median, range, standard deviation, and coefficient of variation. The coefficient of variation is defined as the standard deviation divided by the mean and gives the analyst an indication as to the degree of dispersion exhibited by the data points. The lower the coefficient of variation, the lower the dispersion of the data points, and the better the valuation multiple is as an indicator of value. Note that the equity/book value valuation multiple has the lowest coefficient of variation. The analyst should note that this result can also be eyeballed by noting the range of this multiple compared to the range of the other three multiples: The difference between the lowest equity/book value valuation multiple (1.50) and the highest (6.50) is approximately a factor of 4. The equity/sales valuation multiple has the next lowest coefficient of variation with a difference between its lowest value (0.18) and highest value (1.72) of approximately a factor of 9. This clearly indicates that the equity/book value valuation multiple exhibits less dispersion. Exhibit 9.8 illustrates the guideline company market value of invested capital multiples.

Exhibit 9.7 Guideline Company Equity Multiples

	Equity	Equity/Sales	Equity/GCF[a]	Equity/Net Income	Equity/Book Value
Cumulus	$8,942,500	1.72	25.55	59.62	2.50
Nimbus	$6,187,500	0.18	4.46	10.55	4.50
Cirrus	$13,000,000	0.20	1.82	2.31	6.50
Stratus	$42,000,000	0.72	12.59	15.84	4.00
Stormy	$33,675,000	0.35	3.50	7.04	1.50
Mean	$20,761,000	0.63	9.59	19.07	3.80
Median	$13,000,000	0.35	4.46	10.55	4.00
Range	$6.1MM–$42.0MM	0.18–1.72	1.82–31.18	2.31–103.02	1.50–6.50
Std Dev		0.65	9.84	23.20	1.92
C of V[b]		1.02	1.03	1.22	0.51

[a] Gross cash flow = net income + noncash charges.

[b] Coefficient of variation = standard deviation / mean.

Exhibit 9.8   Guideline Company Market Value of Invested Capital Multiples

	MVIC[a]	MVIC/ Sales	MVIC/ EBITDA	MVIC/ EBIT	MVIC/ Book Value
Cumulus	$13,942,500	2.68	17.43	23.24	1.63
Nimbus	$13,187,500	0.38	5.99	9.42	1.57
Cirrus	$28,200,000	0.43	2.37	2.72	1.64
Stratus	$42,500,000	0.73	8.57	9.94	3.86
Stormy	$54,675,000	0.57	3.79	5.69	1.26
Mean	$30,501,000	0.96	7.63	10.20	1.99
Median	$28,200,000	0.57	5.99	9.42	1.63
Range	$13.1MM–$54.7MM	0.38–2.68	2.37–17.43	2.72–23.24	1.26–3.86
Std Dev		0.97	5.96	7.86	1.06
C of V[b]		1.02	0.78	0.77	0.53

[a] Assumes market value of debt = book value of debt.
[b] Coefficient of variation = standard deviation / mean.

Exhibit 9.9 replicates Exhibit 9.7 except that Exhibit 9.9 does not include Cumulus Company. Based on Cumulus' great divergence from the other four companies' multiples, it has been eliminated from our consideration and the remaining four have prevailed. Similarly, Exhibit 9.10 replicates Exhibit 9.8 except that Exhibit 9.10 also does not include Cumulus.

Exhibit 9.9   Guideline Company Equity Multiples Less Cumulus

	Equity	Equity/Sales	Equity/GCF[a]	Equity/Net Income	Equity/Book Value
Nimbus	$6,187,500	0.18	4.46	10.55	4.50
Cirrus	$13,000,000	0.20	1.82	2.31	6.50
Stratus	$42,000,000	0.72	12.59	15.84	4.00
Stormy	$33,675,000	0.35	3.50	7.04	1.50
Mean	$23,715,625	0.36	5.59	8.93	4.13
Median	$23,337,500	0.27	3.98	8.80	4.25
Range	$6.2MM–$42.0MM	0.18–0.72	1.82–12.59	2.31–10.55	1.50–6.50
Std Dev		0.25	4.79	5.71	2.06
C of V[b]		0.70	0.86	0.64	0.50

[a] Gross cash flow = net income + noncash charges.
[b] Coefficient of variation = standard deviation / mean.

Exhibit 9.10 Guideline Company Market Value of Invested Capital Multiples Less Cumulus

	MVIC[a]	MVIC/Sales	MVIC/EBITDA	MVIC/EBIT	MVIC/Book Value
Nimbus	$13,187,500	0.38	5.99	9.42	1.57
Cirrus	$28,200,000	0.43	2.37	2.72	1.64
Stratus	$42,500,000	0.73	8.57	9.94	3.86
Stormy	$54,675,000	0.57	3.79	5.69	1.26
Mean	$34,640,625	0.53	5.18	6.94	2.08
Median	$35,350,000	0.50	4.89	7.55	1.61
Range	$13.2MM–54.7MM	0.38–0.73	2.37–8.57	2.72–9.94	1.26–3.86
Std Dev		0.16	2.71	3.39	1.20
C of V[b]		0.30	0.52	0.49	0.57

[a] Assumes market value of debt = book value of debt.
[b] Coefficient of variation = standard deviation / mean.

Subject Company to Comparative Transactions in *Pratt's Stats*™

Data from the four databases of privately held company sales (*Pratt's Stats*™, *Done Deals, BIZCOMPS*®, and the *IBA Market Data Base*) can be consulted in the guideline merger and acquisition method of business valuation when investigating actual privately held company sale transactions in the market. Because the transactions used are usually controlling interests, it is most directly applicable for valuing other controlling ownership interests, although it can be used for minority interest valuations with proper adjustments.

See Exhibit 9.11 and Exhibit 9.12 as illustrative examples of valuation tables using *Pratt's Stats*™ data. Exhibit 9.11 represents the use of equity prices from the *Pratt's Stats*™ database whereas Exhibit 9.12 depicts the use of deal prices from the *Pratt's Stats*™ database. The lowest coefficient of variation occurs in the deal price/EBITDA valuation multiple in Exhibit 9.12. The implied value based on this valuation multiple is shown as well. In a full valuation report, extensive discussion should revolve around the data in these tables.

SUMMARY

We have presented various tables that an analyst may want to use in a final valuation report. We reviewed the invested capital procedure and the direct equity valuation procedure, and created samples of the different types of valuation tables.

Exhibit 9.11 Automobile Dealer Equity Price Valuation Multiples from *Pratt's Stats*™

	Equity / Sales	Equity / Gross Cash Flow	Equity / EBT	Equity / Net Income	Equity / Discretionary Earnings
Mean	0.20	22.28	NM[a]	NM	NM
Median	0.18	10.74	11.60	12.20	6.94
Range	0.10–0.66	4.80–246.70	loss–40.33	loss–54.77	3.68–14.69
Std Dev	0.11	44.60	378.17	379.17	3.03
C of V[b]	0.53	2.00	NM	NM	0.38
Multiplication Factor[c]	$55,857,000	$443,000	$542,000	$371,000	$1,857,000
Implied Value	$9,858,761	$4,758,307	$6,289,802	$4,525,755	$12,879,595

Note: Data are based on 29 selected guideline companies from *Pratt's Stats*™. Used with permission.

[a] Not meaningful.

[b] Coefficient of variation = standard deviation / mean.

[c] Multiplication factor represents value by which the valuation multiple's median value is multiplied (e.g., multiplication factor for equity price / sales is sales = $55,857,000; this value multiplied by 0.18 equates to the implied value).

Exhibit 9.12 Automobile Dealer Price Valuation Multiples from *Pratt's Stats*™

	Deal Price[a] / Sales	Deal Price / EBITDA	Deal Price / EBIT	Deal Price / Total Assets
Mean	0.21	8.41	9.91	0.91
Median	0.18	7.65	9.14	0.79
Range	0.10–0.66	3.67–14.69	4.06–26.04	0.44–1.92
Std Dev	0.11	3.04	4.62	0.38
C of V[b]	0.52	0.36	0.47	0.42
Multiplication Factor[c]	$55,857,000	$728,000	$656,000	$15,457,000
Implied Value	$10,037,503	$5,571,748	$5,993,544	$12,248,127

Note: Data are based on 29 selected guideline companies from *Pratt's Stats*™. Used with permission.

[a] Deal price in *Pratt's Stats*™ equates to market value of invested capital.

[b] Coefficient of variation = standard deviation / mean.

[c] Multiplication factor represents value by which the valuation multiple's median value is multiplied (e.g., multiplication factor for deal price / sales is sales = $55,857,000; this value multiplied by 0.18 equates to the implied value).

We reviewed data based on the guideline company method (ClearSkies example) and the merger and acquisition method (auto dealer from *Pratt's Stats*™).

It is important to remind the reader that in a final valuation report, an effective discussion of the information compiled from the tables is required. We have concentrated on the creation of effective tables in this chapter—the analyst will use his or her knowledge and the information located throughout this book to create an effective discussion of the relevant matters for any valuation.

Chapter 10

Selecting, Weighting, and Adjusting Market Value Multiples

Many analysts tend to lean toward market value of invested capital (MVIC) multiples when valuing controlling interests and equity value multiples when valuing minority interests, although that is not always the case. As noted in Chapter 9, many analysts use only the invested capital procedure whether valuing a minority or a controlling interest.

Apart from the question of control or minority value, the choice of which multiples ultimately to rely on is largely a function of two factors:

1. Size and nature of the company or industry
2. Availability and nature of comparative pricing data

SIZE AND NATURE OF COMPANY

Equity Value Multiples

Generally speaking, when choosing among possible equity value multiples, the smaller the company, the more we choose multiples higher, rather than farther down, on the income statement.

For many very small companies, especially service companies, price/sales gets the primary weight. It is usually the most reliable number for small companies, and the most available. Many buyers feel that for a given "book of business," they already know how much they can bring down to the bottom line. Probably some of the best examples are property and casualty insurance agencies, which tend to have a high degree of customer persistence.

The next most commonly used multiple for very small businesses is discretionary earnings (earnings before interest, taxes, noncash charges, and all compensation and benefits to one owner/operator). For many very small businesses, any income number beyond this may be negative or so small as to be meaningless.

As company size begins to increase, however, discretionary earnings tend to become meaningless. Although there are no precise guidelines as to the size level at which discretionary earnings becomes meaningless, most analysts would not use it for companies valued over $5 million, and some would use it only for companies valued under $1 or $2 million. Also, the number of owner/operators is important. The definition of discretionary earnings is before compensation to *one* owner. To the extent that there are two, three, or more owners/operators, it becomes less meaningful.

As company size continues to increase, there may be positive gross cash flow, even though earnings may be meaningless or nonexistent. This is often the case because many companies are able to "bonus out" most of their earnings without exceeding the reasonable compensation levels of the Internal Revenue Service. With larger companies, net income tends to become a meaningful measure of earnings.

Invested Capital Multiples

For invested capital multiples, similar principles tend to be true. For very small companies, there often is no debt, so the equity multiples are equal to the invested capital multiples. In other words, if there is no debt, invested capital is equal to equity. Therefore, MVIC/sales is equal to price/sales, and MVIC/discretionary earnings is equal to price/discretionary earnings.

Invested capital multiples are useful when the subject company is highly leveraged or when the subject company leverage differs considerably from the guideline companies' leverage.

There is some tendency to prefer MVIC/EBITDA to MVIC/EBIT. This is because MVIC/EBITDA eliminates the effect of different policies with respect to accounting for noncash charges, and it is almost impossible to completely eliminate these differences by financial statement adjustments. However, both measures convey information about the companies. Also, EBIT may be available when EBITDA is not. The analyst usually will consider both measures and emphasize whatever is judged to be most meaningful.

AVAILABILITY OF DATA

Availability of data can be a compelling factor in choice of multiples. For many very small companies, sales or sales and discretionary earnings are the only operating performance variables available. For industries that have tended to lose money, there may be no or only a few companies that have positive net income. The preference is to use variables for which the most guideline companies have meaningful numbers.

For some companies, price to gross profit (sales less cost of goods sold) provides a meaningful valuation metric. This is often positive even when EBITDA is negative. Research in 2004 by Franz Ross found that this metric had the lowest dispersion (as measured by the coefficient of variation) in many industries.[1] As a consequence, *Pratt's Stats*™ has now added this valuation multiple to its transaction database.

DISPERSION OF MARKET VALUE MULTIPLES

When market value multiples among companies in an industry are tightly clustered, this suggests that these are the multiples that the market pays most attention to in pricing companies and stocks in that industry. That is, the denominator that creates the tightly clustered multiple is the financial variable that tends to drive the market value. Therefore, a tight clustering of market value multiples may suggest that those multiples tend to deserve more weight than other multiples.

We measure the degree of dispersion by a statistic called the *coefficient of variation* (CV), which is defined as the standard deviation divided by the mean. The standard deviation is the square root of the variance, and the variance is the sum of the squares of the deviations from the average. Although the formula for standard deviation is a bit complicated, most pocket calculators are programmed to compute it simply by entering the observations and pressing "STD DEV." The mean, of course, is just the sum of the values of the observations divided by the number of observations. Then the CV is just a simple division. Based on the theory that the multiples with the least dispersion should get most weight, those with the lowest coefficients of variation would be accorded the greatest weight.

As a practical matter, many analysts do not go through the mechanics of computing a coefficient of variation, but simply apply the principle by eyeballing the relative dispersion and emphasizing the multiples with the tightest clustering.

THE HARMONIC MEAN AS A MEASURE OF CENTRAL TENDENCY

As an alternative to the mean or median, the harmonic mean can be used to give equal weight to each guideline company in summarizing ratios that have stock price or MVIC in the numerator. It is the reciprocal of the average of the reciprocals of the guideline company multiples. Consider the situation with P/E (price/earnings) multiples of 15 and 5. The reciprocal of the P/E multiple of 15 is .0667, the reciprocal of the P/E multiple of 5 is .200, the average of the two reciprocals is .1334, and the reciprocal of the average is 7.5. This P/E multiple of 7.5 is the same as the P/E of a $200 portfolio with $100 invested (for $6.67 of earnings at a P/E multiple of 15) in the first company, and $100 invested (for $20 of earnings at a P/E multiple of 15) in the second company. With the $200 invested equally in each guideline company, the total earnings are $26.67, and the P/E multiple is 7.5.

Although the harmonic mean is not used frequently, probably because it is unfamiliar to most readers of valuation reports, it is conceptually a very attractive alternative measure of central tendency.

ADJUSTING FROM OBSERVED MARKET VALUE MULTIPLES

In Chapter 9, we left our market value tables showing means, medians, standard deviations, and coefficients of variation for each market value multiple that we considered. In the earlier sections of this chapter, we have discussed the selection of relative weighting of various market multiples. We now must come to grips with making the challenging judgment as to the value to be used for each market multiple selected.

As a measure of central tendency for most statistics that we use in business valuation, we tend to prefer the median over the mean, primarily to avoid distortions from outliers. We might also use the harmonic mean to avoid distortions.

However, simply applying the chosen measure of central tendency of a group of guideline company multiples more often than not fails to capture differences in characteristics between our subject company and the guideline companies as a group. This is the point at which we want to use our comparative financial analysis for guidance.

Each multiple used should be accorded individual attention. It is possible that some selected multiple should be above the guideline averages, while some other selected multiple should be below guideline averages. For example, a company with an above-average return on sales usually would be accorded an above-average price/sales or MVIC/sales multiple. The same company could have a below-average return on book value, which may suggest a below-average price/book value or MVIC/book value multiple.

One must keep in mind that the two factors that influence the selection of multiples of operating variables the most are the growth prospects of the subject company relative to the guideline companies and the risk of the subject company relative to the guideline companies. The analyst should review the comparative financial analysis to try to assess these relationships.

Two procedures are often employed in selecting multiples to apply to the subject company relative to multiples observed from the guideline companies:

1. Select a subset of the guideline companies with financial characteristics (growth, margins, volatility, etc.) most like the subject company and select multiples close to those of the most comparable companies.
2. Assess the growth and risk characteristics relative to the guideline company group as a whole, and accordingly apply median multiples where appropriate or adjust multiples upward or downward from the medians based on the comparative analysis.

One might adjust an observed multiple upward or downward by a percentage, or may go toward the upper or lower end of the range (e.g., use the upper quartile of the range). In extreme situations, a multiple outside the observed range may be selected. In any case, the analyst should provide a narrative explanation for the value of the multiple to be applied to the subject company's financial data.

ILLUSTRATIVE ESTIMATE OF VALUE USING MATHEMATICAL WEIGHTING

A simple table supporting a mathematically weighted estimate of value by the market approach is presented as Exhibit 10.1. This exhibit derives median market multiples from Exhibit 9.10 on page 133 and the fundamentals to which the multiples are applied from Exhibits 9.1 and 9.2 on page 126.

We elected to use the market value of invested capital (MVIC) procedure for this illustration because the subject company (ClearSkies) is fairly highly leveraged, at least on a book-value basis: $7,500,000 book value of debt versus $5,000,000 book value of equity. Also, we judged ClearSkies as being approximately equivalent to

Exhibit 10.1 Illustrative Mathematical Weighting of Indications of Value from the Transaction Method

	Fundamentals of Value for ClearSkies[a]		Median Valuation Multiple[b]		Indication of Value		Weight[c]		Weighted Indication of Value
MVIC/Sales	$48,000,000	×	.50	=	$24,000,000	×	.50	=	$12,000,000
MVIC/EBITDA	5,800,000	×	4.89	=	28,362,000	×	.30	=	8,508,600
MVIC/BVIC	12,600,000	×	1.61	=	20,286,000	×	.20	=	4,057,200
Total weighted indications of value for MVIC									$24,565,800
Less: long-term debt									7,500,000
Indicated Value of Equity by Transaction Method									$17,065,800

[a]From Exhibit 9.2.
[b]From Exhibit 9.10.
[c]See text for explanation.

the average of the guideline companies in terms of growth prospects and risk, so we selected median multiples, although comparative analysis would tend to lend to different selection of multiples in most cases, as discussed in the previous section.

We accorded 50% of the weight to MVIC/sales because that multiple had by far the lowest coefficient of variation, as shown in Exhibit 9.10. We accorded 30% of the weight of MVIC/EBITDA because this metric is relied on more heavily than MVIC/EBIT and the coefficients of variation were quite close between the two measures. We accorded 20% of the weight to MVIC/book value of invested capital because we felt that the assets should be given some weight.

These calculations result in the $17,065,800 estimate of the market value for ClearSkies by the transaction method, as shown in Exhibit 10.1. This table is presented for illustrative purposes only, and much more analysis would be in order to make the final selection of which market multiples should be used, adjustments (if any) to the median multiples, and the relative weight to be accorded each.

SUMMARY

With the market approach encompassing a wide variety of market value multiples to choose from, the analyst must make a reasoned choice of which ones to use in each case.

With income-related variables, the smaller the company, the more the analyst tends to rely on variables near the top of the earnings measurement spectrum, such as sales and discretionary earnings. As the company size becomes larger, the analyst tends to rely more on measures further down the income statement.

For invested capital multiples, the more the accounting treatment of noncash charges varies among companies, the more the analyst tends to prefer EBITDA over EBIT, assuming that the information is available for both.

The less the dispersion of observed multiples in an industry, the more the industry seems to rely on that particular multiple for pricing companies and stocks. Therefore, when using the market approach, the analyst often computes the coefficient of variation for each market value multiple, giving more weight to those multiples with the lowest coefficients of variation, or applying the general principle by eyeballing the distributions and according more weight to those that are most clustered.

Finally, a value for each multiple must be selected. Here the analyst draws on the comparative financial analysis to guide the final judgment as to the appropriate value for each multiple.

Notes

1. Franz Ross, " 'Just One Thing': The Most Reliable Variable for Use in the Market Approach," *Shannon Pratt's Business Valuation Update* (Portland, OR: Business Valuation Resoures, 2004). Full text available at www.BVLibrary.com.

Chapter 11

Control Premiums and Minority Discounts

Using the market approach, we have arrived at one or more estimates of value. Each estimate implies certain ownership characteristics, namely control ownership or minority ownership, depending on the market approach method used.

We can summarize how the various market approach methods imply either control or minority ownership as

- Guideline public company method—minority*
- Guideline merged and acquired company method—control
- Past transactions—control or minority, depending on whether transactions were control or minority
- Rules of thumb—control

---

*One school of thought says that minority interests in public companies are tantamount to control because public company policies prevent exploitation of minority stockholders. It is certainly true that extreme abuses of control that may be common in private companies are rare in public companies. Nevertheless, the minority owner in a public company does not enjoy the prerogatives of control. However, the interests of management and minority owners tend to be aligned through stock options to maximize shareholder wealth.

Exhibit 11.1   "Levels of Value" in Terms of Characteristics of Ownership

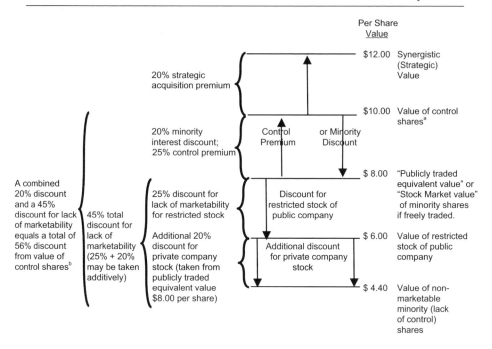

Notes:

[a] Control shares in a privately held company may also be subject to some discount for lack of marketability, but usually not nearly as much as minority shares.

[b] Minority and marketability discounts normally are multiplicative rather than additive. That is, they are taken in sequence:

$ 10.00	Control Value
- 2.00	Less: Minority interest discount (.20 x $10.00)
$ 8.00	Marketable minority value
- 3.60	Less lack of Marketability discount (.45 X 8.00)
$ 4.40	Per-share value of non-marketable minority shares

Source: Copyright © 2005 by Practioners Publishing Company. Reprinted with permission from *Guide to Business Valuations,* 15th ed. (January 2005). For product information call 800-323-8724.

- Buy-sell agreement—usually minority, but sometimes control depending on the interests to which it applies
- Offers to buy—usually control, but depend on the interest for which the offers were/are made

The general concept of levels of value is shown schematically in Exhibit 11.1.

PREROGATIVES OF CONTROL OWNERSHIP

The differential in value between control shares and minority shares exists because the control owner enjoys many potentially valuable prerogatives that the minority owner does not. Some of the most important of these are

- Appoint or change operational management
- Determine management compensation and perquisites
- Set operational policy and strategic policy and change the course of the business
- Acquire, lease, or liquidate business assets, including plant, property, and equipment
- Select suppliers, vendors, and subcontractors with whom to do business and award contracts
- Sell or acquire treasury shares
- Register the company's debt securities for an initial or secondary public offering
- Declare and pay cash and/or stock dividends
- Change the articles of incorporation or bylaws[1]

For any given company, the difference between the value of control shares and minority shares depends to a great extent on how these prerogatives of control are exercised. For example, if cash that could be available for dividends is given as a bonus to the control owner, the difference in value between control and minority shares is likely to be substantial.

QUANTIFYING CONTROL PREMIUMS AND MINORITY DISCOUNTS

Unfortunately, there is no completely satisfactory way to quantify control premiums and minority discounts. As suggested in the previous section, the percentage difference in value between control shares and minority shares is quite different from one company to another depending on the facts and circumstances peculiar to that company.

Public Company Acquisition Premiums

The most popular empirical data on control/minority price differentials observed in market transactions are published by *Mergerstat®/Shannon Pratt's Control Premium Study™*. These studies show the acquisition price paid compared with the public market trading price prior to the acquisition.

Exhibit 11.2 shows the median acquisition premium paid and implied minority discount for each year from 1998 through 2004. If these data are to be used, we prefer the median to the mean average, because the mean is upwardly biased by a few very big premiums paid. These data are also available broken down by industry group.

Exhibit 11.2 Median Premium and Minority Discount by Year, 1998–2004

Year	Medium Premium	Implied Median Minority Discount
1998	19.6%	16.4%
1999	29.2%	22.6%
2000	32.0%	24.2%
2001	29.9%	23.0%
2002	34.0%	25.4%
2003	38.9%	28.0%
2004	24.6%	19.7%

Data compiled using domestic deals and including negative control premiums.

Source: Mergerstat®/Shannon Pratt's Control Premium Study,™ www.bvmarketdata.com.

Although these are the best data available, a major problem is that the acquisition premium includes whatever premium was paid for synergy, as well as the premium for the prerogatives of control, and there is no way to separate these two elements. Chris Mercer, in a paper presented at the 1998 Canadian Institute of Chartered Business Valuators/American Society of Appraisers joint conference, which can be found on BVLibrary.com, suggested that control premiums in typical appraisals of closely held businesses are not as large as we have previously thought. It has been estimated that upward of 80% of public company acquisitions in the 1990s were synergistic acquisitions (far higher than is the case for purchases of small businesses).

Steven Garber addressed this problem in a paper presented at the American Society of Appraisers annual meeting in June 1998. He suggested that transactions of public companies "going private" (e.g., management leverage buyouts [LBOs]) were more representative of fair market value than synergistic acquisitions, which incorporate the synergistic elements of investment value. He researched the P/E (price/earnings) ratios paid in LBOs versus all transactions from 1988 through 1997. The results are shown in Exhibit 11.3.

Garber concluded that the acquisition premiums, conceptually, are too high as evidence of premiums for control (not including synergies) and that going private transactions, which have lower average premiums, provide better evidence of premiums for control.[2]

Factors Affecting Level of Control Premiums and Minority Discounts

The extent to which the prerogatives of control are exercised (or could be exercised) for the maximization of benefit to all shareholders has a major bearing on the magnitude of the potential control premium or minority discount for any given company.

Exhibit 11.3 LBO versus Synergistic Acquisition Premiums

Is There a Difference?

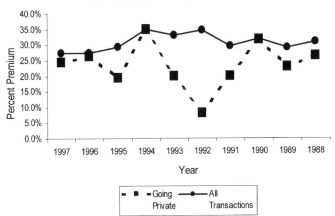

Price/Earnings — Strategic versus Going Private

Average P/E			
Year	Going Private	All Transactions	Percent Difference
1997	23.6	27.4	16.1%
1996	28.9	26.2	-9.3%
1995	30.8	23.8	-22.7%
1994	24.5	24.5	0.0%
1993	14.8	24.4	64.9%
1992	15.2	22.7	49.3%
1991	13.2	20.0	51.5%
1990	15.5	20.1	29.7%
1989	17.8	20.9	17.4%
1988	21.1	21.6	2.4%

Median P/E			
Year	Going Private	All Transactions	Percent Difference
1997	19.9	22.9	15.1%
1996	23.1	20.3	-12.1%
1995	17.2	19.1	11.1%
1994	20.2	20.2	0.0%
1993	14.9	20.0	34.2%
1992	12.7	18.1	42.5%
1991	10.7	14.0	30.8%
1990	13.6	16.7	22.8%
1989	15.5	17.3	11.6%
1988	17.9	18.0	0.6%

Source: Steven Garber, "Control vs. Actual Premiums: Is There a Difference?" presented at the ASA Annual Conference, June 1998. Reprinted with permission of the American Society of Appraisers.

147

If the company is run efficiently, assets well utilized, no largess to control parties, and payouts distributed to stockholders, there may be little difference between the value of control and minority shares. If the company is inefficient, there are significant nonproducing excess assets, the control parties are enjoying substantial excess compensation, and there are no payouts to minority owners, then the difference in value between control and minority shares probably is significant.

Some analysts would adjust earnings and cash flows to reflect estimated control factors, thus eliminating the need for a further control premium adjustment.

HOW THE STANDARD OF VALUE AFFECTS CONTROL PREMIUMS AND/OR MINORITY DISCOUNTS

The applicable standard of value may have a significant or even controlling impact on whether to apply a control premium or a minority discount. The potential impact of different standards of value is discussed here briefly, and examples are included in Chapter 19.

Fair Market Value

Fair market value is the statutory standard of value for virtually all federal tax valuations and is widely used in many other valuation contexts.

Fair market value is defined in U.S. Treasury regulations as

> The net amount which a willing purchaser whether an individual or corporation would pay for the interest to a willing seller, neither being under any compulsion to buy or to sell and both having reasonable knowledge of relevant facts.[3]

Fair market value assumes conditions as they actually exist and a hypothetical buyer and seller, with no special, unique motivations or circumstances. Therefore, under fair market value, one would apply a control premium or minority discount if a discount would logically apply under the facts and circumstances, assuming a buyer and seller with no special motivations.

Investment Value (Value to the Owner or a Particular Buyer)

Investment value is defined in the *International Glossary of Business Valuation Terms* as "the value to a particular investor based on individual investment requirements and expectations."[4]

Investment value is not found anywhere as a statutory standard of value. It is often used as a standard of value in family law courts, whether identified by that name or not. It may reflect the family relationship between a minority owner and a control owner or any of many other special characteristics that make the business more valuable to that owner than to someone else.

Investment value is also sometimes called *acquisition value,* in the context of synergistic mergers and acquisitions. In such cases, the value would be something over and above control value, reflecting an *acquisition premium* or *synergistic premium* consisting of the value of perceived synergies included in the transaction price, over and above the control value of the acquiree on a stand-alone basis.

Fair Value

Fair value is the standard of value for most dissenting stockholder suits and minority oppression actions.

Fair value is defined in the Revised Model Business Corporation Act (RMBCA) of 1984 as

> the value of the shares immediately before the effectuation of the corporate action to which the dissenter objects, excluding any appreciation or depreciation in anticipation of the corporate action unless exclusion would be inequitable.

A majority of states have adopted this definition: Alabama, Arizona, Arkansas, Colorado, Hawaii, Illinois, Indiana, Kentucky, Massachusetts, Michigan, Missouri, Montana, Nebraska, Nevada, New Hampshire, North Carolina, Oregon, South Carolina, South Dakota, Vermont, Virginia, Washington, and Wyoming. Wisconsin uses this definition with respect to dissenters' shares other than in a business combination; fair value with respect to dissenters' shares in a business combination is defined as market value.

A minority of states have adopted the 1984 RMBCA definition, but without the phrase "unless exclusion would be inequitable": Georgia, New Mexico, Rhode Island, Tennessee, and Utah. Other states have adopted the minority definition, but have added a clause stating that the court should consider all relevant factors in determining fair value: Delaware, Oklahoma, and Pennsylvania. Other states have other relatively minor variations: for example, California, Kansas, Maryland, New Jersey, and Ohio.

In 1999, the RMBCA was revised to include this definition:

> "Fair value" means the value of the corporation's shares determined:
> (i)   immediately before the effectuation of the corporate action to which the shareholder objects;
> (ii)   using customary and current valuation concepts and techniques generally employed for similar businesses in the context of the transaction requiring appraisal; and
> (iii)   without discounting for lack of marketability or minority status except, if appropriate, for amendments to the articles pursuant to section 13.02(a)(5).[5]

Several states have adopted the 1999 RMBCA definition: Connecticut, Idaho, Iowa, Maine, Mississippi, and West Virginia. Others have adopted a hybrid definition: Florida incorporates the first two clauses of the 1999 definition, but then adds the last clause of the 1984 definition.

None of the statutes addresses the issue of control premiums or minority discounts. By the nature of the actions, the interests being valued are almost always minority interests. However, many state courts have interpreted the fair value standard to mean that the minority shares are to be valued as if they were worth a pro rata portion of controlling interest value. It is necessary for the analyst to study the relevant case law to determine the extent to which control premiums and/or minority discounts are applicable.

Some of the various court positions include

- Applying a control premium because the base data are minority interests when using the guideline public company method
- Disallowing the guideline merged and acquired company method because that method reflects synergies above a stand-alone control value, thus violating the statutory definition of value
- Regularly allowing minority interest discounts
- Regularly disallowing minority interest discounts
- Declaring that the question of minority interest discounts is a matter to be decided on a case-by-case basis depending on the facts and circumstances of each case

Some states do not yet have case law addressing the application of control premiums or minority discounts in dissenting stockholder and/or minority oppression suits. When the issue comes up as a matter of first impression, states tend to look for guidance to precedential cases from other states with similar statutes.

The latest positions of any state can be researched by key word on Business Valuation Resources Online Library, www.BVResources.com.

THE CONTROL VERSUS MINORITY ISSUE COVERS A SPECTRUM

The control versus minority issue is not black and white, but, rather, covers a spectrum of possibilities. Consider these scenarios:

- 100% control
- Nearly 100%
- Less than 80% (cannot consolidate statements)
- 65% in a state requiring two-thirds supermajority for certain corporate actions
- 50%
- One-third with two other one-third owners
- Swing vote bloc

The state laws, or articles of incorporation governing voting rights, and the distribution of the stock can make quite a difference. For example, a small bloc with a swing vote can have some element of control, hence some small premium over a typical minority bloc. However, a 49% bloc where a single owner has the other 51% and supermajorities are not required would be in an inferior minority position. Also, if there are two 50% owners, and the operating/ partnership agreement states that unanimous consent is required for all significant decisions, then both interests are non-controlling interests.

SUMMARY

The indications of value from the market approach, before adjustments for the subject interest's control or minority status, may be on either a minority or control basis. If the subject interest basis is different from the basis for the market data observed, it might be necessary to adjust by either a control premium or a minority discount.

The market data available for guidance in quantifying this adjustment are limited by two qualifications:

1. Most acquisitions of a public company include some premium for synergistic value over and above a pure premium for control, and it is hard to sort out the synergistic versus the pure control portion of the premium paid.
2. The differential in value between control and minority shares differs greatly from one company to another depending on the facts and circumstances.

Therefore, the ultimate quantification of any control premium or minority discount should be tempered by judgment and analysis of the relevant facts and circumstances.

In addition to the facts and circumstances of the company, the application of control premiums or minority discounts may be imposed by the legal context and appropriate standard of value, such as fair market value, investment value, or fair value. Guidance in this respect is found in relevant case law.

Finally, there is a spectrum of possibilities between pure 100% control and a tiny minority interest, which may affect the magnitude of a control premium or minority interest.

Notes

1. Shannon P. Pratt, Robert F. Reilly, and Robert P. Schweihs, *Valuing a Business,* 4th ed. (New York: McGraw-Hill, 2000), 347–348.
2. Steven D. Garber, "Control vs. Acquisition Premiums: Is There a Difference?" presented at the American Society of Appraisers Annual Conference, Maui, Hawaii, June 1998. Available on *Business Valuation Resources* Web site, www.BVResources.com.
3. 26CPR20.2031-3(1992).

4. *The International Glossary of Investment Value Terms,* a joint publication of the American Institute of Certified Public Accountants, American Society of Appraisers, Canadian Institute of Chartered Business Valuators, National Association of Certified Valuation Analysts, and The Institute of Business Appraisers. Distributed as a supplement to *Shannon Pratt's Business Valuation Update*™ (February 2000). Available on the *Business Valuation Resources* Web site, www.BVResources.com.

5. *Model Business Corporation Act Annotated* 3d ed. §13.01 (Chicago: Section of Business Law of the American Bar Association, 1999).

Discounts for Lack of Marketability

Investors cherish liquidity, that is, the ability to convert the investment asset to cash quickly and at a relatively certain amount. Conversely, investors loathe lack of liquidity.

Consequently, other things being equal, investors pay more, often much more, for an investment that is highly liquid than for an otherwise comparable investment that is not liquid. Conversely, investors usually demand a substantial discount to attract their money to an illiquid investment compared with an otherwise similar liquid investment.

DEFINING DISCOUNT FOR LACK OF MARKETABILITY

Although some authors make a minor distinction between the terms *liquidity* and *marketability,* we will use the two terms synonymously in this book.[1] The

International Glossary of Business Valuation Terms defines marketability as "the ability to quickly convert property to cash at a minimal cost."[2] Many people also include in the concept of marketability the notion of a high degree of certainty regarding the amount that will be realized from the sale.

The *International Glossary of Business Valuation Terms* defines *discount for lack of marketability* as "an amount or percentage deducted from the value of an ownership interest to reflect the relative absence of marketability."

APPLYING THE DISCOUNT FOR LACK OF MARKETABILITY

Throughout our discussion, we have been dealing with actual observed transactions, generally either publicly traded minority interests or sales of controlling interests. The efficient stock markets in the United States give stocks representing minority interests in publicly traded companies an extremely high degree of liquidity (i.e., call a stock broker and have cash in one's account in three business days, at or very near a price observed in the market). The merged and acquired companies achieved liquidity for the sellers in the sense that a sale took place, and they received cash or some other consideration.

Most of the businesses or financial interests that we are valuing do not enjoy immediate liquidity. We thus face the task of making an adjustment from the value we have estimated from the transactions observed in the market approach to account for the lack of marketability of the business or business interest that we are valuing. That adjustment is what we refer to as the *discount for lack of marketability.*

As implied in the glossary definition, this discount usually is a deduction from the value estimated through the market approach. Some analysts build the discount for lack of marketability into the market multiple. In other words, if a market multiple was 10 times a certain financial variable, and they estimated the discount for lack of marketability at 30%, they would use a multiple of 7 times ($10 \times [1 - .30] = 7$). However, most analysts apply a percentage discount to the value otherwise indicated by the market approach. Either method effectively increases the rate of return received (or at least expected) by the investor in a privately held interest compared to a publicly held interest.

The guideline public company method produces a fully marketable minority value. Therefore, if valuing a closely held minority interest starting with an indicated value as if publicly traded, one would subtract a discount for lack of marketability.

The merged and acquired company method produces a value on a control basis. A controlling interest is not as readily marketable as a publicly traded stock. Therefore, if valuing a controlling interest, some discount for lack of marketability may be warranted, although if so, it generally would not be as great a percentage as would be appropriate for a minority interest; in fact, it probably would be substantially less. If the analyst chooses to apply a marketability discount to a control transaction, an explanation as to the elements included in the discount should be given.

If the merged and acquired company method is used for valuing a minority interest, usually both a discount for lack of control and also a discount for lack of marketability would be applied, as shown in the schematic levels of value in Exhibit 11.1. These discounts would be applied consecutively, usually first the discount for lack of control to get a minority value and then the discount for lack of marketability. For example, if the control price was $100 per share, the discount for lack of control were 20%, and the discount for lack of marketability 40%, the computation would be

Control price	$100
Discount for lack of control (20% of $100)	– 20
Marketable minority value	$ 80
Discount for lack of marketability (40% of $80)	– 32
Minority, nonmarketable value	$ 48

In the above example, the consecutive discounts of 20% and 40% results in a combined discount of 52% from the control value per share. Combined discounts in excess of 50% are not at all uncommon. The discount can be substantial or may be relatively small depending on the facts and circumstances of each appraisal.

MARKET EVIDENCE REGARDING THE DISCOUNT FOR LACK OF MARKETABILITY FOR MINORITY INTERESTS

Fortunately, there is a huge body of empirical data available to assist in quantifying the discount for lack of marketability for minority interests. These data are based on two lines of studies, each of which uses a certain type of observed market transactions:

1. Restricted stock studies
2. Pre-IPO studies (studies of private transactions before initial public offerings)

Restricted Stock Studies

Most public companies have some stock outstanding that is either unregistered or registered but for various reasons restricted from public trading. When a company has an IPO, often much of the insiders' stock is not registered because the underwriters do not want the insiders to "bail out." Unregistered stock frequently is issued in acquisitions and private financings.

Although this unregistered or restricted stock cannot be sold on the open market, it can be sold in blocks in private placements. The stock is identical in every way to the publicly traded stock except for the restrictions on its sale. Therefore, the concept of the restricted stock studies is to compare the private block sale prices of the restricted stock to the same-day public trading price, with the difference being a proxy for a discount for lack of marketability.

A large number of such studies have been undertaken, independent of each other, starting with the Securities and Exchange Commission (SEC) Institutional Investor Study dating from the late 1960s to the present. The results of these studies are summarized in Exhibit 12.1. The average discounts range from 13% to 45.0%, with most clustered between 31% and 36%.[3]

Since 1990, the restrictions on "restricted stocks" have been increasingly relaxed. In 1997, the required holding period for stock restricted by SEC Rule 144 was reduced from two years to one year. A study conducted by Columbia Financial Advisors found that restricted stock discounts since that change dropped to an average of about 13 to 15%.[4] This increased liquidity on the part of restricted stocks means that average discounts on such stock in recent years are no longer representative of discounts required for privately held stocks that enjoy no such liquidity.

Pre-IPO Studies

Stocks in the restricted stock studies are those of public companies. In most cases, the stock will eventually be registered for public trading or the restrictions will be removed. What about stocks of companies that are not public? Wouldn't people expect that the discount for lack of marketability should be greater?

To address this question, two firms independently undertook a line of studies know as the pre-IPO studies. When a company goes public, it is required to disclose in its registration statement all transactions in the stock within three years prior to the public offering. In the studies, the prices of the transactions before there was a public market were compared to the public offering price to estimate a discount for lack of marketability.

As one might expect, the average discounts were higher, tending to cluster around 45%.

Emory Studies.   John Emory started, and continues to update, a series of studies comparing transaction prices of stocks up to five months prior to an IPO to the public offering price. The results of the Emory studies are summarized in Exhibit 12.2.[5]

Willamette Management Associates' Studies.   Willamette Management Associates used transactions as much as three years prior to the IPO, but eliminated all insider transactions and any other transactions that did not appear to be arm's length. Because of the time difference between the transactions observed while the company was private and the IPO date, adjustments were made for changes in the companies' earnings and for changes in the industries' P/E ratios between the private company transaction date and the IPO date. The results of the Willamette studies are summarized in Exhibit 12.3.[6]

Exhibit 12.1   Summary of Restricted Stock Studies

Empirical Study	Years Covered in Study	Average Price Discount (%)
SEC overall average[a]	1966–1969	25.8
SEC Nonreporting OTC companies[a]	1966–1969	32.6
Gelman[b]	1968–1970	33.0
Trout[c]	1968–1972	33.5
Moroney[d]	N/A[k]	35.6
Mahr[e]	1969–1973	35.4
Standard Research Consultants[f]	1978–1982	45.0[l]
Willamette Management Associates[g]	1981–1984	31.2[l]
Silber[h]	1981–1988	33.8
FMV Opinions Inc.[i]	1979–April 1992	23.0
Management Planning[j]	1980–1996	27.1
Johnson[m]	1991–1995	20.0
Columbia Financial Advisors[n]	1996–1997	13.0

[a] "Discounts Involved in Purchases of Common Stock (1966–1969)," *Institutional Investor Study Report of the Securities and Exchange Commission,* H.R. Doc. N.64, part 5, 92nd Cong., 1st session, 1971, 2444–2456.

[b] Milton Gelman, "An Economist-Financial Analyst's Approach to Valuing Stock in a Closely Held Company," *Journal of Taxation* (June 1972): 353.

[c] Robert R. Trout, "Estimation of the Discount Associated with the Transfer of Restricted Securities," *Taxes* (June 1997): 381–385.

[d] Robert E. Moroney, "Most Courts Overvalue Closely Held Stocks," *Taxes* (March 1973): 144–155.

[e] Michael J. Maher, "Discounts for Lack of Marketability for Closely Held Business Interests," *Taxes* (September 1976): 562–571.

[f] William F. Pittock and Charles H. Stryker, "Revenue Ruling 77-276 Revisited" *SRC Quarterly Reports* (Spring 1983): 1–3.

[g] Willamette Management Associates study (unpublished), Portland, OR.

[h] William L. Silber, "Discounts on Restricted Stock: The Impact of Illiquidity on Stock Prices," *Financial Analysts Journal* (July–August 1991): 60–64.

[i] Lance S. Hall and Timothy C. Polacek, "Strategies for Obtaining the Largest Valuation Discounts," *Estate Planning* (January/February 1994): 38–44.

[j] Robert P. Oliver and Roy H. Meyers, "Analysis of Restricted Stocks of Public Companies: 1980–1995," The Management Planning Study, chap. 12, in *Quantifying Marketability Discounts,* Z. Christopher Mercer (Memphis: Peabody Publishing, LP, 1997). Used with permission.

[k] Although the years covered in this study are likely to be 1969 to 1972, no specific years were given in the published account.

[l] Median discounts.

[m] Bruce Johnson, "Restricted Stock Discounts, 1991–1995," *Shannon Pratt's Business Valuation Update* (March 1999): 1–3. See also Bruce Johnson, "Quantitative Support for Discounts for Lack of Marketability," *Business Valuation Review,* (December 1999): 152–155.

[n] Kathryn Aschwald, "Restricted Stock Discounts Decline as Result of 1-Year Holding Period," *Shannon Pratt's Business Valuation Update* (May 2000): 1–5. This study focuses on the change in discounts as a result of the holding period reduction from two years to one year.

Exhibit 12.2   The Value of Marketability as Illustrated in Initial Public
Offerings of Common Stock

Study	Number of IPO Prospectuses Reviewed	Number of Qualifying Transactions	Discounts (%) Mean	Discounts (%) Median
1997–2000	92	53	54	54
1995–1997	732	91	43	42
1994–1995	318	46	45	45
1991–1993	443	54	45	44
1990–1992	266	35	42	40
1989–1990	157	23	45	40
1987–1989	98	27	45	45
1985–1986	130	21	43	43
1980–1981	97	13	60	66
All 9 studies	2333	363	47%	44%

Source: John D. Emory, "The Value of Marketability as Illustrated in Initial Public Offerings of Common Stock, November 1995 through April 1997," *Business Valuation Review* (September 1997): 125. Reprinted with permission of the American Society of Appraisers, and John D. Emory, Sr., F. R. Dengel III, and John D. Emory, Jr., "The Value of Marketability as Illustrated in Dot.Com IPOs, May 1997–March 2000," *Shannon Pratt's Business Valuation Update* ® (July 2000): 1–2.

REGULATORY AND COURT ACCEPTANCE OF EMPIRICAL LACK OF MARKETABILITY STUDIES

The empirical studies on discounts for lack of marketability have been recognized as probative evidence by both the Internal Revenue Service (IRS) and the courts.

Revenue Ruling 77-287

In 1977, the IRS published Revenue Ruling 77-287 "to provide . . . guidance to taxpayers, Internal Revenue Service personnel, and others concerned with the valuation . . . of securities that cannot be immediately resold because they are restricted from resale pursuant to Federal securities laws." The ruling specifically referenced the SEC Institutional Investors study (the only study of such transactions available at the time) as providing guidance.

Court Recognition of Restricted Stock and Pre-IPO Studies

None of the pre-IPO studies existed in 1977 when Revenue Ruling 77-287 was issued, but since then there has been court recognition of both the restricted stock and pre-IPO studies.

Exhibit 12.3 Summary of Discounts for Private Transaction P/E Multiples Compared with Public Offering P/E Multiples Adjusted for Changes in Industry P/E Multiples

Time Period	Number of Companies Analyzed	Number of Transactions Analyzed	Standard Mean Discount (%)	Trimmed Mean Discount[a] (%)	Median Discount (%)	Standard Deviation (%)
1975–1978	17	31	34.0	43.4	52.5	58.6
1979	9	17	55.6	56.8	62.7	30.2
1980–1982	58	113	48.0	51.9	56.5	29.8
1983	85	214	50.1	55.2	60.7	34.7
1984	20	33	43.2	52.9	73.1	63.9
1985	18	25	41.3	47.3	42.6	43.5
1986	47	74	38.5	44.7	47.4	44.2
1987	25	40	36.9	44.9	43.8	49.9
1988	13	19	41.5	42.5	51.8	29.5
1989	9	19	47.3	46.9	50.3	18.6
1990	17	23	30.5	33.0	48.5	42.7
1991	27	34	24.2	28.9	31.8	37.7
1992	36	75	41.9	47.0	51.7	42.6
1993	51	110	46.9	49.9	53.3	33.9
1994	31	48	31.9	38.4	42.0	49.6
1995	42	66	32.2	47.4	58.7	76.4

Source: Willamette Management Associates.

[a] Excludes the highest and lowest deciles of indicated discounts.

Estate of Gallo.   The pre-IPO studies were first recognized by the U.S. Tax Court in *Estate of Gallo.* Experts for both the taxpayer and the IRS had relied exclusively on the guideline publicly traded company method. The IRS expert claimed a discount of 10% for lack of marketability. Experts for the taxpayer claimed a discount of 36% to 45% for lack of marketability, based on restricted stock transactions and a Willamette Management Associates study of pre-IPO transactions within five years prior to the estate's valuation date. The court determined a discount of 36%, for lack of marketability, the highest discount *purely* for lack of marketability up to that time.[7]

Howard v. Shay.   In the case of *Howard v. Shay,* the appraiser applied a 50% discount for lack of marketability on the sale of a block of employee stock ownership plan (ESOP) stock constituting about 38% of the outstanding stock. In successfully defending the suit brought by beneficiaries for alleged undervaluation, the defendants' expert used the Willamette pre-IPO database, isolating transactions constituting 25% to 49.9% of the outstanding stock.[8]

Estate of Mandelbaum.   In *Estate of Mandelbaum,* the parties stipulated to a minority as if publicly traded value, so the only issue was the discount for lack of marketability. The expert witness for the IRS cited only restricted stock studies, but the witness for the taxpayer cited restricted stock studies and both the Emory and Willamette pre-IPO studies. The court used the studies cited by the taxpayer's expert (35% average discount for restricted stock studies and 45% average discount for private transactions prior to IPOs). The court then listed nine factors (now often referred to as the *Mandelbaum factors*) that might cause the marketability discount in a given instance to be higher or lower than the benchmark averages. The court concluded that, on balance, the factors led to a lower discount, and determined a 30% discount for lack of marketability.[9]

Estate of Davis.   In *Estate of Davis,* the expert for the IRS used only restricted stock studies and testified to a 23% discount for lack of marketability. The experts for the taxpayer used both restricted stock and pre-IPO studies and testified to a 35% discount for lack of marketability. The court concluded about 32%, noting "[the IRS' expert] should have considered the . . . data reflected in those pre-IPO studies because they, together with the restricted stock studies, would have provided a more accurate base range and starting point for determining the appropriate lack-of-marketability discount."[10]

Okerlund v. United States.   In *Okerlund,* involving two valuation dates, both the IRS expert and the taxpayer expert relied on two sources of empirical data for aid in quantifying the discount for lack of marketability: discounts on sales of restricted shares of publicly traded companies and discounts on private transactions prior to initial public offerings. Based on these studies, the taxpayer expert (Dr. Pratt, the author of this book) concluded that a 45% discount for lack of marketability was appropriate, and the IRS expert concluded that a 30% discount was justified. The court found discounts for lack of marketability of 40% on one gift date and 45% on another gift date based on a combinate of restricted stock and pre-IPO date, in addition to a 5% discount for nonvoting stock. In reaching this conclusion, the court said:

> Dr. Pratt's expert reports contain a far more detailed analysis of the empirical studies of trading prices of restricted shares and pre-initial public offering transactions than the AVG Report. . . . According to Dr. Pratt, the discounts observed in restricted stock studies reflect the existence of a public market for the stock once the temporary restrictions lapse. For a variety of reasons, . . . purchasers of restricted stock "generally expect to be able to resell the stock in the public market in the foreseeable future." Pre-IPO discounts, on the other hand, are based on purely private transactions before a company enters the public market, a situation more comparable to closely held companies.

The court accepted the taxpayer's expert's opinion because it found that the expert's detailed analysis of the relevant empirical studies and the shareholder risks was persuasive.[11]

This case demonstrates the importance of a thorough analysis and explanation of both the restricted stock and the pre-IPO studies when supporting a discount for lack of marketability. Other cases, although not relying on the restricted stock and pre-IPO studies, have said as much. In *McCord v. Commissioner,*[12] the taxpayer's expert opined that a 35% marketability discount was appropriate based on his analysis of the restricted stock studies, including the SEC study, the Silber study, the Standard Research Consultants study, and the Hertzel & Smith study. He also testified that pre-IPO studies, including the Willamette Management Associates study and the Emory studies, supported this discount. Although the court rejected the pre-IPO studies, it did review the taxpayer's expert's restricted stock study analysis and found a number of flaws in his reasoning and methodology. Expressly because of these errors, the court rejected his restricted stock analysis. Nonetheless, the court did not completely reject the restricted stock studies as a source of marketability discount data, but concluded that the expert had not adequately analyzed the data from the studies in reaching his 35% discount.

The court echoed this sentiment in *Peracchio v. Commissioner,* saying:

> While restricted stock studies certainly have some probative value in the context of marketability discount analysis, see, e.g., McCord v. Commissioner, 120 T.C. at 390–393, Mr. Stryker makes no attempt whatsoever to analyze the data from those studies as they relate to the transferred interests. Rather, he simply lists the average discounts observed in several such studies, effectively asking us to accept on faith the premise that the approximate average of those results provides a reliable benchmark for the transferred interests. Absent any analytical support, we are unable to accept that premise, particularly in light of the fundamental difference between an investment company holding easily valued assets (such as the partnership) and the operating companies that are the subject of the restricted stock studies.[13]

Also, in *Estate of Green v. Commissioner,* the court said that although it believed that pre-IPO studies were "entitled to some consideration," it did not find that they justified a discount greater than 35%.[14]

FACTORS AFFECTING MAGNITUDES
OF MARKETABILITY DISCOUNTS

Empirical studies indicate several factors that influence the magnitudes of discounts for lack of marketability. Primary factors include

- Dividend yield or partnership withdrawals
- Company size
- Company profitability
- Depth of trading market
- Restrictions on transferability
- Size of transaction as a percent of shares outstanding

It is only reasonable that the amount of payout is the most important factor, because the greater the payout the less dependent the investor is on being able to sell to realize some return. Studies such as the Johnson study (see Exhibit 12.1) show that the smaller the company, the greater the discount for lack of marketability. These studies also show that stocks of more profitable companies tend to have lower discounts for lack of marketability. The SEC study showed the lowest average discounts for New York Stock Exchange companies, rising up to the highest average discounts for small over-the-counter companies. It is reasonable that stocks with greater restrictions on transferability would suffer greater discounts for lack of marketability than those with less or no restrictions.

The Mandelbaum factors are:

- Financial statement analysis
- Dividend policy
- Nature of the company, its history, its position in the industry, and its economic outlook
- Management
- Amount of control in the transferred shares
- Restrictions on transferability
- Holding period for the stock
- Company's redemption policy
- Costs associated with a public offering[15]

Many analysts believe, however, that some of these factors (e.g., financial analysis, nature of the company, management) could represent "double counting" because they would already be reflected in the publicly traded minority value. It is not clear how the costs of a public offering apply, because a minority stockholder cannot register a public offering.

As a check for reasonableness, the analyst may wish to check to see how the discount for lack of marketability increases the overall expected rate of return for the privately held interest.

DISCOUNTS FOR LACK OF MARKETABILITY FOR CONTROLLING INTERESTS

All of the empirical studies we have discussed—restricted stock and pre-IPO studies—relate entirely to minority interests. Controlling interests may also suffer from lack of marketability (one cannot call the broker and sell the company in three days), but determining the magnitude of the discount relies on an entirely different analysis. Unlike discounts for lack of marketability for minority interest, there are no directly observable market data to quantify discounts for lack of marketability for controlling interests.

One must keep in mind that the observed controlling interest merger and acquisition data represent *completed transactions.* The transaction data provide evidence of what one might expect to realize once one had done everything that the sold companies did. Preparing the company for sale and accomplishing the sale involves substantial time and costs, for example:

- Legal costs
- Accounting costs
- Management time
- Transaction costs
- Inability to hypothecate
- Holding period risks
- Time value of holding period, if not offset by dividends or appreciation

Furthermore, there is risk that once these costs are incurred, the company might not be able to realize the amount indicated by the historically observed merger and acquisition transactions. In determining a discount for lack of marketability, if any, for a controlling interest, one should attempt to quantify these costs and risks, relative to the amounts one might expect to eventually receive, not try to use the minority interest transaction studies.

SUMMARY

Using the guideline publicly traded stock method, the analyst arrives at an indicated value as if the stock were publicly traded. If valuing a minority interest in a closely held company, a discount for lack of marketability usually would be applied, because investors generally are only willing to pay a significantly lower amount for an interest that lacks liquidity than for one that is readily marketable.

There is a substantial body of market data available to quantify this discount:

- Restricted stock studies (average discounts about 35%)
- Pre-IPO studies (average discounts about 45%)

However, analysts today should not just use these "benchmark averages." They should access the available databases (for example, for restricted stocks the FMV database and for IPO transactions the Valuation Advisors and/or Emory databases) and extract transactions in those companies with characteristics as close as possible to their subject company.

Using the guideline merged and acquired company method, the analyst arrives at an indicated value for a controlling interest. Even a controlling interest may suffer from lack of marketability. If valuing a controlling interest, the analyst could consider the costs of preparing the company for sale, transaction costs, and the risk of not receiving the expected proceeds as factors in quantifying a discount for lack of marketability from the value of the expected proceeds.

If the analyst is using the guideline merged and acquired company method to value a minority interest, then *both* a discount for lack of control and a discount for lack of marketability usually are appropriate. These are taken multiplicatively, not additively; that is, they are taken sequentially. Usually the discount for lack of control is applied to get to a minority value, and then the discount for lack of marketability is applied to the minority value.

Notes

1. For a discussion of those who do make some distinction between marketability and liquidity, see Pratt, Reilly, and Schweihs, "Discounts for Illiquidity and Lack of Marketability," chap. 17 in *Valuing a Business,* 4th ed. (New York: McGraw-Hill, 2000).
2. The *International Glossary of Business Valuation Terms,* a joint publication of the American Institute of Certified Public Accountants, American Society of Appraisers, Canadian Institute of Chartered Business Valuators, National Association of Certified Valuation Analysts, and The Institute of Business Appraisers, distributed as a supplement to *Shannon Pratt's Business Valuation Update* (February 2000).
3. For detail on each of these studies, as well as the pre-IPO studies, *see* note 1.
4. Kathryn F. Aschwald, "Restricted Stock Discounts Decline as Result of 1-Year Holding Period," *Shannon Pratt's Business Valuation Update* (May 2000): 1–5.
5. These studies are also known as the Baird & Co. studies because they were started when John Emory was with Baird & Co., a Milwaukee investment banking firm. He now continues the studies through the business valuation firm that he heads, Emory Business Advisors, LLC.
6. A detailed review of the restricted stock and pre-IPO studies can be found in Z. Christopher Mercer, *Quantifying Marketability Discounts: Developing and Supporting Marketability Discounts in the Appraisal of Closely Held Business Interests,* chaps. 2 and 3 (Memphis: Peabody

Publishing, 1997). See Appendix D, "The Quantitative Marketability Discount Model," for a summary of the basic concepts of Chris Mercer's book by the same title.

7. *Gallo v. Commissioner,* 50 T.C.M. (CCH) 470, T.C.M. (RIA) 85363 (July 22, 1985).

8. *Howard v. Shay,* 100 F3d 1484 (9th Cir., November 22, 1996).

9. *Mandelbaum v. Commissioner,* 69 T.C.M. (CCH) 2852, T.C.M. (RIA) 95, 255 (June 12, 1995).

10. *Davis v. Commissioner,* 110 T.C. 530 (June 30, 1998).

11. *Okerlund v. United States,* 53 Fed. Cl. 341, 2002 U.S. Claims LEXIS 221 (U.S Ct., Fed. Claims, August 23, 2002).

12. *McCord v. Commissioner,* 120 T.C. No. 13, 2003 U.S. Tax Ct. LEXIS 16 (U.S. Tax Ct., May 14, 2003).

13. *Peracchio v. Commissioner,* T.C. Memo 2003-280 (U.S. Tax Ct., September 15, 2003).

14. *Estate of Green v. Commissioner,* T.C. Memo 2003-348, 2003 Tax Ct. Memo LEXIS 348 (U.S. Tax Ct., December 29, 2003).

15. *Mandelbaum v. Commissioner, see* note 9.

PART IV

Sample Market Approach Cases

Chapter 13

Small-size Service Company Sample Case: Sub Shop

In this sample case, we will explore various small private company market data resources available to the business appraiser and examine the practical application of those data within the scope of the market approach. The case involves the valuation of a small submarine sandwich shop. In particular, we will be valuing the company by using private company merger and acquisition data.

BUSINESS DESCRIPTION

Wildcat Sub Shop was established in November 1994 as a sole proprietorship located in Lexington, Kentucky. The business serves hot and cold made-to-order sandwiches, soups, and sodas to customers between the hours of 11 A.M. and 9 P.M., Monday through Saturday. Wildcat Subs' customer base consists primarily of college students and individuals aged 17 to 28. During the college football season,

Wildcat Sub Shop also serves cold sandwiches and sodas to fans attending home games from a mobile vending cart. Regular operations are conducted from a leased facility with seating for 50, one block away from the main campus of the University of Kentucky. The current lease approximates market rates and expires December 31, 2005, with an option to renew for five years at prevailing market rates. The business employs three full-time employees, including the owner/operator, and two part-time employees. Wildcat Subs' owner/operator received an annual salary equal to the business's reported 1999 net income of $33,000.

VALUATION ASSIGNMENT

Satisfied that Wildcat Subs is on firm financial footing and established in its market, the current owner has expressed a desire to sell the business and pursue other interests. We were retained to value a 100% ownership interest in the assets of the business as of December 31, 1999, and express an opinion as to the fair market value of the business. It is assumed that substantially all of the operating assets and liabilities will be transferred in the sale of Wildcat Subs, with the exception of cash and equivalents.

ECONOMIC OUTLOOK

The sandwich shop's strong association with and close proximity to the university and its campus continue to play an important role in the business's growth and profitability. Management has indicated that expected revenue growth for the next five years should approximate the 14% per annum growth realized over the past five years. This is consistent with the owner's plan to initiate limited delivery service to dormitory residents. Wildcat Subs' immediate competition includes the university's food services, several pizza parlors with and without delivery services, and a number of franchise restaurants. Despite low barriers to entry and intense competition in the local market area, the university's expected student population growth and general economic conditions in the region lend support to management's expectations of revenue growth in the near future.

FINANCIAL STATEMENT ANALYSIS

Wildcat Subs provided historical financial statements, including balance sheets and income statements, reflecting the business's financial condition and the results of operations for each of the years ended December 31, 1995, through December 31, 1999. The historical and common size financial statements reproduced here as Exhibits 13.1 and 13.2 have been adjusted with input from management and are consistent with the purpose of this valuation assignment. In particular, extraordinary

Exhibit 13.1 Wildcat Sub Shop Balance Sheets

| | Fiscal Years Ended December 31 | | | | | Fiscal Years Ended December 31 | | | | |
	1999	1998	1997	1996	1995	1999 (%)	1998 (%)	1997 (%)	1996 (%)	1995 (%)
Current Assets										
Cash & Equivalents	6,200.00	5,700.00	5,100.00	3,700.00	3,500.00	6.6	6.5	6.3	5.1	5.1
Accounts Receivable	2,600.00	2,800.00	3,400.00	3,000.00	1,600.00	2.8	3.2	4.2	4.1	2.3
Inventory	2,100.00	1,700.00	1,400.00	1,000.00	800.00	2.2	1.9	1.7	1.4	1.2
Other Current Assets	13,100.00	10,400.00	11,600.00	8,500.00	7,700.00	13.9	11.9	14.2	11.6	11.2
Total Current Assets	24,000.00	20,600.00	21,500.00	16,200.00	13,600.00	25.5	23.5	26.4	22.1	19.8
Furniture, Fixtures & Equipment, Net	60,000.00	54,000.00	49,000.00	47,000.00	46,000.00	63.8	61.6	60.1	64.2	67.1
Other Noncurrent Assets, Net of Amort.	10,000.00	13,000.00	11,000.00	10,000.00	9,000.00	10.6	14.8	13.5	13.7	13.1
Total Assets	94,000.00	87,600.00	81,500.00	73,200.00	68,600.00	100.0	100.0	100.0	100.0	100.0
Current Liabilities										
Trade Payables	16,900.00	14,800.00	13,100.00	11,300.00	9,900.00	18.0	16.9	16.1	15.4	14.4
Wages Payable	12,400.00	11,200.00	10,600.00	9,000.00	7,900.00	13.2	12.8	13.0	12.3	11.5
Other Current Liabilities	15,400.00	14,000.00	12,600.00	8,300.00	7,000.00	16.4	16.0	15.5	11.3	10.2
Total Current Liabilities	44,700.00	40,000.00	36,300.00	28,600.00	24,800.00	47.6	45.7	44.5	39.1	36.2
Long-term Debt	-	-	-	-	-	0.0	0.0	0.0	0.0	0.0
Shareholders Equity	49,300.00	47,600.00	45,200.00	44,600.00	43,800.00	52.4	54.3	55.5	60.9	63.8
Total Liabilities and Shareholders Equity	94,000.00	87,600.00	81,500.00	73,200.00	68,600.00	100.0	100.0	100.0	100.0	100.0

Exhibit 13.2 Wildcat Sub Shop Income Statements

	Fiscal Years Ended December 31					Fiscal Years Ended December 31				
	1999	1998	1997	1996	1995	1999 (%)	1998 (%)	1997 (%)	1996 (%)	1995 (%)
Net Sales	169,000.00	148,000.00	129,000.00 $	113,000.00	99,000.00	100.0	100.0	100.0	100.0	100.0
Cost of Revenues	51,000.00	45,000.00	39,000.00	35,000.00	31,000.00	30.2	30.4	30.2	31.0	31.3
Gross Profit	118,000.00	103,000.00	90,000.00 $	78,000.00	68,000.00	69.8	69.6	69.8	69.0	68.7
Yearly Rent	27,000.00	27,000.00	27,000.00	27,000.00	27,000.00	16.0	18.2	20.9	23.9	27.3
Owner's Compensation	-	-	-	-	-	0.0	0.0	0.0	0.0	0.0
Other Operating Expenses	53,000.00	42,000.00	32,000.00	23,000.00	17,000.00	31.4	28.4	24.8	20.4	17.2
Depreciation & Amortization	5,000.00	5,000.00	5,000.00	5,000.00	4,000.00	3.0	3.4	3.9	4.4	4.0
Total Operating Expenses	85,000.00	74,000.00	64,000.00	55,000.00	48,000.00	50.3	50.0	49.6	48.7	48.5
Income (Loss) from Operations	33,000.00	29,000.00	26,000.00 $	23,000.00	20,000.00	19.5	19.6	20.2	20.4	20.2
Interest Expense	-	-	-	-	-	0.0	0.0	0.0	0.0	0.0
Income (Loss) before Taxes	33,000.00	29,000.00	26,000.00 $	23,000.00	20,000.00	19.5	19.6	20.2	20.4	20.2
Provision (Benefit) for Taxes	-	-	-	-	-	0.0	0.0	0.0	0.0	0.0
Net Income	33,000.00	29,000.00	26,000.00 $	23,000.00	20,000.00	19.5	19.6	20.2	20.4	20.2

and nonrecurring income and expenses and nonoperating assets and related income and expenses have been eliminated. Depreciation expense and owner compensation were reviewed and deemed appropriate given the level of fixed assets and service performed, respectively. See Chapter 7 for a discussion of financial statement adjustments.

Trend Analysis

Wildcat Subs' income statements show that the business has been profitable for each of the last five years, with revenues, gross profit, and net income growing at roughly 14% per annum.

The income statement accounts have remained relatively stable with the exception of rent expense and other operating expenses, which have decreased to 16% and increased to 31% respectively. Rent expense is fixed for the near term and therefore will continue to decline as a percent of sales with an increase in sales. Other operating expenses include variable costs that are positively correlated with sales and therefore will increase with an increase in sales. The changes in these two accounts have largely offset one another, leaving total operating expenses at roughly 50% and operating profit at approximately 20% largely unaffected to this point. It should be noted that other operating expenses have grown faster than sales, 33% versus 14%, over the last four years. This trend is not expected to continue as the primary component of other operating expenses, payroll expense, should remain stable for the near-term future.

Exhibit 13.3 includes several financial ratios calculated using data from Wildcat Subs' adjusted financial statements. The current and quick ratios have declined minimally, suggesting that Wildcat Subs' liquidity has done so as well. This is particularly worrisome because inventory turnover has fallen from 39× to 27×. With the exception of inventory turnover, the remaining activity ratios have improved over recent years. Fixed-charge coverage improved modestly, from 1.7× to 2.2× over the same time period. Despite these concerns, gross profit and net profit margins have remained steady at 70% and 19% respectively, while return on total assets before owner's compensation improved to 36% from 32%.

Peer Comparison

Using data published in the 1998 *RMA Annual Statement Studies* and the 1999 *Restaurant Industry Operation Report,* Wildcat Subs' financial condition and operating performance was carefully compared to that of other restaurants similar in size and characteristics. Most notable among the observations made using both sources of data was the fact that Wildcat Subs exhibited typical gross profit margins and superior operating profit margins, 70% and 19% respectively, while maintaining relatively typical operating expenses at 50% (see Exhibits 13.4 and 13.4A), as well as above-normal occupancy costs at 16%.

Exhibit 13.3   Wildcat Sub Shop Ratio Analysis

	Fiscal Years Ended December 31				
	1999	1998	1997	1996	1995
LIQUIDITY RATIOS					
Current Ratio	0.54	0.52	0.59	0.57	0.55
Quick Ratio	0.20	0.21	0.23	0.23	0.21
ACTIVITY RATIOS					
Inventory Turnover	26.8	29.0	32.5	38.9	N/A[a]
Average Inventory Turnover Period	13.6	12.6	11.2	9.4	N/A
Accounts Receivable Turnover	62.6	47.7	40.3	49.1	N/A
Average Collection Period	5.8	7.6	9.1	7.4	N/A
Fixed Asset Turnover	3.0	2.9	2.7	2.4	N/A
Asset Turnover	1.9	1.8	1.7	1.6	N/A
COVERAGE/LEVERAGE RATIOS					
Total Debt to Total Assets (%)	47.6	45.7	44.5	39.1	36.2
Fixed-Charges Coverage[b]	2.2	2.1	2.0	1.9	1.7
PROFITABILITY RATIOS (%)					
Gross Profit Margin	69.8	69.6	69.8	69.0	68.7
Operating Profit Margin	19.5	19.6	20.2	20.4	20.2
Net Profit Margin	19.5	19.6	20.2	20.4	20.2
Cash Flow to Sales[c]	22.5	23.0	24.0	24.8	24.2
Return on Total Assets[d]	36.3	34.3	33.6	32.4	N/A
Return on Equity	66.9	60.9	57.5	51.6	45.7

[a] Not available.
[b] Fixed-charges coverage assumes rent expense equals fixed charge.
[c] Cash flow = net income plus depreciation and amortization expense.
[d] Tax rate of 30% used in return on total assets calculation.

Risk Management Associates (RMA) also publishes ratios corresponding to the survey sample's liquidity, coverage, leverage, operations, and expenses—presented here as Exhibit 13.5. Although some of the ratios published by RMA are calculated using conventional methods, a few differ due to the source and nature of the data collected. Readers should be cautioned that in some cases adjustments must be made to conventional ratio calculation methods in order to avoid apples-to-oranges comparisons. In particular, the ratios presented in Exhibit 13.5 were calculated using only the corresponding year's financial information and therefore will differ from those ratios presented in Exhibit 13.3.

A comparison of Wildcat Subs' liquidity ratios to those reported by RMA for restaurants of similar size reveals that our subject ranks above the bottom 25% of respondents in terms of its current, quick, and cost of sales to inventory relationships. Wildcat Subs' depreciation expense is typical of that reported by RMA, and owner's compensation is above normal relative to the sample. In terms of leverage ratios, Wildcat Subs compares more favorably to its selected peers, ranking among the top

Exhibit 13.4 Wildcat Subs RMA Common Size Comparison

	1998 Subject	1998 RMA	1997 Subject	1997 RMA	1996 Subject	1996 RMA	1995 Subject	1995 RMA
Number of Observations	1	125	1	142	1	176	1	144
Average Asset Size ($000)	88	285	82	258	73	255	69	234
Average Sales Volume ($000)	148	609	129	628	113	598	99	619
	%	%	%	%	%	%	%	%
Common Size Income Statements								
Net Sales	100.0	100.0	100.0	100.0	100.0	100.0	100.0	100.0
Cost of Goods Sold	30.4		30.2		31.0		31.3	
Gross Profit	69.6	61.0	69.8	62.2	69.0	62.7	68.7	60.7
Operating Expenses	50.0	52.8	49.6	55.3	48.7	57.4	48.5	54.6
Operating Income	19.6	8.2	20.2	6.9	20.4	5.4	20.2	6.1
Other Income (Expense), Net	0.0	1.8	0.0	2.0	0.0	2.1	0.0	1.5
PRETAX PROFIT	19.6	6.4	20.2	4.9	20.4	3.3	20.2	4.6
Common Size Balance Sheets								
ASSETS								
Current Assets:								
Cash & Equivalents	6.5	14.1	6.3	15.4	5.1	12.4	5.1	15.0
Accts. & Notes Receivable (Trade)	3.2	1.5	4.2	0.8	4.1	0.8	2.3	0.7
Inventory	1.9	4.6	1.7	4.7	1.4	5.7	1.2	4.8
All Other Current Assets	11.9	1.0	14.2	1.8	11.6	3.1	11.2	1.5
Total Current Assets	23.5	21.1	26.4	22.8	22.1	22.1	19.8	22.0
Net Fixed Assets	61.6	59.4	60.1	54.8	64.2	57.9	67.1	57.2
Net Intangible Assets	14.8	11.8	13.5	11.8	13.7	11.0	13.1	10.0
Net Other Assets		7.7		10.6		9.0		10.9
TOTAL ASSETS	100.0	100.0	100.0	100.0	100.0	100.0	100.0	100.0

(continued)

Exhibit 13.4 Wildcat Subs RMA Common Size Comparison *(continued)*

	1998		1997		1996		1995	
	Subject	RMA	Subject	RMA	Subject	RMA	Subject	RMA
LIABILITIES & EQUITY								
Liabilities:								
Current Liabilities:								
Notes Payable		8.0		6.7		10.6		2.8
Current Mat. LTD		5.2		5.2		6.2		5.4
Accounts & Notes Payable (Trade)	16.9	6.9	16.1	8.5	15.4	8.0	14.4	6.8
Income Taxes Payable		0.3		0.2		0.2		0.3
All Other Current Liabilities	28.8	10.9	28.5	11.8	23.6	14.6	21.7	13.2
Total Current Liabilities	45.7	31.3	44.5	32.3	39.1	39.6	36.2	28.5
Total Long-term Debt	0.0	36.4	0.0	31.2	0.0	32.1	0.0	37.4
Total Other Noncurrent Debt		2.5		5.1		4.2		4.0
Total Liabilities	45.7	70.2	44.5	68.6	39.1	75.9	36.2	69.9
Total Equity	54.3	29.8	55.5	31.4	60.9	24.1	63.8	30.1
TOTAL LIABILITIES & EQUITY	100.0	100.0	100.0	100.0	100.0	100.0	100.0	100.0

Source: Data from *RMA Annual Statement Studies*, 1999. Used with permission of Risk Management Associates.

Exhibit 13.4A   Wildcat Subs Restaurant Industry Operations Report Common Size Comparison

	1999	
	Subject	Restaurant Industry Operations Report
Number of Observations	1	33
	%	%
Common Size Income Statements		
Net Sales	100.0	100.0
Cost of Goods Sold	30.2	33.8
Gross Profit	69.8	66.2
Restaurant Occupancy Costs	16.0	6.6
Depreciation	3.0	1.5
Total Operating Expenses	50.3	54.7
Operating Income	19.5	N/A
Other Income (Expense), Net	0.0	N/A
PRETAX PROFIT	19.5	6.5

Source: 1999 Restaurant Industry Operations Report, National Restaurant Association and Deloitte & Touche LLP, 1999. Reprinted with permission from the National Restaurant Association.

25% of respondents in this category. A comparison of operating ratios presented mixed results. Specifically, Wildcat Subs compares favorably in terms of return to net worth and total assets, but less so in terms of asset turnover measures.

Conclusion of Financial Statement Analysis

Provided with an understanding of Wildcat Subs' recent operating results and the insights gleaned from industry statistics, two important observations can be made about our subject:

1. Wildcat Subs exhibits relatively higher business risk characteristics than the average restaurant of similar size.
2. Wildcat Subs has consistently enjoyed above-average gross and operating profit margins relative to its peers.

IDENTIFICATION AND SELECTION OF MARKET DATA

According to the American Society of Appraisers, Business Valuation Standard BVS-V, Market Approach to Business Valuation, transaction data used in

Exhibit 13.5 Wildcat Subs RMA Ratio Comparison

		1998		1997		1996		1995	
		Subject	RMA	Subject	RMA	Subject	RMA	Subject	RMA
Number of Observations		1	125	1	142	1	176	1	144
Average Asset Size ($000)		88	285	82	258	73	255	69	234
Average Sales Volume ($000)		148	609	129	628	113	598	99	619
Liquidity Ratios									
Current Ratio	High		1.5		1.4		1.4		1.6
	Median	0.52	0.6	0.59	0.5	0.57	0.6	0.55	0.7
	Low		0.2		0.2		0.2		0.3
Quick Ratio	High		1.4		1.0		0.9		1.0
	Median	0.21	0.4	0.23	0.3	0.23	0.3	0.21	0.5
	Low		0.1		0.1		0.0		0.1
Cost of Sales/Inventory	High		63.0		66.7		61.2		63.4
	Median	26.5	40.0	27.9	38.7	35.0	39.1	38.8	38.7
	Low		25.2		28.0		26.0		26.0
Cost of Sales/Payables	High		UND		UND		UND		167.8
	Median	3.0	44.3	3.0	36.7	3.1	32.8	3.1	31.7
	Low		10.9		10.2		11.5		11.5

Leverage Ratios								
Fixed/Worth								
High		1.0		1.0		1.1		1.2
Median	1.1	4.0	1.1	2.9	1.1	3.6	1.1	2.7
Low		(18.2)		(20.9)		(19.2)		53.8
Debt/Worth								
High		1.1		0.9		0.9		1.1
Median	0.8	4.5	0.8	4.3	0.6	4.9	0.6	3.6
Low		(21.8)		(17.9)		(15.7)		NM
Operating Ratios								
% Profit Before Taxes/Tangible Net Worth								
High		119.1		148.0		128.2		108.1
Median	83.8	46.2	76.0	48.3	66.5	40.2	57.5	57.0
Low		5.9		15.6		16.9		14.7
% Profit Before Taxes/Total Assets								
High		29.0		31.5		25.6		27.5
Median	33.1	11.4	31.9	11.2	31.4	7.7	29.2	12.5
Low		0.0		0.9		0.3		1.5
Sales/Net Fixed Assets								
High		11.4		22.8		21.3		14.7
Median	2.7	5.9	2.6	9.2	2.4	5.9	2.2	6.3
Low		2.2		2.6		2.2		3.0
Sales/Total Assets								
High		4.7		6.5		6.5		5.3
Median	1.7	3.0	1.6	3.8	1.5	3.0	1.4	2.9
Low		1.5		1.6		1.7		1.9

(continued)

Exhibit 13.5 Wildcat Subs RMA Ratio Comparison (*continued*)

Expense to Sales Ratios		1998 Subject	1998 RMA	1997 Subject	1997 RMA	1996 Subject	1996 RMA	1995 Subject	1995 RMA
% Depr., Dep., Amort./Sales	High		1.8		1.7		2.0		1.6
	Median	3.4	3.0	3.9	2.8	4.4	3.2	4.0	3.0
	Low		4.6		4.0		5.1		4.5
% Officers', Directors', Owners' Comp/Sales	High		4.3		3.4		4.5		3.4
	Median	19.6	5.9	20.2	5.0	20.4	6.1	20.2	5.9
	Low		9.2		9.8		8.7		9.4

Source: Data from *RMA Annual Statement Studies*, 1999. Used with permission of Risk Management Association.

arriving at a value conclusion by means of the market approach should exhibit "sufficient similarity of qualitative and quantitative investment characteristics" to provide a reasonable basis for comparison. With this in mind, we will initially define the parameters of our search for market data by industry and company size, specifically Standard Industrial Classification (SIC) code 5812 (restaurants) and annual sales of $500,000 or less.

Three private company transaction databases report data on the sales of restaurants similar in size to Wildcat Subs. Furthermore, the level of value, specifically controlling interest, indicated by using data from private company transaction databases is the appropriate level of value for our particular valuation assignment. Therefore, we will rely on the three private company transaction data providers, *BIZCOMPS*® Business Sale Statistics, Institute of Business Appraisers' *IBA Market Data Base,* and *Pratt's Stats™* Private Business Sale Transaction Database, to identify similar, recently acquired companies that can be used in the valuation of Wildcat Subs.

BIZCOMPS® Business Sale Statistics

Using the broad criteria defined in the last section, our search for market statistics reported by *BIZCOMPS*® yielded 109 restaurant sale transactions. After a close examination of the search results, the number of transactions was further pared down to include only those sales that involved restaurants described as Deli-Sandwiches, Deli-Sub Shops, Deli-Sandwich Shops, or Deli-Submarines located in the eastern and southeastern portion of the United States. Finally, any transaction consummated before 1993 was also excluded from our consideration. The resulting subset of *BIZCOMPS*® transactions included 12 sales and is presented here as Exhibit 13.6.

Wildcat Subs' revenues fit nicely within the range of revenues (Ann Gross) reported, from $80,000 to $346,000. Indeed, the median revenue of the sample was just marginally higher than that of our subject, $197,000 versus $169,000. Conversely, Wildcat Subs' seller's discretionary cash flow (SDCF) of $38,000 is substantially higher than the median reported by BIZCOMPS®, of $32,000. However, on a common size basis, we find that Wildcat Subs' SDCF/Sales ratio is very similar, at 22%, to that of the median SDCF/Sales ratio reported by BIZCOMPS®, at 21%. The same cannot be said of Wildcat Subs' Rent/Sales expense ratio, which is among the highest, at 16%, with 75% of the sample reporting lower Rent/Sales expense. However, because Wildcat Subs' lease terms are fixed for the near future, the risk factor is somewhat mitigated. Provided sales continue to grow, rent expense as a percentage of sales will continue to decline.

Qualitatively, the match between our subject and the selected transactions is much harder to define. To a great extent, we must rely on sound selection criteria to support an assertion of qualitative similarity. In this case, we have focused our qualitative selection criteria on the business description, location, and date of sale. Certainly the business descriptions are a close match. Location may not provide as

Exhibit 13.6 Selected *BIZCOMPS*® Business Sale Statistics

SIC #	BUS TYPE	ASK PRICE (000)	ANN GROSS (000)	SDCF (000)[a]	SDCF/ GROSS SALES	SALE DATE	SALE PRICE (000)[b]	% DOWN	TERMS	SALE/ GROSS SALES	SALE/ SDCF	INV AMT	FF&E (000)	RENT/ SALES	AREA
5812.22	Deli-Sandwiches	123	210	32	0.15	4/29/98	120	10%	4 Yrs @ 8.5%	0.57	3.8	2	107	13%	Cary, NC
5812.22	Deli-Sub Shop	80	152	27	0.18	11/30/96	51	46%	5 Yrs @ 6%	0.34	1.9	5	19	20%	Central Florida
5812.22	Deli-Sub Shop	70	110	40	0.36	7/31/96	52	29%	2.5 Yrs @ 10%	0.47	1.3	1	35	13%	Central Florida
5812.22	Deli-Sandwiches	98	226	40	0.18	9/30/95	82	100%	N/A[c]	0.36	2	3	10	7.9%	Central Virginia
5812.22	Deli-Sandwiches	147	346	101	0.29	5/31/95	97	67%	N/A	0.28	1	3	45	19.1%	Central Florida
5812.22	Deli-Sandwiches	247	346	100	0.29	2/28/95	147	60%	N/A	0.42	1.5	3	70	17.3%	Central Florida
5812.22	Deli-Sandwiches	55	116	26	0.22	3/31/94	51	45%	5 Yrs @ 8%	0.44	2	1	40	9.9%	Palm Beach, Florida
5812.22	Deli-Submarines	90	125	25	0.20	2/28/94	85	47%	5 Yrs @ 8%	0.68	3.4	0		5.5%	Central Florida
5812.22	Deli-Sandwiches	80	184	27	0.15	6/30/93	55	100%	N/A	0.30	2		15	10%	Central Florida
5812.22	Deli-Sandwich Shop	87	224	31	0.14	5/31/93	52	25%	4 Yrs @ 9%	0.23	1.7	3	41	12%	Pittsburgh, PA
5812.22	Deli-Sandwiches	50	80	20	0.25	4/30/93	49	48%	5 Yrs @ 9%	0.61	2.5	2	17	10.6%	Southwest Florida
5812.22	Deli-Sandwiches	118	232	53	0.23	2/28/93	101	49%	5 Yrs @ 8%	0.44	1.9	2	10	7%	Central Florida
	Maximum		346	101	0.36					0.68	3.8			20%	
	Minimum		80	20	0.14					0.23	1			5.5%	
	Mean		196	44	0.22					0.43	2.08			12.1%	
	Median		197	32	0.21					0.43	1.95			11.3%	
	Coefficient of Variation		0.44	0.64	0.31					0.32	0.39			0.38	
	Standard Deviation		87	28	0					0.14	0.81			0.05	

Note: BIZCOMPS® available online at www.BVMarketData.com

[a] Seller's discretionary cash flow (net profit before taxes *and any compensation to owner* plus amortization, depreciation, interest, other noncash expense, and non-business-related expense. Assumes one working owner).

[b] Sale Price does not include cash, accounts receivable, or accounts payable. Inventory has also been excluded but the actual amount of inventory at the time of sale is shown for each business sale.

[c] Not available.

close a match as one might hope. Nonetheless, if too-stringent criteria are used, the number of observations important in understanding overall market activity would be less reliable due to dwindling sample sizes.

IBA Market Data Base

Using the same criteria set as that employed in our *BIZCOMPS®* search, we have narrowed our search results from the *IBA Market Data Base* from 152 transactions to 10 sales. Each sale involved a restaurant with the business description of Deli-Sandwich Shop, Sub Shop, or Sandwich Shop consummated after 1992 with the geographic dispersion specified in our criteria. Five of the transactions were also reported in the *BIZCOMPS®* database, so we ended up with five additional transactions. One weakness of the data is that the latest sandwich shop sale reported was in 1994. Exhibit 13.7 contains the reported transaction details for each sale selected.

The sales data reported by the IBA exhibits a much tighter range of revenue than that of the *BIZCOMPS®* sample, $150,000 to $203,000. Given our subject's sales of $169,000, Wildcat Subs ranks well within the range of this sample.

There is some ambiguity as to the *IBA Market Data Base* definition of *earnings*. If one reads the definition literally, it would be after expense for noncash charges, such as depreciation. However, for the five transactions that the *IBA Market Data Base* and *BIZCOMPS®* have in common, the earnings in the IBA database are the same as the SDCF reported in *BIZCOMPS®* (which is defined the same way as discretionary earnings reported in *Pratt's Stats™*). We interviewed several brokers who contribute data to both databases, and they indicated that they report the same way to both. Therefore, for the purpose of our analysis, we will assume that annual earnings as reported by the IBA, SDCF as reported by *BIZCOMPS®*, and discretionary earnings as reported by *Pratt's Stats™* are defined identically to each other.

Consequently, we find that the absolute value of Wildcat Subs discretionary earnings, at $38,000, is only 5% lower than the median Annual Earnings of our selected IBA transactions. When measured as a percentage of sales, we find that Wildcat Subs' earnings, 22.5%, is almost equal to the reported median for annual earnings/sales in this sample, 22.2%. Clearly the earnings for our sample transactions and subject are substantially similar, according to the quantitative information provided.

Due to the similar nature of the data provided by the *IBA Market Data Base* and *BIZCOMPS®*, the arguments made with respect to the qualitative similarity between our subject and the *BIZCOMPS®* sample also hold for our subject and the *IBA Market Data Base* sample.

Pratt's Stats™ Private Business Sale Transaction Database

Following the same parameters that we used in our previous two searches, *Pratt's Stats™* Private Business Sale Transaction Database, the official completed sale database of the International Business Brokers Association, returned 36 restaurant sales, which were subsequently reduced to 5 transactions that satisfied our narrowed

Exhibit 13.7 Selected *IBA Market Data Base* Business Sale Transactions

Business Type	Annual Gross $000's	Annual Earnings $000's[a]	Owner's Comp. $000's	Sales Price $000's	Price/Gross	Price/Earnings	Geographic	Yr/Mo of Sale	Annual earnings as a percentage of gross sales
Sub shop	150	55		45	0.30	0.82	FL	94/08	36.7%
Sandwich Shop	169	48		85	0.50	1.77	FL	94/10	28.4%
Subshop	180	40		85	0.47	2.13	FL	94/03	22.2%
Deli - Sandwich Shop	203	37		44	0.22	1.19	PA	93/06	18.2%
Deli - Sandwich Shop	190	35		68	0.36	1.94	PA	94/04	18.4%
Number of observations	5	5		5	5	5			5
Maximum	203	55		85	0.50	2.13			36.7%
Minimum	150	35		44	0.22	0.82			18.2%
Mean	178	43		65	0.37	1.57			24.8%
Median	180	40		68	0.36	1.77			22.2%
Coefficient of Variation	0.11	0.19		0.31	0.32	0.35			0.315
Standard Deviation	20	8		20	0.12	0.55			0.078

Source: Data from "Market Analysis Portfolio Report of Eating Places (Sub Shops), SIC Code-5812," 1999. Used with permission of the Institute of Business Appraisers.

[a] Reported annual earnings before owner's compensation, interest, and taxes.

criteria set. An example of the information provided for each transaction reported by *Pratt's Stats™* appears here as Exhibit 13.8 with a summary of selected information for each transaction presented in Exhibit 13.9. One obvious difference between the data reported by *Pratt's Stats™* and that of the previously reviewed resources is the amount of quantitative and qualitative information provided for each transaction. Afforded this level of detail, we can compare our subject to the selected sample using many of the same techniques employed in our initial financial statement analysis.

As presented in Exhibit 13.9, revenues for the sample of *Pratt's Stats™* transactions ranged from $90,000 to $340,000, with the median revenue reported, $189,000, only slightly higher than that of our subject. As we can see from Exhibit 13.10, a common size comparison of our subject's and sample's income statements, Wildcat Subs has a relatively higher gross profit margin and an EBIT (earnings before interest and taxes) substantially higher than the median reported for the selected *Pratt's Stats™* transactions. Just the opposite is true of DE (defined by *Pratt's Stats™* as net income plus owner's compensation, noncash charges, interest, and taxes) as a percent of sales.

A comparison of financial ratios of Wildcat Subs' and the *Pratt's Stats™* transactions yields results similar to our conclusions reached using RMA data. In particular, Exhibit 13.11 shows that Wildcat Subs' activity ratios were the lowest reported for our sample, indicating a relative underutilization of the business's assets.

Furthermore, despite having no interest expense, the impact of Wildcat Subs' relatively high rent expense results in a low fixed-charge coverage ratio. Finally, in regard to measures of profitability, we see once again that our subject's gross profit, net profit margin and return on total assets ratios are typical or above that of the median for our sample. Certainly we can make the case that Wildcat Subs is similar quantitatively to the *Pratt's Stats™* sample transactions despite exhibiting relatively higher risk characteristics.

With respect to issues of qualitative comparison, we can see from Exhibit 13.12 that *Pratt's Stats™,* although reporting fewer transactions that meet the tightened comparative criteria, provides considerably more insight per transaction than does either *BIZCOMPS®* or the *IBA Market Data Base*. It is also worth noting that all of the *Pratt's Stats™* transactions are from 1997 forward, while only one of the *BIZCOMPS®* transactions and none of the IBA transactions are later than 1996. Specifically, in addition to providing sale dates and business locations, other qualitative issues addressed by *Pratt's Stats™* include:

- Age of the business at the time of sale
- Number of employees
- Business structure
- Description of lease agreements

Given the information gleaned from our management interview we can conclude that Wildcat Subs is substantially similar to our sample of *Pratt's Stats™* transactions according to these criteria.

Exhibit 13.8 *Pratt's Stats™* Transaction Record

Pratt's Stats™ Transaction Report Prepared: 12/20/2004 12:13:37 PM (PST)

Transaction Details

Intermediary Name	Town, James A.	Company Name	N/A
Firm Name	Prime Business Investments	Sale Location	Fulton, GA, United States
SIC	5812 Eating and Drinking Places	Years in Business	1
NAICS	722211 Limited-Service Restaurants	Number Employees	3
Business Description	Sandwich Shop	Report Date	6/28/1999

Income Data

Data is "Latest Full Year" Reported	No
Data is Restated (see Notes for any explanation)	Yes
Income Statement Date	12/31/1998
Net Sales	$189,000
COGS	$66,150
Gross Profit	$122,850
Yearly Rent	$14,196
Owner's Compensation	N/A
Other Operating Expenses	$0
Noncash Charges	$0
Total Operating Expenses	$69,930
Operating Profit	$52,920
Interest Expenses	$0
EBT	$52,920
Taxes	$0
Net Income	$52,920

Asset Data

Data is Latest Reported	Yes
Data is "Purchase Price Allocation agreed upon by Buyer and Seller"	No
Balance Sheet Date	12/31/1998
Cash Equivalents	N/A
Trade Receivables	$0
Inventory	$500
Other Current Assets	N/A
Total Current Assets	$500
Fixed Assets	$27,000
Real Estate	N/A
Intangibles	N/A
Other Noncurrent Assets	$25,000
Total Assets	$52,500
Long-term Liabilities	N/A
Total Liabilities	N/A
Stockholder's Equity	N/A

Transaction Data

Date Sale Intiated	8/14/1998
Date of Sale	3/5/1999
Asking Price	$95,000
Equity Price*	$55,000
Market Value of Invested Capital*	$55,000
Liabilities Assumed	N/A
Employment Agreement Value	N/A
Noncompete Value	N/A
Amount of Down Payment	$25,000
Stock or Asset Sale	Asset
Company Type	Sole Proprietorship
Was there an Employment/Consulting Agreement?	No
Was there an Assumed Lease in the sale?	Yes
Was there a Renewal Option with the Lease?	No

*Includes noncompete value; excludes real estate and employment/consulting agreement values.

Additional Transaction Information

Was there a Note in the consideration paid?	Yes
Was there a personal guarantee on the Note?	No
Terms	$30,000 note
Balance of Assumed Lease (Months)	47
Terms of Lease	Five years. Rent negotiable. 1,141 square feet.
Noncompete Length (Months)	36
Noncompete Description	3 mile radius.
Employment/Consulting Agreement Description	Seller will train for 2 weeks.
Additional Notes	Estimated fair value of assets acquired is $25,000. Income Data is annualized. Assets acquired include inventory, license fee and fixed assets. Seller owned business since inception. Operation licensed from Restaurant Developers & Management, Inc.(RDM), who holds the lease. RDM licenses several shops in office buildings for initial fee and royalty of 5%.

Valuation Multiples

Equity Price/Net Sales	0.291
Equity Price/Gross Cash Flow	1.039
Equity Price/EBT	1.039
Equity Price/Net Income	1.039
Equity Price/Book Value of Equity	N/A
MVIC/Net Sales	0.291
MVIC/Gross Profit	0.448
MVIC/EBITDA	1.039
MVIC/EBIT	1.039
MVIC/Discretionary Earnings	N/A
MVIC/Book Value of Invested Capital	N/A

Financial Ratios

Net Income/Sales	0.280
EBIT/Sales	0.280
Sales/Total Assets	3.600
Sales/Fixed Assets	7.000
EBIT/Interest Expense	N/A
Long-term Debt/Total Assets	N/A
Return on Assets	1.008
Return on Equity	N/A

N/A = Not Available

Exhibit 13.9 Selected *Pratt's Stats*™ Transaction Data

SIC Code	Business Description	Income Statement Date	Asking Price (000)	Net Sales (000)	DE (000)	DE/Net Sales	Sale Date	Sale Price (000)	Sale Price/ Net Sales	Sale Price/ DE	Inventory Balance (000)	Rent/Net Sales	AREA
5812	Deli	12/31/96	254	340	106	0.31	8/7/97	186	0.55	1.75	N/A	12.4%	N/A
5812.0305	Sandwich Shop	N/A	67	119	14	0.12	7/24/97	37	0.31	2.64	0.5	9.4%	Venice, FL
5812.09	Deli Sandwiches	12/31/98	64	90	9	0.10	4/20/99	35	0.39	3.89	4.0	13.4%	Greenville, SC
5812.0313	Sandwich Shop	12/31/98	95	189	53	0.28	3/5/99	55	0.29	1.04	0.5	7.5%	Fulton, GA
5812.0313	Sandwich Shop	12/31/99	160	277	73	0.26	6/18/99	160	0.58	2.19	2.0	6.5%	Cobb, GA
Maximum			254	340	106	0.31		186	0.58	3.89		13.4%	
Minimum			64	90	9	0.10		35	0.29	1.04		6.5%	
Mean			128	203	51	0.21		95	0.42	2.30		9.8%	
Median			95	189	53	0.26		55	0.39	2.19		9.4%	
Coefficient of Variation			0.63	0.52	0.80	0.46		0.77	0.31	0.46		0.30	
Standard Deviation			80	105	41	0.10		73	0.13	1.07		2.98%	

Exhibit 13.10   *Pratt's Stats™* Common Size Income and Cash Flow Comparison

		Selected *Pratt's Stats™* Transactions				Median	Wildcat Subs
	#1	#2	#3	#4	#5		
	12/31/96	N/A	12/31/98	12/31/98	12/31/99		12/31/99
	(%)	(%)	(%)	(%)	(%)	(%)	(%)
Cost of Goods Sold	36.1	66.4	35.0	36.5	40.4	36.5	30.2
Gross Profit	63.9	33.6	65.0	63.5	59.6	63.5	69.8
Rent	12.4	9.4	7.5	13.4	6.5	9.4	16.0
Oper. Exp.	32.8	24.2	37.0	53.2	43.7	37.0	50.3
EBIT	31.1	9.4	28.0	10.3	15.9	15.9	19.5
Net Income	31.1	9.4	28.0	10.3	15.9	15.9	19.5
DE*	31.1	11.5	28.0	10.3	26.4	26.4	22.5

Source: Pratt's Stats™. Used with permission of Business Valuation Resources.

[a] Discretionary earnings defined by *Pratt's Stats™* as net income plus owner's compensation, noncash charges, interest and taxes. Using this definition Wildcat Subs' DE = $38,000 in 1999.

IDENTIFICATION AND SELECTION OF VALUATION MULTIPLES

Now that we are satisfied with the comparative analysis of our subject relative to the selected guideline transactions, we can start the process of evaluating the various pricing multiples reported by each of the data services. According to the third edition of *Valuing Small Businesses and Professional Practices*,[1] the selection and

Exhibit 13.11   *Pratt's Stats™* Ratio Comparison

	Selective *Pratt's Stats™* Transactions				Wildcat Subs
	Number of Observations	Upper Limit of Range	Lower Limit of Range	Median	
Activity Ratios[a]					
Inventory Turnover	4	157.8	8.2	94.2	26.5
Fixed Asset Turnover	3	7.0	3.4	5.6	2.7
Total Asset Turnover	4	3.6	2.6	2.9	1.7
Leverage Ratio					
Fixed-Charges Coverage[b]	5	4.7	1.8	3.4	2.2
Profitability Ratios					
Gross Profit Margin	5	65.0%	33.6%	63.5%	69.8%
Net Profit Margin	5	31.1%	9.4%	15.9%	19.5%
Return on Total Assets	4	100.8%	26.5%	35.6%	35.1%

Source: Pratt's Stats™. Used with permission of Business Valuation Resources.

[a] Activity ratios calculated using year-end 1999 asset account balances.

[b] Assumes rent expense is equal to fixed charges.

Exhibit 13.12 Qualitative Aspects of Selected *Pratt's Stats*™ Transactions

Date of Sale	Location	Years in Business	Number of Employees	Business Type	Lease Details
6/18/99	Cobb, GA	5	5	S Corporation	9.5 Yrs. Remaining + 5 Yr. Option
4/20/99	Greenville, SC	1	3	L.L.C.	0.5 Yr. Remaining
3/5/99	Fulton, GA	1	3	Sole Proprietorship	4 Yrs. Remaining
8/7/97	N/A	N/A	N/A	Sole Proprietorship	5 Yrs. Remaining
7/24/97	Venice, FL	3	2	S Corporation	3 Yrs. Remaining + 3 Yr. Option
Wildcat Subs					
N/A	Lexington, KY	5	5	Sole Proprietorship	5 Yrs. Remaining + 5 Yr. Option

Source: Pratt's Stats™. Used with permission of Business Valuation Resources.

weighting of valuation multiples hinges on four general aspects of the available information:

1. Number of data points available
2. Comparability of data measurements
3. Comparability of data patterns
4. Apparent market reliance

As we can see from Exhibit 13.13, each of the data services reported sale price/net sales and sale price/DE multiples, providing us with 22 restaurant sale observations.

The second issue raised for consideration is ensuring that a reasonable basis for comparison exists for our subject's fundamental financial data and the selected valuation multiple. This issue was also raised in conjunction with the comparative analysis of our subject and the selected guideline transaction companies. For example, in the course of comparing our subject to the selected *BIZCOMPS®, IBA Market Data Base,* and *Pratt's Stats™* transactions, we adjusted Wildcat Subs' measures of return according to the stated definition of return cited by each of the services used. In this manner we avoided the pitfalls associated with apples-to-oranges comparisons.

The last issue for consideration concerns the apparent market reliance placed on each particular valuation multiple. According to the authors of *Valuing Small Businesses and Professional Practices,* this is often demonstrated by how "tightly clustered or widely dispersed" observed valuation multiples are in relationship to each other.[2] In Exhibit 13.14, each of the selected multiples demonstrated a low coefficient of variation, a statistical measure of dispersion. In particular, the price/sales exhibited the tightest range of coefficient of variation for the reported guideline transactions. Accordingly, we will consider all the multiples discussed in the valuation of Wildcat Subs.

VALUATION OF WILDCAT SUBS

Given the preceding analysis of our subject and selected comparable guideline transactions, we can proceed with valuing a 100% ownership interest in the assets of

Exhibit 13.13 Number of Observations for Selected Valuation Multiples

Valuation Multiple	Price / Sales	Price / DE[a]
BIZCOMPS®	12	12
IBA Market Database	5	5
Pratt's Stats™	5	5

Source: Data from *BIZCOMPS®,* Institute of Business Appraisers *Market Data Base,* and *Pratt's Stats™.* Used with permission.

[a] Discretionary earnings = net income plus owners compensation, noncash charges, interest, and taxes.

Exhibit 13.14   Coefficient of Variation for Selected Valuation Multiples

Valuation Multiple	Price / Sales	Price / DE[a]
BIZCOMPS®	0.32	0.39
IBA Market Database	0.32	0.35
Pratt's Stats™	0.31	0.46

Source: Data from *BIZCOMPS®*, Institute of Business Appraisers *Market Data Base,* and *Pratt's Stats™.* Used with permission.

[a] Discretionary earnings = net income plus owners compensation, noncash charges, interest, and taxes.

Wildcat Subs. Exhibit 13.15 presents the median valuation multiples reported by each of the reviewed data sources that we will use as a starting point for this process.

We will use the comparative analysis of our subject to each of the samples of guideline transactions to adjust each of the median multiples applied to Wildcat Subs' fundamental financial data. For example, Wildcat Subs' SDCF/sales was only marginally higher than the median reported by our sample of *BIZCOMPS®* transactions; accordingly, we will not adjust the price/sales multiple reported by *BIZCOMPS®*.

Because of the similarity between our subject's and the IBA sample's return measure, as well as the limited information regarding the risk characteristics of the selected IBA transactions, we will also elect to use the median price/sales multiple reported by the IBA.

The results of our comparative analysis using data from *Pratt's Stats™* provided mixed results. Indeed, Wildcat Subs' risk characteristics were considerably worse, as evidenced by a comparison of activity ratios, than those of the guideline transactions.

In particular, our subject's DE as a percentage of sales was 15% lower than the median indicated for the sample of *Pratt's Stats™* transactions. Nevertheless, Wildcat Subs' profitability measures were somewhat similar to the median reported for the selected *Pratt's Stats™* transactions. We will adjust the median price/sales multiple reported by *Pratt's Stats™* downward by 15% to account for the relative differences in risk characteristics.

Finally, we have elected to use the median discretionary earnings multiple calculated for each of the services as there is insufficient quantifiable information with respect to the observed businesses' risk characteristics to make meaningful adjustments.

Exhibit 13.15   Median Guideline Transaction Valuation Multiples

Median Valuation Multiple	Price / Sales	Price / DE[a]
BIZCOMPS®	0.43	2.0
IBA Market Database	0.36	1.8
Pratt's Stats™	0.39	2.2

Source: Data from *BIZCOMPS®*, Institute of Business Appraisers *Market Data Base,* and *Pratt's Stats™.* Used with permission.

[a] Discretionary earnings = net income plus owners compensation, noncash charges, interest and taxes.

Exhibit 13.16 Application of Indicated Pricing Multiples to Wildcat Subs Fundamental Financial Data

	Price/Sales			Price/DE		
	BIZCOMPS®	IBA	*Pratt's Stats*™	*BIZCOMPS®*	IBA	*Pratt's Stats*™
Median Multiple	0.43	0.36	0.39	2.0	1.8	2.2
Adjustment Factor	--	--	-15%	--	--	--
Adjusted Multiple	0.43	0.36	0.33	2.0	1.8	2.2
Wildcat Sub's Fundamental	$169,000	$169,000	$169,000	$38,000	$38,000	$38,000
Indicated Value	$72,670	$60,840	$55,770	$76,000	$68,400	$83,600

Source: Data from *BIZCOMPS®*, Institute of Business Appraisers *Market Data Base*, and *Pratt's Stats*™. Used with permission.

Exhibit 13.17 Application of Valuation Multiples

	BIZCOMPS®			IBA Market Database			Pratt's Stats™		
	Value Indication	Weighting Factor	Weighted Value	Value Indication	Weighting Factor	Weighted Value	Value Indication	Weighting Factor	Weighted Value
Price/Sales	$72,670	0.50	$36,335	$60,840	0.50	$30,420	$55,770	0.50	$27,885
Price/DE	$76,000	0.50	$38,000	$68,400	0.50	$34,200	$83,600	0.50	$41,800
Weighted Value			$76,435			$64,620			$69,685

Source: Data from BIZCOMPS®, Institute of Business Appraisers Market Data Base, and Pratt's Stats™. Used with permission.

[a] Weighted value includes $2,100 inventory balance.

RECONCILING VALUE CONCLUSIONS

Exhibit 13.16 provides a visual recap of the adjustments discussed previously and presents the resulting implied values for Wildcat Subs. The indicated values range from $55,770 to $83,600, with the lowest indicated values resulting from the application of the various adjusted price/sales multiples to Wildcat Subs' fundamental financial data. Nonetheless, given the relatively low coefficient of variation for the reported price/sales multiples, a 50% weighting factor is appropriate for this multiple. Provided the business continues to be operated in its present fashion, the reported price to discretionary earnings multiples should reflect the risk characteristics inherent in this type of business. Furthermore, earnings represent the primary potential return available to a prospective investor and therefore should be afforded considerable weight in reaching an ultimate value conclusion. Therefore, we will equally weight the reported price/sales and price/earnings multiples. The weighting of each multiple and the resultant range of value indications is presented in Exhibit 13.17. The value indication reached using *BIZCOMPS*® data was adjusted upward by $2,100 to reflect the assumed transfer of Wildcat Subs' inventory as part of the proposed sale transaction. Considering the narrow range of values indicated using the merger and acquisition method, we will appraise Wildcat Submarine Shop at $70,000.

ADDENDUM IF VALUING FOR OTHER PURPOSES

The analysis presented was for the purpose of pricing the company for sale and therefore excluded cash and accounts receivable, because they would not be transferred, and did not subtract liabilities, because they would not be assumed by the buyer. If valuing for some other purpose, such as divorce, one would have to add the cash and accounts receivable to the indicated value and subtract the liabilities.[3]

Notes

1. Shannon P. Pratt, Robert F. Reilly, and Robert P. Schweihs, *Valuing Small Businesses and Professional Practices,* 3rd ed. (New York: McGraw-Hill, 1998), 323–324.
2. Id., at 32.
3. A complete valuation report would contain exhibits showing the adjustments and reasons for each, but they have been omitted here for brevity.

Chapter 14

Medium-size Service Company Sample Case— Software Developer*

Valuation Assignment
    Objective and Purpose of the Appraisal
    Definition and Premise of Value
    Summary Description of Colossal Software Corporation
    Valuation Terms and Conditions

Economic Outlook
    United States Economic Outlook
    Computer Software Industry Outlook

Fundamental Position of the Company
    History
    Employees
    Capitalization and Ownership
    Dividend Policy
    Prior Transaction in Colossal Software's Stock

Selection of Market Data
    Guideline Public Company Data
    Merger and Acquisition Data

Financial Statement Analysis
    Balance Sheets
    Income Statements
    Ratio Analysis
    Peer Comparison
        Industry Statistics
        Guideline Public Companies
        Guideline Transactions

Identification and Application of Valuation Multiples
    MVIC Multiple Adjustments
    Common Equity Pricing Multiple Adjustments

Valuation of Colossal Software

*This hypothetical case study takes place in early 1999.

Colossal Software is a hypothetical company contrived to illustrate the guideline public company and merger and acquisition methods of the market approach. Any resemblance between Colossal Software and other real-world companies is purely coincidental. Readers should not be concerned whether the fact pattern presented resembles the reader's perception of reality in the software industry.

VALUATION ASSIGNMENT

On March 27, 1999, the minority shareholders of Colossal Software Corporation (CSC, or "the company") were offered $45 per share in a squeeze-out merger and are concerned that this offer represents a substantial discount from the value of their ownership interest.

Objective and Purpose of the Appraisal

At the request of the minority shareholders of Colossal Software, we have conducted a limited appraisal of CSC's common equity with the objective of determining the value of five minority interests totaling 49% of the beneficial ownership interest in the common stock of CSC as of March 27, 1999.

The purpose of our limited appraisal is to assist the minority shareholders in deciding whether to proceed with a dissenting stockholder action against the majority shareholder of CSC.

Definition and Premise of Value

CSC's state of incorporation is Delaware. Under Delaware's appraisal rights statute, the shares in a dissenting shareholder action must be valued under the fair value standard.[1] The statute directs the court to determine "fair value exclusive of any element of value arising from the accomplishment or expectation of the merger or consolidation" and to take into account "all relevant factors."[2]

A proceeding under Delaware's appraisal statute, *8 Del. C. § 262*, requires that the Court of Chancery determine the "fair value" of the dissenting stockholders' shares. The fairness concept has been said to implicate two considerations: fair dealing and fair price. *Weinberger v. UOP Inc.*, 457 A.2d at 711. Since the fairness of the merger process is not in dispute, the Court of Chancery's task here was to value what has been taken from the shareholder: "viz. his proportionate interest in a going concern." *Tri-Continental Corp. v. Battye*, Del. Supr., 31 Del. Ch. 523, 74 A.2d 71, 72 (1950). To this end the company must be first valued as an operating entity by application of traditional value factors, weighted as required, but without regard to post-merger events or other possible business combinations. *See Bell v. Kirby Lumber Corp.*, Del. Supr., 413 A.2d 137 (1980). The dissenting shareholder's proportionate interest is determined only after the company as an entity has been valued. In that determination the Court of Chancery is not required to apply further weighting factors at the shareholder level, such as discounts to minority shares for asserted lack of marketability.[3]

Additionally, CSC's stock is to be valued under the assumption that the business will continue to be operated as a going-concern for the foreseeable future.

Summary Description of Colossal Software Corporation

Colossal Software is a closely held C Corporation specializing in performing contract programming services for the development and support of custom electronic enterprise planning (ERP) software for small to midsize manufacturing companies. Operations are conducted from a leased facility located in Boston, Massachusetts. As of the company's fiscal year ended December 31, 1998, CSC reported operating and net income of $3.6 million and $2.3 million, respectively, on revenues of $69.5 million.

Valuation Terms and Conditions

Audited and unaudited financial data with respect to CSC's financial position and results of operations were provided by CSC and have been accepted without independent verification or confirmation. Furthermore, this appraisal was limited to consideration of only that data available as of March 27, 1999, and deemed relevant in the application of the guideline public company and merger and acquisition methods of the market approach.

The valuation opinion expressed in this limited appraisal is prepared solely for the purpose stated herein and is not intended for use under any other circumstance or fact set than that outlined in the preceding sections.

ECONOMIC OUTLOOK

In conducting our appraisal of the fair value of CSC's common equity, we considered the consensus forecasts for the U.S. economy and software industry that prevailed as of March 27, 1999.

United States Economic Outlook

The overall economic outlook for the United States at the end of 1998 appeared to be guardedly optimistic for Colossal Software's business. In particular, third-quarter 1998 gross domestic product (GDP) increased at a 3.7% annualized rate versus 3.0% in the third quarter of 1997 and was expected to decline somewhat in 1999. Consumer price index (CPI) and producer price index (PPI), key indicators of inflation for the U.S. economy, remained steady between the second and third quarters of 1998, easing inflationary concerns. Indeed, inflation, measured at 1.5% as of November 1998, had actually decreased from 1.8% in November of 1997 and was expected to remain at similar levels for 1999. Unemployment rates also improved modestly during the same time period, decreasing from 4.6% in 1997 to 4.4% in 1998. Interest rates, as measured by the 30-year U.S. Treasury yield, also inched lower in 1998, ending the year at 5.09%. This trend was expected to continue in 1999, with the 30-year U.S. Treasury yield projected to approach 4.85% toward the latter part of the year. Business-to-business sales increased 6% between October of 1997 and 1998 and were expected to remain strong during 1999. Finally, most major stock market indices posted strong double-digit growth in 1998, with the Standard & Poor's (S&P) 500 and NASDAQ Composite indices recording growth of 31.5% and 44.3%, respectively. Although estimates of growth for these two market indices in 1999 varied depending on the source, most predictions were bullish in their outlook.

Computer Software Industry Outlook

Although macroeconomic conditions in the United States at the end of 1998 indicated that the business environment would remain moderately favorable, microeconomic indicators for the computer software industry were decidedly much more promising. U.S. Market Trends and Forecasts estimated that the value of the data processing and network services market would increase 104%, from $42.7 billion in 1997 to $86.9 billion in 2003. Additionally, the compound annual growth rate (CAGR) for the data processing services market over the same time period was forecasted to be 12.6%. According to AMR Research Inc., a Boston-based consulting firm, the ERP market was expected to top $16 billion in 1998, with 1999 growth predicted to approximate 22%. Year 2000 (Y2K) preparedness spending continued to soften demand for ERP software products in the near term; nonetheless, AMR expected long-term market growth to accelerate to 35% after 2000 with the market value reaching a projected $66.6 billion by 2003. Despite increasing competition and the rapid pace of technological advances in the computer software industry, by most accounts, the outlook for well-positioned companies with differentiated markets, products, or services remained overwhelming positive at the end of 1998.

FUNDAMENTAL POSITION OF THE COMPANY

Headquartered in Boston, Massachusetts, Colossal Software was incorporated in Delaware on September 5, 1991. The company's primary line of business centers on the development, implementation, and support of ERP software solutions for midsize manufacturing companies with annual revenues between $3 million and $1 billion. CSC's software solutions and services facilitate the enterprise-wide management of resources and information to reduce order fulfillment cycles, improve operating efficiencies, and measure performance against defined objectives.

History

Colossal Software's short history dates back to 1985, when the company was founded by Peter Wilson, chief executive officer (CEO) and chairman of the board. During the mid- to late 1980s, CSC sustained consistent operating losses while developing and promoting market acceptance for its software products. The company recorded its first profitable year in 1990 and, with the exception of 1995, continues to anticipate profitable growth for the near-term future.

According to CSC's management team, much of the company's recent success has been in large part due to its strategy of focusing marketing and development resources on industries inadequately served by ERP software providers. Nonetheless, CSC faced increasing competition in almost all of its core market segments. To combat the threat posed by new entrants, CSC's management team has sought to strengthen the company's competitive position by merging with or acquiring companies with complementary technologies and/or markets. To execute this strategy, CSC borrowed $10 million in 1995, bearing interest at 8.5% and payable in quarterly installments of principal and interest.

On January 1, 1997, CSC acquired substantially all of the assets of ERPWare, a development-stage corporation, for a cash consideration of $2.5 million. The company's second substantial acquisition occurred on June 4, 1998, when CSC purchased the exclusive rights to license certain proprietary technologies developed by Controlled Process Production for $4.5 million in cash. Each of the acquisitions was expected to enhance CSC's core services offerings.

Employees

At the end of 1998, CSC's workforce consisted of 35 salaried professionals, 60 hourly or contract employees, and 15 part-time employees. Of the 95 regular employees, roughly 15% were software engineers, 25% support engineers, 30% sales associates; the remaining 30% fulfilling support roles.

Colossal Software's organizational structure had remained relatively flat with each manager reporting directly to the CEO, Peter Wilson. Key management personnel consisted of

- *Peter Wilson* (58), founder, president, and CEO of CSC, responsible for corporate strategy and financial planning.
- *James Watts* (42), vice president and director of marketing, responsible for overseeing the sales and marketing staff as well as assisting in corporate planning.

- *George Grevelis* (36), director of software development, responsible for over-seeing engineering activities as well as assisting in corporate planning.
- *David Laken* (37), operations manager, responsible for human resource planning and oversight.

Capitalization and Ownership

Colossal Software was capitalized with one class of voting common stock. As of the valuation date, CSC had issued an outstanding 1 million of an authorized 10 million shares of $0 par value voting common stock. Table 14.1 shows beneficial ownership of CSC's common stock on March 27, 1999.

Table 14.1

Shareholder	Number of Shares Owned	Percentage of Total Outstanding Shares
Peter Wilson	510,000	51%
Craig Brown	150,000	15%
Devoe Family Trust	140,000	14%
James Watts	100,000	10%
George Grevelis	50,000	5%
David Laken	50,000	5%
Total	1,000,000	100%

Dividend Policy

Historically, Colossal Software had retained all of its earnings to help fund growth, and is expected to continue this policy for the foreseeable future.

Prior Transactions in Colossal Software's Stock

No sales of the company's stock have occurred in the preceding six years before the appraisal date.

SELECTION OF MARKET DATA

We elected to value CSC's stock by using both the guideline public company and merger and acquisition methods of the market approach. In particular, we will use the observed prices that investors are willing to pay for an ownership interest in a company substantially similar to CSC to develop pricing multiples to apply to our subject's fundamental financial data, thereby estimating the value of a like ownership interest in Colossal Software.

To establish a reasonable basis for comparison between our subject and the selected guideline companies and transactions, market data was selected according to these criteria:

- Primary SIC (Standard Industrial Classification) code of 7371, 7372, or 7373
- Similar business description or market
- Revenues between $1 million and $750 million
- Positive operating earnings for the latest reported fiscal year-end
- Positive cash flow (defined as net income plus depreciation) for the latest reported fiscal year-end
- Businesses located in the United States

Guideline Public Company Data

A search was conducted for companies with a primary SIC code of 7371 to 7373. Each filing identified was subsequently examined to determine whether the business described therein satisfied our stated search criteria. Finally, of the businesses that met our initial search criteria, only those companies with actively traded stocks, as evidenced by listing on a major exchange, and at least five years of financial data were considered for this valuation.

A brief description of each of the selected three guideline companies follows:

- *Best Software, Inc.* (Best), incorporated in Virginia in 1982. Best is a leading supplier of corporate resource management software solutions, designed to help corporations better manage their people, assets, and budgeting processes. Best reported operating income and net income of $6.8 million and $5.3 million on revenues of $69.3 million for its fiscal year ended December 31, 1998.
- *IDX Systems Corporation* (IDX), incorporated in Vermont in 1969. IDX offers health care information solutions that enable health care organizations to redesign patient care and other work-flow processes in order to improve efficiency and quality. IDX reported operating income and net income of $47.1 million and $30.2 million on revenues of $321.7 million for its fiscal year ended December 31, 1998.
- *Symix Systems Inc.* (Symix), founded in 1979. Symix designs, develops, markets, and supports integrated manufacturing, supply chain management, and financial and e-commerce software solutions for midsize manufacturing and distribution companies. Symix reported operating and net income of $2.0 million and ($1.4) million on revenues of $97.6 million for its fiscal year ended June 30, 1998.

Merger and Acquisition Data

Merger and acquisition data used to value Colossal Software were selected from transactions reported in the publications listed in Table 14.2.

Table 14.2

Publication/Data Service	Publisher
Done Deals Data	Practitioner's Publishing Co.
Pratt's Stats™ Private Business Sale Database	Business Valuation Resources

Transactions were initially screened according to the general criteria previously described. In addition, transactions exhibiting any of these characteristics were excluded from our consideration:

- Asset sale
- Sale of less than 100% of the outstanding common equity
- Contingent purchase price

Of the 250 plus transactions identified in our initial screening process, only 5 satisfied our narrowed criteria. It should also be noted that while all of the data services provided an efficient and easy method of screening potential guideline transactions, ultimately we relied on SEC filings for our analysis of each of the selected transactions.

A brief description of each of the selected guideline transactions follows.

- *BGS Systems Inc.* (BGS), a public corporation, was purchased by BMC Software on March 27, 1998, for a cash consideration of $285.0 million. BGS was organized in Massachusetts in 1975 and designs, develops, markets, and supports performance and capacity management software support. BGS reported operating and net income of $13.0 million and $9.1 million on revenues of $48.6 million for its fiscal year ended January 31, 1997.

- *Eclipse Information Systems Inc.* (Eclipse), a private subchapter S corporation, was purchased by New ZMax Corporation on December 14, 1998 for a cash and stock consideration of $7.4 million. Located in Illinois, Eclipse was incorporated in 1990 and performs management and information systems consulting services as well as resells certain hardware and software products to its customers. Eclipse reported operating and net income of $1.9 million and $0.1 million on revenues of $5.4 million for its fiscal year ended December 31, 1997.

- *Interactive Group Inc.* (Interactive), a public corporation, was purchased by Dataworks Corporation on September 29, 1997, for a stock consideration of $57.0 million. Located in San Diego, California, Interactive develops, markets, implements, and supports integrated business information systems that allow manufacturers to manage their enterprise-wide information requirements. Interactive reported operating and net income of $2.0 million and $1.3 million on revenues of $56.2 million for its fiscal year ended December 31, 1996.

- *Logic Works Inc.* (Logic), a public corporation, was purchased by Platinum Technology, Inc., on May 28, 1998, for a stock consideration of $174.8 million. Located in Princeton, New Jersey, Logic provides client/server database design and business process modeling software. Logic reported operating and net income of $6.0 million and $4.6 million on revenues of $50.5 million for its fiscal year ended December 31, 1997.

- *PCM Inc.* (PCM), a private subchapter S corporation, was purchased by Aztec Technology Partners, Inc., on July 29, 1998, for a cash consideration of $54.0 million. Located in Illinois, PCM provides networking services, technical support and maintenance, and hardware and software procurement to business clients. PCM reported operating and net income of $7.2 million and $7.0 million on revenues of $34.7 million for its fiscal year ended December 31, 1997.

FINANCIAL STATEMENT ANALYSIS

Audited financial statements reflecting the company's financial condition and the results of operations for each of the five years ended December 31, 1994, through December 31, 1998, were provided by counsel for the minority shareholders. To the best of our knowledge, these statements accurately reflect the operations and position of the company. After reviewing the statements provided, we adjusted the company's income statement to provide a more accurate picture of CSC's earning capacity. In particular, we eliminated a $78,000 net expense resulting from the settlement of a contract dispute with a customer recorded as an extraordinary expense for the fiscal year ended December 31, 1996. As a result of the adjustment, the reported net income of $921,000 for 1996 was increased to $999,000. No other adjustments were deemed necessary given the nature of the valuation assignment. Colossal Software's adjusted balance sheets and income statements are reproduced here as Exhibit 14.1 and Exhibit 14.2, respectively.

Balance Sheets

Between 1994 and 1998, CSC's assets grew 18.5%, increasing from $29.0 million to $57.0 million. Current assets represented the majority of the company's assets, comprising 68.4% of CSC's total asset balance at the end of 1998. Accounts receivable, the single largest asset account, increased 151% to $17.3 million in 1998 from $6.9 million in 1994, reflecting the company's continued revenue growth.

Exhibit 14.1 Colossal Software Adjusted Balance Sheets

	December 31					December 31				
	1998 ($000)	1997 ($000)	1996 ($000)	1995 ($000)	1994 ($000)	1998 (%)	1997 (%)	1996 (%)	1995 (%)	1994 (%)
Current Assets										
Cash and Cash Equivalents	$ 9,209	$ 9,962	$ 9,080	$ 8,752	$ 6,012	16.1	19.4	20.9	22.1	20.8
Short-term Investments	7,135	6,180	8,289	8,074	5,284	12.5	12.1	19.1	20.4	18.2
Accounts Receivable, Net	17,296	13,963	10,583	9,602	6,892	30.3	27.2	24.4	24.2	23.8
Other Current Assets	5,365	4,948	3,040	3,267	1,583	9.4	9.7	7.0	8.2	5.5
Total Current Assets	$ 39,005	$ 35,053	$ 30,992	$ 29,695	$ 19,771	68.4	68.4	71.5	74.8	68.3
Equipment, Furniture and Fixtures, Net	7,092	6,535	5,280	3,850	3,211	12.4	12.7	12.2	9.7	11.1
Capitalized Software Costs, Net	2,103	2,217	2,408	2,984	2,786	3.7	4.3	5.6	7.5	9.6
Intangible Assets, Net	7,041	6,100	2,928	2,731	2,876	12.3	11.9	6.8	6.9	9.9
Other Assets	1,812	1,360	1,760	413	314	3.2	2.7	4.1	1.0	1.1
Total Assets	$ 57,053	$ 51,265	$ 43,368	$ 39,673	$ 28,958	100.0	100.0	100.0	100.0	100.0
Current Liabilities										
Accounts Payable	$ 4,001	$ 3,589	$ 2,420	$ 1,325	$ 1,563	7.0	7.0	5.6	3.3	5.4
Other Accrued Liabilities	3,909	3,159	2,180	1,742	1,449	6.9	6.2	5.0	4.4	5.0
Deferred Revenue	9,335	7,969	5,230	3,567	2,890	16.4	15.5	12.1	9.0	10.0
Current Portion of Long-term Liabilities	856	787	724	665	0	1.5	1.5	1.7	1.7	0.0
Total Current Liabilities	$ 18,101	$ 15,504	$ 10,554	$ 7,299	$ 5,902	31.7	30.2	24.3	18.4	20.4
Deferred Income Taxes	1,014	816	523	391	212	1.8	1.6	1.2	1.0	0.7
Long-term Liabilities	6,967	7,824	8,611	9,335	0	12.2	15.3	19.9	23.5	0.0
Total Liabilities	$ 26,082	$ 24,144	$ 19,688	$ 17,025	$ 6,114	45.7	47.1	45.4	42.9	21.1
Shareholders' Equity										
Common Stock	22,181	20,625	19,334	19,301	19,001	38.9	40.2	44.6	48.7	65.6
Retained Earnings	8,790	6,496	4,346	3,347	3,843	15.4	12.7	10.0	8.4	13.3
Total Shareholders' Equity	$ 30,971	$ 27,121	$ 23,680	$ 22,648	$ 22,844	54.3	52.9	54.6	57.1	78.9
Total Liabilities and Shareholders' Equity	$ 57,053	$ 51,265	$ 43,368	$ 39,673	$ 28,958	100.0	100.0	100.0	100.0	100.0

Exhibit 14.2 Colossal Software Adjusted Income Statements

	Fiscal Years Ended December 31					Fiscal Years Ended December 31				
	1998 ($000)	1997 ($000)	1996 ($000)	1995 ($000)	1994 ($000)	1998 (%)	1997 (%)	1996 (%)	1995 (%)	1994 (%)
Revenues										
Software Licenses	$ 35,209	28,944	21,153	$ 17,544	$ 12,351	50.7	49.5	52.9	58.8	57.1
Support & Other Services	34,272	29,523	18,848	12,294	9,275	49.3	50.5	47.1	41.2	42.9
Total Revenues	$ 69,481	58,467	40,001	$ 29,838	$ 21,626	100.0	100.0	100.0	100.0	100.0
Cost of Revenues										
Software Licenses	6,750	5,553	3,937	4,229	3,500	9.7	9.5	9.8	14.2	16.2
Support & Other Services	22,848	19,477	12,347	9,374	7,517	32.9	33.3	30.9	31.4	34.8
Total Cost of Revenues	$ 29,598	25,030	16,284	$ 13,603	$ 11,017	42.6	42.8	40.7	45.6	50.9
Gross Profit	$ 39,883	33,437	23,717	$ 16,235	$ 10,609	57.4	57.2	59.3	54.4	49.1
Operating Expenses										
Sales and Marketing	16,883	14,244	10,008	7,006	4,745	24.3	24.4	25.0	23.5	21.9
Research and Development	9,914	7,329	5,008	3,330	2,096	14.3	12.5	12.5	11.2	9.7
General and Administrative	7,352	5,959	4,124	3,063	2,016	10.6	10.2	10.3	10.3	9.3
Depreciation and Amortization	2,086	1,737	1,177	839	546	3.0	3.0	2.9	2.8	2.5
Total Operating Expenses	$ 36,235	29,269	20,317	$ 14,238	$ 9,403	52.2	50.1	50.8	47.7	43.5
Income (Loss) from Operations	$ 3,648	4,168	3,400	$ 1,997	$ 1,206	5.3	7.1	8.5	6.7	5.6
Interest Expense	638	707	771	829	0	0.9	1.2	1.9	2.8	0.0
Other Income (Expense), Net	814	123	(625)	(610)	(317)	1.2	0.2	(1.6)	(2.0)	(1.5)
Income (Loss) before Income Taxes	$ 3,824	3,584	2,004	$ 558	$ 889	5.5	6.1	5.0	1.9	4.1
Provision (Benefit) for Income Taxes	1,530	1,434	1,005	1,054	756	2.2	2.5	2.5	3.5	3.5
Income before Extraordinary Item	$ 2,294	2,150	999	$ (496)	$ 133	3.3	3.7	2.5	(1.7)	0.6
Extraordinary Item, Net of Taxes	0	0	0	0	0	0.0	0.0	0.0	0.0	0.0
Net Income	$ 2,294	2,150	999	$ (496)	$ 133	3.3	3.7	2.5	(1.7)	0.6
Income (Loss) before Extraordinary Gain per Common Share - Basic	$ 2.29	2.15	1.00	$ (0.50)	$ 0.13					
Common shares outstanding (000)	1,000	1,000	1,000	1,000	1,000					
Income (Loss) before Extraordinary Gain per Common Share - Diluted	$ 2.29	2.15	1.00	$ (0.50)	$ 0.13					
Common shares outstanding assuming dilution (000)	1,000	1,000	1,000	1,000	1,000					

Relative to the company's other assets, cash and short-term investments remained stable during the same time period, accounting for 29% of total assets as of December 31, 1998. With the exception of capitalized software costs, CSC's non-current assets also exhibited strong growth in the years preceding 1999, increasing 96% from $9.2 million in 1994 to $18.0 million in 1998.

As of December 31, 1998, the company's current liabilities and total liabilities amounted to $18.1 and $26.1 million, implying a compound annual growth rate of 32.3% and 43.7%, respectively. Deferred revenue, the largest current liability account, consisted primarily of ongoing support agreements with clients and was expected to continue to approximate 27% of support revenues for the near-term future. Similarly, accounts payable and accrued liabilities were each expected to stabilize at 6% of total revenues for fiscal 1999 and beyond.

As of December 31, 1998, long-term liabilities totaled 12% of total liabilities and equity. Consistent with management's long-term growth strategy, leverage was expected to remain an important component of the company's capital structure. Shareholder's equity had grown modestly since 1994, totaling $31.0 million as of December 31, 1998. Nonetheless, equity represented only 54% of CSC's liabilities and equity, down from 79% as of December 31, 1994.

Income Statements

CSC's year-to-year revenue growth had dropped from 38% in 1994 to 19% in 1998, reflecting decreased revenues associated with increased competition and Y2K spending. Despite this trend, CSC's CAGR for revenues remained well above that of the industry as a whole, at 34%. With revenue growth in the ERP industry expected to reach 35% after 2000, CSC's 1999 revenue growth was predicted to approximate 27% due in large part to continued strong software sales growth, 22% in 1998.

Cost of goods sold had decreased from 51% of sales in 1994 to 43% of sales in 1998, primarily as a result of decreasing software licensing expense over the same time period, and was expected to stabilize at approximately 45% of sales for the 1999 fiscal year. Operating expenses, however, had increased relative to sales from 44% in 1994 to 52% in 1998. Much of the growth in operating expenses resulted from increased research and development and general and administrative expenses associated with expansion activities. Operating expenses were expected to decrease from 52% to 46% of sales during 1999 as recent acquisitions were assimilated into operations.

Colossal Software's net profit margin exhibited a pattern of uneven growth over the five years ended December 31, 1998. In particular, CSC's reported net profit margin had increased from less than 1% in 1994 to just over 3% in 1998. Given management's growth and operating expectations for 1999, CSC's net profit margin was projected to approximate 5% of sales in 1999.

Ratio Analysis

Upon review of Colossal Software's financial and operating ratios for the years ended December 31, 1994, through 1998 (presented here as Exhibit 14.3), we find that CSC's liquidity dropped as measured by the current and quick ratios. This trend was in large part due to the growth of deferred revenues relative to that of current assets. However, at 2.2× and 1.9× current liabilities, both the current and quick ratios were within reasonable limits as of December 31, 1998. Furthermore, working capital was expected to remain stable at roughly $20 million during 1999 and 2000.

Exhibit 14.3   Colossal Software Financial and Operating Ratio Analysis

	Fiscal Years Ended December 31				
	1998	1997	1996	1995	1994
LIQUIDITY RATIOS					
Current Ratio	2.2	2.3	2.9	4.1	3.3
Quick Ratio	1.9	1.9	2.6	3.6	3.1
Working Capital ($MM)	20.9	19.5	20.4	22.4	13.9
ACTIVITY RATIOS					
Accounts Receivable Turnover	4.4	4.8	4.0	3.6	N/A[a]
Average Collection Period	82.1	76.6	92.1	100.9	N/A
Fixed Asset Turnover	10.2	9.9	8.8	8.5	N/A
Asset Turnover	1.3	1.2	1.0	0.9	N/A
Working Capital Turnover	3.4	2.9	1.9	1.6	N/A
COVERAGE/LEVERAGE RATIOS					
Total Debt to Total Assets (%)	45.7	47.1	45.4	42.9	21.1
Long-term Debt to Equity (%)	22.5	28.8	36.4	41.2	N/A
Times Interest Earned	5.7	5.9	4.4	2.4	N/A
PROFITABILITY RATIOS (%)					
Fixed-charges Coverage Ratio[b]	1.8	2.0	1.7	1.2	2.0
Gross Profit Margin	57.4	57.2	59.3	54.4	49.1
Operating Profit Margin	5.3	7.1	8.5	6.7	5.6
Net Profit Margin	3.3	3.7	2.5	(1.7)	0.6
Cash Flow to Sales[c]	6.3	6.6	5.4	1.1	3.1
Return on Total Assets[d]	4.9	5.4	3.5	0.0	N/A
Return on Equity	7.4	7.9	4.2	(2.2)	0.6

[a] Not available.

[b] Fixed-charges coverage includes rent expense of $1.25 ($MM) per annum.

[c] Cash flow = net income plus depreciation and amortization expense.

[d] Tax rate of 40% used in return on assets calculation.

Activity ratios indicated that CSC's asset utilization was generally improving over the four fiscal years ended 1998. In particular, receivables turnover improved to 4.4× in 1998 versus 3.6× in 1995. This implied that the average collection period required for recovery of accounts receivable fell from 101 days to 82 days over the corresponding time frame. Fixed asset turnover, total asset turnover, and working capital turnover improved between 1995 and 1998, indicating that CSC was utilizing its assets more effectively.

Total debt as a percentage of total assets increased dramatically in 1995, reflecting the addition of long-term debt to CSC's capital structure. After 1995, the company's total liabilities fluctuated around 46% of total assets, and as of fiscal 1998, long-term debt had decreased to 23% of equity and 12% of total assets versus 41 and 24% in 1995, respectively. Interest expense coverage also improved subsequent to 1995, and at the end of 1998, CSC's EBIT (earnings before interest and taxes) was 5.7× its annual interest expense.

Profitability measures were for the most part mixed for CSC. In particular, fixed-charges coverage improved modestly over the interim period of 1996 through 1997 after the addition of long-term debt to the company's capital structure in 1995. However, in 1998, due to slowed revenue growth, fixed-charges coverage declined by 10% from 1997 levels. As previously discussed, CSC's gross profit margin of 57% was expected to decline to 55% of revenues by 1999 due to expected increases in cost of goods sold. Operating profit margin, despite successive declines in 1997 and 1998, was expected to approach 1996 levels once the company assimilated recent acquisitions into ongoing operations. Measures of return based on Colossal's net income (i.e., net profit margin, return on total assets, and return on equity) improved between 1994 and 1998 despite exhibiting a greater degree of volatility relative to other profitability measures. In particular, other income and expenses, consisting primarily of long-term investment income, contributed to the volatility observed in CSC's net income.

Peer Comparison

In addition to analyzing CSC's financial and operating trends over time, we also considered our subject's performance relative to other firms in the computer programming services industry. The insights provided by this analysis follows in the sections below.

Industry Statistics. Colossal Software's financial condition and operating performance was compared to that of similarly sized computer programming services companies as reported by Risk Management Association's *Annual Statement Studies* (RMA) and are presented here as Exhibit 14.4A and 14.4B. It should be noted that the ratios presented for CSC in Exhibit 14.4B were calculated using only the corresponding year's year-end financial data to provide a reasonable basis for comparison to RMA calculations and therefore will differ from the ratios presented in Exhibit 14.3.

As we can see from the common-size comparison of CSC and RMA balance sheet data, our subject company was substantially similar in terms of asset composition to that of the average firm reported by RMA. Indeed, Colossal Software's total current assets and fixed asset base were just below the averages reported by RMA at 68.4% versus 70.5% and 12.4% versus 15.5%, respectively. Furthermore, CSC's total liabilities as of December 31, 1998, were very similar to that of the RMA sample at 45.7% and 46.7%, respectively. However, the composition of the liabilities was significantly different with current liabilities as a percentage of assets for CSC, 20% lower than that of the RMA sample. In particular, this difference was attributable to CSC's lack of short-term borrowings and relatively low accounts payable. Finally, our subject's long-term debt, while considerably reduced since 1995, was 3.7× greater than the average reported by RMA.

A common-size comparison of our subject's income statements and RMA income statement data reveal that operating expenses (involving cost of goods sold) were marginally higher for our subject than that reported by RMA, 94.8% versus 93.2% in 1998. As a result operating and net income were slightly lower than the average reported by RMA.

An analysis of CSC's financial and operating ratios relative to those reported by RMA indicated that our subject exhibited typical liquidity levels, as measured by the current and quick ratios relative to other firms in the industry. Nonetheless, the impact of Colossal's debt service resulted in considerably lower coverage ratios than that of the average computer programming services firm. Consistent with our common size comparison of RMA industry statistics and CSC's financial data, we also found that our subject's overall leverage is similar to that of the average reported by RMA as measured relative to net worth for companies in this industry.

The most notable differences between our subject and those firms surveyed by RMA are found in the various measures of return reported by RMA relative to those calculated for CSC. In particular, Colossal Software ranked near the bottom 25% of all RMA respondents for both pretax return on tangible equity and on assets. The relatively low returns were due primarily to CSC's low asset turnover compared to the RMA sample, as well as its relatively higher interest expense.

Guideline Public Companies.   A comparison of Colossal Software's financial condition and operating performance with that of the selected guideline public companies is presented in Exhibits 14.5A and 14.5B.

As was the case with the comparative analysis conducted using RMA data, CSC's balance sheet composition as of December 31, 1998, was found to be substantially similar to that of the selected guideline public companies. In particular, our subject's current assets represented 68.4% of total assets relative to a median of 77.3% of total assets for the selected guideline public companies. Differences between the two were due primarily to CSC's lower short-term investments and

Exhibit 14.4A Colossal Software and RMA Common Size Financial Statements: SIC Code 7371—Services, Computer Programming

	1998		1997		1996		1995		1994	
	Subject	RMA	Subject	RMA	Subject	RMA	Subject	RMA	Subject	RMA
Number of Observations	1	54	1	59	1	39	1	25	1	26
Average Asset Size ($MM)	57	62	51	57	43	56	40	53	29	49
Average Sales Volume ($MM)	69	117	58	83	40	91	30	89	22	88
	%	%	%	%	%	%	%	%	%	%
Common Size Income Statements										
Net Sales	100.0	100.0	100.0	100.0	100.0	100.0	100.0	100.0	100.0	100.0
Cost of Goods Sold	42.6		42.8		40.7		45.6		50.9	
Gross Profit	57.4		57.2		59.3		54.4		49.1	
Operating Expenses	52.2	93.2	50.1	94.3	50.8	92.8	47.7	93.5	43.5	91.6
Operating Income	5.3	6.8	7.1	5.7	8.5	7.2	6.7	6.5	5.6	8.4
Other Income (Expense), Net	0.3	0.7	(1.0)	0.2	(3.5)	(0.4)	(4.8)	0.0	(1.5)	1.2
PRETAX PROFIT	5.5	7.5	6.1	5.5	5.0	7.6	1.9	6.5	4.1	7.2

Common Size Balance Sheets

ASSETS

Current Assets:										
Cash & Equivalents	28.6	22.1	31.5	23.9	40.1	19.7	42.4	17.3	39.0	17.7
Accts. & Notes Receivable (Trade)	30.3	41.2	27.2	38.1	24.4	40.1	24.2	39.2	23.8	45.9
Inventory	9.4	1.5	9.7	3.9		2.7		3.4		3.2
All Other Current Assets		5.8		5.8	5.5	5.5	8.2	6.0	5.5	4.0
Total Current Assets	68.4	70.5	68.4	71.7	71.5	67.9	74.8	65.9	68.3	70.8
Net Fixed Assets	12.4	15.5	12.7	14.4	12.2	16.2	9.7	18.7	11.1	14.1
Net Intangible Assets	12.3	7.5	11.9	4.8	6.8	5.8	6.9	7.7	9.9	8.0
Net Other Assets	6.9	6.6	7.0	9.1	9.6	10.1	8.6	7.7	10.7	7.1
TOTAL ASSETS	100.0	100.0	100.0	100.0	100.0	100.0	100.0	100.0	100.0	100.0

LIABILITIES & EQUITY

Liabilities:										
Current Liabilities:										
Notes Payable		8.7	1.5	4.9	1.7	7.4	1.7	5.1	0.0	4.2
Current Mat. LTD	1.5	1.0	7.0	3.7	5.6	1.1	3.3	1.6		2.2
Accounts & Notes Payable (Trade)	7.0	9.9		11.7		12.3		11.2	5.4	11.3
Income Taxes Payable		0.9		1.5		0.8		1.4		2.3
All Other Current Liabilities	23.2	18.9	21.7	21.7	17.1	22.4	13.4	17.0	15.0	20.9
Total Current Liabilities	31.7	39.4	30.2	43.4	24.3	43.9	18.4	36.3	20.4	40.9
Total Long-term Debt	12.2	3.3	15.3	4.3	19.9	6.0	23.5	3.2	0.0	5.4
Total Other Noncurrent Debt	1.8	4.0	1.6	5.3	1.2	6.3	1.0	5.8	0.7	6.0
Total Liabilities	45.7	46.7	47.1	53.1	45.4	56.2	42.9	45.3	21.1	52.3
Total Equity	54.3	53.3	52.9	46.9	54.6	43.8	57.1	54.8	78.9	47.7
TOTAL LIABILITIES & EQUITY	100.0	100.0	100.0	100.0	100.0	100.0	100.0	100.0	100.0	100.0

Exhibit 14.4B Colossal Software and RMA Financial and Operating Ratio Analysis: SIC Code 7371—Services, Computer Programming

		1998		1997		1996		1995		1994	
		Subject	RMA	Subject	RMA	Subject	RMA	Subject	RMA	Subject	RMA
Number of Observations		1	54	1	59	1	39	1	25	1	26
Average Asset Size ($MM)		57	62	51	57	43	56	40	53	29	49
Average Sales Volume ($MM)		69	117	58	83	40	91	30	89	22	88
Liquidity Ratios											
Current Ratio	High		3.5		2.9		3.3		3.1		3.1
	Median	2.2	1.9	2.3	1.6	2.9	1.6	4.1	1.8	3.3	2.0
	Low		1.3		1.1		1.2		1.3		1.2
Quick Ratio	High		2.9		2.7		2.7		2.9		2.6
	Median	1.9	1.7	1.9	1.5	2.6	1.3	3.6	1.5	3.1	1.6
	Low		1.2		1.1		0.9		1.0		1.1
Sales/Receivables	High		7.0		6.5		6.8		7.3		6.3
	Median	4.0	4.8	4.2	5.2	3.8	5.2	3.1	5.5	3.1	5.2
	Low		3.7		3.7		3.7		3.8		3.3
Sales/Working Capital	High		3.0		2.9		3.7		3.7		4.3
	Median	3.3	8.3	3.0	7.1	2.0	9.8	1.3	6.6	1.6	7.1
	Low		21.4		32.3		34.3		17.0		22.0
Coverage Ratios											
EBIT/Annual Int. Expense	High		60.7		31.5		22.4		31.3		58.4
	Median	5.7	16.1	5.9	9.9	4.4	10.4	2.4	9.8	N/A	14.7
	Low		3.0		2.3		2.1		4.2		7.7
Net Profit + Depr., Dep.,	High		44.5		38.9		12.0				
Amort./Cur. Mat. LTD	Median	5.1	7.7	4.9	7.3	3.0	4.6	0.5		N/A	
	Low		3.4		1.2		3.1				

Ratios		Med. 5	Group 5	Med. 4	Group 4	Med. 3	Group 3	Med. 2	Group 2	Med. 1	Group 1
Leverage Ratios											
Fixed/Worth	High		0.2		0.1		0.2		0.1		0.2
	Median	0.2	0.3	0.2	0.3	0.2	0.4	0.2	0.2	0.1	0.4
	Low		0.8		0.7		1.1		0.8		0.8
Debt/Worth	High		0.4		0.5		0.4		0.6		0.6
	Median	0.8	1.0	0.9	0.9	0.8	1.3	0.8	0.9	0.3	1.4
	Low		3.2		4.7		5.0		1.5		3.3
Operating Ratios											
% Profit Before Taxes/Tangible Net Worth	High		54.8		51.6		81.5		56.3		60.4
	Median	16.0	34.9	17.0	28.0	9.7	35.6	2.8	30.8	4.5	39.9
	Low		8.9		11.1		16.6		11.8		22.5
% Profit Before Taxes/Total Assets	High		28.0		20.9		26.5		26.0		25.9
	Median	6.7	14.0	7.0	11.7	4.6	11.4	1.4	12.7	3.1	16.8
	Low		3.7		1.2		3.4		5.2		8.7
Sales/Net Fixed Assets	High		36.3		25.9		22.4		54.4		29.9
	Median	9.8	15.8	8.9	15.8	7.6	16.6	7.8	15.6	6.7	13.8
	Low		8.5		8.2		8.0		7.5		9.4
Sales/Total Assets	High		3.5		2.6		2.5		2.8		2.8
	Median	1.2	1.8	1.1	1.6	0.9	2.1	0.8	2.0	0.7	2.3
	Low		1.1		1.0		1.1		1.6		1.4
Expense to Sales Ratio											
% Depr., Dep., Amort./Sales	High		0.8		1.3		1.2		0.9		1.1
	Median	3.0	1.9	3.0	2.8	2.9	2.3	2.8	2.5	2.5	3.5
	Low		3.8		5.2		4.0		3.6		4.9

213

Exhibit 14.5A Colossal Software and Selected Guideline Public Company Common Size Comparison

Fiscal Year Ended	Best Software 12/31/98 (%)	IDX Systems 12/31/98 (%)	Symix Systems 6/30/98 (%)	Median (%)	Colossal Software 12/31/98 (%)
Size					
Assets ($MM)	75	284	66	75	57
Revenues ($MM)	69	322	98	98	69
Balance Sheets					
ASSETS					
Cash & Equivalents	39.6	3.9	9.2	9.2	16.1
Short-term Investments	22.4	39.9		31.2	12.5
Accounts Receivable, Net	11.0	34.9	49.6	34.9	30.3
Other Current Assets	4.2	3.4	4.3	4.2	9.4
Total Current Assets	77.3	82.2	63.1	77.3	68.4
Fixed Assets, Net	5.8	11.2	9.8	9.8	12.4
Capitalized Software Costs, Net		0.2	16.6	8.4	3.7
Intangible Assets, Net	9.6		7.7	8.6	12.3
Other Assets	7.3	6.4	2.9	6.4	3.2
TOTAL ASSETS	100.0	100.0	100.0	100.0	100.0
LIABILITIES & EQUITY					
Accounts Payable	8.4	5.1	20.0	8.4	7.0
Other Accrued Liabilities	10.7	5.8	2.4	5.8	6.9
Deferred Revenue	25.9	6.4	19.8	19.8	16.4
Current Portion of LTD	0.2	0.0	0.4	0.2	1.5
Total Current Liabilities	45.3	19.3	42.6	42.6	31.7
Deferred Income Taxes		0.0	3.7	1.9	1.8
Long-term Debt	0.2	0.0	3.5	0.2	12.2
Total Liabilities	46.2	22.4	52.8	46.2	45.7
Shareholders' Equity	53.9	77.6	47.2	53.9	54.3
TOTAL LIABILITIES & EQUITY	100.1	100.0	100.0	100.0	100.0
Income Statements					
Net Sales	100.0	100.0	100.0	100.0	100.0
Cost of Sales	19.4	50.7	36.6	36.6	42.6
Gross Profit	80.6	49.3	63.4	63.4	57.4
Depreciation Expense	4.3	3.5	6.4	4.3	3.0
Operating Expenses	70.8	34.7	61.4	61.4	52.2
Operating Profit	9.8	14.7	2.1	9.8	5.3
Interest Expense		0.0		0.0	0.9
Other Income (Expenses), Net	3.4	1.6	(0.2)	1.6	1.2
Pretax Income	13.2	16.3	1.9	13.2	5.5
Income Taxes	(5.0)	6.9	3.3	3.3	2.2
NET INCOME	8.1	9.4	(1.4)	8.1	3.3

Exhibit 14.5B Colossal Software and Guideline Public Company Financial and Operating Ratio Analysis

Fiscal Year Ended	Best Software 12/31/98	IDX Systems 12/31/98	Symix Systems 6/30/98	Median	Colossal Software 12/31/98
LIQUIDITY RATIOS					
Current Ratio	1.7	4.3	1.5	1.7	2.2
Quick Ratio	1.6	4.1	1.4	1.6	1.9
Working Capital ($MM)	23.9	178.7	13.6	23.9	20.9
ACTIVITY RATIOS					
Accounts Receivable Turnover	10.8	3.9	3.6	3.9	4.4
Average Collection Period	33.8	94.1	102.1	94.1	82.1
Fixed Asset Turnover	21.3	10.7	16.0	16.0	10.2
Asset Turnover	1.1	1.2	1.8	1.2	1.3
Working Capital Turnover	2.8	2.0	9.1	2.8	3.4
COVERAGE/LEVERAGE RATIOS					
Total Debt to Total Assets (%)	46.2	22.4	52.8	46.2	45.7
Long-term Debt to Equity (%)	0.3	0.0	3.5	0.3	22.5
Times Interest Earned	75.6	1096.4	5.4	75.6	5.7
Fixed-charges Coverage Ratio	30.3	906.8	3.5	30.3	1.8
PROFITABILITY RATIOS					
Gross Profit Margin (%)	80.6	49.3	63.4	63.4	57.4
Operating Profit Margin (%)	9.8	14.7	2.1	9.8	5.3
Net Profit Margin (%)	8.1	9.4	(1.4)	8.1	3.3
Cash Flow to Sales (%)[a]	12.4	12.9	5.0	12.4	6.3
Return on Total Assets (%)[b]	8.6	11.6	(2.0)	8.6	4.9
Return on Equity (%)	14.0	15.2	(4.3)	14.0	7.4

[a] Cash flow = net income plus depreciation and amortization expense.
[b] Tax rate of 40% used in return on assets calculation.

accounts receivable balances. With respect to long-term assets, CSC exhibited higher fixed and intangible assets and lower capitalized software costs and other assets balances relative to the median guideline public company. It is often appropriate to remove capitalized software costs and recorded intangible assets, with resulting operating statements influences, from balance sheets of guideline companies in the technology industry to ensure consistency, and recalculate ratios. We have not removed these items here to maintain simplicity.

Exhibit 14.5A also revealed that CSC's total liability level reasonably approximated that of the median for our selected guideline public companies, at 45.7% of total assets versus 40.5% of total assets respectively. The most notable differences in the composition of liabilities between CSC and the average guideline public company were evidenced by CSC's substantially lower accounts payable balance and higher long-term debt balance.

Comparative analysis of Colossal Software's common size income statement as of December 31, 1998, to those of the selected guideline public companies revealed that CSC's gross operating and net profit margins were considerably lower than the median calculated for our guideline companies. Specifically, our subject's reported operating and net income as a percent of sales for the fiscal year ended December 31, 1998, were 46% and 60% lower than the median calculated using the selected guideline public company data, respectively. The most obvious explanation for this discrepancy could be found in CSC's relatively higher cost of sales, at 42.6% versus 36.6%.

Exhibit 14.5B illustrates Colossal Software's ability to meet its short-term obligations, which was typical of the selected guideline companies as evidenced by CSC's current and quick ratios. Furthermore, we can see from Exhibit 14.5B that Colossal Software's activity ratios were only marginally different from the median computed for our sample of guideline companies. However, due to Colossal's relatively high debt load, most of the guideline companies exhibited substantially more favorable coverage and leverage ratios than those of our subject. Similarly, CSC was outperformed by all but Symix Systems according to operating and net profit margin ratios calculated for our subject and the selected guideline companies.

Guideline Transactions. A comparison of Colossal Software's financial condition and operating performance with that of the selected guideline transactions is presented in Exhibits 14.6A and 14.6B. It should be noted that the ratios presented for CSC in Exhibit 14.6B were calculated using only year-end financial data to provide a reasonable basis for comparison to guideline transaction ratio calculations, and therefore will differ from the ratios presented in Exhibit 14.3 and 14.5B.

The common-size balance sheet data presented in Exhibit 14.6A revealed that as of December 31, 1998, Colossal's asset mix was considerably less current-asset-oriented than the median of the guideline transactions. In particular, CSC's accounts receivable at 30.3% of total assets was much lower than that of the median acquired companies, at 52.9%. Intangible assets, however, were substantially higher for CSC. Colossal's liabilities relative to assets were marginally lower than the median guideline transaction, despite having twice the long-term debt of any reported transaction data. CSC's current liabilities were considerably lower than the median transaction data primarily as a result of lower accounts payable and other current liabilities.

Comparative income statement analysis served to reiterate the findings of our RMA and guideline public company income statement comparisons. Colossal exhibited below-average operating and net profit margins despite enjoying a higher gross profit margin than the calculated median for the selected acquired companies.

Comparative ratio analysis using transaction data yielded similar conclusions to earlier like exercises. In particular, relative to guideline public company and guideline transaction data, Colossal Software exhibited

- Average to above-average liquidity
- Average receivable turns

Exhibit 14.6A Common Size Comparison of Selected Guideline Transactions and Colossal Software

Fiscal Year Ended	BGS Systems 1/31/97 ($000)	PCM 12/31/97 ($000)	Eclipse Infomation Systems 12/31/97 ($000)	Interactive Group 12/31/96 ($000)	Logic Works 12/31/97 ($000)	Median ($000)	Colossal Software 12/31/98 ($000)
Size							
Assets ($MM)	40.9	9.4	1.7	29.0	59.5	29.0	57.1
Revenues ($MM)	48.6	34.7	5.4	56.2	50.5	48.6	69.5
Balance Sheets							
ASSETS							
Cash & Equivalents	31.8	38.0	1.3	12.7	64.5	31.8	28.6
Accounts Receivable, Net	35.4	52.9	80.3	55.4	18.9	52.9	30.3
Other Current Assets	4.3	1.3	2.5	7.3	6.3	4.3	9.4
Total Current Assets	71.4	97.1	84.1	75.4	89.7	84.1	68.4
Fixed Assets, Net	25.4	0.8	14.1	10.6	7.2	10.6	12.4
Capitalized Software Costs, Net	3.1	0.0	0.0	0.0	0.8	0.0	3.7
Intangible Assets, Net	0.0	0.0	0.0	8.1	0.0	0.0	12.3
Other Assets	0.0	2.1	1.7	5.9	2.2	2.1	3.2
TOTAL ASSETS	100.0	100.0	100.0	100.0	100.0	100.0	100.0

(continued)

217

Exhibit 14.6A Common Size Comparison of Selected Guideline Transactions and Colossal Software
(continued)

Fiscal Year Ended	BGS Systems 1/31/97 ($000)	PCM 12/31/97 ($000)	Infomation Systems 12/31/97 ($000)	Interactive Group 12/31/96 ($000)	Logic Works 12/31/97 ($000)	Median ($000)	Colossal Software 12/31/98 ($000)
LIABILITIES							
Accounts Payable	3.8	23.0	25.5	23.4	3.2	23.0	7.0
Accrued Expenses	9.1	5.8	0.0	16.7	11.7	9.1	6.9
Deferred Revenue	40.1	0.5	0.0	6.5	11.4	6.5	16.4
Other Current Liabilities	1.2	10.0	20.2	11.4	0.8	10.0	1.5
Total Current Liabilities	54.2	39.3	45.7	58.1	27.2	45.7	31.7
Long-term Debt	0.0	0.0	2.6	5.8	0.0	0.0	12.2
Total Liabilities	55.4	39.3	48.3	64.5	27.2	48.3	45.7
Stockholders' Equity	44.6	60.7	51.7	35.5	72.8	51.7	54.3
Total Liabilities and Stockholders' Equity	100.0	100.0	100.0	100.0	100.0	100.0	100.0
Income Statements							
Net Sales	100.0	100.0	100.0	100.0	100.0	100.0	100.0
Cost of Sales	29.5	71.9	62.9	50.4	12.5	50.4	42.6
Gross Profit	70.5	28.1	37.1	49.6	87.5	49.6	57.4
Depreciation Expense	3.2	0.0	0.9	2.5	3.9	2.5	3.0
Operating Expenses	43.8	7.5	34.3	46.0	75.6	43.8	52.2
Operating Profit	26.7	20.6	2.8	3.6	11.9	11.9	5.3
Interest Expense	0.0	0.1	0.1	0.5	0.6	0.1	0.9
Other Income (Expenses), Net	2.2	0.1	(0.1)	0.1	3.3	0.1	1.2
Pretax Income	28.9	20.5	2.5	3.2	14.6	14.6	5.5
Income Taxes	10.2	0.3	0.2	1.0	5.5	1.0	2.2
NET INCOME	18.8	20.2	2.4	2.2	9.1	9.1	3.3

Exhibit 14.6B Financial Ratio Comparison of Selected Guideline Transactions and Colossal Software

Fiscal Year Ended	BGS Systems 1/31/97	PCM 12/31/97	Eclipse Infomation Systems 12/31/97	Interactive Group 12/31/96	Logic Works 12/31/97	Median	Colossal Software 12/31/98
LIQUIDITY RATIOS							
Current Ratio	1.3	2.5	1.8	1.3	3.3	1.8	2.2
Quick Ratio	1.2	2.3	1.8	1.2	3.1	1.8	1.9
Working Capital ($MM)	7.1	5.5	0.6	5.0	37.2	5.5	20.9
ACTIVITY RATIOS							
Accounts Receivable Turnover	3.4	7.0	4.0	3.5	4.5	4.0	4.0
Average Collection Period	108.7	52.4	90.2	104.3	81.0	90.2	90.9
Fixed Asset Turnover	4.7	454.1	23.0	18.3	11.7	18.3	9.8
Asset Turnover	1.2	3.7	3.2	1.9	0.8	1.9	1.2
Working Capital Turnover	6.9	6.4	8.4	11.2	1.4	6.9	3.3

(continued)

Exhibit 14.6B Financial Ratio Comparison of Selected Guideline Transactions and Colossal Software
(continued)

Fiscal Year Ended	BGS Systems 1/31/97	PCM 12/31/97	Infomation Systems 12/31/97	Interactive Group 12/31/96	Logic Works 12/31/97	Median	Colossal Software 12/31/98
COVERAGE/LEVERAGE RATIOS							
Total Debt to Total Assets (%)	55.4	39.3	48.3	64.5	27.2	48.3	45.7
Long-term Debt to Equity (%)	0.0	0.0	5.1	16.5	0.0	0.0	22.5
Times Interest Earned	nmf[a]	151.0	19.5	7.2	19.5	19.5	5.7
Fixed-charges Coverage Ratio[b]	10.6	37.1	4.6	1.7	3.1	4.6	2.6
PROFITABILITY RATIOS							
Gross Profit Margin (%)	70.5	28.1	37.1	49.6	87.5	49.6	57.4
Operating Profit Margin (%)	26.7	20.6	2.8	3.6	11.9	11.9	5.3
Net Profit Margin (%)	18.8	20.2	2.4	2.2	9.1	9.1	3.3
Cash Flow to Sales (%)[c]	21.9	20.2	3.2	4.8	13.0	13.0	6.3
Return on Total Assets (%)[d]	22.3	74.7	8.0	4.9	8.1	8.1	4.7
Return on Equity (%)	50.0	122.5	15.0	12.3	10.6	15.0	7.4

[a] Not meaningful.
[b] Fixed-charges coverage includes rent expense.
[c] Cash Flow = net income plus depreciation and amortization expense.
[d] Tax rate of 40% used in return on assets calculation.

- Below-average asset turns
- Average total debt
- High long-term debt
- Low but adequate coverage
- Above-average gross profit margin
- Below-average operating and net profit margins
- Below-average return on total assets and equity

IDENTIFICATION AND APPLICATION OF VALUATION MULTIPLES

In conducting the preceding comparative analysis of Colossal Software relative to the selected market data, we found that CSC as of December 31, 1998, was considerably more leveraged than the selected peer data. Therefore, when using adjusted, historical financial data, we elected to value the company's common equity on an invested capital basis. In particular, CSC's common stock was valued using multiples of deal price based on the market value of invested capital (MVIC). Benefit streams available to all classes of stakeholders (including debt and equity) were considered in calculating market multiples. As a result, the ultimate determination of Colossal's common equity value was arrived at by reducing the indicated dollar value of MVIC by the market value of CSC's long-term debt, approximately $7.0 million as of December 31, 1998. Market multiples calculated for the purpose of pricing Colossal's MVIC included

- MVIC/sales
- MVIC/EBITDA (earnings before interest, taxes, depreciation, and amortization)
- MVIC/EBIT
- MVIC/DFCF (debt-free cash flow)

In addition to considering multiples based on historical financial data, we have used analysts' estimates and the revenue and expense projections discussed in our analysis of CSC's financial statements to prepare projected fiscal 1999 income statements for our subject and the selected guideline public companies, presented here as Exhibit 14.7. Because of the lack of information with respect to the guideline companies' long-term debt, interest expense, and depreciation expense, we elected to value CSC's common equity on a levered basis when using forward-looking pricing multiples. In particular, the company's common equity was valued using multiples of price based on the expected market value (price) of the guideline public companies' common equity as of each of their respective fiscal 1999 year-ends. Furthermore, only those benefit streams available to common equity holders were considered in determining the corresponding market multiples.

Market multiples calculated for the purpose of pricing Colossal's common equity on a leveraged basis included

- Price/sales
- Price/pretax income (EBT)
- Price/net income (NI)

MVIC Multiple Adjustments

As we can see from Exhibit 14.8, the majority of the selected MVIC multiples considered exhibited a relatively tight range of values as evidenced by low coefficient of variation (CV). All else being equal, multiples exhibiting low CV tend to more accurately reflect market consensus with respect to value.

Data used to determine the MVIC and resultant pricing multiples for each of the selected guideline public companies and guideline transactions are presented in Exhibits 14.9A to 14.9E and 14.10, respectively. Exhibit 14.9A demonstrates the calculation of MVIC for the guideline public companies, which in turn is used in the determination of the four selected MVIC multiples presented in Exhibits 14.9B to 14.9E. Guideline transactions MVIC and concomitant pricing multiples are presented together in Exhibit 14.10.

Exhibit 14.7   Fiscal 1999 Year-End Income Statements

| | Projected | | | | |
	Best Software	IDX Systems	Symix Systems	Median	Colossal Software
Sales	92,645	324,731	133,255	133,255	88,241
Percent Increase	*33.6*	*1.0*	*36.5*	*33.6*	*27.0*
Operating Profit	15,372	19,504	11,919	15,372	7,942
Percent of Sales	*16.6*	*6.0*	*8.9*	*8.9*	*9.0*
Pretax Income (EBT)	17,619	23,604	12,010	17,619	7,379
Percent of Sales	*19.0*	*7.3*	*9.0*	*9.0*	*8.4*
Taxes	7,048	9,442	4,804	7,048.0	2,952
Tax Rate	*40.0*	*40.0*	*40.0*	*40.0*	*40.0*
Net Income (NI)	10,571	14,162	7,206	10,571	4,427
Percent of Sales	*0.11*	*0.04*	*0.05*	*0.05*	*0.05*
Shares Outstanding (000)	12,426	27,224	7,373		1,000

Exhibit 14.8   Coefficient of Variation and Median MVIC Valuation Multiples

Selected Pricing Multiple	Coefficient of Variation		Median Pricing Multiples	
	LTM Guideline Public Company Data	Merger & Acquisition Data	LTM Guideline Public Company Data	Merger & Acquisition Data
MVIC/Sales	0.41	0.74	1.3	1.6
MVIC/EBITDA	0.39	0.59	13.4	18.1
MVIC/EBIT	0.81	0.56	23.6	28.4
MVIC/DFCF	0.37	0.50	18.5	25.9

The following sections summarize our analysis, adjustment, and subsequent weighting of the selected MVIC multiples and are organized here according to the nature of the underlying data, specifically guideline public company and guideline transaction.

Guideline Public Company MVIC Multiples

- *MVIC/sales.* In addition to the data presented in Exhibit 14.9B, regression analysis was conducted using EBITDA/sales as the independent variable and MVIC/sales as the dependent variable. However, the explanatory power of this model was quite low, as evidenced by an R^2 equal to 0.06%, and therefore was rejected in favor of analysis of the median LTM (latest twelve months) multiple. Due to CSC's consistent low returns to sales and increased risk relative to the guideline public company data, we elected to adjust the median LTM multiple downward by 20%.

  The resulting multiple received a weight of 20% reflecting our opinion that the average investor is primarily concerned with returns on investments versus revenue growth.

- *MVIC/EBITDA.* Comparative financial analysis revealed that CSC underperformed relative to the selected guideline companies with respect to asset utilization and operating profit. We see from Exhibit 14.9C that our subject's 1998 LTM EBITDA actually decreased relative to that reported for 1997; only one of the guideline companies reported lower 1998 EBITDA levels. Additionally, CSC's EBITDA growth was marginally lower than the median calculated for the selected guideline companies. Therefore, we reduced the median MVIC/EBITDA multiple by 15%.

  Given the relatively low CV demonstrated by the MVIC/EBITDA multiple, we will accord this multiple a weight of 30%.

Exhibit 14.9A Guideline Public Company Market Value of Invested Capital

Company	Mkt./Sym.	FYE	Lat. Qtr. BV IBD ($000)	Lat. Qtr. MV IBD ($000)	As of or for Period Ending	Bid/Close Price per Common Share 3/26/99 ($)	Common Shares Outstanding (000)	MV Common Equity ($000)	MVIC ($000)
Best Software	NASD/BEST	12/31/98	125	125	3/26/99	13.750	11,640	160,050	160,175
IDX Systems	NASD/IDXC	12/31/98	0	0	3/26/99	15.437	26,493	408,972	408,972
Symix Systems	NASD/SYMX	6/30/98	2,305	2,305	3/26/99	16.125	6,711	108,215	110,520
Colossal Software	N/A	12/31/98	6,594	6,594	3/26/99				

Exhibit 14.9B Guideline Public Company MVIC/Sales

Company	LTM Sales ($000)	Ending	Sales					5-Yr. Avg. Annual Compound Growth (%)	MVIC[a] ($000)	MVIC/ LTM Sales
			1998 ($000)	1997 ($000)	1996 ($000)	1995 ($000)	1994 ($000)			
Best Software	69,330	12/31/98	69,330	46,707	39,229	35,023	27,541	26.0	160,175	2.3
IDX Systems	321,676	12/31/98	321,676	251,417	206,879	175,285	104,706	32.4	408,972	1.3
Symix Systems	97,597	6/30/98	97,597	65,772	45,759	42,828	35,486	28.8	110,520	1.1
Mean								29.1		1.6
Median								28.8		1.30
Standard deviation								3.2		0.6
Coefficient of Variation								0.11		0.41
Colossal Software	69,481	12/31/98	69,481	58,467	40,001	29,838	21,626	33.9		

[a]From Exhibit 14.9A.

Exhibit 14.9C Guideline Public Company MVIC/EBITDA

Company	LTM EBITDA ($000)	Ending	Earnings before Interest, Taxes, Depreciation and Amortization (EBITDA)					5-Yr. Avg. Annual Compound Growth (%)	MVIC[a] ($000)	MVIC/ LTM EBITDA
			1998 ($000)	1997 ($000)	1996 ($000)	1995 ($000)	1994 ($000)			
Best Software	9,772	12/31/98	9,772	8,668	5,777	7,814	2,943	35.0	160,175	16.4
IDX Systems	58,320	12/31/98	58,320	19,486	29,953	25,856	10,624	53.1	408,972	7.0
Symix Systems	8,238	6/30/98	8,238	9,665	6,555	1,393	2,603	33.4	110,520	13.4
Mean								40.5		12.3
Median								35.0		13.4
Standard deviation								10.9		4.8
Coefficient of Variation								0.27		0.39
Colossal Software	5,734	12/31/98	5,734	5,905	4,577	2,836	1,752	34.5		

aFrom Exhibit 14.9A.

226

Exhibit 14.9D Guideline Public Company MVIC/EBIT

Company	LTM EBIT ($000)	Ending	Earnings before Interest and Taxes (EBIT)					5-Yr. Avg. Annual Compound Growth (%)	MVIC[a] ($000)	MVIC/ LTM EBIT
			1998 ($000)	1997 ($000)	1996 ($000)	1995 ($000)	1994 ($000)			
Best Software	6,800	12/31/98	6,800	7,380	1,997	2,338	2,943	23.3	160,175	23.6
IDX Systems	47,144	12/31/98	47,144	10,614	22,626	19,038	6,928	61.5	408,972	8.7
Symix Systems	2,018	6/30/98	2,018	5,072	3,491	(1,362)	792	26.3	110,520	54.8
Mean								37.0		29.0
Median								26.3		23.6
Standard deviation								21.2		23.5
Coefficient of Variation								0.57		0.81
Colossal Software	3,648	12/31/98	3,648	4,168	3,400	1,997	1,206	31.9		

[a]From Exhibit 14.9A.

Exhibit 14.9E Guideline Public Company MVIC/DFCF

Company	LTM DFCF ($000)	Ending	Debt-free Cash Flow (DFCF)					5-Yr. Avg. Annual Compound Growth (%)	MVIC[a] ($000)	MVIC/ LTM DFCF
			1998 ($000)	1997 ($000)	1996 ($000)	1995 ($000)	1994 ($000)			
Best Software	8,649	12/31/98	8,649	7,258	7,457	7,088	2,519	36.1	160,175	18.5
IDX Systems	41,430	12/31/98	41,430	16,952	24,119	27,649	8,653	47.9	408,972	9.9
Symix Systems	5,088	6/30/98	5,088	7,861	5,401	2,146	2,432	20.3	110,520	21.7
Mean								34.8		16.7
Median								36.1		18.5
Standard deviation								13.8		6.1
Coefficient of Variation								0.40		0.37
Colossal Software	4,763	12/31/98	4,763	4,311	2,639	840	679	62.7		

[a]From Exhibit 14.9A.

- *MVIC/EBIT.* Exhibit 14.9D indicated that our subject's 1998 EBIT increased relative to that reported for 1997; all but one of the guideline public companies reported lower 1998 EBIT levels. In addition, CSC exhibited moderately higher EBIT growth relative to that of the median selected guideline company. However, because of CSC's relatively low asset utilization and operating margin, we elected to adjust the MVIC/EBIT multiple downward by 5%.

  The weight accorded the MVIC/EBIT multiple was 20% due to the relatively higher CV demonstrated by this multiple.

- *MVIC/DFCF.* As can be seen from Exhibit 14.9E, CSC exhibited much higher DFCF growth over the past five years than that of any of the selected guideline public companies. However, CSC's year-to-year DFCF growth had fallen off considerably by 1998. Similarly, two of the three selected guideline public companies also exhibited declines in year-to-year DFCF growth as of 1998. Given this analysis, we elected not to adjust the MVIC/DFCF.

  The MVIC/DFCF multiple was accorded a weight of 30% on the basis of its low CV.

Guideline Transactions MVIC Multiples (Exhibit 14.10)

- *MVIC/sales.* Regression analysis (not shown) of MVIC/sales relative to EBITDA/sales resulted in an indicated multiple only marginally lower than the median presented in Exhibit 14.10, 1.5 versus 1.6. Additionally, the R^2 of this regression was determined to be equal to .74, indicating a significant correlation between MVIC/sales and EBITDA/sales. Given this relationship, we elected to value CSC using a MVIC/sales multiple of 1.5 calculated according to the regression equation.

  We elected to weight the MVIC/sales multiple 20% due to the relatively high CV exhibited by this multiple.

- *MVIC/EBITDA.* CSC's EBITDA as a percentage of sales was substantially lower than that of the median for the selected guideline transactions, 8.3% versus 18.1%. In addition, as was noted in our comparative analysis of our subject relative to the guideline transactions, CSC exhibited considerably higher leverage to support fewer productive assets than did its peers. Therefore, we estimated that the median reported multiple should be reduced by 15%.

  The MVIC/EBITDA multiple was accorded a weight of 20% due to its relatively high CV.

- *MVIC/EBIT.* Similarly, CSC's very low operating profit margin and less desirable risk characteristics convinced us to reduce the reported median MVIC/EBIT multiple by 15% as well.

  Given the relatively low CV demonstrated by the MVIC/EBIT multiple, we will weight this multiple 30%.

- *MVIC/DFCF.* An analysis of CSC's DFCF/sales relative to that of the median guideline transaction revealed that at 25.9%, the median guideline transaction

Exhibit 14.10 Selected Guideline Transactions Pricing Multiples

	BGS Systems ($000)	PCM ($000)	Eclipse Infomation Systems ($000)	Interactive Group ($000)	Logic Works ($000)	Median ($000)	Coefficient of Variation
Equity Purchase Price	285,000	54,000	7,400	57,000	174,800	57,000	
Assumed Long-term Debt	0	0	0	0	0	0	
MVIC	285,000	54,000	7,400	57,000	174,800	57,000	
Net Sales	48,578	34,737	5,380	56,191	50,514	48,578	0.74
EBITDA	15,591	7,192	190	3,502	9,634	7,192	0.59
EBIT	12,981	7,154	149	2,006	6,017	6,017	0.56
DFCF	10,644	7,061	178	2,842	6,754	6,754	0.50
MVIC/Net Sales	5.9	1.6	1.4	1.0	3.5	1.6	
MVIC/EBITDA	18.3	7.5	39.0	16.3	18.1	18.1	
MVIC/EBIT	22.0	7.5	49.7	28.4	29.1	28.4	
MVIC/DFCF	26.8	7.6	41.5	20.1	25.9	25.9	

Exhibit 14.11   Guideline Market Data MVIC Multiple Adjustments

Selected Pricing Multiple	Median Pricing Multiple	Adjustment Factor	Adjusted Pricing Multiple	Multiple Weight
Guideline Public Company Data				
MVIC/Sales	1.3	−20%	1.0	20%
MVIC/EBITDA	13.4	−15%	11.4	30%
MVIC/EBIT	23.6	−5%	22.4	20%
MVIC/DFCF	18.5	0%	18.5	30%
Guideline Transaction Data				
MVIC/Sales	1.5	0%	1.5	20%
MVIC/EBITDA	18.1	−15%	15.4	20%
MVIC/EBIT	28.4	−15%	24.1	30%
MVIC/DFCF	25.9	−25%	19.4	30%

generated close to 4× the DFCF generated by our subject, 6.9%. Therefore, the median MVIC/DFCF multiple reported was reduced by 25%.

We elected to weight the MVIC/DFCF multiple 30% on the strength of its low CV.

Exhibit 14.11 provides a tabular summary of the preceding analysis.

Common Equity Pricing Multiple Adjustments

Using estimates of each of our selected guideline public companies' fiscal 1999 year-end operating results in addition to forecasted price to earnings (P/E) ratios, we were able to develop several common equity pricing multiples based on forecasts for the year ahead. As we can see from Exhibit 14.12A, each of the selected common equity multiples exhibited relatively tight ranges of value as evidenced by the calculated CV.

The following discussion summarizes our analysis, adjustment, and subsequent weighting of the selected common equity multiples.

Guideline Public Company Common Equity Multiples

- *Price/sales.* As we can see from Exhibit 14.7, CSC's 1999 sales growth was estimated to be 20% lower than that of the median guideline public company. Additionally, due to CSC's consistent low returns to sales and increased risk relative to the guideline company data, we elected to adjust the median price/sales multiple downward by 20%.

  The resulting multiple was accorded a weight of 20% due to its relatively higher CV value.

Exhibit 14.12A   Guideline Public Company Common Equity Pricing Multiples Based on Forecasted Results

	Best Software	IDX Systems	Symix Systems	Median	Coefficient of Variation
Sales per Share	$7.46	$11.93	$18.07		
EBT per Share	$1.42	$0.87	$1.63		
Net Income per Share	$0.85	$0.52	$0.97		
Shares Outstanding (000)	12,426	27,224	7,373		
Price/Sales	2.3	1.4	1.3	1.4	0.39
Price/EBT	12.0	19.5	14.9	14.9	0.25
Price/NI	20.0	32.5	25.0	25.0	0.25
Implied Price per Share	$17.000	$16.900	$24.250		

- *Price/pretax income.* Similarly, although our subject's 1999 pretax income improved considerably relative to that of the median guideline public company since 1998, it was still close to 10% lower than the estimated 9% of sales calculated for the guideline company data. Therefore, we elected to reduce the price/pretax income multiple by 10%.

  Because of the relatively low CV indicated for this multiple, we elected to weight the resulting price/pretax income multiple at 40%.

- *Price/net income.* According to Exhibit 14.7, CSC's 1999 net income as percent of sales was expected to approximate the 5% calculated for our selected guideline companies. However, due to the higher risk associated with CSC's earnings, we felt that a 10% discount for this multiple was warranted. Given the low CV value associated with this multiple, we elected to weight the adjusted price/net income multiple at 40%.

  Exhibit 14.12B provides a tabular summary of the preceding analysis.

VALUATION OF COLOSSAL SOFTWARE

According to the description of this valuation assignment, we are to value five blocks of minority interest ownership in the common stock of Colossal Software, totaling 49% of CSC's outstanding common stock. The standard of value applicable to this assignment is *fair value,* in accordance with Delaware State laws for dissenting shareholder actions. In particular, although not explicitly clear on the

Exhibit 14.12B   Guideline Public Company Common Equity Pricing Multiples
Adjustments

Selected Pricing Multiple	Median Pricing Multiple[a]	Adjustment Factor	Adjusted Pricing Multiple	Multiple Weight
Guideline Public Company Data				
Price/Sales	1.4	−20%	1.1	20%
Price/Pretax Income	14.9	−10%	13.4	40%
Price/Net Income	25.0	−20%	20.0	40%

[a]From Exhibit 14.12A.

subject, the Delaware Chancery Court has generally found the appropriate level of value for determining the fair value of a minority interest to be control value. Indeed, it is generally accepted that the fair value of a minority interest under Delaware dissenting stockholder statutes is equal to the pro rata value of all outstanding common stock ownership interests.

To estimate the pro rata value of CSC's outstanding common stock, we must first subtract the market value of any outstanding long-term debt from the indicated values produced using MVIC (see Exhibit 14.13A and 14.13B). Provided that CSC's long-term debt was roughly $6.9 million as of March 27, 1999, the fair value of Colossal Software's aggregate common equity was estimated to be $69.3 million and $85.6 million, according to the guideline public company MVIC and guideline transaction MVIC methods, respectively. The value estimate reached using guideline public company common equity multiples, $94.4 million need not be adjusted, as the indicated value reflects the effect of CSC's leverage (see Exhibit 14.13C).

Marketability discounts have not received support from the Delaware courts and thus will not be used to reach our ultimate common equity value conclusion. Additionally, we will price Colossal Software's common equity as if valuing a controlling interest in the company.

The guideline public company methods of the market approach produce an indication of minority marketable value. In order to translate this level of value to control value, we applied a control premium of 15% to the price indicated using both guideline public company methods, that is, guideline public company MVIC method and guideline public company common equity method.[4] We believe that the magnitude of the selected control premium is reasonable in light of the relatively strong performance and high earnings multiples generated by technology stocks relative to other sectors of the broader markets. The resulting product indicates that the fair value of Colossal Software's common equity using the MVIC method is roughly $79.7 million and $108.5 million using the common equity method. Merger and acquisition data, however, produces an indication of control value; therefore, we will not adjust the indicated price of $85.6 million (rounded) arrived at by using guideline transaction data.

Exhibit 14.13A Guideline Public Company Method Weighting and MVIC Multiple Calculation

Selected Pricing Multiple	Adjusted Pricing Multiple	Colossal Software Fundamental ($000)	Indicated Value ($000)	Multiple Weight	Weighted Method Value ($000)
Guideline Public Company Data					
MVIC/Sales	1.0	69,481	69,481	20%	13,896
MVIC/EBITDA	11.4	5,734	65,368	30%	19,610
MVIC/EBIT	22.4	3,648	81,715	20%	16,343
MVIC/DFCF	18.5	4,763	88,112	30%	26,434
Guideline Public Company MVIC					76,283
Less: Market value of interest-bearing debt (1998)					6,967
Equals: Indicated value of Common Equity					69,316
Plus: Control Premium (15%)					10,397
Equals: Control value base on Guideline Public Company common equity					79,713

Exhibit 14.13B Guideline Transaction Method Weighting and MVIC Calculation

Selected Pricing Multiple	Adjusted Pricing Multiple	Colossal Software Fundamental ($000)	Indicated Method Value ($000)	Multiple Weight	Weighted Method Value ($000)
Guideline Transaction Data					
MVIC/Sales	1.5	69,481	104,222	20%	20,844
MVIC/EBITDA	15.4	5,734	88,304	20%	17,661
MVIC/EBIT	24.1	3,648	87,917	30%	26,375
MVIC/DFCF	19.4	4,763	92,398	30%	27,719
Guideline Transaction MVIC					92,599
Less: Market value of interest-bearing debt (1998)					6,967
Equals: Control value base on Guideline Transaction common equity					85,632

Exhibit 14.13C Guideline Public Company Common Equity Method Weighting Multiple Calculation

Selected Pricing Multiple	Adjusted Pricing Multiple	Colossal Software Fundamental ($000)	Indicated Method Value ($000)	Multiple Weight	Weighted Method Value ($000)
Guideline Public Company Data					
Price/Sales	1.1	88,241	97,065	20%	19,413
Price/Pretax Income	13.4	7,379	98,879	40%	39,552
Price/Net Income	20.0	4,427	88,540	40%	35,416
Forecasted Guideline Public Company common equity value					94,381
Plus: Control Premium (15%)					14,157
Equals: Control value base on forecasted Guideline Public Company common equity					108,538

Using our previous assessment of the micro- and macroeconomic environments as of the beginning of 1999, specifically that growth and competition will play an increasingly significant role in the computer services industry over the near term, we weighted the various methods of valuing CSC's common equity to reflect those expectations. In particular, greater weight was accorded to multiples calculated using forward-looking revenue and income value measures. We believe that this places an appropriate emphasis on the role that future expectations play in pricing a company in a high-growth industry. Table 14.3 presents the selected weights and resulting values for each of the methods.

Table 14.3

Method	Indicated Value	Method Weight	Weighted Value
Guideline Public Company			
MVIC method	$ 79,713,000[a]	30%	$23,913,900
Guideline Transaction MVIC method	85,623,000[b]	30%	25,689,600
Guideline Public Company Common	108,538,000[c]	40%	43,415,200
Equity method			
Total		100%	$93,018,700

[a]From Exhibit 14.13A
[b]From Exhiibit 14.13B
[c]From Exhibit 14.13C

Given the outlined method weighting scheme, Colossal Software's aggregate common equity was valued at $93 million.

According to common share data provided in Exhibit 14.2, Colossal Software had 1 million shares outstanding as of December 31, 1998. Provided that no new shares were issued between December 31, 1998, and March 27, 1999, the fair value of Colossal Software's common stock was $93 per share. Finally, Table 14.4 presents the fair value of the five minority interest holdings of Colossal Software common stock.

Table 14.4

Shareholder	Number of Shares Owned	Fair Value of Shares
Craig Brown	150,000	$13,953,000
Devoe Family Trust	140,000	$13,022,800
James Watts	100,000	$9,302,000
George Grevelis	50,000	$4,651,000
David Laken	50,000	$4,651,000

Notes

1. 8 Del. C. §262(a)(1999).
2. Id. at 262(h).
3. *Cavalier Oil Corp. v. Harnett,* 564 A. 2d 1137, 1146 (September 5, 1989).
4. Adding a control premium to a value derived by the public company guideline method to eliminate the implicit minority discount is consistent with Delaware procedure. [See, for example, *Borruso v. Communications Telesystems International,* 1999 Del. Ch. Lexis 197 (September 24, 1999).] One school of thought would not add a control premium to the results to the guideline public company method on the theory that the public companies are already selling at control value or else they would be taken over.

PART V

Important Aspects of Using the Market Approach

Chapter 15

Reconciling Market Approach Values with Income and Asset Approach Values

One of the hardest things to do is to reconcile indications of value when there are divergent results between or among the income, market, and asset approaches. Unfortunately, there are no easy answers, no cookie-cutter procedures to reach a satisfactory reconciliation.

Although this chapter is primarily aimed at reconciling internal differences, the points may also be applied to reconciliation of divergent results between the work of one appraiser and another.

DID WE APPRAISE THE CORRECT PROPERTY?

A common error found in the asset approach is simply to appraise the assets and not take account of the corporate or partnership entity structure intervening between the owner and the assets. That is, it is not uncommon to overlook that what should be appraised is stock or a partnership interest, not direct ownership of assets.

It must be recognized that, unless control is involved, the stock or partnership owner cannot force liquidation or redeployment of the assets. Also, if assets are to be liquidated or redeployed, significant costs are likely to be involved. These may include, but are not limited to, management time, appraisal costs, legal and accounting costs, transaction costs, and capital gains and/or ordinary income taxes incurred on disposal. Furthermore, discounts often are warranted for the elapsed time to consummate the process and the risk of whether the estimated values actually can be realized.

Ownership of any business or business interest is really a bundle of rights. The appraiser must make sure that the correct bundle of rights is being appraised.

CONFORMANCE TO THE REQUIRED DEFINITION OF VALUE

It is important to examine whether all the methods and the procedures used to implement them conform to the applicable standard of value and either actual ownership characteristics or ownership characteristics required to be assumed by the definition of value sought.

For example, did some procedure used in one valuation method bring in elements of control when a minority valuation was sought, or vice versa? Or did some procedure used in one valuation method bring in elements of investment value when fair market value was the applicable standard? Although these two are the most common departures from the stated appraisal assignment, there can be many other variations.

If a procedural departure from the methodology indicated by the appraisal assignment has been incorporated in the implementation of one appraisal method, correction of that procedure may bring the results of the method more in line with results of other methods.

RELATIVE ADEQUACY AND RELIABILITY OF DATA

If a divergent result from one method is based on data that are significantly less extensive or well supported than data from another method, it is often quite reasonable that the method supported by adequate and reliable data is deemed to dominate.

For example, if there are very good guideline companies but no or very unreliable projections of operating results, the market approach may be the only approach ultimately relied on. Conversely, if there are no good guideline companies but there are excellent projections, the discounted cash flow method may be the single method ultimately used.

Caution: The appraiser should not eliminate an approach for lack of data without thorough investigation. For example, as noted in the Chapters 5 and 6 on gathering data, there are far more guideline public company and acquired company data than most people realize. There are many publicly traded companies with sales under $10 million. One should not eliminate the market approach until all reasonable sources have been checked. Appraisers risk violating Revenue Ruling 59-60 if there is not a vibrant effort to locate companies that can qualify as similar to the subject.

CHECK FOR ERRORS

When results from different approaches to value diverge, the very first thing to do is to check all the arithmetic, then check for other kinds of errors. An incorrect number of shares could have been used in computing the market value of equity for a guideline company, especially if secondary sources were used. Errors can creep in numerous ways.

CHECK ASSUMPTIONS

Having checked for errors, the next logical step is to reexamine assumptions. For example, in the income approach, were the projections that were relied on overly aggressive or conservative? Was the discount or capitalization rate possibly a little high or low, not realistically reflecting the subject company risk factors? Were the numbers used in the asset approach adequately supported? Do the guideline companies used to derive multiples closely mirror the risk and growth prospects of the subject company, or, if not, were adequate adjustments made when selecting multiples to apply to the subject company?

RELATIONSHIP BETWEEN MARKET MULTIPLES
AND DISCOUNT OR CAPITALIZATION RATES

When income and market approach results diverge, one should check carefully whether the analysis leading to the choice of market multiples is consistent with the analysis leading to the choice of discount or capitalization rates.

Discount rates and market value multiples both reflect risk. The higher the risk, the higher the discount rate and the lower the market value multiple, and vice versa. Capitalization rates and market value multiples both reflect not only risk, but also anticipated growth. Given equal risk, the higher the anticipated growth, the lower the capitalization rate and the higher the market value multiple, and vice versa. We will examine this relationship more carefully, because much of the reconciliation of divergent income and market approach results can be mitigated by reconciliation of the quantification of market multiples relative to discount or capitalization rates.

Although many analysts, the author included, prefer to use net cash flow as the measure of earnings in the income approach, we will use net income for our illustration here in order to make a direct comparison between income approach analysis and market approach analysis.

In our companion book, *Cost of Capital,*[1] we explained the basic discounted future benefits model:

Formula 15.1

$$PV = \frac{NI_1}{(1 + k_{ni})} + \frac{NI_2}{(1 + k_{ni})^2} + \cdots + \frac{NI_n}{(1 + k_{ni})^n}$$

where

PV	= Present value
$NI_1 \ldots NI_n$	= Projected net income for each period 1 through n, n being the final net income in the life of the investment
k_{ni}	= Discount rate (cost of capital) for equity capital when net income is the measure of earnings being discounted

In Formula 15.1, the discounting method, all expected future changes in the level of income are reflected in the numerator, *NI*. The level of risk is reflected in the denominator, k_{ni}, the cost of equity capital, in this case using net income as the measure of earnings.

The discount rate is the market's *total required rate of return.* It is developed by either the build-up method or the capital asset pricing model (CAPM).

To review briefly, in the build-up model, the discount rate is the sum of any or all of four components:

1. Risk-free rate
2. General equity risk premium
3. Size factor
4. Specific company and/or industry risk adjustment factor

The CAPM is similar to the build-up model, but the general equity risk premium is modified by multiplying it by a factor called *beta,* a measure of *systematic risk,* or the sensitivity of returns for the subject company relative to an index of returns on large company stocks. Because the beta may incorporate some of the size risk and some specific industry and company factors, the numbers for those factors may be different in the CAPM than in the build-up model.[2]

The *Cost of Capital* also showed some alternative procedures for developing a discount rate.[3] The important thing is that the *discount rate,* however estimated, represents the *total expected annualized rate of return over the life of the investment.*

We also explained that the income capitalization model was a shortcut version of the discounting model. Starting with a discount rate, one can estimate a *capitalization rate* by subtracting from the discount rate the estimated long-term sustainable rate of growth in the variable being capitalized. In a formula, using net income as the earnings variable, this would be expressed as

Formula 15.2

$$c_{ni} = k_{ni} - g_{ni}$$

where

c_{ni} = Capitalization rate applicable to a single period's net income
k_{ni} = Discount rate (cost of capital) for equity capital when net income is the measure of earnings being discounted
g_{ni} = Growth in net income, expressed as the expected annualized long-term percentage (technically in perpetuity), proceeding from the period being capitalized

Therefore, the capitalization rate, unlike the discount rate, reflects the long-term growth rate expectation in the denominator rather than the numerator.

With this formula, we can compute what the income approach tells us the price/earning (price/net income) multiple *ought* to be. For example:

k_{ni} = 20% (required total return with net income used as measure of return)
g_{ni} = 8% (long-term expected annualized growth in net income from the period being capitalized)

Therefore, substituting these figures in Formula 15.2, we have

Formula 15.3

$$c_{ni} = .20 - .08$$
$$= .12$$

We noted earlier that multiples are the reciprocals of capitalization rates. Therefore, to convert the capitalization rate to a multiple, we divide 1 by the capitalization rate:

Formula 15.4

$$P/NI = \frac{1}{c_{ni}}$$

where

P/NI = Price/net income multiple (price/earnings)

c_{ni} = Capitalization rate applicable to a single period's net income, but reflecting expectations as to long-term growth in the variable being capitalized.

Substituting in Formula 15.4, we have

Formula 15.5

$$\frac{1}{.12} = 8.3$$

Therefore, with the above assumptions, the income approach indicates that the P/E multiple should be 8.3×.

Alternately, we can start with the observed market multiple and compute what the market approach tells us the implied discount rate should be. We will again use an 8.3 market multiple and an 8% expected growth rate. Since the capitalization rate is the reciprocal of the multiple, the capitalization rate can be computed by dividing 1 by the multiple:

Formula 15.6

$$c_{ni} = \frac{1}{P/NI}$$

Substituting in Formula 15.6, we have

Formula 15.7

$$c_{ni} = \frac{1}{8.3}$$

$$= .12$$

The implied discount rate can now be calculated by adding the expected long-term growth rate to the capitalization rate:

Formula 15.8

$$k_{ni} = c_{ni} + g_{ni}$$

Substituting in Formula 15.8, we have

Formula 15.9

$$k_{ni} = .12 + .08$$

$$= .20$$

If this analysis results in a substantial discrepancy between the discount rate used in the income approach and the discount rate implied by the market approach, or a substantial discrepancy between the multiple used in the market approach and the multiple implied by the income approach, the inputs to the models should be carefully examined. Might the discount rate be too high or too low? Might the estimated growth rate be too high or too low? Or could the cost of capital and/or expected growth rates for the guideline companies be significantly more or less than for the subject company, and the multiples observed not adequately adjusted to reflect these differences? This analysis may result in some adjustments to the discount rate, the estimated growth rate, and/or the market multiples selected, thus narrowing the divergence in indicated value between the income and market approaches.[4]

In this example, we have used net income as the operative financial variable. If the income approach used net cash flow, and the analyst estimated that over the long run net cash flow would equal net income, then no adjustments are necessary to perform this comparative analysis. If, however, net cash flow and net income are not expected to be equal, the income approach discount rate and the implied market approach discount rate should be just different enough from each other to account for the difference between expected net cash flow and expected net income. This is not a precise exercise, but it should be close enough for its purpose, that is, to help reconcile significant differences between values indicated by the income approach and values indicated by the market approach.

The same general reconciliation exercise can be conducted if the analysis has been done on an invested capital basis. In this case, the operative market approach variable would be EBITDA (earnings before interest, taxes, depreciation, and amortization), and the operative discount rate would be the weighted average cost of capital (WACC). If the analyst estimates that net cash flow to invested capital would equal EBITDA (noncash charges would be equal to capital expenditures plus additions to net working capital), then no adjustments are necessary. If, however, net cash flow to invested capital and EBITDA are not expected to be equal, the weighted average cost of capital and the implied market approach weighted average cost of capital should vary enough to account for the difference between expected net cash flow to invested capital and expected EBITDA. Again, this is not a precise exercise, but it should be close enough to be helpful in the reconciliation analysis.

WHAT TO DO WHEN RECONCILIATION EFFORTS FAIL

Once all attempts at reconciliation have been made and significant divergence still exists, the analyst has to decide whether one or two approaches should dominate the final valuation or whether some weight should be accorded to each. This decision requires an examination of the purpose of the appraisal, the standard of value, the actual or assumed ownership characteristics (e.g., minority versus control), and the premise of value (e.g., going concern versus liquidation).

When the Asset Approach Differs Significantly from Others

If appraising on a going-concern basis, and the asset approach value is significantly lower than both the income approach and market approach values, the answer usually is that there is some intangible value that was not fully captured in the asset approach. One might attempt to identify and value the intangible asset(s). However, the usual solution is to accord all the weight to the market and/or income approach. When this is done, there should be a statement in the report explaining the rationale for giving no weight to the asset approach.

If the asset approach results in a significantly higher value, the resolution may depend on whether a controlling or minority interest value is being sought. Stockholders or partners have no direct claim on the assets and no ability to force the company to redeploy them. The last time I backed my van up to the brewery loading dock and tendered my stock in the brewery to exchange it for beer, I was unsuccessful. The public stock market accords little or no value to excess or non-operating assets. In a minority interest valuation, the asset approach may be given little or no weight, especially given operating assets that generate a low earnings stream. The assets could be recognized by a slight upward adjustment in market multiples to reflect the company's asset strength, or by a specific weighting being applied to the asset approach when reconciling value.

In a controlling-interest situation, the control owner has the power to redeploy assets. Therefore, in some situations, the liquidation value of the assets, after all costs of liquidation and recognition of attendant risk, could be accorded some weight or even be considered a floor valuation figure. However, if liquidation clearly is not a prospect, then the asset value could be accorded some weight or the asset strength be reflected by some upward adjustment to multiples.

When the Market Approach Differs Significantly from Others

In the roaring public stock market and merger and acquisition market of the last decade, it is not uncommon for the market approach to produce a higher indicated value than either the income or asset approach. If this happens, the first thing to do is to reexamine the characteristics of the guideline public and merged and acquired companies relative to the subject company. Does the subject company really have the characteristics that it could go public? If so, could it be at the multiples of the guideline public companies? Is the subject company really a candidate to be acquired in the current merger market environment? If so, could it realize the multiples achieved by the guideline merged and acquired companies?

If the answer to these questions is yes, the resolution may depend on whether the assignment is a control or minority valuation. A minority stockholder cannot force either a public offering or a sale of the company. Therefore, in a minority valuation, the market approach may be accorded less weight, or, perhaps more commonly, the divergence in value may suggest higher minority and/or marketability discounts applied to the market approach indicated value. If valuing a controlling interest and the answers to the previous questions were yes, substantial weight to the market approach would seem to be appropriate.

If the answer to these questions is no, then some adjustment probably should be made to the market approach multiples to account for the differences, or the market approach should be accorded less weight if the other approaches have strong support. Conversely, market approach multiples may most realistically reflect buyer and seller motivations and economic/industry concerns as of the valuation date, and the cause of differences may lie in less realistic elements in the discount rate construction or the calculated level of earnings used in income-based methods.

EXPLICIT VERSUS IMPLICIT WEIGHTING

Finally, if the analyst concludes that no single approach should dominate, then there is the choice of according the results of the approaches explicit mathematical weights or weighting subjectively.

Explicit Mathematical Weights

The advantage of explicit mathematical weights is that they quantify the thinking of the analyst as to how much weight should be accorded to each approach. A typical valuation conclusion on a per-share basis could be

	Value	Weight	Weighted Value
Income Approach	$10.00	.30	$ 3.00
Market Approach	12.00	.50	6.00
Asset Approach	6.00	.20	1.20
Concluded Value			$10.20

This presentation also has the advantage of making it easy for the reader to compute an alternate value based on different weightings.

Implicit Weighting

Revenue Ruling 59-60 comes down on the side of implicit weighting:

Sec. 7 Average of Factors

Because valuations cannot be made on the basis of a prescribed formula, there is no means whereby the various applicable factors in a particular case can be assigned mathematical weights in deriving the fair market value. For this reason, no useful purpose is served by taking an average of several factors (for example, book value, capitalized earnings and capitalized dividends) and basing the valuation on the result. Such a process excludes active consideration of other pertinent factors, and the end result cannot be supported by a realistic application of the significant facts in the case except by mere chance.[5]

An implicit weighting might be presented by showing the results of each method and then providing a narrative analysis of the relative applicability of each and concluding with the final estimate of value.

It is true that there is no empirical basis for assigning mathematical weights to the results of different valuation approaches. Therefore, if an explicit weighting is used, there should be a disclaimer statement that the weightings are presented to help the reader understand the thinking of the analyst. It is also imperative, in any case, to be sure that all relevant factors have been considered.

SUMMARY

The reconciliation of divergent results from different valuation approaches presents an important challenge to the valuation analyst. This chapter covered suggested analyses that may lead to modified results to reduce the divergence among the approaches and the question of how to handle divergences that continue to persist; it also addressed reaching the final conclusion of value by mathematical weighting of results from the different approaches versus reaching the final conclusion by a qualitative analysis of the merits of each presented in the form of a narrative discussion.

The analyst should first check to be sure that the correct property was appraised. For example, we sometimes encounter an appraisal of assets without consideration of the effect of the corporate or partnership entity that intervenes between the assets and the owner.

We should also be sure that all the procedures conform to the applicable standard of value. The analyst also should check the adequacy and reliability of underlying data, and check for any possible errors. The validity of assumptions also should be questioned.

The chapter then presented relatively simple steps to evaluate whether the multiples used in the market approach were in reasonable accord with the discount or capitalization rates used in the income approach, with suggestions for reconciling discrepancies.

When all reconciliation efforts fail, the analyst must examine the purpose of the valuation, the applicable definition of value, the actual or assumed control or minority basis of valuation, and the applicable going-concern or liquidation premise of value to seek guidance as to which approach(es) conform to these factors.

Finally, the analyst must decide whether to present the conclusion of value as a mathematical weighting of the results of different approaches or a qualitative discussion of the different approaches supporting a subjective final conclusion of value.

Notes

1. Shannon P. Pratt, *Cost of Capital: Estimation and Applications,* 2nd ed. (Hoboken, NJ: John Wiley & Sons, 2002). Reprinted by permission of John Wiley & Sons, Inc.
2. Pratt, "Build-up Models," chap. 8, and "The Capital Asset Pricing Model (CAPM)," chap. 9, in Pratt, *Cost of Capital,* 57–79.
3. Pratt, "The DCF Method of Estimating Cost of Capital," chap. 12, in Pratt, *Cost of Capital,* 96–103.
4. Z. Christopher Mercer, "The Adjusted Capital Asset Pricing Model for Developing Capitalization Rates: An Extension of Previous 'Build-up' Methodologies Based Upon the Capital Asset Pricing Model," *Business Valuation Review* (December 1989): 147–156.
5. Revenue Ruling 59-60, 1959-1, C.B.237.

Does Size Matter? Evidence from Empirical Data

Does size matter?

In a word, yes.

Smaller companies in most industries tend to sell at lower multiples of most financial variables than larger companies in the same industry.

This conclusion, reached from analysis of market data, is consistent with income approach (cost of capital) research, which shows that smaller companies have higher costs of capital (higher discount rates) than larger companies. Higher discount rates in the income approach should mean lower multiples in the market approach, and this relationship does, indeed, hold true.

This phenomenon was further verified by the consensus of two middle-market financiers on a panel at a meeting of the Association for Corporate Growth:

- Companies with $2 to $3 million EBITDA (earnings before interest, taxes, depreciation, and amortization) are easier to sell than companies with $1 to $1.5 million EBITDA.
- Companies with $2 to $3 million EBITDA command higher pricing multiples on average than companies with $1 to $1.5 million EBITDA.[1]

EVIDENCE FROM MARKET APPROACH DATA

Studies of sales of both privately held and publicly traded companies bear out the size effect on valuation multiples.

Evidence From Sales of Private Companies

Studies that we have undertaken on the private company transaction databases (*Pratt's Stats*™ and *BIZCOMPS*®) quite consistently bear out the phenomenon that larger companies tend to sell for higher multiples. For example, the comparisons of average transaction data from one edition of *BIZCOMPS*® are typical.[2]

	Sale Price/Ask Price	Sale Price/Sales	Sale Price/SDCF[3]
Businesses sold for under $100K	76.6%	.34	1.5
Businesses sold for over $500K	91.8%	.53	2.6

We also did a study of multiples from *BIZCOMPS*® and multiples from *Pratt's Stats*™ for several industry subgroups that had approximately comparable definitions between the two databases. The results are shown in Exhibit 16.1. As the exhibit shows, the median size as measured by sales was much higher in the *Pratt's Stats*™ database in all categories. As the size phenomenon would suggest, price/sales and price/discretionary earnings (SDCF) multiples were, with some minor exceptions, generally significantly higher for the *Pratt's Stats*™ transactions.[4]

Evidence from Sales of Public Companies

As Exhibit 16.2 shows, companies under $50 million sold for considerably lower P/E (price/earnings) multiples than companies from $50 to $500 million, and companies over $500 million sold for higher multiples than those from $50 to $500 million. The sample size for this study shown in the exhibit is sufficient to make meaningful conclusions. Larger companies are less risky and, therefore, are priced in the market reflecting lower discount rates and higher market multiples.

Other work written by Jerry Peters and published in the *Business Valuation Review* in 1992 and 1995 addresses the matter of adjusting price/earnings ratios from public companies for differences in company size.[5]

Evidence from Sales of Cable Companies

Exhibit 16.3 shows the relationship between size, as measured by number of subscribers, and multiples of operation cash flows for the cable companies in 1998 and 1999. The companies are a mixture of private and public companies.

Exhibit 16.1 Median Pricing Multiples from *BIZCOMPS*® and *Pratt's Stats*™ Data

Business Type	SIC Code	BIZCOMPS® Data					PRATT'S STATS™ DATA				
		Count	Median Sale Price/Annual Gross	Median Sale Price/SDE	Median Sale Price (in 000)	Median Annual Gross (in 000)	Count	Median MVIC/Net Sales	Median MVIC/Gross Profit	Median MVIC (in 000)	Median Net Sales (in 000)
Building Contractors	1521-1542	26	0.285	1.864	$425	$1,537	24	0.4	1.604	$1,455	$4,100
Publishing and Printing	2711-2759	229	0.54	2.034	$158	$300	165	0.73	1.49	$850	$1,205
Pharmaceutical Manufacturing	2834	2	0.458	1.935	$705	$2,228	42	2.679	4.148	$22,483	$2,507
Machine Shops	3599	59	0.684	2.438	$270	$500	29	0.708	1.572	$1,050	$1,787
Industrial Supplies Distributor	5085	33	0.248	1.716	$250	$1,050	17	0.546	1.754	$1,620	$4,134
Grocery Stores	5411	191	0.205	1.737	$115	$489	90	0.239	1.06	$225	$917
Restaurants	5812	1355	0.354	1.799	$100	$300	427	0.389	0.63	$120	$330
Bars/Nightclubs	5813	189	0.378	1.855	$105	$258	45	0.346	0.54	$155	$387
Pharmacy/Drug Store	5912	13	0.173	1.302	$173	$983	28	0.331	1.018	$1,747	$4,597
Florist	5992	133	0.356	1.671	$76	$238	46	0.372	0.665	$93	$237
Coin Operated Laundry	7215	127	0.806	2.258	$80	$101	41	0.929	0.945	$87	$86
Carwashes	7542	49	0.671	2.043	$149	$250	29	1.051	1.468	$550	$508
Dentist Offices	8021	2	0.374	1.582	$110	$295	306	0.623	0.623	$400	$752
Day Care Centers	8351	120	0.439	1.85	$95	$239	50	0.518	0.558	$146	$323

Source: BIZCOMPS®.

Exhibit 16.2 Average P/E Multiples Relative to Sales

Deal Size	Number of Deals 12 Months Ended 4/30/2004	4/30/2003	Aggregate Value ($Bil) 12 Months Ended 4/30/2004	4/30/2003	Average P/E
$1 Billion +	104	72	$424.1	$235.4	30.3
$500M to $999.9M	110	72	$76.3	$52.5	27.2
$250M to $499.9M	185	140	$64.7	$49.0	24.9
$100M to $249.9M	367	311	$56.7	$48.0	24.6
$50M to $99.9M	369	327	$26.1	$23.1	25.3
$25M to $49.9M	418	397	$14.9	$14.2	24.6
$10M to $24.9M	551	617	$8.9	$9.9	21.1
Under $10M	1,044	1,076	$4.2	$4.4	20.2
Value Not Disclosed	5,632	4,896	N/A	N/A	N/A
Grand Total	**8,780**	**7,908**	**$675.8**	**$436.6**	**24.3**

Source: Factset Flashwire Monthly (May 2004).

EVIDENCE FROM INCOME APPROACH DATA

Income approach data are consistent with market approach data in concluding that size does matter, that is, smaller companies do, indeed, have higher costs of capital (which translate into lower market multiples).

Ibbotson Associates Studies

For recent years, Ibbotson Associates has broken down NYSE (New York Stock Exchange) stock returns into deciles by size, as measured by the aggregate

Exhibit 16.3 Cable Acquisitions, July 1998–March 1999

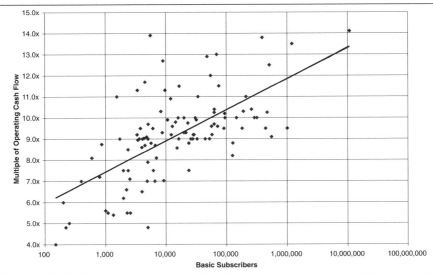

Source: Gil Matthews, compiled from data from Kagan.

market value of the common equity. The excess returns over the riskless rate increase dramatically with decreasing size, as shown in Exhibit 16.4. The fact that stocks of smaller companies have higher excess returns, that is, higher costs of capital, is consistent with the observations of lower market valuation multiples.

This excess return (higher cost of capital) is especially noticeable for the smallest 10% of the companies. Exhibit 16.5 shows the market capitalizations of the largest company in each of the respective decile groups. Exhibit 16.6 shows the size composition of the NYSE decile breakdowns.

Standard and Poor's Corporate Value

Roger Grabowski and David King of Consulting (CVC) Risk Premium Report (formerly the PricewaterhouseCoopers Risk Premium Report) have extended the study of the small-stock phenomenon to encompass additional detail. In particular:

- They have studied more size categories. They have broken down the stocks into 25 size groups, each representing 4% of the stocks by size included in the NYSE, instead of the 10 groupings used by Ibbotson Associates.

Exhibit 16.4 Long-Term Returns in Excess of CAPM Estimation for Decile Portfolios of the NYSE (1926–2003 [Perms.])

Decile	Beta[a]	Arithmetic Mean Return	Realized Return In Excess of Riskless Rate[b]	Estimated Return In Excess of Riskless Rate	Size Premium (Return In Excess of CAPM)[c]
1-Largest	0.91	11.43%	62.10%	6.54%	–0.34%
2	1.04	13.16%	79.40%	7.44%	0.50%
3	1.10	13.78%	85.50%	7.88%	0.67%
4	1.13	14.43%	92.00%	8.09%	1.11%
5	1.16	14.91%	96.80%	8.32%	1.36%
6	1.18	15.32%	10.09%	8.50%	1.59%
7	1.23	15.65%	10.42%	8.85%	1.57%
8	1.28	16.64%	11.42%	9.16%	2.25%
9	1.34	17.76%	12.53%	9.63%	2.90%
10-Smallest	1.41	21.73%	16.50%	10.16%	6.34%
Mid-Cap, 3-5	1.12	14.16%	89.30%	8.02%	0.91%
Low-Cap, 6-8	1.22	15.67%	10.44%	8.74%	1.70%
Micro-Cap, 9-10	1.36	18.98%	13.75%	9.74%	4.01%

[a] Betas are estimated from monthly portfolio total returns in excess of the 30-day U.S. Treasury bill total return versus the S&P 500 total returns in excess of the 30-day Treasury bill, January 1926–December 2003.

[b] Historical riskless rate is measured by the 78-year arithmetic mean income return component of 20-year government bonds (5.23 %)

[c] Calculated in the context of the CAPM by mutiplying the equity risk premium by the beta. The equity risk premium is estimated by the arithmetic mean total return of the S&P 500 (12.41 %) minus the arithmetic mean income return component of 20-year government bonds (5.23 %) from 1926–2003.

- They have introduced seven additional size criteria, in addition to market value of equity. These size criteria are:
  - ◆ Market value of equity
  - ◆ Book value of equity
  - ◆ Five-year average net income
  - ◆ Market value of invested capital
  - ◆ Book value of invested capital (while articles published in *Business Valuation Review* and *Shannon Pratt's Business Valuation Update*™ use book value of invested capital, PwC has replaced this with total assets in the updates published on the Cost of Capital section of the Ibbotson Associates Web site (http://valuation.ibbotson.com).
  - ◆ Five-year average EBITDA
  - ◆ Sales
  - ◆ Number of employees

The CVC data cover the years 1963 (the first year of *Compustat* data) through the present, as compared with 1925 through the present for the Ibbotson data. In addition to NYSE companies, the PwC study also includes AMEX and NASDAQ companies. The PwC set of companies also differs from Ibbotson in that PwC has screened out companies with certain poor financial characteristics. Two results of the PW studies seem strikingly significant:

1. In spite of the different time period and somewhat different set of companies, the average results are very close to the Ibbotson results.
2. The results are significantly similar for all eight measures of company size.

The results of the CVC size study through 1996 is shown in Exhibit 16.7. Recent updates are available on the Cost of Capital section of the Ibbotson Associates web site (http://valuation.ibbotson.com). PwC has also compiled data for a separate set of financially distressed companies, that is, any company with one or more of these characteristics:

- In bankruptcy or liquidation
- Negative book value of equity
- Debt to total capital >80% (debt measured at book value; equity at market value)
- Negative five-year average net income (before extraordinary items)

Returns for these companies with high financial risk are shown at the bottom of the tables in Exhibit 16.7.

Exhibit 16.7 shows both the actual premium for each size group and the

Exhibit 16.5 Size-Decile Portfolios of the NYSE, AMEX/NASDAQ, Largest Company and Its Market Capitalization by Decile (September 30, 2003)

Decile	Market Capitalization of Largest Company (in thousands)	Company Name
1-Largest	$286,638,305	General Electric Co.
2	$11,366,767	Masco Corp.
3	$4,794,027	EOG Resources Inc.
4	$2,585,984	Toys R Us Inc.
5	$1,720,959	International Rectifier Corp.
6	$1,166,799	Thor Industries Inc.
7	$795,983	Granite Construction Inc.
8	$507,820	Steelcase Inc.
9	$330,608	Sterling Bancorp
10-Smallest	$166,414	Ethly Corp.

Source: © 2004 CRSP® Center for Research in Security prices. Graduate School of Business. The University of Chicago. Used with permission. All rights reserved. www.crsp.uchicago.edu.

Exhibit 16.6 Size-Decile Portfolios of the NYSE, Size and Composition (1926–2003)

Decile	Historical Average Percentage of Total Capitalization [a]	Recent Number of Companies [b]	Recent Decile Market Capitalization (in thousands) [b]	Recent Percentage of Total Capitalization [b]
1-Largest	63.33%	168	$7,419,638,030	64.91%
2	13.99%	186	$1,471,629,952	12.87%
3	7.57%	198	$746,716,927	6.53%
4	4.74%	200	$451,145,013	3.95%
5	3.24%	221	$337,041,577	2.95%
6	2.37%	277	$290,452,647	2.54%
7	1.72%	343	$238,327,258	2.08%
8	1.27%	379	$171,437,318	1.50%
9	0.97%	613	$168,889,652	1.48%
10-Smallest	0.80%	1,724	$136,028,242	1.19%
Mid-Cap 3-5	15.55%	619	$1,534,903,517	13.43%
Low-Cap 6-8	5.36%	999	$700,217,223	6.13%
Micro-Cap 9-10	1.77%	2,337	$304,917,894	2.67%

Source: © 2004 CRSP® Center for Research in Security prices. Graduate School of Business. The University of Chicago. Used with permission. All rights reserved. www.crsp.uchicago.edu.

[a] Historical average percentage of total capitalization shows the average, over the last 78 years, of the decile market values as a percentage of the total NYSE/AMEX/NASDAQ calculated each month.

[b] Number of companies in deciles, recent market capitalization of deciles, and recent percentage of total capitalization are as of September 30, 2003.

Exhibit 16.7   Summary Results of S&P CVC Size Effect Study

Historical Equity Risk Premiums: Averages Since 1963
Data for Year Ending December 31, 1996

Portfolio Rank by Size	Market Value of Equity			Book Value of Equity			5-Year Average Net Income			Market Value of Invested Capital		
	Average ($ mils.)	Arithmetic Average Premium	Smoothed Average Premium	Average ($ mils.)	Arithmetic Average Premium	Smoothed Average Premium	Average ($ mils.)	Arithmetic Average Premium	Smoothed Average Premium	Average ($ mils.)	Arithmetic Average Premium	Smoothed Average Premium
1	40,860	5.21%	2.29%	10,225	5.43%	3.75%	1,572	5.62%	3.90%	52,246	5.02%	2.51%
2	12,776	3.94%	4.17%	4,664	5.01%	4.94%	575	5.81%	5.24%	17,601	3.49%	4.25%
3	7,619	3.53%	5.00%	2,866	5.80%	5.68%	367	5.19%	5.84%	10,828	4.48%	5.03%
4	5,069	6.16%	5.66%	2,104	5.24%	6.14%	238	5.15%	6.41%	6,883	4.54%	5.75%
5	4,280	4.20%	5.93%	1,575	6.52%	6.58%	188	5.78%	6.73%	5,608	5.37%	6.08%
6	3,288	6.26%	6.36%	1,335	7.50%	6.83%	141	8.57%	7.11%	4,532	8.36%	6.42%
7	2,502	6.74%	6.80%	1,087	6.82%	7.14%	110	6.74%	7.44%	3,733	7.12%	6.73%
8	2,156	7.52%	7.04%	893	6.31%	7.44%	95	7.61%	7.65%	2,958	6.21%	7.10%
9	1,957	6.16%	7.19%	752	6.02%	7.70%	76	7.05%	7.93%	2,483	6.44%	7.38%
10	1,610	7.94%	7.51%	652	7.62%	7.91%	67	6.44%	8.11%	2,124	7.47%	7.63%
11	1,368	8.01%	7.77%	577	9.39%	8.10%	55	9.72%	8.36%	1,896	6.47%	7.81%
12	1,181	8.55%	8.01%	472	9.50%	8.40%	46	8.12%	8.60%	1,676	8.37%	8.01%
13	1,017	7.53%	8.25%	415	7.61%	8.59%	37	9.14%	8.88%	1,438	8.81%	8.25%
14	864	8.79%	8.51%	363	8.68%	8.80%	33	7.90%	9.06%	1,188	8.73%	8.56%
15	710	8.60%	8.83%	314	9.00%	9.02%	28	9.46%	9.27%	996	9.64%	8.84%
16	586	9.25%	9.14%	281	9.89%	9.18%	24	9.21%	9.46%	832	9.53%	9.13%
17	496	8.07%	9.41%	237	8.83%	9.44%	20	10.99%	9.70%	673	8.91%	9.46%
18	408	10.56%	9.72%	208	8.48%	9.64%	16	10.44%	9.98%	572	7.57%	9.72%
19	344	9.21%	10.00%	174	9.52%	9.91%	14	9.22%	10.22%	494	10.20%	9.96%
20	285	9.21%	10.30%	146	10.70%	10.17%	11	10.72%	10.47%	396	11.14%	10.31%
21	225	11.32%	10.68%	125	10.00%	10.41%	9	11.45%	10.81%	316	10.34%	10.67%
22	170	10.34%	11.14%	100	11.62%	10.74%	7	12.13%	11.19%	237	11.71%	11.13%
23	130	12.10%	11.56%	84	10.72%	11.00%	5	11.52%	11.63%	186	10.43%	11.52%
24	85	12.45%	12.26%	60	11.52%	11.50%	3	12.11%	12.20%	126	12.25%	12.14%
25	30	15.83%	13.92%	24	14.17%	12.91%	1	13.67%	13.58%	46	15.55%	13.77%
High financial risk	14.63%			14.09%			14.63%			14.63%		
Constant		19.42%			17.70%			13.71%			19.86%	
Slope		-3.71%			-3.48%			-3.07%			-3.68%	

(continued)

"smoothed" premium. The smoothed premium is based on regression analysis. In most parts of the size range, the smoothed premium is probably most appropriate to use.

It is important to note, however, that we find a pronounced jump in the premium in the smallest 4% of companies. This is of interest to many business valuators, since this jump occurs in a size category in which, as a practical matter, many more valuation assignments are performed. For seven of the eight size measures, the actual premium for the smallest group was greater than the smoothed premium, generally by a considerable margin. It remains a matter of analyst's judgment, after analyzing the risk characteristics of the subject company, whether to lean toward the actual premium for the smallest group or the smoothed premium.

SUMMARY

Size does matter.

The smaller the company, the higher the average cost of capital and the lower the average market valuation multiple.

Exhibit 16.7 Summary Results of the S&P CVC Size Study *(continued)*

Portfolio Rank by Size	Book Value of Invested Capital			5-Year Average EBITDA			Sales			Number of Employees		
	Average ($ mils.)	Arithmetic Average Premium	Smoothed Average Premium	Average ($ mils.)	Arithmetic Average Premium	Smoothed Average Premium	Average ($ mils.)	Arithmetic Average Premium	Smoothed Average Premium	Average ($ mils.)	Arithmetic Average Premium	Smoothed Average Premium
1	22,397	4.64%	3.36%	4,860	5.92%	4.21%	33,180	6.43%	5.29%	181,966	5.98%	5.81%
2	9,282	4.43%	4.69%	1,856	5.29%	5.48%	11,821	5.37%	6.41%	59,133	6.66%	6.86%
3	5,790	5.10%	5.40%	1,213	5.84%	6.04%	8,159	7.14%	6.82%	40,819	7.17%	7.20%
4	4,173	6.28%	5.89%	788	5.61%	6.62%	5,673	7.58%	7.22%	31,672	7.93%	7.43%
5	2,978	6.58%	6.39%	603	6.76%	6.97%	4,174	8.69%	7.55%	24,425	8.52%	7.67%
6	2,323	7.72%	6.77%	472	8.31%	7.29%	3,344	7.85%	7.79%	17,962	8.43%	7.96%
7	1,896	6.81%	7.07%	361	7.76%	7.65%	2,776	7.74%	8.00%	15,419	7.42%	8.10%
8	1,646	5.56%	7.28%	318	6.42%	7.81%	2,332	7.06%	8.19%	12,828	7.68%	8.27%
9	1,383	6.16%	7.55%	264	6.47%	8.06%	2,007	6.77%	8.35%	10,385	8.98%	8.47%
10	1,241	7.40%	7.71%	226	7.48%	8.27%	1,596	7.94%	8.60%	8,437	9.04%	8.66%
11	1,018	7.70%	8.01%	189	8.68%	8.51%	1,345	8.87%	8.79%	6,863	9.01%	8.85%
12	815	8.13%	8.34%	157	9.55%	8.75%	1,128	11.00%	8.98%	6,260	8.95%	8.93%
13	741	8.07%	8.48%	141	10.46%	8.89%	1,003	11.77%	9.11%	5,417	9.31%	9.07%
14	630	10.54%	8.73%	112	8.52%	9.20%	892	7.84%	9.23%	4,655	8.61%	9.21%
15	526	8.87%	9.00%	92	8.27%	9.45%	753	9.00%	9.42%	3,938	9.98%	9.36%
16	469	8.78%	9.17%	84	10.49%	9.57%	678	8.37%	9.53%	3,520	9.60%	9.47%
17	407	9.55%	9.38%	69	10.01%	9.83%	583	10.45%	9.70%	2,928	8.63%	9.64%
18	342	10.91%	9.64%	59	10.21%	10.05%	521	8.99%	9.82%	2,438	8.63%	9.81%
19	285	10.39%	9.92%	50	10.55%	10.25%	420	9.46%	10.05%	2,173	7.92%	9.91%
20	243	10.14%	10.16%	40	8.84%	10.56%	336	9.85%	10.30%	1,787	11.21%	10.10%
21	198	8.86%	10.47%	33	10.52%	10.81%	279	9.21%	10.50%	1,446	9.91%	10.29%
22	152	10.27%	10.86%	27	11.68%	11.10%	235	9.75%	10.69%	1,101	10.75%	10.54%
23	121	11.03%	11.21%	20	12.80%	11.50%	177	13.09%	11.00%	875	10.98%	10.76%
24	88	12.24%	11.68%	13	12.82%	12.08%	123	11.38%	11.39%	595	10.65%	11.11%
25	36	14.03%	13.05%	5	13.09%	13.40%	47	13.55%	12.44%	223	13.55%	12.02%
High financial risk	14.27%			14.86%			14.64%			15.22%		
Constant		18.41%			15.44%			16.65%			17.03%	
Slope		−3.46%			−3.05%			−2.51%			−2.13%	

Source: Data originally presented by David King of PricewaterhouseCoopers at the American Society of Appraisers Annual International Conference in Houston, Texas, June 1997. Table published in Shannon P. Pratt, *Cost of Capital: Estimations and Applications,* © 1998 John Wiley & Sons. Reprinted with permission of PricewaterhouseCoopers and John Wiley & Sons. Updates to this data, including the 2004 edition of the CVC Size Study and the CVC Risk Study are available on Ibbotson's cost of capital Web site, http://valuation.ibbotson.com.

This phenomenon has been shown by Ibbotson Associates Cost of Capital studies, based on NYSE data, for many years. In recent years, it has been further supported by a series of studies by PricewaterhouseCoopers, whose studies also include AMEX and NASDAQ companies.

As shown by examples in this chapter, recent studies using market multiples observed in acquisitions show that smaller companies tend to sell at lower multiples than their larger counterparts. This is true both for acquisitions of private companies and for acquisition of public companies.

Notes

1. Jay C. Vester, FPC Investors, and Stuart D. Matthews, Metapoint Partners, Inc., Association for Corporate Growth, annual meeting, Ponte Vedra Beach, Florida, April 1998. Quoted in *Shannon Pratt's Business Valuation Update™* (May 1998), 1 et seq.

2. *BIZCOMPS*® analysis presented in *Shannon Pratt's Business Valuation Update*™ (March 1999).

3. *BIZCOMPS*® uses SDCF to stand for seller's discretionary cash flow. It is defined the same way as the International Business Brokers Association's definition of discretionary earnings, that is, EBITDA plus all compensation to one owner/operator.

4. *Shannon Pratt's Business Valuation Update*™ (March 1999).

5. Jerry Peters, "Adjusting Price/Earnings Ratios for Differences in Company Size," *Business Valuation Review* (March 1992): 3–4, and "Adjusting Price/Earnings Ratios for Difference in Company Size—An Update," *Business Valuation Review* (September 1995): 121–123. See also update by Peters in June 1999 *Business Valuation Review*.

Chapter 17

Common Errors in Implementing the Market Approach

If the analyst implements market approach methodology using the procedures described in this book, the errors discussed in this chapter should not occur.

Nevertheless, reading this chapter, which is somewhat in the nature of review, may help the analyst to avoid falling into any of these frequently encountered traps.

Moreover, the chapter may prove useful in a disputed valuation setting when any of these errors is encountered in a report by an opposing valuation analyst. The chapter provides concrete material for getting errors corrected, which may help to facilitate settlement. In the context of litigation, the chapter offers a basis for deposition questions, cross-examination questions, rebuttal testimony, and lawyers' briefs critiquing an opposing expert's testimony or report methodology.

INADEQUATE SELECTION OF GUIDELINE COMPANIES

Probably the most common shortcoming in implementation of the market approach is one that takes place near the beginning of the exercise: poor selection of guideline companies.

Defining Too Narrow a Population

The problem of defining too narrow a population of guideline companies from which to choose can occur with either the guideline public company method or the guideline merged and acquired company method.

Guideline Public Companies. There are over 15,000 public companies reporting to the Securities and Exchange Commission (SEC), not to mention as many more that are public but fall below the SEC reporting requirement as measured by either asset size or number of stockholders. However, none of the major secondary services covers every one of the reporting companies, and services such as Value Line cover only a small subset of the largest companies. Consequently, analysts often overlook some of the smaller guideline public companies that are likely to be most comparable to the subject being valued.

Guideline Merged and Acquired Companies. Getting a comprehensive list of guideline merged and acquired companies can be even more difficult than getting a good list of guideline public companies because there is no single comprehensive source. Appendix B should help the analyst in this respect. Also, for smaller companies, the emergence and expansion of the four private company databases discussed in this book should make the company selection more comprehensive for small and midsize companies (mom-and-pop businesses up to those valued under $100 million).

Guideline Limited Partnerships. The Partnership Profiles database contains over 315 real estate–related limited partnerships. The publicly registered limited partnerships include commercial, apartments, insured mortgages, leases, parking lot, and retail real estate properties. It is common to find guideline limited partnerships that are similar in size, leverage, and profitability to family limited partnerships.

Inadequate Comparative Analysis

Many times in court, one analyst's market approach has been accepted and another's rejected because of the relative degree of comparability of the guideline companies selected. After the initial selection, comparative analysis of both the nature of operations and the financial characteristics should be undertaken to reach a final group of guideline companies. On occasion, the initial selection criteria may even be widened to allow one or a few more companies with investment characteristics similar to the subject.

INDISCRIMINATE USE OF AVERAGE (OR MEDIAN) MULTIPLES

One of the most common errors in implementation of the market approach is naively applying either mean or median guideline company multiples to subject company data with little or even no comparative analysis.

Once in a while, the subject company will have characteristics almost identical to the average of the guideline companies, but not often. Even if it does, the analyst should point out analysis that leads to the conclusion of this similarity.

But more often, differences between the guideline and subject companies would lead to applying multiples that are not identical to the guideline averages. That is why we do comparative financial analysis and conduct site visits and management interviews. As discussed in Chapter 10 on selecting and weighting multiples, one might choose the multiples of the most comparable subset of guideline companies; might increase or decrease multiples by a percentage; might choose a point in the observed range, such as upper or lower quartile or quintile; or possibly (but rarely) even justify multiples outside the observed range.

A related error is unexplained adjustments, such as blindly adjusting all multiples by exactly the same percentage or in exactly the same manner. It may be appropriate to adjust some multiples differently from others. The most obvious example would be a company that had a high return on sales but a low return on equity relative to the guideline companies. This situation would suggest a price/sales ratio above the guideline averages, but a price/book value ratio below the guideline averages.

FAILING TO CONSIDER GUIDELINE COMPANY FINANCIAL STATEMENT ADJUSTMENTS

A common error in implementing the guideline public company method (or the guideline merger and acquisition method using acquired public companies) is to make proper adjustments to the subject company financial statements but ignore possible comparable adjustments to the guideline company statements.

Many types of adjustments should be made for valuation purposes that would not be classified as extraordinary under generally accepted accounting principles (GAAP). Some of these would include

- Nonrecurring items, which should be eliminated to get comparable, normalized operating results
  - Major gains or losses on the sale of assets
  - Effect of strikes
  - Effect of lawsuits
- Results of discontinued operations

Also, if some companies are on last in, first out (LIFO) inventory accounting and some on first in, first out (FIFO), all should be adjusted to FIFO to put them on a comparable basis.

None of these factors will show up if the analyst relies on secondary sources to compile financial data for the guideline companies. This is one important reason why it is desirable to use original company documents, such as 10-Ks and 10-Qs, if this level of detail is required.

FAILURE TO CONDUCT A SITE VISIT AND MANAGEMENT INTERVIEWS

If possible, site visits and management interviews are equally important for the income approach and the market approach and, in many instances, even for the asset approach. There are, of course, situations where the site visit and management interviews cannot be conducted due to the restrictions of time or hostility of the parties.

The analyst has the responsibility of selecting the guideline companies. Seeing the operations and interviewing management should help guide the analyst's judgment as to which potential guideline companies are satisfactorily comparable. Also, management may have some suggestions as to guideline companies that the analyst may have overlooked or may have some valid reasons to consider rejecting certain guideline companies that the analyst was considering.

Furthermore, the analyst must exercise judgment to decide on the types and levels of market multiples to apply to the subject company relative to the multiples observed for the guideline public or merged and acquired companies. The analyst almost inevitably gains some insight on the subject company's strengths and weaknesses relative to its peers by observing the premises and operations and interviewing the management (and sometimes even customers and other related outside parties, such as suppliers, bankers, accountants, attorneys, and competitors). These insights, along with the comparative financial analysis, should guide the analyst's judgment in choosing the types and levels of market multiples to apply to the subject company relative to the peer group guideline companies selected.

Most of us like to do the first pass at the financial statement adjustments and the comparative financial analysis (described in Chapters 7 and 8) before the site visit and management interview. This exercise usually results in questions to ask management to gain greater insight about observed data and the implications for future changes. (After all, valuation is to assess the present value of the future benefits of investing in the company, and a study of the past is really to help assess that future.) The visit and interviews also may result in some revisions to or additions to (or even elimination of) some preliminary financial statement adjustments.

Site visits and management interviews are especially important if there is actual or possible litigation. Courts tend to accord considerably more credibility to an analyst who has visited the premises and operations and interviewed management than to one who has not.

There are instances, of course, when site visits are not possible or practical. We suggest that, in such cases, the analyst should disclose it in the report and note the reason for omitting the site visit.

MAKING INAPPROPRIATE OR UNSUPPORTED FINANCIAL STATEMENT ADJUSTMENTS

The standard of value and the assumed ownership characteristics often dictate whether certain financial statement adjustments are warranted in a particular situation. In any case, if adjustments are made (or might potentially be made but are rejected), the analyst should provide adequate support for the reason and amount of the adjustment.

Inappropriate Adjustments

When valuing a minority interest under the standard of fair market value, many analysts would consider it an error to make financial statement adjustments that only a control owner can make. The most common example is excess compensation. For example, if the control owner is taking excess compensation and will continue to do so, that money will not be available to minority stockholders; therefore, the analyst would take the position that the statements should not be adjusted as if it would be.

One argument in favor of a compensation adjustment when using the public guideline company method is to put the subject company on a basis that is comparable to the guideline companies. If that is done when there is excess compensation, then there should be a minority interest discount, even though the public companies are minority interests, to reflect the distribution of the excess compensation to the control owner.

If the standard of value is fair value, and if case law indicates that a pro rata portion of control value is appropriate, then there would be justification for an adjustment for things like excess compensation even though the shares that are being valued are minority shares.

Inadequately Supported Adjustments

It is important that the magnitude of any financial statement adjustments be supported, using the best empirical data available. Again, an adjustment for reasonable compensation is both the most common and the most controversial. There are many sources of compensation data, and the analyst should try to choose the source most germane.[1]

APPLYING MULTIPLES TO INCONSISTENTLY DEFINED DATA

There are many levels of the income statement and balance sheet from which data for market value multiples may be drawn. Furthermore, each of the variables may be before or after possible adjustments as discussed in Chapter 7. The possible mismatches between the variable as defined for the guideline companies and the variable as defined for the subject company are too numerous to catalog in this book, but it is essential to be on the lookout for possible mismatches.

FAILURE TO MATCH TIME PERIODS

Measuring financial variables over different time periods for the guideline companies from the subject company can lead to very distorted results. This can be especially true with cyclical or seasonal companies, and especially true if the effective valuation date is near the turning point in a cycle.

Failure to Match Historical Time Periods

Public companies report operating results quarterly. About half of them have calendar fiscal years, while the other half have fiscal years somewhat scattered throughout the calendar. The analyst usually uses subject company data as near as possible to the effective valuation date. If public company fiscal quarters coincide with the date of the subject company data, that data should be used, not the public company's prior fiscal year data. If the fiscal quarters do not coincide, then it is usually best to use data from the closest available date. In some situations, being off by only a single quarter distorted results to the point of being meaningless at a turning point in a cyclical industry. Some analysts also use only the public companies' latest full-year data when more recent quarterly data are available.

When using merger and acquisition data, dates necessarily will not coincide: An adjustment for changes in industry conditions may be needed.

Applying a Multiple Derived from Average Data to a Single Period's Data

If, for example, the analyst creates a multiple based on a current stock price times the average of five years' past earnings for each guideline company, common sense would dictate that the multiple should be applied to the last five years' average earnings for the subject company. Yet sometimes such a multiple is applied to a single year's earnings (or some other variable) for the subject company. If there is any kind of a trend or cyclicality for either the guideline company or subject companies' earnings (which is usually true), this mismatch will result in a distorted indication of value.

Applying a Multiple from Historical Data to Forecast Data

The price/earnings (P/E) multiple, as it is published for thousands of companies in the national and world financial press, represents the current price times the latest reported 12 months' trailing earnings. Some analysts, however, take those reported P/Es and apply them to their subject company's coming-year projected earnings. Assuming that the industry is expecting growing earnings, this produces an upwardly biased indication of value.

If the financial variable to be used for the subject company is next year's projected earnings, then this must be matched with guideline company multiples consisting of the valuation date price times the *projected* earnings for each respective guideline company. (Sources for such forecasts are included in Appendix B.)

RELIANCE ON RULES OF THUMB

If there is a widely used rule of thumb for valuation in an industry, it should be considered. However, it should not be relied on as the only method. Rather, it is more appropriately used as a "sanity check" on the value as determined using other appropriate valuation methods.

In his book on valuation formulas for small businesses, Glenn Desmond emphasizes this point:

> Formulas and rule-of-thumb multiplier ranges change because of new forms of competition, influences from regional or national inflation or recession, changes in popularity and marketability of businesses, and refinements in valuation methodology and data sources.
>
> Since the 1988 edition of this handbook, there has been a general decline in the value of small businesses. As of late 1992, declines of 25% to 30% are common. . . .[2]

> [F]ormula valuations are not substitutes for careful consideration of other appropriate valuation methods that are applicable to the business being appraised.[3]

Nobody knows how most rules of thumb were derived.

We have included them in this book on the market approach because some people think that they represent a consensus of actual market activity. However, it may be more accurate to say that they may represent what business brokers anticipate or owners hope to realize on a sale versus what owners in the industry typically realize on a sale.

The author has conducted two major tests of rules of thumb, one for the property management industry and the other for the car rental franchise industry. In each case, a valuation rule of thumb was developed by an extensive survey of business owners in the industry. Then an extended study of actual transactions of sales of the companies in the industry was made. In the case of the property management companies, the actual transactions were at an average of about 65% of the value that the consensus rule of thumb indicated. In the case of the car rental franchises, the actual transactions were at an average of about 50% of the values that the consensus rule of thumb indicated.

Based on this limited anecdotal evidence, one might conclude that rules of thumb tend to be upwardly biased, and this could be so. Many people are interested in this question, so the author has planned a lengthy series of empirical tests. Recently and over the next several years, we have and will test published valuation rules of thumb against actual transactions, using *Pratt's Stats™* and other private transaction databases, and publish the results.[4]

FAILURE TO ACCOUNT FOR EXCESS OR DEFICIENT CASH

Market multiples based on financial operating results (e.g., price/earnings, market value of invested capital/earnings before interest, taxes, depreciation, and amortization [MVIC/EBITDA]) do not directly reflect differences in the cash positions from one company to another. A common error is failure to make any adjustment when the subject company has significantly more or less cash or cash equivalents than the guideline companies.

There are at least three ways to handle significant cash differences:

1. Adjust multiples up or down to reflect greater or less financial strength.
2. Add or subtract a specific dollar amount for an estimate of excess or deficient cash.
3. Subtract out all the cash of both guideline and subject companies before the comparative analysis, and then add the subject company's cash back at the end: the investment banker's method.

FAILURE TO ADJUST FOR DIFFERENCES IN DEAL TERMS AND STRUCTURE

All too often, we find that the prices at which the guideline merger and acquisition transactions took place are not adjusted for differences in transaction terms or for differences in the property being transferred.

Differences in Deal Terms

Most small businesses are not sold for cash. The seller often accepts a note from the buyer, and the interest on the note usually is at rates below those that would be available in an arm's-length commercial loan. The price of such a deal should be adjusted by computing the present value of the seller's note using a market rate of interest. Both *Pratt's Stats™* and *BIZCOMPS®* provide the transaction terms necessary to make this adjustment. The analyst must make an estimate as to what a market rate of interest would be. Failure to make such an adjustment, where appropriate, usually results in overstatement of the value of the guideline transaction, thus resulting in overstated multiples.

A related problem arises when the terms of the guideline transaction contain contingencies. The most common contingency is retention of existing clients, commonly found in sales of professional practices, such as accounting practices. If enough information is available, the analyst should adjust the transaction price to the present value of the best estimate of the expected proceeds. If such an estimate cannot be made, the analyst might consider dropping the transaction from the guideline list.

Differences in Property Transacted

The different middle-market and small-company databases have different policies about what is assumed to be included in the transaction price, as discussed in Chapter 6. This is especially true with respect to current assets and current liabilities transferred or assumed.

It is important to compare what is assumed to be included in the subject transaction and adjust for the value of any differences between it and what was included in the guideline transaction.

One of the most commonly overlooked differences is noncompete and employment contracts. In most cases, the property that the analyst is appraising does *not* include either a noncompete or an employment agreement. However, the transaction prices for a significant portion of small businesses and professional practice sales *do* include noncompete and/or employment agreements. If the guideline transactions do include such agreements and the subject property does not, the value of such agreements should be subtracted from the guideline company transaction prices and the multiples recomputed before applying the multiples to the subject property. Failure to make this adjustment results in overstatement of the value of the subject property. Most *Pratt's Stats™* and *BIZCOMPS®* transactions include the information necessary to make these adjustments.

Failure to make these adjustments is a common problem in valuations for divorces. Noncompete and employment agreements are regarded as personal rather than marital property in most states. Nevertheless, we often see valuations of businesses and practices that are based on guideline transactions without any reduction in price for the inclusion of those valuable intangible assets.

"ASSETS PLUS . . ." RULES

The chapter section "Reliance on Rules of Thumb" noted that some rules are in the form of "assets plus a multiple of some operating variable." Such rules never address a value less than the net asset value, and they usually assume (at least loosely) that the asset values are somewhere near current replacement value.

Many businesses are worth much less than the replacement value of their assets, all the way down to liquidation value. A business is worth something more than the value of its assets only to the extent that it can earn more than a reasonable return on the asset value. That is the concept of the *excess earnings method,* where the capitalized value of earnings over a reasonable return on assets is added to the asset value. But we never hear anyone speak of the *deficient earnings method,* where one might subtract the capitalized value of an earnings deficiency from the value of the assets.

Goodwill is not only a function of continuing patronage, but also is dependent on being able to make a return on that patronage over and above a reasonable return on tangible assets. Many small business owners with established patronage but poor returns do not understand why they cannot sell their businesses for the current value of their assets plus some "blue sky" for the customer base. One very highly regarded small women's clothing chain, however, wisely chose to liquidate when it realized that its competition was strong enough that it could not even earn a reasonable profit relative to the liquidation value of its assets.

FAILING TO APPLY APPROPRIATE DISCOUNTS AND PREMIUMS

We sometimes see a failure to adjust, or make proper adjustments, to get from the level of value indicated by the market approach results to the level of value required in the assignment. Often the nature of the adjustment is perfectly appropriate, but there is no, or inadequate, data presented to support the magnitude of the adjustment. Chapters 11 and 12 on discounts and premiums should help the analyst avoid this important category of errors.

SUMMARY

The opportunities to go awry in the implementation of the market approach are legion. Sometimes the toughest ones to spot are errors of omission, such as failing to consider the full population of potentially useful guideline companies, failure to make certain adjustments, or failure to use all of the best data available to support certain adjustments, such as reasonable compensation or a discount for lack of marketability.

Some of the most common errors are

- Inadequate guideline company selection
- Failure to analyze and adjust guideline company data
- Failure to conduct site visit and management interviews
- Making inappropriate or unsupported financial statement adjustments
- Applying multiples to inconsistently defined data
- Failure to match time periods
- Reliance on rules of thumb
- Failure to account for excess or deficient cash
- Using an "assets plus" rule when the company's returns are not even adequate to support the assets employed
- Applying improper (or *not* applying proper) discounts and premiums, or not adequately supporting the amounts of the discounts or premiums applied

We hope that this chapter will help the analyst avoid any of these shortcomings. Moreover, we hope that this chapter will help spot errors in opposing valuations and have them corrected or convincingly brought to the attention of the decision maker or court.

Notes

1. Many general and specialized sources of compensation data are included regularly in "Where to Find It: Business Valuation Data Directory," published as a supplement to *Shannon Pratt's Business Valuation Update™*.
2. Glenn Desmond, *Handbook of Small Business Valuation Formulas and Rules of Thumb*, 3rd ed. (Camden, ME: Valuation Press, 1993), 4. Reprinted with permission of Marshall & Swift, LP.
3. Id. at 3.
4. Results have been published in *Shannon Pratt's Business Valuation Update™*.

Chapter 18

The Dismal Track Record of U.S. Market Acquisitions

The most difficult decision an executive faces in negotiating an acquisition is the price to be paid.[1]

Joseph Marren, in *Mergers & Acquisitions: A Valuation Handbook,* continues: "Acquisitions, on average, have not worked out well for corporate acquirors."[2] Marren's rule is

Don't overpay! There are many things that can be changed in a deal after it is done, including management, the product line, and facilities. However, once the purchase price has been paid, you have to live with it. If you significantly overpaid because you got too emotional over the opportunity, you have dug a very deep hole to climb out of.[3]

ACQUIRORS TEND TO OVERPAY

It has been well documented over the last two decades that buyers of businesses, on average, pay too much. Studies conducted on the public markets show that acquisitions do increase total shareholder value, on average. That is, the average postacquisition value of the combined acquirer and acquiree companies is greater than the sum of their separate preacquisition market values. However, *more than 100% of the total market value increases tend to go to the shareholders of the acquiree companies with the acquirer companies' shareholders losing market value.*

The most comprehensive study to date demonstrating the widespread tendency to overpay was done by Mark Sirower, a professor at New York University. He analyzed 91 deals between 1979 and 1990 for his book, *The Synergy Trap: How Companies Lose the Acquisition Game.*[4] He found that two-thirds of those deals destroyed value for acquiring company shareholders.

In commenting on Sirower's work, Al Rappaport says "while there is no comparable body of event studies for the 1990s at this time, there is no shortage of 'value-destroying' acquisition examples."[5]

University of Chicago professor Steven Kaplan researched 70 large deals completed from 1993 to 1995. He concluded that the mergers created 13% added value, in the sense that the market value of the combined company was 13% more than the total of the companies' respective separate values before the mergers. However, this net 13% increase was comprised of a 21% gain to the target companies' stockholders and an 8% average loss in value to the buying companies' stockholders (see Exhibit 18.1).[6]

Commenting on 1998 mergers, a *Fortune* article opined, "[A]t the prices acquirors are paying, most deals still won't work." The article explained:

Attend a press conference for one of today's megamergers, and it's hard to resist being swept up in it all: the two imperial CEOs and their soaring strategic vision; the solemn assurances that this is all for the good of the shareholders; the infectious camaraderie radiating from the podium. (Hey, he didn't sell just because he stood personally to make $30 million; he sold because he really likes the other CEO.) The press adores the big story, and Wall Street, never inclined to impede an oncoming gravy train, adds its strong backing.

Exhibit 18.1 Bidder Returns, Target Returns, and Combined Returns after 70 Large Acquisition Announcements, 1993–1995

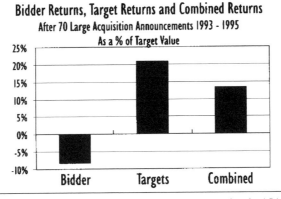

Source: Steven Kaplan, "Valuation Issues in Control Transactions," presented at the ASA Advanced Business Valuation Conference, Boston, November 3, 1995. Abstracted in *Shannon Pratt's Business Valuation Update* (December 1995), 5. Reprinted with permission of the American Society of Appraisers.

It's all so positive, so full of good feeling, that you'd have to be a complete curmudgeon to spoil the mood by questioning the deal's price.

But maybe it's time for the curmudgeons to take the floor. As no less crusty a customer than Warren Buffett observed in one of his memorable Berkshire Hathaway shareholder letters, "A too-high purchase price for the stock of an excellent company can undo the developments." In other words, "strategic fit" ain't enough. The plan is seamless integration, and a harmonious blend of cultures—all the elements that you need to achieve synergies. But if the acquirer overpaid, it doesn't matter. The shareholders still lose.[7]

WHY BUYERS OVERPAY: THE HUBRIS EFFECT

In a 1983 article titled "The Hubris Hypothesis of Corporate Takeovers," Richard Roll states that "*the hubris hypothesis* is very simple: Decision makers in acquiring firms pay too much for their targets on average in the samples we observe."[8]

Roll explains:

The mechanism by which takeover attempts are initiated and consummated suggests that at least part of the large price increases observed in target firm shares might represent a simple transfer from the bidding firm, that is, that the observed takeover premium (tender offer or merger price less preannouncement market price of the target firm) overstates the increase in economic value of the corporate combination.[9]

Webster defines *hubris* as an " 'exaggerated pride or self-confidence, often resulting in retribution.' Hubris derives from Greek mythology . . . [where] those who were excessively confident, presumptuous [toward the gods], blindly ambitious or otherwise lacking humility were relentlessly struck down by the gods."[10] Hubris is a convenient concept that can be applicable in many contexts.

In the context of merger and acquisition pricing, Columbia University professor Donald Hambrick along with doctoral candidate Mathew Hayward conducted a study of 106 transactions in which they conclude that high chief executive officer (CEO) hubris leads to payment of high acquisition premiums. They also concluded, "Not only did the acquiring firms lose value, . . . but the larger the premium paid, the greater the [shareholder] loss."[11]

Four Factors Evidence CEO Hubris

The authors tested factors associated with CEO hubris leading to high acquisition premiums on the basis of four hypotheses:

1. *Recent organizational success.* The better the recent performance of the acquiring firm (as measured by its LTM stockholder returns), the higher the premium it will pay.

2. *CEO media praise.* The greater the recent media praise for the firm's CEO, the higher the premium paid. (This was based on the number and strength of articles favorable to the CEO in certain national media.)

3. *CEO inexperience.* The shorter the tenure of the acquiring firm's CEO, the higher the premium paid.

4. *CEO self-importance.* The greater the CEO's self-importance, as reflected by his or her compensation relative to the second highest paid officer, the greater the premium paid.

The Columbia University study found strong correlations between CEO hubris and the payment of high acquisition premiums when they measured hubris by these factors. They found even stronger correlations when a great deal of media praise or high relative pay for the CEO existed in combination with a board of directors largely composed of insiders. The model is shown schematically in Exhibit 18.2.

Egos Frequently Outpace Logic

Hayward and Hambrick note that "acquiring managers' egos frequently outpace their logic during a takeover campaign." They add, "[B]idding managers infected with hubris overestimate their ability to manage the target firm and hence overpay for it." Here premiums reflect acquirer management arrogance.

Other observations include:

Exhibit 18.2   A Model of CEO Hubris and Acquisition Premiums

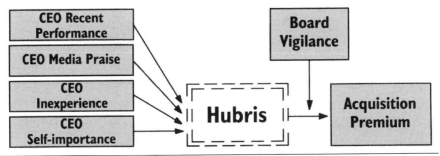

Source: Reprinted from "Explaining Premiums Paid for Large Acquisitions: Evidence of CEO Hubris" by Matthew L. Hayward and Donald C. Hambrick, published in *Administrative Science Quarterly* 42(1) by *Administrative Science Quarterly.* © 2000 by Cornell University. Presented in *Shannon Pratt's Business Valuation Update®* (October 1995), 8.

- "Some CEOs have systematically inflated views of their abilities . . . often to the point of delusions of grandeur."

- "It seems that some CEOs who pay extremely large acquisition premiums, on the assumption that they have the talent to recoup the extraordinary outlays, [have] literally come to believe their own press."

- "Some CEOs have an extreme sense of potency, verging on arrogance . . . and that these CEOs will be relatively likely to inject their arrogance into their strategic choices, including the prices they pay for large acquisitions."

The authors conclude that "the evidence is substantial that this exceedingly 'economic' phenomenon acquisition pricing, typically involving huge sums of money—is due more to social, psychological, and institutional forces than to financial optimization."[12]

CEO Hubris Leads to Investment Value

The primary difference between *fair market value* and *investment value* is that fair market value is the value to a *typical* or *hypothetical* buyer or seller, while investment value is the value to a *particular* buyer or seller. It would seem that the greater the CEO hubris, the more the transaction price leans toward investment value versus fair market value.

When evaluating acquisition transactions in the implementation of the market approach, the analyst might consider investigating the extent of CEO hubris as a clue to the extent to which the transaction represents investment value rather that fair market value.

THE FROG-KISSING PRINCESS

In his book, *Creating Shareholder Value,* Al Rappaport concluded his chapter on mergers and acquisitions with this quote from Warren E. Buffett:

> In the past, I've observed that many acquisition-hungry managers were apparently mesmerized by their childhood reading of the story about the frog-kissing princess. Remembering her success, they pay dearly for the right to kiss corporate toads, expecting wondrous transfigurations. Initially, disappointing results only deepen their desire to round up new toads. ("Fanaticism," said Santayana, "consists of redoubling your effort when you've forgotten your aim.") Ultimately, even the most optimistic manager must face reality. Standing knee-deep in unresponsive toads, he then announces an enormous "restructuring" charge. In this equivalent of a Head Start program, the CEO receives the education but the stockholders pay the tuition.[13]

SUMMARY

It has been well documented that, on balance, far more actual company sales are overpriced than are underpriced. This is often because of buyers' overestimation of the values of synergies between the selling company and the buying company, or overestimation of the earning capacity that the buyer can realize from the company being purchased.

Studies attempting to analyze reasons for this phenomenon often have centered on the hubris effect, or an unjustified and overconfident optimism about the results that the buyer can expect to obtain from the company being bought.

The author hopes that readers will benefit in arriving at reasonable prices by objectively applying the principles of the market approach espoused in this book and the principles of the income approach as explained in his earlier book, *Cost of Capital.*[14] Of course, if you are a seller, you want to find a buyer with lots of hubris!

Notes

1. Joseph K. Marren, *Mergers & Acquisitions: A Valuation Handbook* (Homewood, IL: Business One Irwin, 1993), v.
2. Id. at ix.
3. Id. at 33.
4. Mark Sirower, *The Synergy Trap: How Companies Lose the Acquisition Game* (New York: The Free Press, 1997), 145–56.
5. Alfred Rappaport, *Creating Shareholder Value,* rev. ed. (New York: The Free Press, 1998), 145. Original source of quote: Mark L. Sirower, *The Synergy Trap* (New York: The Free Press, 1997).
6. Steven Kaplan, "Valuation Issues in Control Transactions," presented at American Society of Appraisers Advanced Business Valuation Conference, Boston, November 3, 1995. Abstracted in *Shannon Pratt's Business Valuation Update™* (December 1995): 5.
7. Shawn Tully and Eileen P. Gunn, "Special Report: Megamergers," *Fortune,* January 11, 1999, 99. Reprinted with permission of Time Life Syndication.
8. Richard Roll, "The Hubris Hypothesis of Corporate Takeovers," *Journal of Business* 59, no. 2 (1986): 212. Reprinted with permission of the University of Chicago Press.
9. Id. at 198.
10. Matthew L. Hayward and Donald C. Hambrick, "Explaining the Premiums Paid for Large Acquisitions," *Administrative Science Quarterly* 42, no. 1 (March 1997): 103–125. © 2000 by Cornell University. Reprinted with permission.
11. Id.
12. Id.
13. Letter to shareholders in the 1992 annual report of Berkshire Hathaway. See note 5, 162. Reprinted with permission of Warren E. Buffett.
14. Shannon P. Pratt, *Cost of Capital: Theory and Applications,* 2nd ed. (Hoboken, NJ: John Wiley & Sons, 2002).

The Market Approach in the Courts

The cases in this chapter use the market approach and are generally representative of the various courts' reactions to various aspects of its application. The full text of most federal and state appellate valuation cases since 1990, and earlier landmark cases, are included on the BV Library section of BVResources.com, where one can search by keyword, such as *market approach, guideline company method,* or *guideline merged and acquired company method.*

U.S. TAX COURT

The U.S. Tax Court has widely accepted the market approach.[1] However, disputes commonly occur concerning expert choices of guideline companies, what control premium or minority discount to use, or whether to use either at all, and whether prices set in buy-sell agreements are true indications of value.

Choosing Guideline Companies

At issue in *Caracci v. Commissioner* was the value of a home health care agency and related entities that were transferred into S corporations.[2] The Internal Revenue Service (IRS) expert used the market approach, considering two types of transfers: valuation of comparable publicly traded home health care agencies and valuation of merged or acquired companies. As a basis for valuations under the market approach, the expert estimated the subject company's market value of invested capital (MVIC), using a price/revenue multiple. The court favored this approach, saying: "We believe that the best evidence of the value of [the company] arises from the use of the comparable value method employed by both experts. . . . use of the MVIC approach to compare the privately held [company] entities to similar publicly traded businesses is especially appropriate here. . . ."

In *Estate of Leichter*, both experts used comparables for an importer and wholesale distributor.[3] The IRS expert compared the subject company to five publicly traded firms and discounted the value of the subject to match more accurately the comparables. Although the court found that his conclusion was "within a reasonable range," it also found some weakness in his analysis, most notably his use of guideline companies that were not similar to the subject.

At issue in *Hess v. Commissioner* was the value of the stock of a closely held corporation.[4] In his guideline companies analysis, the IRS expert relied solely on price/earnings (P/E) ratios to compare the subject company to the guideline companies. The taxpayers argued that use of P/E ratios was erroneous, claiming that P/E ratios are a "crude measure" for calculating value and do not consider important differences in interest levels, tax levels, and depreciation levels between the subject company and the guideline companies. The court agreed that the IRS expert's guideline companies method would have been more complete and more persuasive if it had employed additional measures of comparison. However, the court also noted that it is clear that P/E ratios bear a well recognized relationship in the valuation of companies and that reliance on P/E ratios was not inherently flawed. The P/E ratios of publicly held companies do not compare to the P/E ratios of a closely held company if the companies themselves are not comparable. Whether the stock price of one company with a given earnings stream will be similar to that of another company with the same earnings depends on a wide variety of factors, including management policy, management ability, past performance, and dividend policy. Although taxpayers suggested that the guideline companies did not compare to the subject company, the court pointed out that two of the four guideline companies used by the IRS expert in his analysis were companies used by the subject to "benchmark" its performance and three of the four guideline companies were also used by the taxpayers' expert in his market comparable analysis. Accordingly, the court found that the guideline companies, when properly adjusted, were comparable to the subject company.

The value of the stock of a small, one-branch bank in Boonville, Indiana, was at issue in the *Estate of Hendrickson* case.[5] Even though the subject bank was commercial, it acted more like a thrift. Thrifts usually provide a lesser range of banking services than commercial banks, are frequently owned by a bank holding company owning one or more institutions, and stock companies account for more than 66% of their assets. The court accepted the guideline companies of petitioner's expert, because his selection criteria were limited to thrifts comparable in size to the subject bank. However, the Tax Court rejected the guideline companies chosen by the expert for the IRS, because his principal criterion was "geography, rather than size, financial, or operating characteristics." Five of the seven companies the IRS expert chose were bank holding companies, engaged in a wide range of personal and commercial banking services. And even though two of the selected companies were thrifts, they had multiple branches and had much greater assets than those of the subject bank.

The subject company in *Estate of Brookshire* owned a chain of grocery stores, two food and merchandise distribution centers, two bakery plants, one milk processing plant, and a photo processing center.[6] The court determined that three guideline public companies the expert for the IRS chose were not comparable, because they had "significant sales in markets other than retail grocery." Therefore, the expert overstated the value of the company's stock.

The court accepted the guideline companies for all three experts in *Estate of Gallo,* even though only one of the comparables was in the same business as the subject company.[7] The subject company was a winery, and experts for both sides found that there was only one publicly traded winery that was "even remotely comparable" to the subject company. Revenue Ruling 59-60 states that in valuing closely held stock, one of the factors to consider in the analysis is:

> The market price of stocks of corporations engaged in the same or a similar line of business having their stocks actively traded in a free and open market, either on an exchange or over-the-counter.[8]

All experts chose distilling and brewing companies. In addition to these companies, the IRS expert chose companies in the food processing industry. Petitioner's first expert reasoned that these were useful comparables, because they operated in the same regulated environment as the subject company, and those products competed with those of the subject company. In addition to choosing comparables in the soft drink industry, petitioner's second expert chose producers of single discretionary food products because of the competitive market conditions and those companies were also subject to fluctuations in agricultural raw material prices.

Hallmark Cards, Inc., was the subject company in *Estate of Hall.*[9] At the time of the valuation date, there existed only one publicly traded greeting card company, American Greetings. Respondent's expert and petitioner's experts all chose American Greetings as a comparable. Petitioner's experts also chose comparable companies, which the court accepted, that "produced brand name consumer goods, were leading companies in their industries, had publicly traded common stock, had financial characteristics similar to Hallmark," and were "highly regarded by the investment community for their quality management, leading market positions, and excellent financial conditions." Examples of these guideline public companies include Avon, McDonald's, Anheuser-Busch, IBM, and Coca-Cola.

The expert for the IRS in *Hall* used only American Greetings as a comparable. The court did not accept this, and it rejected the IRS's argument that it was " 'simply wrong as a matter of law' to look beyond the single, publicly held company engaged in the sale of greeting cards to other companies engaged in the sale of other types of consumer nondurable goods or having similar financial characteristics." The court wrote that the IRS's "argument too narrowly construes the concept of comparability and ignores the use of 'similar' as well as 'same' " in Section 2031 of the Estate Tax regulations. One comparable does not constitute a market—no matter how good it is. "Any one company may have unique individual characteristics that may distort the comparison. Similarly, the good fortune of one company in an industry may be at the expense of its direct competitors."[10]

Even if experts for both sides use the guideline public company method, the court will not necessarily accept either expert's comparables or methodology, as in *Rakow v. Commissioner.*[11] The court rejected the methodology used by petitioner's expert, because his calculations did not focus on the period of time close to the valuation date of the subject company. Because the subject company was so small compared to the guideline companies chosen by the IRS expert, he made numerous adjustments to the ratios. Therefore, the court found the market approach unreliable in this case and "more prone to error" than a discounted cash flow (DCF) analysis, which the IRS expert also used.

"Because value under the guideline method is developed from the market data of similar companies, the selection of appropriate comparable companies is of paramount importance."[12] These words, written by the court in *Hendrickson,* sum up the importance of selecting comparable guideline companies. Even though a company may seem to be an appropriate comparable at first glance, the court looks at it as a whole. All the characteristics of the guideline company should be considered before an analyst chooses it to conduct a valuation.

Buy-Sell Agreements

Courts have long recognized that the value of corporate stock may be limited for gift and estate tax purposes by an enforceable buy-sell agreement that fixes the price that the stock may be offered for sale to the remaining shareholders. In *Estate of Lauder,* the court outlined several requirements to test whether the price in the buy-sell agreement is binding:

- The price must be fixed and determinable under the agreement
- The agreement must be binding on the parties during life and after death.
- The agreement must have been entered into for a bona fide business reason.
- It must not be a substitute for a testamentary disposition.[13]

The *Lauder* court found that the buy-sell agreement was indeed intended to be a testamentary device, so the court did not uphold the agreement price for estate tax purposes. This particular buy-sell agreement used a formula based on book value for the shares of the cosmetic company of Estee Lauder, Inc. The court rejected the agreement price because there was no formal appraisal, the parties did not consider the trading prices of comparable companies, there was no evidence that the parties negotiated with respect to the formula, and the formula did not include the value of intangible assets, which are significant components of aggregate value for cosmetic companies.

In *Estate of Blount,* the Tax Court disregarded a buy-sell agreement in determining decedent's interest in a closely held company on the date of his death.[14] The agreement restricted the transfer of stock at death and set a fixed, lump-sum purchase price. The only other shareholder was the company's employee stock ownership plan (ESOP). The estate's expert concluded that the buy-sell agreement was similar to other such agreements negotiated at arm's length. The Tax Court, however, ignored the agreement's set value because decedent had the unilateral ability to modify it, thus failing to satisfy the requirement that it be binding during life. The court also disregarded the agreement under Internal Revenue Code Section 2703, which requires that to be included in a valuation, a buy-sell agreement's terms must be "comparable to similar arrangements entered into by persons in an arm's-length transaction." Here the court concluded that the parties were "related" and had not engaged in arm's-length bargaining.

In *Estate of True,* one issue was whether the book value price specified in the buy-sell agreements controlled estate and gift tax values of the subject interests in several family companies gifted and deeded to children.[15] The analysis focused on the *Lauder* factors. The court found that the fact that the children did not have independent legal or accounting advice, while not dispositive, reasonably suggested less than arm's-length dealings. The court was critical that the companies' buy-sell agreements did not provide a mechanism for periodic review or adjustment to the tax book value formula. The court also considered an analysis under the adequacy of consideration test. This test requires that the formula price (1) be comparable to what persons with adverse interests dealing at arm's length would accept and (2) bear a reasonable relationship to fair market value. As the court said, "[T]hese standards must be applied with the heightened scrutiny imposed on intrafamily agreements restricting transfers of closely held businesses." The court concluded that "[t]he True family buy-sell agreements do not satisfy the Lauder II test, because they are substitutes for testamentary dispositions. As a result, under Section 2031 and the related regulations, the tax book value buy-sell agreement price does not control estate tax values of interests in the True companies at issue in the estate tax case." The court also determined that the buy-sell agreements were not controlling for the gift tax case. The Tenth Circuit affirmed on appeal.

However, in *Hutchens Non-Marital Trust,* the Tax Court upheld the redemption price pursuant to an agreement because the agreement negotiations were at arm's length and in the ordinary course of business.[16] The importance of the agreement being in the ordinary course of business is stated in Section 25.2512-8 of the Gift Tax Regulations:

> [A] sale, exchange, or other transfer of property made in the ordinary course of business (a transaction which is bona fide, at arm's length, and free from any donative intent), will be considered as made for an adequate and full consideration in money or money's worth.[17]

Even though the parties to the agreement in *Hutchens* were family members, the court found the stock price valid, because an outside appraiser had valued the stock using the guideline public company method, the family members were not on good terms and were individually represented by attorneys during negotiations, and the parties' interests were "clearly divergent."

The Tax Court rejected petitioner's argument that the buy-sell agreement price should be controlling in *Bommer Revocable Trust*.[18] The court concluded that the agreement price was fixed and not subject to reevaluation, the decedent had bargained for that fixed price, and the fixed price and the generous payment terms were evidence of the agreement being a testamentary device. The petitioners in *Bommer* tried to persuade the court to follow the Southern District of Indiana's holding in *Rudolph v. United States,* where the court found the buy-sell agreement price indicative of the stock value.[19] The *Bommer* court distinguished the facts in *Rudolph* by stating that "the agreement at issue in *Rudolph* provided for review of the stock purchase price at the annual stockholders meeting. In addition, the District Court found in *Rudolph* that there was no intent to escape payment of estate taxes; there was no evidence in the record with respect to any discussion of the tax consequences that would result from the buy-sell agreement."

Buy-sell agreements among family members are scrutinized carefully. For a buy-sell agreement price to be evidence of value, several factors are persuasive. These include obtaining an independent appraisal, negotiating the price at arm's length, and showing that the agreement was not entered into as a testamentary device to limit tax liability.

Other Issues

Choosing the appropriate guideline companies and determining whether a price in a buy-sell agreement is controlling are not the only market approach issues that arise in estate and gift cases.

In *Estate of Renier v. Commissioner,* the court rejected a market approach method known as the business broker method.[20] The business broker method postulates that the purchase price of a business equals the market value of the inventory and fixed assets plus a multiple of the seller's discretionary cash flow, defined as the total cash flow available to the owner of the business. The court rejected the expert's application of this method because he failed to justify the multiple he applied to the company's discretionary cash flow. He used "his own judgment" rather than providing adequate supporting data. Accordingly, the court found that "on this record the reliability of the business broker method has not been established."

Although not a U.S. Tax Court case, *Church v. United States* was the first family limited partnership case to be tried in a federal district court.[21] In that case, in addition to determining whether the partnership agreement was valid, the court was presented with evidence of value based on the market approach that used closed-end funds and real estate limited partnerships as comparables. The court ultimately found that when the facts of the case can be supported by law and the business purpose can be reasonably explained, a limited partnership is a valid entity that cannot be disregarded for estate tax purposes.

In *Estate of Thompson,* the estate's experts found that no comparables were available, whereas the IRS's expert identified 11 companies that were appropriate comparables.[22] The expert took reported financial information for each company and created four multiples: (1) stock price to net income, (2) stock price to cash flow, (3) stock market value to tangible, and (4) intangible assets and stock price to revenue. He calculated the median multiple for the comparables and applied the medians to the subject company's averages over a five-year period. The court, however, criticized both experts for their lack of experience and for the general credibility of their valuations. The court revalued the company based on a capitalization of the subject company's estimated sustainable net income.

MARITAL DISSOLUTIONS

One of the most cited cases for the proposition that the market approach should not be used to value private companies in marital dissolution cases is *Lotz v. Lotz.*[23] The subject company, Your Own Things, was a corporation that manufactured women's clothing. The *Lotz* court rejected the guideline publicly traded company method because of these reasons:

> There are enormous differences between the two types of corporations. The stock in publicly traded corporations is much higher than the volume of closely held corporations. The stock in a publicly traded corporation has liquidity value because its owners can sell stock and get money in a matter of days, whereas the stock in "Your Own Things" has no liquidity value. There is less risk in owning stock in public corporations because they can "miss on two or three lines" without being hurt too much. Finally, the cost "to go public" is between $150,000 and $200,000 for legal and accounting fees. Therefore, there is no substantial support for the use of the above formula in evaluating a closely held corporation, even considering the attempts to adjust the formula.[24]

However, this statement is not as sweeping as it may seem at first glance. First, in using the guideline public company method, the wife's expert focused solely on the price earnings ratios of these companies, which has been rejected in later decisions.[25] He also made no effort to find guideline closely held companies, using the guideline merged and acquired company method. This case was decided in 1981, and since that time much more data on merged and acquired companies are available, as discussed in Chapter 3.

Even though another widely cited case, *Hewitson v. Hewitson,* followed the holding in *Lotz,* the *Hewitson* court realized that there are no clear-cut methods and Revenue Ruling 59-60 should be followed:

> We recognize the determination of value of infrequently sold, unlisted, closely held stock is a difficult legal problem. Most of the cases illustrate there is no one applicable formula that may be properly applied to the myriad factual situations calling for a valuation of closely held stock. . . . Unless there is some statutory or decisional proscription on their use, the factors listed in Revenue Ruling 59-60 should be consulted and used to evaluate closely held stock.[26]

Thus, the market approach has been introduced in marital dissolution cases. For example, in *In re the Marriage of Cutler,* the issue was the value of husband's "captive" auto insurance company agency.[27] The wife's expert used comparable companies consisting exclusively of multiline insurance agencies, rather than captive agencies. The husband's expert, however, searched various comparable sales databases to find captive agency sales for use in the market approach but did not find any, and his conclusion that there was no comparable market value was bolstered by the testimony of two individuals who had owned captive insurance agencies. On appeal, the appellate court rejected the trial court's acceptance of the wife's expert's use of the market approach because he had failed to determine the fair market value of the agency and therefore, had not laid a proper foundation for his evidence.

In other marital dissolution cases, the market approach was attempted, but yielded no comparables,[28] was used as one of several approaches,[29] or was disregarded by the court.[30]

BANKRUPTCY

The market approach has been used successfully in some bankruptcy proceedings. In *Peltz v. Hatten,* involving an adversarial proceeding in bankruptcy, the primary issue was whether the debtor's purchase of $68 million of Connecticut Telephone and Connecticut Mobilecom stock constituted a fraudulent transfer, that is, whether the debtor received "reasonably equivalent value" for the $68 million it paid.[31] The court favored the market approach to determine the value of the stock at the time the debtor acquired it and accepted testimony based on comparable sales closest in time to the sale of the stock.

At issue in *In re Coram Healthcare Corp.* was the value of two debtor corporations for the purpose of determining whether the bankruptcy trustee's plan was "fair and equitable."[32] Both parties provided expert testimony during trial and used the same methodologies: comparable public company analysis, comparable transaction analysis, and discounted cash flow analysis. The court, however, sided with the party whose valuation was within the range of reasonableness, rather than with the party that "took aggressive and optimistic views regarding the valuation and strength of the Debtors."

CONDEMNATION

The market approach also has its place in condemnation cases. In *L.A. Unified School District v. Chong Mo Chong dba My Tina,* the litigation was over whether the government's offer in eminent domain proceedings for the goodwill of a closely held company was unreasonable.[33] Both parties employed experts to value the goodwill of the company and to testify at trial. In addition, both experts used the market approach and the excess earnings method when valuing the goodwill of the company—but with disparate outcomes. The government expert derived a market multiplier of 3 based on comparables of small businesses over the last 10 years, but she did not use comparables that involved publicly traded companies because, in her opinion, they were not comparable. The company's expert derived a multiplier of 14 from a survey of three companies that had been purchased by publicly traded companies. The trial court found that the government's offer had been reasonable. This holding was affirmed on appeal.

DISSENTING STOCKHOLDER, MINORITY OPPRESSION, AND OTHER SHAREHOLDER DISPUTES

Fundamental corporate changes, such as mergers, usually can occur with the approval of the majority of the shareholders. Dissenters from these actions usually have an appraisal remedy available to them under state statutory law.

Standard of Value

The standard of value in dissenting shareholder actions is usually fair value. However, state statutes often do not provide much guidance about how to determine fair value. Delaware, a leader in corporate law, directs its courts to determine "fair value exclusive of any element of value arising from the accomplishment or expectation of the merger or consolidation" and to take into account "all relevant factors."[34] And according to Delaware case law, a shareholder is entitled to a proportionate share of the corporation as a going concern, rather than on a liquidated basis.[35] See Chapter 11 for a discussion of the fair value standards in the states.

Accepted Valuation Methods

The Chancery Court of Delaware has expressed a general preference for the discounted cash flow method of valuation, provided that reliable inputs for the method are available. The reliable inputs that that court prefers are management projections made in the normal course of business at the time reasonably proximate to the valuation date (the day immediately preceding the action to which the dissenter objects). When such projections either are not available or are suspect for some reason, the court usually turns to the market approach.

For example, in a 2004 case, *Dobler v. Montgomery Cellular Holdings Co. Inc.,* the court ultimately attributed 65% of the weight to the transaction method, 30% to the discounted cash flow method, and 5% to the guideline public company method.[36] Several other cases have relied primarily on the market approach.[37]

Discounts and Premiums

A highly debated issue is whether fair value is the enterprise value of a company, or the value as a going concern or if any discounts should be applied in calculating fair value. In *Swope v. Siegel-Robert,* the parties argued that the Missouri District Court should look to different jurisdictions when deciding this issue.[38] The plaintiffs asked the court to look at states like Delaware, Nebraska, Maine, Minnesota, and Washington, whose courts have disallowed discounts, whereas defendant chose the states of Illinois, Mississippi, Kansas, and Oregon for the proposition that the application of discounts is proper. Ultimately, the court looked to Missouri case law for the notion that a minority discount would be reasonable in this case. However, the court disallowed a marketability discount. The court stated that "the court action creates a market" for the shares and that the plaintiffs "should not be further penalized by being denied . . . a fair value for their interest."

On appeal, the Eighth Circuit ruled that the lower court did not err in declining to apply a marketability discount, reasoning that absent exceptional circumstances, the marketability of the stock is not relevant when determining fair value, and no extraordinary circumstances warranted a discount for lack of marketability in the instant case. However, the court did hold that the district court erred in discounting the value of the stock to account for the stock's minority status. Although intermediate Missouri appellate courts had allowed such a discount, the court concluded that the state's supreme court would not.[39]

In *Pueblo Bancorporation v. Lindoe, Inc.,* the Colorado Supreme Court held that the term *fair value,* for the purpose of Colorado's dissenters' rights statute, means the dissenting shareholder's proportionate interest in the corporation valued as a going concern.[40] The court ruled that the trial court must determine the value of the corporate entity and allocate the dissenting shareholder his or her proportionate ownership interest of that value, without applying a marketability discount at the shareholder level.

In *Matthew G. Norton Co v. Smyth,* a case of first impression in Washington, the issue was the propriety of discounts for lack of marketability and built-in capital gains in a dissenters' rights proceeding.[41] The trial court held that, as a matter of law, the company could not apply a lack of marketability discount or a discount for future taxation of imbedded capital gains in determining "fair value" of the dissenters' shares. On appeal, however, the appellate court held that discounts for lack of controlling interest or lack of marketability are appropriate on a corporate level, and if the trial court order intended to preclude these discounts on a corporate level, the decision was reversed. The court of appeals further held that if the trial court intended to preclude the possibility of any lack of marketability discount at the shareholder level, even in the face of extraordinary circumstances (i.e., a "bright-line rule"), the decision was also reversed. However, the court of appeals also held that the trial court's decision would be affirmed to the extent that the trial court's order was intended to declare that, absent extraordinary circumstances, no such discount can be applied at the shareholder level. The court of appeals held that the trial court's "bright-line ruling" with respect to the tax discount issue was too broad as well.

In *Agranoff v. Miller,* the Delaware Chancery Court explained that the comparable companies' analysis generates an equity value that includes an inherent minority trading discount, because the method depends on comparisons to market multiples derived from trading information for minority blocks of the comparable companies.[42] In an appraisal action, the court must correct this minority trading discount by adding back a premium designed to offset it. This correction is necessarily an imprecise one. In order to determine what the implicit minority discount in a comparable companies' analysis is, one is forced to look at the prices paid for control blocks. Such prices are frequently paid in connection with a merger or other fundamental transaction. The court found that this source of data therefore is problematic, because the premiums arguably reflect value that is not related to the value of the acquired companies as going concerns under their preexisting business plans, such as synergistic values attributable to transactionally specific factors. As a practical matter, however, the court acknowledged that it is impossible to make precise determinations about what motivated an acquiror to pay a control premium. The court ultimately decided that the adjustment should be 30%, but proved no basis for that decision.

In *Applebaum v. Avaya, Inc.,* the Delaware Chancery Court rejected such an approach in a case involving a cash-out of fractional shareholders.[43] The plaintiff in this case sought a control-premium adjustment similar to the one made in appraisal actions, but the court said:

> This argument ignores the fundamental difference between the circumstances leading to an appraisal under Section 262 and the factual predicate of the transaction at issue here. The cases dealing with control premiums in the context of appraisal actions all tacitly assume that the shares in question are no longer available for purchase in that same marketplace by the person whose shares are being appraised. Otherwise, the award of a premium over

market would constitute an unwarranted windfall, since the stockbroker could repurchase shares subject to the appraisal in the market without paying any premium. For that reason, the court is unpersuaded that . . . in the circumstances of this case, market price is not "fair value" for the purposes of Section 155(2) [the fractional share statute].

The court also rejected the plaintiff's statutory construction argument that the phrase "fair value" as used in Section 155(2) must be given the same meaning as in an appraisal action, an argument advanced in order to invoke the appraisal-derived rule that market value cannot be the sole determinant of "fair value."

In *In re Valuation of Common Stock of Penobscot Shoe Company,* a dissenters' rights action involving a small, closely held business, the court rejected the application of a small-business risk discount as a proper valuation method in a company-to-company (market approach) comparison.[44] However, the court permitted a control premium adjustment, noting that the two adjustments are distinct, and there is no persuasive reason why if one discount cannot be applied properly, the other adjustment is also unavailable. For these reasons, the court concluded that the control premium could properly be used as an upward adjustment of the value of the subject company's shares when compared to similar companies in the industry.

The Delaware Court of Chancery, in *Borruso v. Communications Telesystems,* held that a control premium should be added, but a discount for lack of marketability (called *private company discount* in the case) was not warranted in this dissenting shareholder action.[45] Because the guideline public company method inherently reflects a minority discount, the court stated that the value derived from this method "is not fully reflective of the intrinsic worth of the corporation on a going concern basis." The court then chose a 30% control premium "to reflect the elimination of impermissible elements of postmerger value."

The respondent in *Borruso* argued that a 20% marketability discount was warranted at the "corporate level." This was argued in response to the Delaware Supreme Court's ruling in *Cavalier Oil Corp. v. Harnett* that "it is wrong to apply a discount 'at the shareholder level,' for a lack of marketability of shares."[46]

Some states hold that no minority discount[47] or marketability discount[48] is applied to a buyout of an oppressed shareholder's shares. Other states have held that, in exceptional circumstances, a marketability discount is applied to a buyout of an oppressed shareholder's shares. For example, in *Advanced Communication Design, Inc. v. Follett,* the Minnesota Supreme Court, noting that the value assigned by the trial court must be "fair and equitable to all parties," rejected a "bright-line rule" rejecting the application of a marketability discount in all cases.[49] The court indicated that "a bright-line rule that would foreclose consideration of a marketability discount in all circumstances could lead to a valuation that is unfair to the remaining shareholders." The court gave as an example of "extraordinary circumstances" the possibility of an unfair wealth transfer, as where the exercise of a minority shareholder's appraisal rights in a financially strained corporation with illiquid assets would yield a price far greater than the price that would actually be paid for the shares in a market transaction. Finding such extraordinary circumstances in the case, the court directed that the discount should be somewhere between 35% and 55%.

In *Balsamides v. Protameen Chemicals,* the trial court found that plaintiff was an oppressed shareholder and was entitled to a buyout of defendant's interest in Protameen Chemicals, Inc.[50] The issue in the New Jersey Supreme Court was whether the fair value of plaintiff's stock should reflect a marketability discount. The court looked to *Lawson Mardon Wheaton v. Smith,*[51] decided in the same court on the same day, for the proposition that "there is no clear consensus on whether a marketability discount should be applied" in a statutory appraisal action.[52] The court looked to Delaware courts, and based on its "review of the history and policies behind dissenter's rights and appraisal statutes [it] found most persuasive those cases holding that marketability discounts generally should not be applied in determining the 'fair value' of a dissenting shareholder's stock in an appraisal action . . . there is even less consensus about whether discounts should be applied in oppressed shareholder actions."[53] The appellate court refused to apply a marketability discount, but the New Jersey Supreme Court overturned this finding, because not allowing the discount would be unfair:

> [T]he Appellate Division ignored the reality that Balsamides is buying a company that will remain illiquid because it is not publicly traded and information about it is not widely disseminated. If it is resold in the future, Balsamides will receive a lower purchase price because of the company's closely-held nature. Because the equities of this case quite clearly lie with Balsamides, it would be unfair to allow Perle to receive Protameen's undiscounted value.

However, the New Jersey Supreme Court did not pronounce that a marketability discount should be allowed in every oppression action, because "each decision depends not only on the specific facts of the case, but 'should reflect the purpose served by the law in that context.' "[54]

SUMMARY

Court decisions are extremely fact driven. Courts are free to reject the methodology of the experts. An analyst should always research the case law of his or her jurisdiction. If there are no statutes or cases directly on point, one should look to other jurisdictions that the court has followed. For instance, in a shareholder dispute case, it is probably wise to look at Delaware law. With cases before the U.S. Tax Court, Revenue Ruling 59-60 should always be a reference. What constitutes a "same" or "similar" company will depend on how unique the subject company is. It is important to realize that courts respect prepared experts who have done their due diligence, and that is probably the most difficult step.

This chapter has quoted just a small representative sample of court cases involving the market approach. The full texts of all cases cited in this chapter as well as hundreds more are available at BVLibrary.com, fully searchable by keyword.

Notes

1. An influential case that accepted the market approach is *The Central Trust Co. v. United States,* 305 F.2d 393, 1962 U.S. Ct. Cl. LEXIS 16 (July 18, 1962). In that case, the Court of Claims said, "Although no two companies are ever exactly alike, it being rare to have . . . almost ideal comparatives . . . so that absolute comparative perfection can seldom be achieved, nevertheless the comparative appraisal method is a sound and well-accepted technique. In employing it, however, every effort should be made to select as broad a base of comparative companies as is reasonably possible, as well as to give full consideration to every possible factor in order to make the comparison more meaningful."
2. *Caracci v. Commissioner,* 118 T.C. 379, 118 T.C. No. 25, 2002 U.S. Tax Ct. LEXIS 25 (U.S. Tax Ct., May 22, 2002).
3. *Estate of Leichter v. Commissioner,* T.C. Memo 2003-66, 2003 Tax Ct. Memo LEXIS 66 (U.S. Tax Ct., March 6, 2003).
4. *Hess v. Commissioner,* T.C. Memo 2003-251 (U.S. Tax Ct., August 20, 2003).
5. *Hendrickson v. Commissioner,* T.C. Memo 1999-278, 78 T.C.M. (CCH) 322, T.C.M. (RIA) 99278 (August 23, 1999).
6. *Brookshire v. Commissioner,* T.C. Memo 1998-365, 76 T.C.M. (CCH) 659 (October 8, 1998).
7. *Gallo v. Commissioner,* T.C. Memo 1985-363, 50 T.C.M. (CCH) 470, T.C.M. (RIA) 85363 (July 22, 1985).
8. Rev. Rul. 59-60 § 4.01(h), 1959-1 C.B. 237, *see also* 26 C.F.R. § 20.2031-2(f)(2).
9. *Hall v. Commissioner,* 92 T.C. 312 (February 14, 1989).
10. Id.
11. *Rakow v. Commissioner,* T.C. Memo 1999-177, 77 T.C.M. (CCH) 2066, T.C.M. (RIA) 99177 (May 27, 1999).
12. *Hendrickson v. Commissioner, see* note 5.
13. *Lauder v. Commissioner,* T.C. Memo 1992-736, 64 T.C.M. (CCH) 1643 (December 30, 1992).
14. *Estate of Blount v. Commissioner,* T.C. Memo 2004-116 (U.S. Tax Ct., May 12, 2004).
15. *Estate of True v. Commissioner,* T.C. Memo 2001-167, 2001 Tax Ct. Memo LEXIS 199 (U.S. Tax Ct. July 6, 2001), *aff'd,* 2004 U.S. App. LEXIS 24844 (10 Cir., December 2, 2004).
16. *Hutchens Non-Marital Trust v. Commissioner,* T.C. Memo 1993-600, 66 T.C.M. (CCH) 1599 (December 16, 1993).
17. 26 C.F. R. § 25.2512-8.
18. *Bommer Revocable Trust v. Commissioner,* T.C. Memo 1997-380, 74 T.C.M. (CCH) 346 (August 20, 1997).
19. *Rudolph v. United States,* 93-1 U.S. Tax Cas. (CCH) Par. 60, 130, 71 A.F.T.R.2d (RIA) 2169 (S.D. Ind. February 5, 1993).
20. *Estate of Renier v. Commissioner,* T.C. Memo 2000-298, 2000 Tax Ct. Memo LEXIS 350 (U.S. Tax Ct., September 25, 2000).
21. *Church v. United States* (I), 2000 U.S. Dist. LEXIS 714 (W.D. Tex., January 18, 2000).
22. *Estate of Thompson v. Commissioner,* 2004 Tax Ct. Memo LEXIS 180 (U.S. Tax Ct., July 26, 2004).
23. *Lotz v. Lotz,* 120 Cal. App. 3d 379, 174 Cal. Rptr. 618 (June 15, 1981).
24. Id. at 384, 621.
25. See *Hewitson,* note 1, and *Sharp v. Sharp,* 143 Cal. App. 3d 714, 192 Cal. Rptr. 97 (June 7, 1983).
26. *Hewitson v. Hewitson,* 142 Cal. App. 3d 874, 888, 191 Cal. Rptr. 392, 401 (May 10, 1983).
27. *In re the Marriage of Cutler,* 334 Ill. App. 3d 731, 778 N.E.2d 762, 2002 Ill. App. LEXIS 973 (October 22, 2002).

28. E.g., *Manelick v. Manelick*, 59 P.3d 259, 2002 Alas. LEXIS 161 (November 22, 2002).

29. E.g., *In re the Marriage of Schleif*, 2002 Minn. App. LEXIS 1339 (December 10, 2002) (experts for both wife and husband, guided by Rev. Rul. 59-60, used the market approach; wife's expert used both the guideline transactions method and the past company transactions method, and husband's expert used the guideline public company method); *Hanson v. Hanson*, 2004 Ore. App. LEXIS 230 (March 10, 2004) (all the experts prepared reports using a combination of the capitalization of earnings method (income approach) and the comparable transaction methods (market approach)); *Covert v. Covert*, 2004 Ohio App. LEXIS 3190 (June 28, 2004) (expert used average of asset value, the excess earnings method, and the market approach to arrive at a fair market value); *Ledwith v. Ledwith*, 2004 Va. App. LEXIS 488 (October 12, 2004) (husband's expert was criticized for using an asset approach to arrive at a value and then applying a market approach to determine what portion of that value was comprised of good-will).

30. E.g., *In re the Marriage of Steinbesser*, 2002 MT 309, 313 Mont. 74, 60 P.3d 441, 2002 Mont. LEXIS 590 (December 12, 2002) (the trial court ignored the only expert testimony, based on a market approach, presented at trial).

31. *Peltz v. Hatten*, 279 B.R. 710, 2002 U.S. Dist. LEXIS 10282 (D. Del., June 5, 2002).

32. *In re Coram Healthcare Corp.*, 2004 Bankr. LEXIS 1516 (U.S. Ct. Fed. Claims, October 5, 2004).

33. *L.A. Unified School District v. Chong Mo Chong dba My Tina*, 2004 Cal. App. Unpub. LEXIS 11468 (December 17, 2004).

34. 8 Del. C. § 262(h).

35. See *Rapid-American Corp. v. Harris*, 603 A.2d 796 (Del. Supr. January 23, 1992).

36. *Dobler v. Montgomery Cellular Holding Co., Inc.*, 2004 Del. Ch. LEXIS 139 (September 30, 2004).

37. *Doft & Co. v. Travelocity.com Inc.*, 2004 Del. Ch. LEXIS 75 (the court rejected the DCF approach of both parties' experts because the most fundamental input used by the experts—the projections of future revenues, expenses, and cash flows—were not shown to be reasonably reliable; instead, the court relied on the comparable company analysis offered by the parties); *Agranoff v. Miller*, 2001 Del. Ch. LEXIS 71 (May 15, 2001) (the court used a comparable companies approach to value the subject company); *Borruso v. Communications Telesystems Int'l.*, 1999 Del. Ch. LEXIS 197 (September 24, 1999) (the court relied on a comparable company analysis because neither expert was comfortable using a DCF analysis to value the company's shares due to the limited financial data of the company available as of the merger date); *Taylor v. Am. Specialty Retailing Group, Inc.*, 2003 Del. Ch. LEXIS 75 (July 15, 2003) (the court averaged the two values derived from the DCF method and the market approach, finding that they were sufficiently similar); *Gray v. Cytokine Pharmasciences, Inc.*, 2002 Del. Ch. LEXIS 48 (April 25, 2002) (the court averaged the two values derived by an independent appraiser from the DCF method and the market approach)

38. *Swope v. Siegel-Robert*, 74 F. Supp 2d 876 (E.D. Mo. June 23, 1999).

39. *Swope v. Siegel-Robert*, 243 F.3d 486, 2001 U.S. App. LEXIS 2760 (8th Cir., February 26, 2001).

40. *Pueblo Bancorporation v. Lindoe, Inc.*, 63 P.3d 353, 2003 Colo. LEXIS 53 (January 21, 2003).

41. *Matthew G. Norton Co v. Smyth*, 112 Wn. App. 865, 51 P.3d 159, 2002 Wash. App. LEXIS 1841 (August 5, 2002).

42. *Agranoff v. Miller*, 2001 Del. Ch. LEXIS 71 (May 15, 2001).

43. *Applebaum v. Avaya, Inc.*, 805 A.2d 209; 2002 Del. Ch. LEXIS 75 (June 27, 2002).

44. *In re Valuation of Common Stock of Penobscot Shoe Company*, 2003 Me. Super. LEXIS 140 (May 30, 2003).

45. *Borruso v. Communications Telesystems Int l,* C.A. No. 16316-NC, 1999 Del. Ch. LEXIS 197 (September 24, 1999).

46. Id.

47. See, e.g., *Tifft v. Stevens,* 162 Or. App. 62, 987 P.2d 1, 1999 Ore. App. LEXIS 1373 (March 11, 1999); *Cooke v. Fresh Express Foods,* 169 Or. App. 101, 7 P.3d 717, 2000 Ore. App. LEXIS 1128 (July 12, 2000).

48. E.g., *Jahn v. Kinderman,* 2004 Ill. App. LEXIS 628 (June 7, 2004).

49. *Advanced Communication Design, Inc. v. Follett,* 615 N.W. 2d 285, 2000 Minn. LEXIS 417 (August 3, 2000).

50. *Balsamides v. Protameen Chemicals,* 160 N.J. 352, 734 A.2d 721 (July 14, 1999).

51. *Lawson Mardon Wheaton v. Smith,* 160 N.J. 383, 734 A.2d 738 (July 14, 1999).

52. *Balsamides,* 160 N.J. at 375.

53. Id. at 376.

54. Id. at 381.

Appendixes

Bibliography

Books

Articles

Periodicals

BOOKS

Agiato Jr., Joseph A., and Michael J. Mard. *Valuing Intellectual Property and Calculating Infringement Damages: Practice Aid.* Jersey City, NJ: American Institute of CPAs, 1999.

Albo, Wayne P., Andrew D. Pigott, and Adam Bryk. *The Purchase and Sale of Privately-Held Businesses,* 3rd ed. Toronto: Canadian Institute of Chartered Accountants, 2000.

American Bar Association. *The Valuation Expert in Divorce Litigation: A Handbook for Attorneys and Accountants.* Chicago: American Bar Association Section of Family Law, 1992.

American Dental Association. *Valuing a Practice: A Guide for Dentists,* rev. ed. Chicago: American Dental Association, 2001.

Blackman, Irving L. *Valuing Your Privately Held Business: The Art & Science of Establishing Your Company's Worth.* Burr Ridge, IL: Irwin Professional Publishing, 1995.

Boer, F. Peter John. *The Valuation of Technology: Business and Financial Issues in R&D.* New York: John Wiley & Sons, 1999.

Brealey, Richard A., Stewart C. Myers, and Alan J. Marcus. *Fundamentals of Corporate Finance,* 6th ed. New York: McGraw-Hill, 2002.

Bumstead, William W. *Buying & Selling Businesses: Including Forms, Formulas and Industry Secrets.* New York: John Wiley & Sons, 1998.

Carmichael, Doug R. *Accountants Handbook,* 2-vol. set. Hoboken, NJ: John Wiley & Sons, 2002.

Commerce Clearing House *IRS Valuation Guide for Income Estate and Gift Taxes.* Chicago: Commerce Clearing House, 1994.

Copeland, Thomas. *Valuation: Measuring and Managing the Value of Companies,* 3rd ed. Hoboken, NJ: John Wiley & Sons, 2004.

Cottle, Sidney, Roger F. Murray, and Frank E. Block. *Graham and Dodd's Security Analysis,* 5th ed. New York: McGraw-Hill, 1988.

Desmond, Glenn M. *Handbook of Small Business Valuation Formulas and Rules of Thumb,* 3rd ed. Camden, ME: Valuation Press, 1993.

Dietrich, Mark O. *Medical Practice Valuation Guidebook.* Framingham, MA: Windsor Professional Information, annual.

Feder, Robert D. *Valuation Strategies in Divorce,* 4th ed. Frederick, MD: Aspen Law & Business, 1997.

Fishman, Jay E., Shannon P. Pratt, et al. *Guide to Business Valuations,* 15th ed. Fort Worth, TX: Practitioners Publishing Company, 2005.

Gaughan, Patrik A. *Mergers Acquisitions and Corporate Restructuring,* 3rd ed. New York: John Wiley & Sons, 2002.

Hawkins, George B., and Michael A. Paschall. *CCH Business Valuation Guide,* 1st ed. Chicago: CCH Incorporated, 1999.

Howitt, Idelle A., and Susan E. Schechter, eds. *Federal Tax Valuation Digest.* Boston: Warren Gorham & Lamont, annual.

Kasper, Larry I. *Business Valuation Advanced Topics.* Westport, CT: Quorum Books, 1997.

Kleeman Jr., Robert E., R. James Alerding, and Benjamin D. Miller. *The Handbook for Divorce Valuations.* New York: John Wiley & Sons, 1999.

Kuhn, Robert Lawrence. *Mergers Acquisitions and Leveraged Buyouts.* Burr Ridge, IL: Irwin Professional Publishing, 1990.

Laro, David, and Shannon P. Pratt. *Business Valuation and Taxes: Procedure, Law and Perspective.* Hoboken, NJ: John Wiley & Sons, 2005.

Marren, Joseph H. *Mergers & Acquisitions: A Valuation Handbook.* Burr Ridge, IL: Irwin Professional Publishing, 1993.

Mercer, Z. Christopher. *Valuing Financial Institutions.* Burr Ridge, IL: Irwin Professional Publishing, 1992.

————. *Quantifying Marketability Discounts.* Memphis, TN: Peabody Publishing, 1997.

Miles, Raymond C. *Basic Business Appraisal.* New York: John Wiley & Sons, 1984.

Pratt, Shannon P. *Business Valuation Body of Knowledge: Exam Review and Professional Reference,* 2nd ed. Hoboken, NJ: John Wiley & Sons, 2002.

————. *Cost of Capital: Estimation and Applications,* 2nd ed. New York: John Wiley & Sons, 1998.

Pratt, Shannon P., Robert F. Reilly, and Robert P. Schweihs. *Valuing a Business: The Analysis and Appraisal of Closely Held Companies,* 4th ed. New York: McGraw-Hill, 2000.

————. *Valuing Small Businesses and Professional Practices,* 3rd ed. New York: McGraw-Hill, 1998.

Pratt, Shannon P., Robert F. Reilly, Robert P. Schweihs, and Jay E. Fishman. *Business Valuation Videocourse.* Jersey City, NJ: American Institute of Certified Public Accountants, 1993. Videotape and course handbook.

Razgaitis, Richard. *Early-Stage Technologies: Risk Management Valuation and Pricing,* 2002 ed. Hoboken, NJ: John Wiley & Sons, 2002.

Reed, Stanley Foster, and Alexandra Reed Lajoux. *The Art of M&A: A Merger and Acquisition Buyout Guide,* 3rd ed. New York: McGraw-Hill, 1998.

Reilly, Robert F., and Robert P. Schweihs. *Valuing Accounting Practices.* New York: John Wiley & Sons, 1997.

———. *Valuing Professional Practices: A Practitioner's Guide.* Chicago: Commerce Clearing House, 1997.

———. *Valuing Intangible Assets.* New York: McGraw-Hill, 1999.

Reilly, Robert F., and Robert P. Schweihs, eds. *Handbook of Advanced Business Valuation.* New York: McGraw-Hill, 1999.

Saret, Lewis J., and Lewis D. Solomon. *Valuation of Closely Held Businesses: Legal and Tax Aspects.* Frederick, MD: Aspen Law & Business, 1998.

Sirower, Mark L. *The Synergy Trap: How Companies Lose the Acquisition Game.* New York: The Free Press, 1997.

Smith, Gordon V. *Trademark Valuation.* New York: John Wiley & Sons, 1996.

Smith, Gordon V., and Russell L. Parr. *Valuation of Intellectual Property and Intangible Assets,* 3rd ed. New York: John Wiley & Sons, 2000.

Tinsley, Reed. *Valuation of a Medical Practice.* New York: John Wiley & Sons, 1999.

Trugman, Gary R. *Conducting a Valuation of a Closely Held Business Practice Aid.* Jersey City, NJ: American Institute of CPAs, 1993.

———. *Understanding Business Valuation: A Practical Guide to Valuing Small to Medium-Sized Businesses,* 2nd ed. Jersey City, NJ: American Institute of CPAs, 2002.

Umbenhaur III, Rexford E. *Selling Your Business Successfully.* New York: John Wiley & Sons, 1999.

Weil, Roman L. *Litigation Services Handbook: The Role of the Accountant as Expert,* 2nd ed. supp. New York: John Wiley & Sons, 2000.

West, Tom, ed. *Business Reference Guide,* Annual. Concord, MA: Business Brokerage Press, 2000.

West, Thomas L., and Jeffrey D. Jones. *Mergers and Acquisitions Handbook for Small and Midsize Companies.* New York: John Wiley & Sons, 1997.

———. *Handbook of Business Valuation,* 2nd ed. New York: John Wiley & Sons, 1999.

White, Gerald I, Ashwinpaul C. Sondhi, and Dov Fried. *The Analysis and Use of Financial Statements,* 3rd ed. Hoboken, NJ: John Wiley & Sons, 2002.

Zukin, James H. *Financial Valuation: Businesses and Business Interests.* Boston, MA: Warren Gotham Lamont, 1990.

ARTICLES

Ackrell, Michael. "How to Price Internet IPOs in these Wild Appreciation Days." *Shannon Pratt's Business Valuation Update*® (August 1999): 1–3.

Agiato, Joseph A. "Mind Games: Trends in the Appraisal of Intellectual Property." Presented at the 1998 Annual Conference of the Institute of Business Appraisers, San Antonio, Texas. Available at www.bvlibrary.com.

Allen, Terry. "Small Business Valuation Issues." Presented at the 1999 AICPA Business Valuation Conference. Summary available at www.bvlibrary.com.

Annin, Michael, and Z. Christopher Mercer. "Control and Synergy Premiums." Presented at the 1998 CICBV/ASA Joint Business Valuation Conference, Montreal, Canada. Available at www.bvlibrary.com.

Aschwald, Kathryn. "Restricted Stock Discounts Decline as Result of 1-Year Holding Period." *Shannon Pratt's Business Valuation Update*® (May 2000): 1–5.

Baliga, Wayne J. "Risk Management for Engagements Involving the Purchase or Sale of a Business." Presented at the 1997 AICPA National Conference on Business Valuation, San Diego, California. Available at www.bvlibrary.com.

Barenbaum, Les, and Bonnie O'Rourke. "Valuing Closely Held Automobile Dealerships Using Public Dealership Acquisitions." *Shannon Pratt's Business Valuation Update*® (November 1999): 1–3.

Barron, Michael S. "When Will the Tax Court Allow a Discount for Lack of Marketability?" *Journal of Taxation* (January 1997): 46–50.

Bates, Mary Ellen. "Where's EDGAR Today? Finding SEC Filings Online." *Database* (June 1996): 41–50.

Becker, Brian C. "Multiple Approaches to a Valuation: The Use of Sensitivity Analysis." *Business Valuation Review* (December 1996): 157–160.

Bielinski, Daniel W. "The Comparable-Company Approach: Measuring the True Value of Privately Held Firms." *Corporate Cashflow Magazine* (October 1990): 64–68.

Bingham, Bruce. "Valuing Start-Up Companies." Presented at the American Society of Appraisers 16th Annual Advanced Business Valuation Conference, San Francisco, California. Available at www.bvlibrary.com.

Bjorklund, Victoria B., and Susan A. Meisel. "Valuation: When Are Comparables Comparable Enough?" *Practical Tax Lawyer* (Spring 1991): 45–47.

Bogdanski, John A. "Further Adventures with the Lack of Marketability Discount." *Estate Planning* (June 1999): 235–239.

Brinig, Brian P. "Business Valuation Litigation: Developing, Documenting, Presenting and Defending Your Opinion." Available at www.bvlibrary.com.

Crow, Matthew R. "Developing Valuation Multiples Using Guideline Companies." *CPA Litigation Service Counselor* (September 1999): 8–9.

Curtiss, Rand M. "The Justification for Purchase Test: An Essential Appraisal Tool." *Business Appraisal Practice* (Fall 1999): 45–50.

DiVittorio, Martha Montes. "Evaluating Sources of U.S. Company Data." *Database* (August 1994): 39–44.

Emory, John D., Sr. "Why Business Valuation and Real Estate Appraisal Are Different." *Business Valuation News* (June 1990): 5–8.

———. "The Value of Marketability as Illustrated in Initial Public Offerings of Common Stock, November 1995 through April 1997." *Business Valuation Review* (September 1997): 125–131.

Emery, John D., Sr., F. R. Dengel, III, and John D. Emory, Jr. "The Value of Marketability as Illustrated in Dot.Com IPOs, May 1997–March 2000." *Shannon Pratt's Business Valuation Update®* (July 2000): 1–2.

"Enhanced EDGAR Site Has Email Capabilities and Integrates with Microsoft Excel 97." *Shannon Pratt's Business Valuation Update®* (September 1997): 5.

Epley, Cathryn. "Moving Targets: Determining the Fair Market Value of Restaurants." *Shannon Pratt's Business Valuation Update®* (February 1999): 1–4.

Fannon, Nancy J. "Thousands of Manufacturing Companies to Value, But the Appraiser Needs to Assess Their Risks." *Shannon Pratt's Business Valuation Update®* (May 1999): 1–3.

Fishman, Jay E. "Appraisal Reports: The Long and the Short of It." Presented at the 1998 CICBV/ASA Joint Business Valuation Conference, Montreal, Canada. Available at www.bvlibrary.com.

———. "The Alternate Market Comparison Approach in Valuing Closely Held Enterprises." *Fair $hare: The Matrimonial Law Monthly* (October 1988): 7–8.

Fowler, Bradley A. "The How You Handle It Column in Business Valuation Review." Presented at the 1997 ASA International Appraisal Conference. *Business Valuation Review* (September 1996): 136–137. Available at www.bvlibrary.com.

———. "The Problem with Rules of Thumb in the Valuation of Closely Held Entities." *Fair $hare: The Matrimonial Law Monthly* (October 1984): 13–15.

Garber, Steven D. "Control Premiums vs. Acquisition Premiums: Is There a Difference?" Available at www.bvlibrary.com.

Goeldner, Richard W. II. "Adjusting Market Multiples of Guideline Companies." Available at www.bvlibrary.com.

———. "Bridging the Gap between Public and Private Market Multiples." *Business Valuation Review* (September 1998): 97–101.

———. "The Public Guideline Company Method." Available at www.bvlibrary.com.

Graham, Michael D. "Selection of Market Multiples in Business Valuation." *Business Valuation Review* (March 1990): 8–12.

Hill, James M. "Small Business Valuation Revisited." Presented at the 1998 International Appraisal Conference of the American Society of Appraisers, Kaanapali Beach, Hawaii. Available at www.bvlibrary.com.

Jefferson, Mozette. "Through EDGAR on the Internet: How to Access SEC Filings

Cheaply and Easily." *Shannon Pratt's Business Valuation Update* (November 1995): 6–7.

———. "Convert Raw Internet Fillings into Easy-to-Read Formatting." *Shannon Pratt's Business Valuation Update*® (December 1995): 7.

Johnson, Bruce A. "Quantitative Support for Discounts for Lack of Marketability." *Valuation Strategies* (January/February 2000): 152–155.

Julius, J. Michael. "Using Control Premium Statistics: Premises of Value and Valuations." *CPA Litigation Service Counselor* (July 1999): 8–10.

Matthews, Gilbert E. "Delaware Court Relies on Comparable Acquisition Method." *Shannon Pratt's Business Valuation Update*® (March 1998): 10.

Mattson, Michael. "Market Approach." *Shannon Pratt's Business Valuation Update*® (January 1999): 5.

McCarter, Mary B. "The Applications and Uses of Discounts and Premia in Business Valuation." Available at www.bvlibrary.com.

McDonagh, Christopher S., and John M. McDonagh. "Valuing a Target's Ability to Compete in the Market." *Mergers & Acquisitions* (September/October 1995): 22–25.

Mercer, Z. Christopher. "Public Multiples/Private Companies: Grappling with the Fundamental Issues." Presented at the 1996 IBA National Conference, Orlando, Florida.

Nath, Eric W. "How Public Guideline Companies Represent 'Control' Value for a Private Company." *Business Valuation Review* (December 1997): 167–171.

O'Leary, Mick. "The Many Faces of Disclosure." *Database* (October/November 1996): 91–92.

Penhollow, John, and Gary Purnhagen. "EDGAR." In *Securities Filings 1996,* by Alan K. Austin. *Practicing Law Institute* (1996): 33–131.

Peters, Jerry O. "Adjusting Price/Earnings Ratios for Differences in Company Size." *Business Valuation Review* (June 1999): 71–85.

Pratt, Shannon P. "Current Tax Court Decisions." Presented at the 1998 AICPA Business Valuation Conference. Available at www.bvlibrary.com.

———. "Drawing a Clear Distinction Between Income and Market Approaches and Methodology." *Shannon Pratt's Business Valuation Update*® (September 1998): 2–4.

———. "Insights on Private-Company Sale Pricing from *Pratt's Stats*™ Database." Presented at the 1998 Canadian Institute of Chartered Business Valuators/American Society of Appraisers Joint Business Valuation Conference. Available at www.bvlibrary.com.

———. "Limited Partnership Study Documents Large Discounts from Net Asset Value: Interview with Spencer Jefferies." *Shannon Pratt's Business Valuation Update*® (September 1996): 1–2.

———. "A Semantic Proposal: When We Should Use 'Multiple' vs. 'Ratio.' " *Shannon Pratt's Business Valuation Update*® (November 1999): 1.

————. "A View from the Street: How Wall Street's Valuation Approaches Differ from Independent Fee Appraisers. Interview with Gil Matthews and Mark Lee." *Shannon Pratt's Business Valuation Update®* (June 1996): 1–4.

Randisi, Martin P. "Comparable Company Method of Valuing a Closely Held Business." *Fair $hare: The Matrimonial Law Monthly* (January 1991): 3–5.

Reilly, Robert F. "Problems in Using Capital Market Data to Value Operating Business Assets." *Valuation Strategies* (January/February 1999): 17–19, 44, 46.

Ross, Franz. "Just One Thing: The Most Reliable Variable for Use in the Market Approach." *Shannon Pratt's Business Valuation Update®* (September 2004). available at www.bvlibrary.com.

"Separating Entity from Personal Intangibles Assets." *Valuation Strategies* (May/June 1999): 5–9.

Slee, Robert T. "Is the Subject Company Similar?" *Valuation Strategies* (May/June 1998): 4–7, 34.

Sliwoski, Leonard J. "Utilizing the IBA Market Database as a Profit Enhancement Tool." Presented at the 1999 National Conference of the Institute of Business Appraisers, Lake Buena Vista, Florida. Available at www.bvlibrary.com.

Spencer, Leslie. "Valuing a Business." *Forbes* (April 11, 1994): 98–99.

Summers, S. Chris. "The Myth of Public Company Comparisons." *Business Valuation Review* (June 1992): 59–62.

Sziklay, Barry S. "Divorce Valuation." Presented at the 1997 AICPA Business Valuation Conference, San Diego, California. Available at www.bvlibrary.com.

Taub, Maxwell J. "Can Market Comparables Be Used in Valuing Small Businesses?" *IBBA Journal* (October 1991): 10–14.

Trugman, Gary R. "Mid-Size Companies—How Do They Differ from Small Businesses and Publicly Held Firms?" *IBBA Journal* (Fall 1993): 25–32.

————. "Using the Market Approach to Value Small and Medium-Sized Businesses." Presented at the 1996 Institute of Business Appraisers National Conference, Orlando, Florida. Available at www.bvlibrary.com.

Tudor, Jan Davis. "For Free SEC Documents, Call EDGAR." *Business Valuation Review* (December 1995): 174–77.

West, Thomas L. "Pricing Businesses: The Use of Comparables." *The Business Broker* (June 1992): 1–4.

PERIODICALS

Shannon Pratt's Business Valuation Update®

The update has provided timely news, views, and resources for better valuations since 1995. Monthly features include legal and court case update, editor's column, news update, data and publications update, reader/editor exchange, guest interviews, cost of capital, and calendar update. Subscription also includes the annually updated Where to Find It—Business Valuation Data Directory. Published by Business Valuation Resources, 7412 S.W. Beaverton-Hillsdale Highway, Suite 106, Portland, OR 97225, (888) BUS-VALU.

BVLibrary.com

Library includes the full searchable text of all issues of *Business Valuation Update,* since inception in 1995, as well as all the issues of *Judges and Lawyers Update.* Also included are thousands of pages of the full texts of court case decisions and summaries featured in all issues of both newsletters, landmark valuation cases, Technical Advice Memorandums, Revenue Rulings, unpublished research, and conference papers. All are searchable by keyword. Published by Business Valuation Resources, 7412 S.W. Beaverton-Hillsdale Highway, Suite 106, Portland, OR 97225, (888) BUS-VALU. Available from www.BVLibrary.com.

ACG Network

Published monthly, except bimonthly issues in May/June and July/August, *ACG Network* offers fresh commentary and news reports on key M&A and internal growth issues. It offers calendars of leading conferences in the United States. and United Kingdom and professional developments about ACG members. Target audience: corporate growth professionals in the middle market. Available from Association for Corporate Growth, 1926 Waukegan Road Suite One, Glenview, IL 60025-1770, (847) 920-9030, www.acg.org.

Business Appraisal Reports Library

Volumes I and II of *Business Appraisal Reports Library* feature eight appraisal reports that represent typical assignments in the appraisal businesses. The reports consist of: Restaurant/Divorce (100% Interest/Limited Scope); Manufacturer/Valued for Gifting (Minority Interest/Formal); FLP/Holding Company Type Assets/Gift (Minority Interest /Formal); Manufacturer/Estate Settlement (100% Interest/Formal); Oppressed Shareholder Action/Fair Value Standard (Minority Interest/Formal); Medical Practice/Divorce (100% Interest/Formal); Contractor/Actual Sale (100% Interest Formal); and High Tech Company/ Valued for ESOP (30% Interest/Formal). The CD-ROM also includes the IBA Data Analyzer, a Glossary of Business Appraisal Terms, IBA Standards, Tutorials on Use of Market Data, the Applicant's Handbooks, and selected Web site links. Available in print and CD-ROM from Institute of Business Appraisers, PO Box 17410, Plantation, Florida 33318, (954) 584-1144, www.instbusapp.org.

Business Valuation Review

Published quarterly, *Business Valuation Review* provides information about the valuation of businesses, professional practices, corporate stock, and tangible/ intangible assets. Includes recent valuation developments, classified ads, book reviews, and research projects. Cumulative index printed yearly (free to subscribers). Updates of the Bibliography of Business Valuation Literature are published annually. Available from Business Valuation Committee of the American Society of Appraisers, 2777 S. Colorado Boulevard, #200, Denver, CO 80222, (303) 975-8895, www.appraisers.org.

CCH Business Valuation Alert

This special quarterly newsletter is free of charge to those who subscribe to Commerce Clearing House's Business Valuation Guide loose-leaf book, but it is also available for separate sale. The 16-page newsletter reports on the latest valuation trends, developments, and techniques. It focuses on changing areas of valuation and provides insights into the practical considerations of the industry. Articles by leading valuation professionals populate each issue. Newsletters include brief stories on late-breaking news plus detailed analytical articles on some of the more complex problems faced by valuation professionals. Available from CCH Incorporated, 4025 W. Peterson Avenue, Chicago, IL 60646, (847) 267-2282, www.cch.com.

CPA Litigation Service Counselor

Published monthly, *CPA Litigation Service Counselor* provides background information, practice management techniques, marketing tips, case studies, and technical data that can be helpful with valuations and other litigation support engagements. Available in print from Harcourt Professional Publishing, Order Fulfillment, 4th floor, 6277 Sea Harbor Drive, Orlando, FL 32887, (800) 831-7799, www.hbpp.com.

Fair $hare: The Matrimonial Law Monthly

Published monthly, this journal covers the latest legal and financial issues divorce attorneys must face. Available from Aspen Law & Business, 7201 Mckinney Circle, Frederick, MD 21704, (800) 638-8437.

Fair Value

Published quarterly, *Fair Value* provides a detailed treatment of current valuation issues and topics and is available gratis to clients and friends (on a selective basis) of Banister Financial, Inc. Requests should be sent by mail, e-mail, or fax. Available from Banister Financial, 1914 Brunswick Avenue, Suite 1-B, Charlotte, NC 28207, (704) 334-4932, www.businessvalue.com.

M&A Today

Published monthly, available in print and online, *M&A Today* is a newsletter for the professional intermediary—and all those involved in the buying and selling of midsize companies. Available from Business Brokerage Press, PO Box 247, Concord, MA 01742, (978) 369-5254.

The Value Examiner

A bimonthly magazine used for professional development, in addition to up-to-date feature articles of a technical nature, this magazine offfers a broad variety of related industry news, including industry trends, economic forecasts, new and useful resources for information, NACVA research and new finds, classified ads, issues in debate, letters to the editor, and marketing ideas. Free to NACVA members. Available from NACVA at (800) 677-2009 or via their Web site, www.nacva.com.

Valuation Strategies

A 48-page bimonthly journal, *Valuation Strategies* is designed to showcase the importance of valuation issues in a myriad of tax, planning, and compliance transactions that CPAs, attorneys, and other business advisors face on a regular basis. To order contact the subscription department at 1 (800) 452-1216, fax 1 (800) 452-9009. Editorial inquiries should be sent to 90 Fifth Avenue, New York, NY 10011, (212) 807-2298, fax (212) 337-4207.

Valuation Survey

The *Valuation Survey* provides comparative data on the value of privately held firms in the architecture, engineering, and environmental consulting industries. Includes profiles of 300+ individual valuation cases and a large database of actual valuations. Value data for each firm are summarized in five ratios: value per employee, value/book value, value/net revenue, value/profit, and value/backlog. Call for information about becoming a survey participant. Available annually in print from Zweig White & Associates, Inc., PO Box 8325, One Apple Hill Drive, Natick, MA 01760-2085, (800) 466-6275, www.wa.com.

Data Resources

Guideline Publicly Traded Company Method
    EDGAR (Electronic Data Gathering, Analysis, and Retrieval)
    Mergent FIS Inc. (previously Moody's)
    Standard & Poor's
    U.S. Government Printing Office

Earnings Forecasts and Related Data for Public and Private Companies
    Value Line
    First Call
    I/B/E/S
    Integra Information
    Standard & Poor's ACE (Analysts' Consensus Estimates)
    Zacks Investment Research

Sources of Financial Ratios and Financial Statement Analysis
    Several sources including publications derived from the Statistics of Income
        (SOI) division of the IRS

Databases
    Compact D
    Global Access

Online Services
    Yahoo! on the Money
    Hoover's Online
    Just Quotes

Public Company Transaction Method Sources of Transactions
    Print Sources
    Electronic Sources

Private Company Sale Transaction Data
    BIZCOMPS®
    Done Deals Data
    Pratt's Stats™
    IBA Market Data Base

Partnership Transaction Data

Compensation Data

Periodicals

GUIDELINE PUBLICLY TRADED COMPANY METHOD

EDGAR (Electronic Data Gathering, Analysis, and Retrieval)

The EDGAR system was established by the Securities and Exchange Commission to allow public access to the filings of public companies. The EDGAR database contains information on more than 15,000 public companies. It can be accessed through the Securities and Exchange Commission Internet home page: www.sec.gov/cgi-gin/srch-edgar, or the New York University Stern School of Business Internet home page: www.edgar.stern.nyu.edu.

Freeware that can be used to reformat EDGAR data to a more usable layout is available from these two sources, as well as from Business Valuation Resources, www.BVResources.com.

Since May 6, 1996, all public domestic companies are required to electronically file on EDGAR, unless they are granted a hardship exemption. A number of sites provide access to the EDGAR data. Many of the sites try to attract users by offering additional features such as enhanced search capability, preformatted printing options, and watch services.

Available free from multiple vendors:

SEC	www.sec.gov
EdgarOnline	www.edgar-online.com
10K Wizard	www.tenkwizard.com
EdgarScan	edgarscan.pwcglobal.com

In addition to the sites listed above, there are several fee-based EDGAR services including:

LIVEDGAR, www.gsionline.com: Powerful search capability, alert service, M&A database, and custom presentation downloads.

EDGAR Online Pro and *Access,* access.edgar-online.com, provides data from SEC filings of over 15,000 companies. Filings can be viewed as a Web page, in the original format as filed with the SEC, as a Microsoft Word file, as an Adobe document, or as a Microsoft Excel file. Filings also can be organized or searched by the filing form, date of the filing, or period covered by the filing. Company profiles give information based on selected portions of the company's most recent 10-K filing, such as business description and management overview.

Edgar Online, www.edgar-online.com: Access to most of site is free but fee is required to access personalization services, formatted downloading options, and hard copy delivery options.

Mergent FIS Inc. (previously Moody's)

Mergent Information Services provides a wide variety of publications on publicly traded companies, including *Moody's Industrial Manual, Moody's Bank & Financial Manual, Moody's OTC Industrial Manual, Moody's OTC Unlisted Manual, Moody's Public Utilities Manual, Moody's Transportation Manual, Mergent Company Data,* and *Mergent Industry Review.*

Moody's Industrial Manual, published annually, is a series of individual manuals presenting detailed company descriptions, financial information, ratios, and other data for nearly 2,000 companies listed on the New York, American, or regional stock exchanges. Monthly supplements are available in *Moody's Industrial News Reports;* weekly *News Reports* at www.fisonline.com

Moody's Bank & Finance Manual, published annually, contains information on over 20,000 national, state, and private banks, savings and loans, mutual funds, unit investment trusts, and insurance and real estate companies in the United States. Entries include company name, headquarters and branch offices, phones, names and titles of principal executives, directors, history, Moody's rating, and extensive financial and statistical data. Monthly supplements are available in *Moody's Bank & Finance News Reports,* weekly *News Reports* at www.fisonline.com.

Moody's OTC Industrial Manual, published annually in September, is composed of individual manuals that present nearly 2,000 companies whose stock is traded over the counter. Entries include detailed company descriptions, financial information, ratios, and other data for several industries. Monthly supplements are available in *Moody's OTC Industrial News Reports,* weekly *News Reports* at www.fisonline.com, weekly supplements in *Moody's Industrial News Reports.*

Moody's OTC Unlisted Manual is published annually in October. Monthly supplements are included in *Moody's OTC Unlisted News Reports,* weekly *News Reports* available at www.fisonline.com. Individual manuals present detailed information on over 2,000 companies not listed on national or regional exchanges. Descriptions include financial information, ratios, and other data for companies in several industries.

Moody's Public Utility Manual is published annually in October. Monthly supplements are included in *Moody's Public Utility News Report,* weekly *News Reports* available at www.fisonline.com. Individual manuals present detailed information on about 560 electric, gas, telephone, and water utility companies. Descriptions include financial information, ratios, and other data for companies in several industries.

Moody's Transportation Manual is published annually in November. Monthly supplements are included in *Moody's Transportation News Reports,* weekly *News Reports* available at www.fisonline.com. Individual manuals present detailed information on about 1,000 railroads, airlines, steamship companies, electric railways, bus and truck lines, oil pipelines, bridge and tunnel operators, and automobile and truck leasing companies. Descriptions include financial information, ratios, and other data for companies in several industries.

Mergent Company Data, published monthly and available on CD-ROM, provides comprehensive and accurate business and operating descriptions with full, "as reported" financials on over 10,000 companies. With included MoodEASE software, users can do their own custom searches and sorts as well as export the results to their spreadsheet. Statistics include history, business, long-term debt, capital stock, income statement, balance sheets, footnotes, number of employees and shareholders, stock price ranges, and dividends.

Mergent Industry Review, published annually with bimonthly updates, covers approximately 3,000 leading companies in nearly 137 industry categories. Every company is ranked within its industry by five financial characteristics (revenues, net income, total assets, cash and marketable securities, and long-term debt) and five ratios (profit margin, return on capital, return on assets, P/E, and dividend yield). Every industry report also provides unranked data, including earnings per share, book value, and 12-year stock price summaries.

These publications are available from Mergent FIS Inc., 60 Madison Ave., 6th Floor, New York, NY 10010, (800) 342-5647, Ext. 7601, www.fisonline.com, www.moodys.com.

Standard & Poor's

Standard & Poor's Corporation provides a wide variety of publications, both print and electronic, on publicly traded companies, including *Compustat, Standard & Poor's Corporation Records, Standard & Poor's Industry Reports, Standard & Poor's Industry Survey, Standard & Poor's Stock Guide, Standard & Poor's Stock Reports, Standard & Poor's Earnings Guide, Standard & Poor's Analysts' Handbook,* and *Standard & Poor's Execacomp.* These are all available from Standard & Poor's Corporation, 7400 South Alton Court, Englewood, CO 80112, (800) 525-8640. Call (212) 438-3648 for pricing information for the following products.

Compustat is an online database with real-time, daily, and weekly updates. Inquire as to online cost and availability: (800) 523-4534 or www.compustat.com.

Compustat (North America) contains comprehensive fundamental market data on more than 18,000 publicly traded U.S. and Canadian companies. Includes 20 years of historic information with updates available on a daily, weekly, or monthly basis.

Compustat (Global) is comprised of financial and market data on more than 11,000 publicly traded companies in 70 countries around the world. Includes annual income statement, balance sheet, cash flow, and supplementary data with up to 12 years of history.

Research Insight is a tool for a comprehensive screening of the *Compustat* database over a wide range of investment and financial criteria. It also provides users options for importing proprietary data, accessing daily updates of more than 50 fundamental items, and securing real-time prices, market statistics, and company news.

Market Insight offers financial professionals companywide, Web-based delivery of integrated company, industry, and country information pulled from throughout the Standard & Poor's organization.

Standard & Poor's Analysts' Handbook, published annually with monthly updates, is available in print and disk. This statistical workbook enables anyone concerned with company or industry performance to conveniently compare the most vital per-share data and financial statistics for the S&P industrial stocks and the industries comprising the index. Also includes transportation, financial, and utility groups. Available with monthly updating.

Standard & Poor's Corporation Records, published annually with daily or monthly updates, is available in print and on CD-ROM. They contain detailed information on both public and closely held companies and supplementary news items.

Standard & Poor's Earnings Guide, published monthly, is available in print. This guide to earnings estimates for over 4,300 publicly traded stocks provides the high and low estimate and computes a mean estimate for each of the next two years, as well as book value, cash flow, estimated five-year projected earnings growth rate, and annual revenue. It is released on the second Tuesday of each month.

Standard & Poor's Execucomp, published quarterly, is available on CD-ROM. Product pricing begins at $5,000, standard reports begin at $500, and custom studies from *Execucomp*'s team of experts begin at $700. *Execucomp* is a comprehensive database that covers S&P 500, S&P midcap 400, and S&P small-cap companies, with data on over 1,600 companies. The study includes over 80 different compensation, executive, director, and company items including breakdowns of salary, bonuses, options, and director compensation information.

Standard & Poor's Industry Reports, published monthly, is available in print. It provides a monthly quick reference "snapshot" of 80 industries and provides evaluations of each industry's near- and long-term investment outlook, including price performance over five years with a seven-month moving average, year-end group ratios with a five-year average for comparison, alphabetical list of stock rankings based on S&P's STARS ranking system, and an industry snapshot to show performance for the last quarter, year, and three years.

Standard & Poor's Industry Survey, published weekly and annually, is available in print and on CD-ROM. It provides information on industry structure, trends, and outlook for 52 broad industry groups, subdivided into 500 subgroups and 115 market sectors.

Standard & Poor's Stock Guide, published monthly, is available in print and on CD-ROM. It contains data on 5,200 common and preferred stocks and 650 mutual funds; preferred stock and mutual bond fund rating system, earnings, and dividends rankings.

Standard & Poor's Stock Reports is available in print, CD-ROM, and online. It provides data on over 6,300 public companies, including stock prices, operating statistics, dividend yields, and betas. The print version has separate volumes for NYSE, ASE, and NASDAQ stocks. CD-ROM price varies based on size and end users.

S&P Web sites:

Compustat—Standard & Poor's Corporation, www.compustat.com

Standard & Poor's Corporation Records and *Standard & Poor's Register*— Standard & Poor's Corporation, www.standardpoor.com

Publications—Standard & Poor's Corporation, www.advisorinsight.com

Demonstrations site—Standard & Poor's products and publications www.netadvantage.standardpoor.com/demo.

U.S. Government Printing Office

SEC Directory, the directory of companies required to file annual reports with the Securities and Exchange Commission under the Securities Exchange Act of 1934, is published annually. It lists the companies alphabetically and classified by industry group according to the Standard Industrial Classification Manual. The latest directory (1999) lists over 12,000 companies required to file annual reports with the SEC. Available from U.S. Government Printing Office, Superintendent of Documents, Washington D.C. 20402, (202) 512-1800, www.gpo.gov.

Statistics of Income: Corporation Income Tax Returns, published annually in October, contains industry average balance sheet, income statement, and tax and investment credit items by major and minor industries, broken down by size of total assets, business receipts, and accounting period. Tables provide detailed industry data on receipts, deductions, net income, taxable income, income tax, tax credits, and assets and liabilities. Published three to five years after subject period. Available from U.S. Government Printing Office, Superintendent of Documents, Washington D.C. 20402, (202) 512-1800, www.gpo.gov.

Statistics of Income Bulletin, published quarterly, provides financial statistics from individual and corporation income tax returns in addition to nonfarm sole proprietorships and partnerships. Historical tables include data from Statistics of Income. Available from U.S. Government Printing Office, Superintendent of Documents, Washington D.C. 20402, (202) 512-1800, www.gpo.gov.

North American Industry Classification System: United States, published annually, is available in print and on CD-ROM. NAICS was adopted by the Office of Management and Budget in 1997 and replaces the old SIC, last updated in 1987. It contains a comprehensive system covering the entire field of economic activities, producing and nonproducing. It includes 350 new industries—1,170 in total, definitions for each industry, tables showing correspondence between the 1997 NAICS and the 1987 Standard Industrial Classification (SIC) codes and vice versa, and an alphabetical list of more than 18,000 businesses and their corresponding NAICS codes. Also included are a directory of NAICS-involved agencies and frequently asked questions. Available from U.S. Government Printing Office, Superintendent of Documents, Washington D.C. 20402, (202) 512-1800, www.gpo.gov.

EARNINGS FORECASTS AND RELATED DATA FOR PUBLIC AND PRIVATE COMPANIES

Value Line

Value Line employs a staff of some 100 independent professional security analysts. Its basic *Value Line Investment Survey* covers 1,700 stocks, and the *Value Line Investment Survey—Expanded Edition* covers an additional 1,800 stocks. In addition to historical financial data and betas, Value Line forecasts revenues, cash flow, earnings, dividends, capital expenditures, book value, shares outstanding, income tax rates, net profit margins, capital structure ratios, returns on both total capital and equity, and a three-to-five-year target price range for the stock. For historical research, the *Value Line Investment Survey* is available on microfiche from 1980 and the *Expanded Edition* from March 1995. This organization has several other print services, including the *Value Line Mutual Fund Survey,* the *Value Line No-Load Fund Advisor,* the *Value Line OTC Special Situations Service,* the *Value Line Options Survey,* and the *Value Line Convertibles Survey.*

Value Line also has an array of electronic publications, starting with Value Line Investment Survey for Windows. The software includes 200 searchable data fields, more than 50 chart and graph options, and more than 100 screening options. An expanded version includes data on more than 5,000 stocks. In addition, there are several other electronic products.

The surveys are also available through CompuServe, and Value Line has an online bulletin board service updated weekly for subscribers. There is a *Value Line Data File* with fundamental data on more than 5,000 companies. It has annual data since 1955, quarterly since 1963, and full 10-Q data since 1985. It includes balance sheet and income data, risk measures, rates of return, and analytic ratios. Value Line is at 220 East 42nd Street, New York, NY 10017, (800) 634-3583 for print services, (800) 284-7607 for electronic services.

First Call

First Call Corporation is a source of earnings estimates, research, and corporate information.

First Call Real Time Earnings Estimates (RTEE) has more than 200 data items, including current and previous analysts' earnings estimates, operating data, expected reporting dates, footnotes, and the First Call consensus estimate. *RTEE* covers more than 17,500 companies, updated from more than 500 brokerage firms worldwide.

Other services include current research from 200 brokerage firms, more than 320,000 full-text research reports (including charts, graphs, color, and formatting), a Recommendations Database, and a Fundamentals Database on more than 7,000 companies updated weekly with balance sheet and income items, pricing and valuation data, and some financial ratios.

First Call has consensus earnings estimates updated weekly for about 6,500 companies via America Online and on the Web at www.firstcall.com/individual. All First Call products are available via flexible delivery options. They can be accessed through a dedicated First Call terminal, a local area network (LAN), via other third-party services, or through First Call On Call, a dial-up method using a standard personal computer and modem. *RTEE* data are also available in various hard copy reports and fax products. First Call is headquartered in Boston, 22 Thomson Place, Boston, MA 02210, (800) 448-2348.

I/B/E/S

I/B/E/S covers 6,000 U.S. companies and 12,000 companies in 47 additional countries. It provides earnings estimates, recommendations, stock charts, current summaries and history, and analyst directories. The U.S. estimates come from a little more than 3,000 analysts in about 230 firms. In addition to earnings per share (EPS), I/B/E/S forecasts include cash flow per share, dividends per share, and pretax profits.

I/B/E/S has a U.S. history database that covers more than 20 years of U.S. earnings estimates and results for more than 10,000 companies. Data items include annual EPS projections and actual results since January 1976, long-term (five-year) growth projections since 1981, and quarterly data since 1984. The database is combined with I/B/E/S Rewind Software compatible with Windows.

I/B/E/S data are distributed through nearly every major source of electronic financial information. Although electronic distribution is emphasized, some products including earnings estimates are also available in print versions.

I/B/E/S also has an array of other financial information available, especially that of a global nature.

In addition, I/B/E/S has supported academic research on earnings estimates for many years and has published an annotated bibliography, edited by Lawrence D. Brown, with abstracts of more than 400 articles and reports on such research. I/B/E/S is at 84 Wooster Street, New York, NY 10012, (212) 334-6686, www.rimes.com.

Integra Information

Integra Information provides private company financial information covering 4 million companies in over 900 industries. Integra's *Business Profiler* and *Industry Reports* are decision-support tools for financial professionals, including accountants, appraisers, and valuation specialists. The following publications are available in print and online from Integra Information, 354 Route 206, Flanders, NJ 07836; (800) 780-2660, www.integrainfo.com.

Business Profiler and Industry Reports provide five years of historical and forecasted revenue growth information. Three-year reports include a three-year historical balance sheet and summary income statement information, graphs of key operating trends, ratios and industry descriptions. Five-year reports provide detailed financial analysis and trending of user-selected private business sectors, five-year historical income statements and balance sheets, four years of cash flow analyses, and over 60 ratios.

3-Year Comparative Reports present comprehensive financial information of private company performance for the latest three-year period. Information includes historical financial statements, financial and operating ratios, and growth trends.

Industry Narrative Reports are available for $650 and $750 for national and regional research, respectively. In addition to delivering customized research in narrative format, the reports also identify key industry trends including relevant economic, social, technological, or regulatory issues.

Standard & Poor's ACE (Analysts' Consensus Estimates)

Standard & Poor's offers its Analysts' Consensus Estimates (ACE) through its *Compustat* distribution system. It provides EPS and five-year growth estimates for more than 5,200 of the 9,700 companies on the *Compustat* database. The EPS estimates for each company also include mean, median, high, low, and standard deviation. The estimates come from more than 2,300 analysts in more than 200 brokerage firms.

The data can be accessed through S&P PC Plus Windows-based software. The S&P ACE file is available electronically for loading to the subscriber's computer system or through several *Compustat* vendors distributing the file electronically. Standard & Poor's Compustat group is at 7400 South Alton Court, Englewood, CO 80112, (800) 525-8640.

Zacks Investment Research, Inc.

Zacks offers two print publications, *Zacks Analysts Watch* and *Zacks Earnings Forecaster*. The *Zacks Analysts Watch* covers just over 6,000 companies while the *Zacks Earnings Forecaster* covers Wall Street's top 1,500 companies, including EPS forecasts and other data. *Zacks Earnings Forecaster* includes EPS histograms (fiscal and quarterly updates), quick fundamentals (valuation ratios, income and balance sheets), rankings (stock price, P/E, EPS estimates/growth), and earnings dates. Zacks is at 155 N. Wacker Drive, Chicago, IL 60606, (800) 767-3771.

SOURCES OF FINANCIAL RATIOS AND FINANCIAL STATEMENT ANALYSIS

Almanac of Business and Industrial Financial Ratios

Presents 22 financial ratios and percentages for different types and sizes of businesses. The information is derived from corporate tax returns in the IRS files. This publication is derived from the Statistics of Income (SOI) division of the IRS. Available from Prentice Hall, 111 8th Ave. New York, NY 10036 (800) 447-1717.

Financial Ratio Analyst

Presents easy-to-follow tables regarding solvency ratios, leverage ratios, profitability ratios, and efficiency ratios. Data are classified by SIC code allowing SIC- driven searches. This publication is derived from the Statistics of Income (SOI) division of the IRS. Available annually on disk from Warren Gorham & Lamont, 31 St. James Ave., Boston, MA 02116, (800) 950-1210, www.wglcorpfinance.com.

Financial Studies of the Small Businesses

Presents 16 ratios and 44 percentages for over 65 different types of small businesses (assets of $1 million or less). Contains asset size, sales volume and most profitable breakdowns. Over 170 pages of historical income data and ratios for over 60 industries presented by sales volume and overall for each industry with a five-year trend. Compiled from 25,000 financial statements submitted by over 1,500 Certified Public Accounting firms. Disk includes client comparative analysis software. This publication is derived from the Statistics of Income (SOI) division of the IRS. Available annually in print and on disk from Financial Research Associates, PO Box 7708, Winter Haven, FL 33883-7708, (800) 422-3782, email: fra_fssb@aol.com.

IRS Corporate Ratios

Includes raw tax data and calculated percentages and ratios from the IRS Source Book Statistics of Income Corporation Income Tax Returns on a two-disk Windows-based program. In addition, an easy-to-follow manual is provided detailing installation, accessing, using, and customizing the database. This publication is derived from the Statistics of Income (SOI) division of the IRS. Available from John Wiley & Sons, 7222 Commerce Drive, Suite 210, Colorado Springs, CO 80919-2632, (719) 548-4900, www.wiley.com.

IRS Corporate Financial Ratios

Presents over 70 financial ratios for each of over 225 industries, calculated from the latest income statement and balance sheet data from over 85,000 corporate tax returns. Ratios are provided for four company sizes within each industry group and companies with profits are separated from those with losses. This publication is derived from the Statistics of Income (SOI) division of the IRS. Available in print and on disk from Schonfield & Associates, 2830 Blackthorn Rd., Riverwoods, IL 60015, (847) 948-8080, www.saibooks.com.

RMA Annual Statement Studies

Risk Management Association member institutions submit over 150,000 financial statements of their borrowing customers. The primary section contains composite balance sheets and income data for more than 600 industries, fully identified by titles and SIC numbers. It also contains five years of comparable historical data, along with current data for each industry. Statement Studies also provides 16 commonly used ratios, computed for most of the size groupings and nearly every industry. Data are now arranged by both sales volume and asset size, and include a section on the CFMA construction industry annual survey. The disk version is also available for six separate regions. Published annually in October. Available in print and on disk from Risk Management Association, One Liberty Place, 1650 Market Street, Philadelphia, PA 19103-9734, (800) 677-7621, www.mahq.org.

Compare2 Financial Statement Analysis

Compare2 is a business analysis tool that allows users to compare financial data on 10, 25, 50, or 100 companies (that the user is entering) to the data in the RMA studies. The data are compiled from over 150,000 businesses included in RMA's Statement Studies. Features include common size statements, ratios, historical, and projected financial statements. Available from Risk Management Association, One Liberty Place, 1650 Market Street, Philadelphia, PA 19103-9734, (800) 677-7621, www.mahq.org.

DATABASES

Compact/D

Compact/D offers four extensive databases proprietary to Primark on CD-ROM or online. Users enter search criteria on pull-down menus and a list of matching companies is returned instantly. Entire database records or specific sections can be viewed.

Disclosure SEC and Company—Includes financial and management information for more than 12,000 companies trading on major U.S. exchanges. Weekly updates available online.

Worldscope—Includes financial and management information for more than 15,000 companies representing over 50 established and emerging markets. Monthly updates available online.

Canada—Includes financial and management information for more than 11,000 Canadian, public, private, and crown companies. Weekly updates available online.

New Issues—Issue-by-issue coverage of every sizable U.S. public company equity or debt offering from January 1990 to the present. Weekly updates available online.

The capabilities offered are of fully searchable databases, full-text searching by keyword, custom reporting of complete database records or just specific sections, and multiple save formats—standard, tagged, comma delimited, tab delimited, or fixed—for easy exporting to spreadsheet, database, or word processing programs. For more information contact Primark, 5161 River Road, Bethesda, MD 20816, (800) 638-8241, info@disclosure.com, www.disclosure.com, www.primark .com/pfid/.

Global Access

Global Access is a Web-based, integrated research tool providing desktop access to a full range of critical company information. Offering more than 12 robust data sets, *Global Access* delivers the high-quality and comprehensive online collection of U.S. and international company coverage. Powerful search, display, and download features allow easy access to such information as the Disclosure database of SEC filings and images of annual reports, I/B/E/S earnings estimates, Multex Research Reports, articles online, and insider trading analysis. The image repository spans five years and 1.2 million filings. *Global Access* is an online research tool capable of combining detailed financial and management information with more than 5 million source documents. *Global Access* can be used to:

- Identify investment opportunities
- Perform competitive analysis
- Qualify M&A prospects
- Assess corporate finances
- Manage investment risk
- Track insider trading activity
- Monitor corporate activity
- Perform case studies

Its modular design means users can tailor a subscription to meet their specific needs or opt for unlimited access to all content modules. Available from Primark, 5161 River Road, Bethesda, MD 20816, (800) 638-8241, info@disclosure.com, www.disclosure.com, www.primark.com/pfid. For additional information on this online financial information tool, call (800) 236-6997, ext. 302 (outside the U.S., call 44-171-566-1900).

ONLINE SERVICES

Yahoo! Finance—http://finance.yahoo.com

Access is free to brief company description with links to company home page, stock quote, financial data, and recent news.

Hoover's Online—www.hoovers.com

The *Hoover's Online* site provides extensive information on public companies in an easy-to-use format. *Hoover's Online* database contains information on more than 42,000 companies. Access to the company capsules is free. Company profiles, in-depth financials, and access to investor tools (i.e., analyst's research reports) are available only to subscribers.

Prophet—www.prophet.net

Profit is a financial data search engine. Users enter ticker symbol or company name and are linked to quotes, charts, news, profiles, earnings estimates, SEC filings, analysts, and research reports: magazine, newspaper, and search engines—and more.

PUBLIC COMPANY TRANSACTION METHOD SOURCES OF TRANSACTIONS

Print Sources

Mergerstat Review is published annually in print. This hardbound volume includes in-depth research and analysis of mergers and acquisitions activity and multiyear trend analysis. Narrative and nearly 100 charts/graphs present actionable data necessary to

- Identify and stay current with M&A trends
- Strategically prepare for a sale or acquisition
- Value a company one is buying or selling
- Learn what companies are really sold for
- Track competitors' or clients' M&A moves

Mergerstat tracks deals involving U.S. companies including privately held, publicly traded, and cross-border transactions plus unit divestitures, management buyouts, and certain assets sales. The *Review* provides trend analysis by seller, type, deal size, and industry, plus 25 years of summary M&A statistics, including average premium and P/E ratio. It also provides aggregate and industry deal activity; industry EBITDA, EBIT, and P/E multiples; premiums paid and payment methods, plus financial and legal advisor rankings. Back issues are available. *Mergerstat Review* is available from FactSet Mergerstat LLC, 2150 Colorado Ave., Suite 150, Santa Monica, California 90404, (310) 315-3100, www.mergerstat.com.

FactSet Mergerstat Online Transaction Roster Online service allows users to search and print from up to two years of deal profiles via the Internet. Access informative profiles of over 7,500 transactions added in 2004, plus regular monthly updates of deals. One can search deal data quickly and easily, including buyer and seller name plus location, buyer/seller SIC and business description, deal announcement and close dates, deal size ($), P/E ratio, deal type, and payment method. FactSet Mergerstat LLC, 2150 Colorado Ave., Suite 150, Santa Monica, California 90404, (310) 315-3100, www.mergerstat.com.

FactSet is published monthly. Each information-packed issue features a graphical, top-down overview of the latest trends in the mergers and acquisitions market as well as bottom-up analysis of the key industry statistics driving today's private and public deals. Regular features include

- MergerMetrics—a market-by-market breakdown of the latest trends in deal activity and value
- Middle Market Monitor—a complete, graphical analysis of the middle market
- M&Active Industries—a spotlight on today's most interesting industries
- M&A Hot Spots—the hottest cities, states, regions, and countries in M&A
- Advisor Rankings—a comprehensive listing of M&A's top dealmakers
- Mega-Mergers—snapshots of the biggest deals of the day

Available from FactSet Mergerstat LLC, 2150 Colorado Ave., Suite 150, Santa Monica, California 90404, (310) 315-3100, www.mergerstat.com.

Mergers & Acquisitions, The Dealmaker's Journal, published bimonthly, covers terminology and techniques in the merger and acquisition field, analyzes specific transactions, and provides data on merger activity. Available from Investment

Dealers' Digest, One State Street Plaza, 27th floor, New York, NY 10004, (212) 803-8200.

Mergers & Acquisitions in Canada, published monthly, includes M&A data and analysis. Available from M&A Publishing, One First Canada Place, 9th floor, PO Box 116, Toronto, Ontario, Canada MSX 1A4, (416) 362-0020.

Mergers & Acquisitions Quarterly is specifically designed to provide M&A sourcebook data on a quarterly basis. It offers purchase price data and ratios to seller's sales, earnings, and net worth data on more than 1,000 corporate growth transactions in all industries. In addition, it has detailed charts and graphs, book reviews, and M&A features not published elsewhere. Available from Quality Services Company, 5290 Overpass Road, Suite 126, Santa Barbara, CA 93111, (800) 266-3888.

Mergers & Acquisitions Sourcebook, published annually, is the most comprehensive source of M&A information (600 pages) available anywhere, with coverage of mergers and acquisitions, joint ventures, initial public offerings (IPOs), restructurings, and strategic minority stakes. Details on more than 3,000 transactions, including purchase price and three-year financial data on seller and buyer organized by seller's SIC code; special sections on leveraged buyouts (LBOs), buybacks, and terminations; M&A and divestiture activity of company divisions; foreign M&A activity; and analysis of industry trends. This publication is available from Nvst.com, 777 108th Avenue, N.E., Suite 1750, Bellevue, WA 98004, (425) 454-3639, www.nvst.com.

The Weekly Corporate Growth Report, 50 issues per year, is a newsletter on corporate growth in the United States, with fast-breaking news of the M&A market, including acquisitions, mergers, divestitures, spin-offs, terminations, management buyouts, restructurings, and methods of increasing shareholder value. This publication is available from Nvst.com, 777 108th Avenue, N.E., Suite 1750, Bellevue, WA 98004, (425) 454-3639, www.nvst.com.

The Merger Yearbook, published annually in March, provides information on tens of thousands of announced and completed deals, including total purchase price, price paid per share, form of payment, division/unit purchased, parent company, acquiring company, type of transaction, SIC number and industry section of target company and acquirer, price to earnings ratio, plus dozens of charts covering transactions by dollar amount and industry. Available from Securities Data Publishing, 40 West 57th Street, New York, NY 10019, (800) 455-5844, www.securitiesdata.com.

Electronic Sources

Dialog Corporation. The Dialog Corporation is a leading provider of Internet-based information, technology, and e-commerce solutions, including the *Dialog* online information service. Several business databases can be accessed through *Dialog.*

Business & Industry (B&I) database contains information with facts, figures, and key events dealing with public and private companies, industries, markets, and products for all manufacturing and service industries at an international level. B&I coverage concentrates on leading trade magazines and newsletters, the general business press, regional newspapers, and international business dailies. The database includes abstracts and full text of relevant articles, and is enhanced with rich indexing that enables highly specific retrieval of relevant articles.

Business Dateline, produced by Bell & Howell Information and Learning, provides the full text of major news and feature stories from 550 regional business publications from throughout the United States and Canada. The regional perspectives reported in the business press make *Business Dateline* an important source of in-depth business information with a local point of view. Multiple aspects of regional business activities and trends are covered in the file, with particular emphasis on economic conditions in selected cities, states, or regions, as well as mergers, acquisitions, company executives, new products, and competitive intelligence.

Business Wire contains the full text of news releases issued by approximately 10,000 corporations, universities, research institutes, hospitals, and other organizations. The file primarily covers U.S. industries and organizations, although some information on international events is included. Records in *Business Wire* vary in length, but typically contain fewer than 500 words. News releases received by *Business Wire* are available in the *Business Wire* database the same day. *Business Wire* is available on the Dialog First Release service (updated continuously throughout the day). *Business Wire* is contained in two databases: Files 610 and 810. File 610 contains current data beginning in March 1999. File 810 contains archive data spanning from 1986 through February 1999.

Gale Group PROMT is a multiple-industry database that provides broad, international coverage of companies, products, markets, and applied technologies for all industries. PROMT is comprised of abstracts and full-text records from the world's important trade and business journals, local newspapers, regional business publications, national and international business newspapers, industry newsletters, research studies, investment analysts' reports, corporate news releases, and corporate annual reports. PROMT abstracts and full-text records cover the international events and activities of public and private companies throughout the world. The database is divided into two files: File 16 covers 1990 to the present, and File 160 covers 1972 through 1989. Begin PROMT to search both files simultaneously.

TFSD Worldwide Mergers & Acquisitions includes information on all partial, completed, or rumored transactions that involve a change in ownership of at least 5%. U.S. and international targets are covered in depth, for both public and private companies, with 60 data items available for each transaction.

Gale Group Trade & Industry is a multi-industry database covering international company, industry, product, and market information, with strong coverage of such areas as management techniques, financial earnings, economic climate, product evaluations, and executive changes. Unique industry subfiles allow users to narrow or broaden their searches to one or more groups of industry specific publications. *Gale Group Trade & Industry Database* complements *Gale Group PROMT* (File 16) by providing in-depth coverage of over 65 major industries, including full-text coverage of management, economic, and other professional journals. Abstracts are available for some records and the complete text is fully searchable for many records from 1983 to the present. The above databases are available from Dialog Corporation, 11000 Regency Parkway # 10, Cary, NC 27511, (800) 334-2564, www.dialog.com.

For more information on *Dialog* databases, go to http://products.dialog.com/products/toolkit/databases.html#b.

Alacra.com™, formerly xls.com, is a source for large and middle transaction data. The databases are searchable by keyword and financial criteria. New databases are added regularly. Available at Alacra.dcom, 88 Pine Street, 3rd floor, New York, New York 10005, (212) 363-9620.

Mergerstat®/Shannon Pratt's Control Premium Study™ is a Web-based tool used to quantify minority discounts and control premiums used in the business valuation, business appraisal, venture capital, and merger and acquisition (M & A) professions. This database currently contains over 4,300 transactions ranging from 1998 through 2004.

The **Public Stats™** transaction database contains data variously described as guideline company, guideline transaction, comparable sales data, business comparable, and/or market data. This database reports the financial and transactional details of the sales of publicly held companies and contains over 1,740 transactions between 1995 through the present.

PRIVATE COMPANY SALE TRANSACTION DATA

There are several databases that cover private company transactions.

BIZCOMPS®

BIZCOMPS® is compiled by Jack R. Sanders of Asset Business Appraisal and is available on the Bizcomps® site, BVResources@www.bvmarketdata.com or at www.bizcomps.com and from John Wiley & Sons ValuSource unit. It contains information on hundreds of small business sales. The database is updated and expanded every year. Deals are sorted by industry and contain revenue and discretionary earnings multiples. *BIZCOMPS*® is published annually in print in four editions: *Western, Central, Eastern, National Industrial.* Data for each sale include SIC, type of business, ask price, sale price, annual sales, seller's discretionary cash flow, percent down, terms, inventory, fixtures and equipment, rent percent of sales, general location, ratio of sale price to gross sales, and sale price to seller's discretionary cash flow. There are also a variety of summaries and averages presented for various subgroups of companies.

BIZCOMPS® 2000 Special Food Service Edition (2005). The special edition of *BIZCOMPS®* is published every three years and is available in print. It includes approximately 1,500 transactions drawn from the overall *BIZCOMPS®* database. Data definitions are the same as in other *BIZCOMPS®* editions, all reported as asset sales and excluding cash, accounts receivable and payable, and inventory. Also provided are mean and median pricing statistics.

BIZCOMPS® 2005 on Disk (2005), available on disk. Windows-driven program cataloging 4,400 transactions. Custom searches for any field in each record are allowed. The program also contains graphing and linear regression analysis. For more information on *BIZCOMPS®* products, contact *BIZCOMPS®*, Asset Business Appraisal, PO Box 711777, San Diego, CA 92171, (858) 457-0366, www.bizcomps.com.

Done Deals Data

Done Deals Data is published quarterly in disk format. It contains information on transactions of privately held companies up to $100 million in size. Reported transactions cover approximately 30 industries. Data include sale price, terms, and ratios. The program is available online and on disk and includes a Deal Navigator, which allows the user to search by SIC code, keywords, location, closing date, price, and seller and buyer name. Transactions include five financial indicators: assets, equity, revenue, net income, and cash from operations. Ratios corresponding to these fields are also provided. *Done Deals* currently has 3,600 transactions with up to 250 added each quarter. Access to *Done Deals* database is available on the Web through Thomson PPC at http://donedeals.nvst.com. For more information, contact Practitioners Publishing Co., Nvst.com/World M&A, 717 D Street, N.W., Suite 300, Washington, D.C. 20004, customer.service@ppcnet.com or (817) 332-3709.

Pratt's Stats™

Pratt's Stats™ is a database of privately held business sales containing detailed information on thousands of businesses. Its differentiating feature is its attention to detail—these details include up to 80 different data fields. Each transaction in *Pratt's Stats™* includes a complete income statement and balance sheet from which 10 valuation multiples are calculated, including: equity price/gross cash flow, equity price/EBT, deal price/EBITDA, and deal price/EBIT. In addition, *Pratt's Stats™* also includes details on any consulting/employment agreements, noncompete agreements, assumed leases, and financing of the purchase. All of these can be useful in creating a cash equivalent value or in providing the user with creative ideas for structuring their deals. A sample transaction can be obtained at the *Pratt's Stats*™ Web site, www.PrattsStats.com. Available from Business Valuation Resources, 7412 S.W. Beaverton-Hillsdale Highway, Suite 106, Portland, OR 97225, (888) BUS-VALU.

IBA Market Data Base

The **IBA Market Data Base** is published regularly with updates from brokers. It contains approximately 18,000 transactions submitted during the last 20 years in over 650 SIC codes. The database contains fields such as annual sales, earnings, owner's compensation, sale price, location, and the year and month of the transaction. Available in print free of charge to members of The Institute of Business Appraisers, PO Box 17410, Plantation, FL 33318, (800) 299-4130, www.instbusapp.org.

PARTNERSHIP TRANSACTION DATA

The Direct Investments Spectrum Newsletter is published bimonthly and is available in print. It tracks the partnership industry, especially focusing on but not limited to real estate partnerships. The May/June issue is a compilation of empirical data concerning discounts from net asset value at which minority interests in real estate partnerships trade in the informal resale market. The other issues are valuable to the partnership industry; however, they are not predominately data compilations. Single issues are available for $95 each. Information for each partnership includes specific property holdings, cash distribution history, debt levels, key operating statistics, and so on. Available from Partnership Profiles, PO Box 7938, Dallas, TX 75209, (800) 634-4614 or via e-mail at support@ partnershipprofiles.com.

COMPENSATION DATA

Officer Compensation Report 2000

Created from the largest national database of small- to medium-size companies, the *Report* provides data on salaries, bonuses, pay increases, ownership levels, and incentives at over 50,000 companies in eight industry groups with gross sales of $2 to $100 million, and over. The survey is mailed in the spring to be printed by the fall each year. Published annually in October. Available in print from Aspen Law & Business, PO Box 990, Frederick, MD 21705, (800) 638-8437, www.aspenpub.com.

Executive Compensation: Survey Results

Executive Compensation presents the results of surveys conducted by National Institute of Business Management. The results are separated into eight top executive categories in small or midsize firms. NIBM's compensation survey differs from others in that NIBM covers predominantly smaller companies. The survey breaks down information into industry categories, positions, firm size, and geographical area. Back issues are available. Published annually in August. Available in print from National Institute of Business Management, 1750 Old Meadow Road, Suite 302, McLean, VA 22102-4315, (800) 762-4924.

The Hay Report: Compensation & Benefits

The *Hay Report* is based on findings from the *Hay Compensation Report* database, *Hay/Huggins Benefits Report,* and the Hay Fall Conference series. The *Hay Report* details the practices of thousands of companies and compensation activity by industry, job level, and function. It includes sections on prevailing compensation levels, team-based compensation, average monthly premium costs, and CEO reward practices. Published annually in December. Available in print from Center for Management Research, The Wanamaker Building, 100 Penn Square East, Philadelphia, PA 19107-3388, (215) 861-2633.

Management Compensation Study for Wholesalers and Large Retailers

This annual report is the industry's survey of management compensation data, covering more than 60 key positions ranging from CEO to meat department manager. Data displayed nationally and regionally. Non-bonus-paying and bonus-paying company breakdowns are also used. Approximately 500 pages. Published annually in the fall. Available in print from Food Marketing Institute, 655 15th Street, Suite 700, N.W., Washington, DC 20005, (202) 452-8444, www.fmi .org.

PERIODICALS

BUYOUTS Newsletter

BUYOUTS is a semimonthly newsletter that is a source of news, data analysis, and interpretation of trends in the buyout industry. Available biweekly from Securities Data Publishing, 1290 Sixth Avenue, 36th floor, New York, NY 10104, (800) 455-5844, www.sdponline.com.

DFS/DMA CD-ROM

Both the *Directory of Buyout Financing Sources* and the *Directory of M&A* intermediaries are available on one CD-ROM with fully searchable features. The CD contains one database of 1,000+ financing sources, all fully accessible by topic, such as investment criteria, location, and assets under management; a second database of more than 850 M&A intermediaries, accessible by topic, such as types of clients serviced, fee policies, and geographic preferences; back issues of two industry newsletters, *Buyouts* and *Mergers & Acquisitions Report;* plus several articles contributed by industry experts, all fully accessible by keyword. Available from Securities Data Publishing, 40 West 57th Street, New York, NY 10019, (800) 455-5844, www.securitiesdata.com.

Mergers & Acquisitions: The Dealmaker's Journal

Mergers & Acquisitions focuses on such key elements as acquisition pricing, valuation, strategy, and taxes; plus, it offers complete listings of all M&A deals, including pricing, deal structure, and sales and profit levels of the merger partners. Available monthly from Thomson Media, One State Street Plaza, 27th floor, New York, NY 10004, (800) 455-5844, www.majournal.com.

Mergers & Acquisitions Report Newsletter

This weekly newsletter gives inside information on mergers, acquisitions, restructurings, and buyouts. Also provided is a summary of actual deal data and the people behind the deals. Available weekly from Thomson Media, One State Street Plaza, 27th floor, New York, NY 10004, (800) 455-5844, www.majournal .com.

Mergers & Acquisitions Report

Laden with news about live deals, *Mergers & Acquisitions Report* covers the latest mergers, acquisitions, corporate restructuring, and bankruptcies, in addition to providing insights into industry trends, strategies, and the firms and people involved. It is an inside source on hundreds of M&A transactions throughout the year. Available weekly from Securities Data Publishing, 1290 Sixth Avenue, 36th floor, New York, NY 10104, (800) 455-5844, www.sdponline.com.

Valuation Survey

Valuation Survey provides comparative data on the value of privately held firms in the architecture, engineering, and environmental consulting industries. It includes profiles of 300+ individual valuation cases and a large database of actual valuations. Value data for each firm are summarized in five ratios: value per employee, value/book value, value/net revenue, value/profit, and value/ backlog. Call for information about becoming a survey participant. Available annually in print from Zweig White & Associates, Inc., PO Box 8325, One Apple Hill Drive, Natick, MA 01760-2085, (800) 466-6275, www.wa.com.

Appendix C

International Glossary of Business Valuation Terms

The following societies and organizations whose members provide business valuation services have adopted the definitions for the terms included in this glossary.[1]

American Institute of Certified Public Accountants

American Society of Appraisers

Canadian Institute of Chartered Business Valuators

The Institute of Business Appraisers
  National Association of Certified Valuation Analysts

The performance of business valuation services requires a high degree of skill, and imposes on the valuation professional a duty to communicate the valuation process and conclusion, as appropriate to the scope of the engagement, in a manner that is clear and not misleading. This duty is advanced through the use of terms whose meanings are clearly established and consistently applied throughout the profession.

If, in the opinion of the business valuation professional, one or more of these terms needs to be used in a manner that materially departs from the following definitions, it is recommended that the term be defined as used within that valuation engagement.

This glossary has been developed to provide guidance to business valuation practitioners who are members of the listed societies, organizations, and others performing valuations of business interests or securities by further codifying the body of knowledge that constitutes the competent and careful determination of value and, more particularly, the communication of how that value was determined.

Departure from this glossary is not intended to provide a basis for civil liability and should not be presumed to create evidence that any duty has been breached.

A

Adjusted Book Value The value that results after one or more asset or liability amounts are added, deleted, or changed from their respective financial statement amounts.

Appraisal   See **Valuation.**

Appraisal Approach   See **Valuation Approach.**

Appraisal Date   See **Valuation Date.**

Appraisal Method   See **Valuation Method.**

Appraisal Procedure   See **Valuation Procedure.**

Asset (Asset-Based) Approach   A general way of determining a value indication of a business, business ownership interest, or security by using one or more methods based on the value of the assets of that business net of liabilities.

B

Benefit Stream   Any level of income, cash flow, or earnings generated by an asset, group of assets, or business enterprise. When the term is used, it should be supplemented by a definition of exactly what it means in the given valuation context.

Beta   A measure of systematic risk of a security; the tendency of a security's returns to correlate with swings in the broad market.

Blockage Discount   An amount or percentage deducted from the current market price of a publicly traded security to reflect the decrease in the per-share value of a block of those securities that is of a size that could not be sold in a reasonable period of time given normal trading volume.

Business   See **Business Enterprise.**

Business Enterprise   A commercial, industrial, service, or investment entity, or a combination thereof, pursuing an economic activity.

Business Valuation   The act or process of determining the value of a business enterprise or ownership interest therein.

C

Capital Asset Pricing Model (CAPM)   A model in which the cost of capital for any security or portfolio of securities equals a risk-free rate plus a risk premium that is proportionate to the systematic risk of the security or portfolio.

Capitalization   A conversion of a single-period stream of benefits into value.

Capitalization Factor   Any multiple or divisor used to convert anticipated benefits into value.

Capitalization Rate   Any divisor (usually expressed as a percentage) used to convert anticipated benefits into value.

Capital Structure   The composition of the invested capital of a business enterprise; the mix of debt and equity financing.

Cash Flow   Cash that is generated over a period of time by an asset, group of assets, or business enterprise. It may be used in a general sense to encompass various levels of specifically defined cash flows. When the term is used, it should be supplemented by a qualifier (for example, *discretionary* or *operating*) and a definition of exactly what it means in the given valuation context.

Control   The power to direct the management and policies of a business enterprise.

Control Premium   An amount (expressed in either dollar or percentage form) by which the pro rata value of a controlling interest exceeds the pro rata value of a noncontrolling interest in a business enterprise that reflects the power of control.

Cost Approach   A general way of estimating a value indication of an individual asset by quantifying the amount of money that would be required to replace the future service capability of that asset.

Cost of Capital   The expected rate of return (discount rate) that the market requires in order to attract funds to a particular investment.

D

Discount   A reduction in value or the act of reducing value.

Discount for Lack of Control   An amount or percentage deducted from the pro rata share of value of 100% of an equity interest in a business to reflect the absence of some or all of the powers of control.

Discount for Lack of Marketability   An amount or percentage deducted from the value of an ownership interest to reflect the relative absence of marketability.

Discount Rate   A rate of return (cost of capital) used to convert a monetary sum, payable or receivable in the future, into present value.

E

Economic Life   The period of time over which property may generate economic benefits.

Effective Date   See **Valuation Date.**

Enterprise   See **Business Enterprise.**

Equity Net Cash Flows   Those cash flows available to pay out to equity holders (in the form of dividends) after funding operations of the business enterprise, making necessary capital investments, and reflecting increases or decreases in debt financing.

Equity Risk Premium   A rate of return in addition to a risk-free rate to compensate for investing in equity instruments because they have a higher degree of probable risk than risk-free instruments (a component of the cost of equity capital or equity discount rate).

Excess Earnings   That amount of anticipated benefits that exceeds a fair rate of return on the value of a selected asset base (often net tangible assets) used to generate those anticipated benefits.

Excess Earnings Method   A specific way of determining a value indication of a business, business ownership interest, or security determined as the sum of (a) the value of the assets obtained by capitalizing excess earnings and (b) the value of the selected asset base. Also frequently used to value intangible assets. See **Excess Earnings.**

F

Fair Market Value   The price, expressed in terms of cash equivalents, at which property would change hands between a hypothetical willing and able buyer and a hypothetical willing and able seller, acting at arm's length in an open and unrestricted market, when neither is under compulsion to buy or sell and when both have reasonable knowledge of the relevant facts. (Note: In Canada, the term *price* should be replaced with the term *highest price.*)

Forced Liquidation Value   Liquidation value at which the asset or assets are sold as quickly as possible, such as at an auction.

G

Going Concern   An ongoing operating business enterprise.

Going-concern Value   The value of a business enterprise that is expected to continue to operate into the future. The intangible elements of going-concern value result from factors such as having a trained workforce, an operational plant, and the necessary licenses, systems, and procedures in place.

Goodwill   That intangible asset arising as a result of name, reputation, customer loyalty, location, products, and similar factors not separately identified.

Goodwill Value   The value attributable to goodwill.

I

Income (Income-based) Approach   A general way of determining a value indication of a business, business ownership interest, security, or intangible asset using one or more methods that convert anticipated benefits into a present single amount.

Intangible Assets Nonphysical assets (i.e., franchises, trademarks, patents, copyrights, goodwill, equities, mineral rights, securities, and contracts as distinguished from physical assets) that grant rights, privileges, and have economic benefits for the owner.

Invested Capital The sum of equity and debt in a business enterprise. Debt is typically (a) long-term liabilities or (b) the sum of short-term interest-bearing debt and long-term liabilities. When the term is used, it should be supplemented by a definition of exactly what it means in the given valuation context.

Invested Capital Net Cash Flows Those cash flows available to pay out to equity holders (in the form of dividends) and debt investors (in the form of principal and interest) after funding operations of the business enterprise and making necessary capital investments.

Investment Risk The degree of uncertainty as to the realization of expected returns.

Investment Value The value to a particular investor based on individual investment requirements and expectations. (Note: In Canada, see **Value to the Owner.**)

K

Key Person Discount An amount or percentage deducted from the value of an ownership interest to reflect the reduction in value resulting from the actual or potential loss of a key person in a business enterprise.

L

Levered Beta The beta reflecting a capital structure that includes debt.

Liquidation Value The net amount that can be realized if the business is terminated and the assets are sold piecemeal. Liquidation can be either "orderly" or "forced."

Liquidity The ability to quickly convert property to cash or pay a liability.

M

Majority Control The degree of control provided by a majority position.

Majority Interest An ownership interest greater than 50% of the voting interest in a business enterprise.

Marketability The ability to quickly convert property to cash at minimal cost.

Marketability Discount See **Discount for Lack of Marketability.**

Market (Market-based) Approach   A general way of determining a value indication of a business, business ownership interest, security, or intangible asset by using one or more methods that compare the subject to similar businesses, business ownership interests, securities, or intangible assets that have been sold.

Minority Discount   A discount for lack of control applicable to a minority interest.

Minority Interest   An ownership interest less than 50 percent (50%) of the voting interest in a business enterprise.

N

Net Book Value   With respect to a business enterprise, the difference between total assets (net of accumulated depreciation, depletion, and amortization) and total liabilities of a business enterprise as they appear on the balance sheet (synonymous with shareholder's equity); with respect to an intangible asset, the capitalized cost of an intangible asset less accumulated amortization as it appears on the books of account of the business enterprise.

Net Cash Flow   A form of cash flow. When the term is used, it should be supplemented by a qualifier (e.g., *equity* or *invested capital*) and a definition of exactly what it means in the given valuation context.

Net Tangible Asset Value   The value of the business enterprise's tangible assets (excluding excess assets and nonoperating assets) minus the value of its liabilities. (Note: In Canada, tangible assets also include identifiable intangible assets.)

Nonoperating Assets   Assets not necessary to ongoing operations of the business enterprise. (Note: In Canada, see **Redundant Assets.**)

O

Orderly Liquidation Value   Liquidation value at which the asset or assets are sold over a reasonable period of time to maximize proceeds received.

P

Portfolio Discount   An amount or percentage that may be deducted from the value of a business enterprise to reflect the fact that it owns dissimilar operations or assets that may not fit well together.

Premise of Value   An assumption regarding the most likely set of transactional circumstances that may be applicable to the subject valuation; for example, going concern, liquidation.

R

Rate of Return   An amount of income (loss) and/or change in value realized or anticipated on an investment, expressed as a percentage of that investment.

Redundant Assets   (Note: In Canada, see **Nonoperating Assets.**)

Replacement Cost New   The current cost of a similar new property having the nearest equivalent utility to the property being valued.

Report Date   The date conclusions are transmitted to the client.

Reproduction Cost New   The current cost of an identical new property.

Residual Value   The prospective value as of the end of the discrete projection period in a discounted benefit streams model.

Risk-free Rate   The rate of return available in the market on an investment free of default risk.

Risk Premium   A rate of return in addition to a risk-free rate to compensate the investor for accepting risk.

Rule of Thumb   A mathematical relationship between or among variables based on experience, observation, hearsay, or a combination of these, usually applicable to a specific industry.

S

Special Interest Purchasers   Acquirers who believe they can enjoy postacquisition economies of scale, synergies, or strategic advantages by combining the acquired business interest with their own.

Standard of Value   The identification of the type of value being utilized in a specific engagement; for example, fair market value, fair value, investment value.

Sustaining Capital Reinvestment   The periodic capital outlay required to maintain operations at existing levels, net of the tax shield available from such outlays.

Systematic Risk   The risk that is common to all risky securities and cannot be eliminated through diversification. When using the capital asset pricing model, systematic risk is measured by beta.

T

Terminal Value   See **Residual Value.**

U

Unlevered Beta   The beta reflecting a capital structure without debt.

Unsystematic Risk   The portion of total risk specific to an individual security that can be avoided through diversification.

V

Valuation   The act or process of determining the value of a business, business ownership interest, security, or intangible asset.

Valuation Approach   A general way of determining a value indication of a business, business ownership interest, security, or intangible asset using one or more valuation methods.

Valuation Date   The specific point in time as of which the valuator's opinion of value applies (also referred to as **Effective Date** or **Appraisal Date**).

Valuation Method   Within approaches, a specific way to determine value.

Valuation Procedure   The act, manner, and technique of performing the steps of an appraisal method.

Valuation Ratio   A fraction in which a value or price serves as the numerator and financial, operating, or physical data serve as the denominator.

Value to the Owner   (Note: In Canada, see **Investment Value.**)

W

Weighted Average Cost of Capital (WACC)   The cost of capital (discount rate) determined by the weighted average, at market value, of the cost of all financing sources in the business enterprise's capital structure.

Note

---

1. Reprinted with permission.

The Quantitative Marketability Discount Model[1]

INTRODUCTION

In the context of the levels of value that appraisers discuss so frequently, the marketability discount is that conceptual valuation discount necessary to entice prospective investors in illiquid securities to purchase them rather than similar investments that are readily marketable.[2] It is the discount that converts an appraisal at the marketable minority (freely traded, freely tradable, as if freely traded) level of value into a nonmarketable minority interest conclusion, as indicated in the levels of value chart reproduced below.

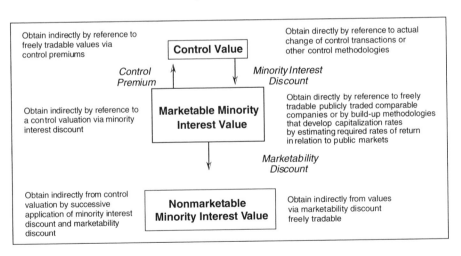

Approached more directly, the nonmarketable minority interest level of value can be developed by valuing cash flows expected to be available to the minority shareholder in the context of a marketable minority interest valuation.

This section summarizes the conceptual logic of one way to simulate the thinking of real or hypothetical investors to develop valuation indications at the nonmarketable minority interest level. The Quantitative Marketability Discount

Model (QMDM) was formally introduced in *Quantifying Marketability Discounts* in 1997.[3]

Unfortunately, many appraisers look at the typical results of the various restricted stock studies, which have had typical discounts in the general range of 30 to 35%, as an *absolute indication* of the magnitude of marketability discounts for minority interests of private companies. *Quantifying Marketability Discounts* makes the point that the relevant economic information from the restricted studies is the implied required holding period returns (discount rates) for investments during the applicable period of illiquidity of the otherwise publicly tradable securities examined. This "relevant economic information" includes the expected holding period, the required returns of investors, and their expectations for growth in value and for interim cash flows. The QMDM enables appraisers to estimate the value of illiquid securities in relationship to their freely tradable value indications and to develop marketability discounts that are both reasoned and reasonable in the context of the facts and circumstances of individual appraisals.

WHAT IS THE QMDM?

The QMDM attempts to look at an investment in a closely held business interest much the way that real-life investors and the hypothetical willing investors of fair market value fame do. There are five key inputs to the QMDM, and they correspond to the basic questions that I believe investors ask about illiquid investments.

The model assumes that the hypothetical willing investor and the business appraiser consider the use of the QMDM in the context of a fully developed business appraisal at the marketable minority interest level. In other words, the basis for comparison of the worth of an illiquid, minority interest in a business is investments in similar, publicly traded companies. It is in the context of such an appraisal that we develop the key assumptions of the QMDM.[4]

Given that we know the marketable minority interest value of a business, the basic questions that investors ask and the corresponding QMDM inputs are

1. *How much can this business grow in value over time?* The QMDM input assumption is the *expected growth rate in value,* from the marketable minority value today.

2. *What can I expect to receive in distributions (i.e., spendable or investable cash) while I wait?* The QMDM assumes dividends on a C corporation equivalent basis, expressed in terms of a yield on the marketable minority interest value derived in the appraisal. This corresponds to the comparable yields on publicly traded companies. For purposes of this brief discussion, we will assume there are no dividends.

3. *Will my distributions grow over time?* The QMDM allows for the appraiser to make an appropriate assumption about the expected growth rate in dividends over the expected holding period.

4. *How long will I have to wait until I can expect to achieve liquidity?* Since there is no active public market for the closely held company, investors desire to know how long before liquidity opportunities are available, whether from a stock repurchase program, an initial public offering, a sale of the business, or some other means.[5] The duration of the expected holding period is usually discussed in terms of an approximate range that is estimated by the appraiser based on the facts and circumstances of a particular company.

5. *What is my discount rate while I wait?* In the QMDM, we call the appropriate discount rate the *required holding period return.* The base for estimating the required holding period return is the equity discount rate in the appraisal at the marketable minority interest level. We then consider additional, specific risks that relate not to the value of the enterprise but specifically, to investors in illiquid interests of the enterprise. It is generally accepted that the markets exact a price (i.e., a price reduction) for illiquidity. The specific risks relating to illiquid investments represent our attempt to begin to measure or quantify that price reduction. We usually express the required holding period return in terms of an approximate range.

While we have introduced these questions in the context of the QMDM, they have broader application. In fact, they are the very same questions that rational investors ask about virtually any type of investment.

The important thing to remember about the QMDM is that it is an *expectational* model. Its commonsense logic is geared to quantify the expectations of returns for rational investors in illiquid, closely held securities. It is, therefore, grounded in expectations for future growth in value and dividends over an expected holding period. We believe that the model reflects how investment decisions actually get made by rational, real-life investors.

The threshold question that investors must ask (and answer) is: *How much am I willing to pay for an illiquid investment with the characteristics of the subject illiquid interest in a closely held enterprise?* This is the essential question addressed by the QMDM. In the process of answering it, we determine the implied marketability discount applicable to the subject interest from the base valuation at the marketable minority interest level of value.

MARKETABLE MINORITY VALUATION CONCEPTS

The Gordon Dividend Discount Model expresses the value of a business in terms of the discounted present value of expected dividends (or cash flows). We can generalize the model as:

$$\text{I. Value} = \frac{\text{Expected Cash Flow}}{(\text{Discount Rate} - \text{Expected Growth Rate of Cash Flow})}$$

or, symbolically, as

$$\text{II.} \quad V = \frac{CF_1}{(R - G)}$$

The present value of a publicly traded security, or the corresponding marketable minority (mm) interest value of a private company, can be expressed as

$$\text{III.} \quad V_{mm} = \frac{CF_{mm}}{(R_{mm} - G_{mm})}$$

The model expressed in Equations I to III is actually a shorthand for a discounted cash flow model that assumes that the expected cash flow of the next period will grow into perpetuity at the constant rate of $G_{mm}\%$. The discount rate (R_{mm}) is an appropriate discount rate for the expected cash flow (CF_{mm}). Appraisers routinely use variations of the Gordon Dividend Discount Model in appraisals to develop marketable minority interest value conclusions.

To put numbers to Equation III, assume that a company has expected earnings next year of $1.00 per share. Assume further that the appropriate equity discount rate, derived using a "build-up" method, is 17.5% (consisting of the long-term Treasury rate of 6.5%, plus a small stock capitalization premium over Treasuries of 10.0%, plus 1.0% of risk attributed to the private company by the appraiser). The expected growth rate of earnings is in the range of 7 to 8%, and the appraiser assumes 7.5%. Value at the marketable minority interest level is, therefore, $10.00 per share, or $1.00 / (17.5% − 7.5%).

Implicit in the use of Equation III is that the cash flows are either reinvested in the company to yield a return equivalent to the discount rate, R_{mm} or distributed to the shareholders of the enterprise, and that shareholders are able to reinvest the distributions at the discount rate.

Some reviewers of the QMDM seem to have a problem at this point. If the discount rate is 17.5%, they suggest, then value should be growing at 17.5% if there are no dividends. This would be true if all earnings were successfully reinvested at the discount rate. However, many private companies pay out large bonuses to the major shareholders, thereby reducing the potential return available to minority shareholders who do not work for the company or who do not receive what may be disguised (and unequal) distributions. Other companies accumulate excess cash and assets because their reinvestment opportunities or inclinations are less than the level available in the marketplace. In the real world, the only ways that investors achieve the full 17.5% return is through the control, the distribution (for reinvestment elsewhere), or the public market capitalization of expected future cash flows. If choices are made that lower the effective returns or add risk to minority shareholders (relative to similar publicly traded shares), these choices should be reflected in the appraisal. These choices get reflected in the QMDM by focusing on cash flows expected to be received by minority shareholders.

The perspective provided by Equation III is the value of an *enterprise,* which is publicly traded. It should be apparent that it is the cash flows of the enterprise that give rise to value. In the context of a publicly traded security, a shareholder does not have access to the cash flows, except as distributed by the company. However, the shareholder has access to the *present value of all expected future cash flows* via the mechanism of the public securities markets.

The markets are continually capitalizing the expected earnings of public companies based on consensus expectations with respect to cash flows, discount rates, and expected growth rates. And shareholders can achieve cash in their brokerage accounts in three days by calling their brokers or executing trades via the Internet. The important point here is that *minority shareholders* in a publicly traded company derive the benefit of 100% of its cash flows through the mechanism of the public markets, even though they lack any aspect of control over the enterprise.

NONMARKETABLE MINORITY VALUATION CONCEPTS

The $10.00 per share value derived using Equation III provides a value indication for a public company. The same equation can be used to develop a value for a private company *as if there were an active public market for its shares.* But we know that no such market exists for the private company.

The situation faced by the shareholder in a private company with no market for its shares is different from that faced by a shareholder of a public company. Assume now that our example relates to a private company. That company has a *hypothetical value* at the marketable minority interest level of $10.00 per share. Appraisers routinely develop *marketable minority interest* value indications for private companies in the process of determining the fair market value of minority interests in those companies at the *nonmarketable minority interest* level of value. The difference between the two levels of value is the so-called *marketability discount* (or, as some prefer to call it, the discount for lack of marketability).

In the context of the Gordon Dividend Discount Model, the simplified situation faced by minority shareholders in closely held companies looks like the following:

$$\text{IV. } V_{sh} = \frac{CF_{sh} \text{ (for all periods)}}{(R_{sh} - G_v) \text{ (discounted for each period)}}$$

Expressed in words, the value, today, for a shareholder of in illiquid interest is the present value of all expected cash flows *to the shareholder,* discounted to the present at the required holding period return (discount rate) applicable to those cash flows. In the case of a non-dividend-paying investment, we would actually capitalize the cash flows expected by the *next buyer* at the point in time that the current, hypothetical, or real investor can expect to sell the interest. That value is then discounted to the present at R_{sh}. The discounting process is simulated by the capitalization of the cash flows at the discount rate less the expected growth rate in the value of the interest.

In the QMDM, we speak of the expected growth rate of value, rather than the expected growth rate in earnings. Since the terminal cash flow will often account for the majority of the present value of an investment in an illiquid security, it is appropriate to focus on the expected growth in value. Earnings growth for the enterprise and growth in the marketable minority interest value can differ, particularly when a company employs extensive leverage or when there is a reasonable expectation for contraction or expansion in the multiple applied to earnings.

This analysis assumes that the subject private company pays no dividends to its shareholders. It can, of course, be expanded to include the payment of dividends. However, we can illustrate how the QMDM works with the no-dividend example.

The investor in the no-dividend example can actually expect *a single cash flow* from his or her investment, the cash flow received on an event of liquidity, at the point in time when the investment can be sold. Unlike in the marketable minority example above, *there are no interim cash flows to be capitalized from the perspective of the shareholder.* So for purposes of our illustration, assume that hypothetical (or real) investors can reasonably expect that the company will be sold in about five years (i.e., a longer expected holding period than the current one-year or the prior two-year period of restriction under Rule 144).

For simplicity, assume that the company will be sold to a financial buyer who has no expectation of acquisition synergies and that the cash flows in developing the marketable minority value indication of $10.00 per share reflected all potential normalizing adjustments. In this example, the expected sale price in the future would correspond to the marketable minority level of value. In other words, there would be no (or virtually no) *control premium* in this example.

Further, assume that there is no difference between the expected growth rates of earnings and value and that value is expected to grow at 7.5% per year, compounded.

Assume that prospective investors look at a base-level equity discount rate of 16.5%, which is identical to that derived in the marketable minority indication, less the 1.0% company-specific risk premium discussed previously. But our prospective investors see different risks that are applicable to the shareholder level. For example, the controlling shareholder could slow down growth by paying abnormally high bonuses to herself (or by retaining large amounts of cash or investing in low-return nonoperating assets). She could also decide not to sell in the indicated five-year time frame.

More personally, the prospective investor(s) might have an emergency need for liquidity. With no market for the shares, a loss could be sustained if the investment had to be sold prematurely. Assume that investors require a specific risk component of 3.0% for these factors. Their *required holding period return* is therefore 19.5%, or the base equity discount rate of 16.5% plus the 3.0% of investment-specific risk.

We can now "value" this example company from the perspective of prospective minority shareholder(s). We know that the marketable minority interest value today is $10.00 per share and that value is expected to grow at 7.5% per year. Value in five years would be expected to be $14.36 per share ($10.00 × (1 + 7.5%)^5). So we know the expected terminal cash flow (future value) that will be received when the company is sold ($14.36 per share). Again, for simplicity, assume the sale will occur at the marketable minority interest level, or with a control premium of zero.

We also know the required holding period return of the prospective investors (19.5%) and the number of years to achieve the cash flow (five years). We can now determine the implied value to the shareholder today by calculating:

Future value	$14.36 per share
Holding period	5 years
Discount rate	19.5%
Present value	$5.89 per share (or, rounded, $6.00 per share)

The value of the subject minority interest to prospective shareholders of our example company is $6.00 per share. In the context of traditional appraisal, we have indirectly developed the appropriate marketability discount. If the hypothetical, marketable minority interest value indication *of the enterprise* is $10.00 per share, and we estimate a value of expected cash flows *to minority shareholders* of $6.00 per share, the implied marketability discount is 40% (1 − $6.00 / $10.00).

As noted, in using the QMDM, we generally recommend that appraisers use reasonable ranges for the assumptions relating to the expected holding period and required holding period return. Ranges for assumptions relating to expected dividends and expected growth rate in value can also be used, of course, but these factors lend themselves to closer estimation in many cases based on management's expected dividend policy and earnings retention and growth policies.

Our example has described the essence of the Quantitative Marketability Discount Model. It comports with financial and valuation theory as well as common sense. And the QMDM can easily be expanded to incorporate the impact of interim distributions or value.

Assumed Market Price of Public Entity		$1.00
Average Management Planning Discount (rounded)	30.0%	($0.30)
Assumed Purchase Price of Restricted Shares		$0.70
Holding Period Until Restricted Shares are Freely Tradable (years)		2.5

Now we can examine a variety of assumptions about the "average" restricted stock transaction in the Management Planning study. This analysis is for purposes of illustration only. Chapters 2 and 3 of *Quantifying Marketability Discounts* raise significant questions about reliance on averages of widely varying transaction indications for both the restricted stock and the pre-IPO studies. The average public price has been indexed to $1.00 per share. As a result, the average MPI transaction price, as indexed, is $.70 per share.

We can estimate the implied returns that were required by investors in restricted stocks based on a variety of assumptions about the expected growth rates in value (or the expected returns of the publicly traded stocks). For purposes of this analysis, we have assumed that the consensus expectations for the public stock returns were somewhere in the range of 0% (no expected appreciation) to 30% compounded. The most relevant portion of this range likely begins at about 10%, since stocks expected to appreciate less than that were probably not attractive for investments in their restricted shares.

Assumed Expected Growth in Value (G)	Expected Future Value in 2.5 Years	Implied Return for Holding Period (R)	Annualized Incremental Return Attributable to Restricted Stock Discount ($R - G$)
0%	$1.00	15.3%	15.3%
5%	$1.13	21.1%	16.1%
10%	$1.27	26.9%	16.9%
15%	$1.42	32.7%	17.7%
20%	$1.58	38.5%	18.5%
25%	$1.75	44.3%	19.3%
30%	$1.93	50.0%	20.0%

Note that the implied holding period returns for the restricted stock transactions, on average, ranged from about 27% per year compounded (with value growing at 10%) to 50% per year compounded (with expected growth of 30%). As noted in Chapter 8 of *Quantifying Marketability Discounts,* the implied returns are in the range of expected venture capital returns for initial investments (not *average* venture capital returns, which include unsuccessful investments). Interestingly, the differential between the implied holding period returns above and the expected growth rate in values used are quite high, ranging from 15.3 to 20.0% (the right column of the table).

This analysis is *ex post.* We do not know how the actual investment decisions were made in the transactions included in the Management Planning study or any of the restricted stock studies. But, *ex post,* it is clear that the investors in the "average" restricted stock transactions were, *ex ante,* either

- Placing very high discount rates on their restricted stock transactions (ranging from 15 to 20% in excess of the expected returns of the public companies they were investing in)

- Questioning the consensus expectations for returns or
- Some combination of the above

We can make several observations about the seemingly high differentials between the restricted stock investors' required returns and the expected value growth of the typical entity:

- The average discounts appear to be indicative of defensive pricing.
- The discounts would likely ensure at least a market return if the expected growth is not realized.
- Very high implied returns as expected growth increases suggests that high growth is viewed with skepticism.
- The implied premiums of R over expected G are substantial at any level, suggesting that the base "cost" of 2.5 years of illiquidity is quite expensive.

Given varying assumptions about holding periods longer than 2.5 years and allowing for entities that pay regular dividends, we would expect some variation from the premium range found in appraisals of private company interests.

By way of comparison, we can make the same calculations for the example applications of the QMDM from Chapter 10 of *Quantifying Marketability Discounts*.

		Average Required Holding Period Return (R)	Expected Growth in Value Assumed (G)	(R – G) Difference	Dividend Yield	Concluded Marketability Discount
Example	Holding Period					
1	5–8 years	20.0%	10.0%	10.0%	0.0%	45.0%
2	5–9 years	20.5%	4.0%	16.5%	8.8%	25.0%
3	7–15 years	18.5%	7.0%	11.5%	8.0%	15.0%
4	1.5–5 years	19.5%	7.5%	12.0%	0.0%	20.0%
5	5–10 years	20.5%	9.8%	10.7%	3.2%	40.0%
6	5–10 years	18.5%	10.0%	8.5%	2.1%	25.0%
7	5–15 years	19.5%	6.0%	13.5%	0.0%	60.0%
8	10–15 years	19.5%	5.0%	14.5%	10.0%	25.0%
9	10 years	26.4%	5.0%	21.4%	0.6%	80.0%
10	3–5 years	22.5%	6.0%	16.5%	0.0%	35.0%
	Averages	20.5%	7.0%	13.5%	3.3%	37.0%
	Medians	19.8%	6.5%	12.8%	1.4%	30.0%

Summary of Results of Applying the QMDM in 10 Example Appraisals

Source: Quantifying Marketability Discounts, Chapter 10.

The range of differences between the average required returns and the expected growth rates in value assumed in the 10 appraisals was from 8.5 to 21.4%, with an average of about 13%. The table also indicates the range of other assumptions that yielded the concluded marketability discounts in the illustrations. We believe that these results, which came from actual appraisals, are consistent with the market evidence from the restricted stock studies. Indeed, the premium returns required by the restricted stock investors, on average, exceeds those applied in these examples, suggesting the conclusions yielded conservative marketability discounts on average.

CONCLUSION

The QMDM, which is used primarily in valuing private companies, develops concrete estimates of expected growth in value of the enterprise and reasonable estimates of additional risk premiums to account for risks faced by investors in nonmarketable minority interests of companies. In its fully developed form, it incorporates expectations regarding distributions of cash flows to assist appraisers in reaching logical, supportable, and reasonable conclusions regarding the appropriate level of marketability discounts for specific valuations.

Marketable minority (and controlling interest) appraisals are developed based on the capitalized expected cash flows of businesses or enterprises. Minority interests in those businesses must be valued based on consideration of the cash flows expected to be available to minority investors. The QMDM allows the business appraiser to bridge the gap between these two cash flow concepts, enterprise and shareholder, to develop reasoned and reasonable valuation conclusions at the nonmarketable minority interest level.

Notes

1. This section was contributed by Z. Christopher Mercer, ASA, CFA, author of *Quantifying Marketability Discounts*. Used with permission.
2. Keep in mind that actual purchasers of illiquid securities do not think in terms of "marketability discounts." They consider the economics of investments and make their investment decisions in light of their analyses and intuitions about the prospects for those investments. Appraisers develop marketability discounts in efforts to simulate the thinking of real life or hypothetical investors.
3. Z. Christopher Mercer, *Quantifying Marketability Discounts: Developing and Supporting Marketability Discounts in the Appraisal of Closely Held Business Interests* (Memphis: Peabody Publishing, L.P., 1997). The book is available directly from the publisher at 1-800-769-0967. A companion diskette designed to facilitate the use of the QMDM is also available.
4. These concepts are discussed in considerable depth in a three-hour tape set with accompanying documentation prepared by Z. Christopher Mercer. See "Theoretical Determinants of Value in the Context of 'Levels of Value,' " available from Peabody Publishing, L.P. at 1-800-769-0967.

5. Note that with restricted stock of publicly traded securities, investors know what the relevant period of restriction is for their investments. Prior to April 1997, the Securities and Exchange Commission required a two-year holding period under Rule 144 for restricted securities before investors could begin to achieve liquidity. Subsequent to April 1997, the holding period was reduced to one year. All but one of the restricted stock studies to date have considered transactions prior to April 1997, or when the holding period was at least two years. A recent study prepared by Columbia Financial Advisers, Inc. considers transactions between April 1997 and 1998. (See Kathryn Aschwald, "Restricted Stock Discounts Decline as Result of 1-Year Holding Period," *Shannon Pratt's Business Valuation Update* [May 2000]: 1.) While Aschwald finds, as expected, that the *absolute value* of restricted stock discounts declined after the shortening of the Rule 144 holding period, the *implied required returns of investors* in those restricted stocks remains substantially in line with the returns discussed later in this section.

Pratt's Stats™ Data Contributors

LOOKING FOR A BROKER?

The following is a partial list of brokers who have contributed to *Pratt's Stats™*. The *Pratt's Stats™* database lists the intermediary along with the transaction in most cases. Subscribers may search the database by intermediary to get a more complete idea of the type of transactions in which the intermediary has been involved.

Broker	Firm Name	City	State	Zip	Association Membership	Professional Designation
Synergy Partners	Synergy Partners, Inc.	Calgary	AB	T2P-3T3		
Business Team	Business Team	San Jose	CA	95128	IBBA, CABB	
Kruse & Associates	Kruse & Associates, P.C.	Nashville	TN	37229-0786	CVA	CPA
Adam, Jeff	Adam Noble Group	Arlington	TX	76016	IBBA	
Adams, C. Dan	Capital Corporation, The	Spartanburg	SC	29302	IBBA	CBI
Adler, Jay	Unison Capital Group	Boulder	CO	80302-6001	IBBA	ASA, IBA, IBI
Alario-Kellemen, Stacy	American Business Brokerage, Inc.	Sarasota	FL	34347	IBBA	
Albano, Vic J.	JVL Business Group	Anaheim Hill	CA	92808		
Allen, Gary	Allen Business Investments	San Ramon	CA	94583		
Anderson, James L.	Anderson & Associates	Alpharetta	GA	30005	GABB	
Anglemyer, Gary R.	Gary R. Anglemyer & Associates	Santa Rosa	CA	95401		
Argiz, Antonio L.	Morrison, Brown, Argiz, & Co., CPA	Miami	FL	33131		
Armstrong, Jack	Sunbelt Business Brokers of New Jersey	Linden	NJ	07036	IBBA	

Name	Company	City	State	Zip	Certifications	
Asadorian, Guy Jr.	Tameracq Partners, Inc.					
Axon, Scott	Americas Group, Inc., The	Springfield	MO	65806		
Ayers, Richard P.	Richard P. Ayers Real Estate Broker/Restaurant Specialist	Denver	CO	80231	CBC, CRA	CBC, FMP
Badal, Fred B.	Allen Business Investments	San Ramon	CA	94583	CABB	
Balis, Phil	Certified Business Brokers	Houston	TX	77092		
Barbarosh, Milton	Stenton Leigh Business Resources, Inc.	Boca Raton	FL	33431	ASA, IBBA	
Barger, Jon	Tucson Business Investment	Tucson	AZ			
Barnes, Walter	Sunbelt Business Consultants	West Hartford	CT	06107		
Barth, J. Richard	Barth Group, The	State College	PA	16805	CBC, IBA, IBBA, PBBA	CBC, CBI
Bateson, Brian T.	Bateson Business Brokerage, Inc.	Altamonte Springs	FL	32714	IBBA, BBF	
Baumgarten, Robert	Spectrum Business Resources, Inc.	Lake Forest	CA	92630-6304		
Bavis, William J.	Clifton Gunderson, LLC	Baltimore	MD	21093	AICPA, NACVA	CPA, CVA

Broker	Firm Name	City	State	Zip	Association Membership	Professional Designation
Beane, Frank E.	New England Business Advisors, Inc.	Rockport	ME	04856	ASA, IBA, IBBA	CBA, FCBI
Beggs, James D.	Becker & Beggs	Cincinnati	OH	45202	IBA, IBBA	
Behm, Bruce	Quazar Capital Corporation	Plymouth	MN	55441	IBBA	
Bellizzi, Ralph A.	Aaron Bell International, Inc.	Aurora	CO	80014		
Berry, Arthur	Arthur Berry & Company	Boise	ID	83706	ASA, IBA, IBBA, other	
Betteto, Jim	Mercorp, Inc.	Burlington	ON	L7N-3M6	IBBA	
Beyer, Kurt	Pedersen Kammert & Company	Darien	CT	06854		
Bhandari, Kapil D.	American Business Connection	Buford	GA	30519	GABB	
Bienert, Catherine	Bottom Line Management, Inc.	Atlanta	GA	30342		
Blair, Kevin	Micro - Merchant Banking Associates	Denver	CO	80221	ACG, IBBA	
Bogard, Jerry	Sunbelt Business Brokers of Northwest Arkansas	Fayetteville	AR	72703		
Bohlmann, David J.	Business Valuations	Miami	FL	33133		
Bowers, Scott	Live Oak Capital Advisors, Inc.	Myrtle Beach	SC	29577	ACG, IBA, IBBA	CBI, CFA
Bragg, Steve	Calhoun Companies-Arrowhead Office	Lutsen	MN	55612		

Name	Company	City	State	Zip		
Bring, Randy	Transworld Business Brokers	Fort Lauderdale	FL	33309		
Brown, Deanne R.	American Business Brokers, Inc.	Federal Way	WA	98003		
Bruss, Ernest	Business Investment Opportunities	Albuquerque	NM	87109	CBC, IBBA	CBC, CBI
Bryant, Mark E	Prime Business Investments	Tucker	GA	30084	GABB	
Bushong, Ned	Bushong Capital Systems, Inc.	Lima	OH	45802	IBA, IBBA	
Butowsky, Howard M.	H. Michael & Associates	Doylestown	PA	18901	IBA, IBBA	
Cagnetta, Andrew	Transworld Business Brokers	Fort Lauderdale	FL	33309	FBBA, IBBA	
Caldwell, Larry	American Business Sales	West Reading	PA	19611	IBBA	
Carlson, Richard	Bray & Company Realtors	Grand Junction	CO	81501	IBBA, CBC, CBB	CBC
Carr, Brad	Prime Business Investments	Tucker	GA	30084	GABB	
Chapman, Keith	Horizon Business Group, LLC	Tyler	TX	75701	IBBA, AICPA, TABB	
Chernak, Ted	Georgia Business Associates, Inc.	Roswell	GA	30076	GABB	
Choi, Stephen	Spectrum Business Resources, Inc.	Lake Forest	CA	92630-6304		
Chugh, Partap	Prime Business Investments	Tucker	GA	30084	GABB	

Broker	Firm Name	City	State	Zip	Association Membership	Professional Designation
Clark, Alan	Hatteras Group, The	Marietta	GA	30060	GABB	
Clayton, Sam	Toledo Group, Inc., The	Perrysburg	OH	43551	IBBA, M&A Source	CPA
Cleary, Terrence P.	Metropolitan Business Brokers	Milwaukee	WI	53214	IBBA	
Clifton, Ted	Aaron Bell International, Inc.	Aurora	CO	80014		
Cooper, Glen J.	Maine Business Brokers Network	Portland	ME	04112	IBBA	
Crader, Linn	Crader & Associates, Inc.	Lake Oswego	OR	97035	CBC, IBBA	CBC, CBI
Cuff, Terry	Business Exchange Center, Inc.	Bellevue	WA	98004	CBC, IBBA	
Cunningham, Don	Cunningham Group, Inc.	Spokane	WA	99201-2428	IBBA, WABB	
Cyliax, Curt A.	Entrepreneurial Edge	Doylestown	PA	18901-2050		CPA
Daigle, Richard J.	Venture Resources, Inc.	Raleigh	NC	27612	IBBA	CBI
Danto, Noel F.	Sunbelt Business Brokers of NW Ohio	Toledo	OH	43606	IBBA, OBBA	
DeGroot, Mark	Compass Advisors	Manhattan	MT	59741	IBBA	
DelVecchio, Jennee	Tucson Business Investments	Tucson	AZ	85711		
DeWitt, Kelly	Sunbelt Business Brokers of Texas	Lewisville	TX	75067	IBBA, TABB	
Diglio, Cress	Corporate Investment International, Inc.	Altamonte Springs	FL	32714		
Dillon, Rick	Dillon Schromm Associates, Ltd.	Overland Park	KS	66214		

Name	Company	City	State	ZIP	Certification	
Doba, Ray	Certified Business Brokers	Houston	TX	77092		
Docena, Del	Business Search Group	San Jose	CA	95126		
Dole, Susan	Kuroman Realty, Inc.	Honolulu	HI	96813	IBBA	ASA
Eardley, Ron	Corporate Finance Associates	Boise	ID	83702	IBBA	
Eggers, Michael J.	American Business Appraisers	San Ramon	CA	94583	IBA	ASA, CPA
Ehrenberg, Robert	The Business Connection, Inc.	Gilford	NH	03249-6686	CIBOR, IBA, IBBA, NEBBA	
Elwood, Ray	Business Brokers Corporation	Omaha	NE	68144	IBBA	
Eshleman, James	Strategic Endeavors, LLC	Landisville	PA	17538		
Evans, Bob	American Business Group, Inc.	Dallas	TX	75251	IBBA, BCB	FCBI
Everingham, Robert	Everingham & Kerr, Inc.	Haddon Heights	NJ	08035	IBA, IBBA	
Finn, Patrick J.	Finn & Associates, Inc.	Wichita	KS	67205	IBBA	CBI
Finsterwald, Philip	National Business Brokers, Ltd.	Colorado Springs	CO	80903	CBC, IBBA, M & A Source	
Fischesser, Donald	DFA Financial Services, Inc.	South Bend	IN	46601		
Flamos, Dick	Certified Business Brokers	Houston	TX	77092		
Fonts, Patricia	American Business Group, Inc.	Dallas	TX	75251	IBBA, BCB	FCBI
Ford, Vanessa L.			GA		GABB	
Fox, Bruce	Fox and Fin Financial Group	Scottsdale	AZ	85250	IBBA	

Broker	Firm Name	City	State	Zip	Association Membership	Professional Designation
Fulford, Steward R.	Fulford Business Brokers, Inc.	Windsor	ON	N8X3T5	CBC, IBBA, RPA	CBI
Gallagher, John J.	Business Acquisition Group	Severna Park	MD	21146-4130	AICPA, CBC	CBC, CPA
Garvin, James T.	Allen Business Investments	San Ramon	CA	94583	IBBA	
Gaspard, Joe	Sunbelt Business Brokers of Northwest Arkansas	Fayetteville	AR	72703		
Gaumer, Laurel	Allen Business Investments	San Ramon	CA	94583		
Geynor, Ronen	Corporate Investment International, Inc.	Altamonte Springs	FL	32714		
Giancola, Donald	Country Business, Inc.	Manchester Center	VT	05255	IBBA	FCBI
Gifford, George	March Group, The	Nashville	TN	37203		
Gluckstern, Michael	West & Feinberg, P. C.	Bethesda	MD	20814	NPA	
Gomez, Rudy						
Gonor, Richard	Certified Business Brokers	Houston	TX	77092		
Grant, Reggie	Sunbelt Business Brokers, Tifton	Tifton	GA	31793	GABB	
Greenblatt, Rich	Allen Business Investments	San Ramon	CA	94583	CABB	
Gregory, . Edmond B	Linton, Shater, & Company	Frederick	MD	21701-5388	IBA	ASA, CPA
Grimes, Carl	Sunbelt Business Brokers of Northwest Arkansas	Fayetteville	AR	72703	IBBA	CBI

Name	Company	City	State	Zip	Affiliations	
Hall, Dan	East Texas Business Brokers	Tyler	TX	75701	IBA, IBBA, BCB, TABB	CBI
Hall, Gloria	Prime Business Investments	Tucker	GA	30084	GABB	
Hamilton, Jeff	International Business Exchange Corporation	Austin	TX	78761	CBC, IBBA, TABB	CBI
Harkins, Patrick	Anchor Business Advisors	Atlanta	GA	30328	GABB	
Harris, Michael E.	Tucson Business Investments	Tucson	AZ	85711	IBBA	
Sams, Kay	Sams & Associates	Minnetonka	MN	55305		
Rogers, Tim	Sunbelt Business Brokers of Sacramento	Sacramento	CA	95841	IBBA	
Janes, Shawn	Alliance Business Brokers	Buford	GA	30518	IBBA	
Daudt, Robert	Sunbelt Business Brokers	Minnetonka	MN	55305	IBBA	
Mullens, Jim	Bundy & Company	Roanoke	VA	24016	IBBA, CVBBA	
Cochrane, Bob	Sunbelt Business Advisors of Indiana, LLC	Indianapolis	IN	46268		
Bass, Matthew	Matthew Bass & Associates, Inc.	New York	NY	10170	IBBA	
Lenhard, Robert E.	Hallmark Business Consultants, Inc.	Tucson	AZ	85718	IBBA	
Wain, Stephen	Woodland Group, The	Morganville	NJ	07751		
Thomas, Ivor	NH Business Sales, Inc.	Meredith	NH	03253	IBBA	
Parker, Leon	NH Business Sales, Inc.	Henniker	NH	03242	IBBA	
Richardson, Kathleen	Florida's Business Connection, Inc.	Spring Hill	FL	34606	IBBA	

Broker	Firm Name	City	State	Zip	Association Membership	Professional Designation
Angulo, Lauren	Island Business Brokers	Hanalei	HI	96714	IBBA	
O'Hara, Paula	New South Business Ventures	Asheville	NC	28801	IBBA	
Riordan, Nathan	Sunbelt Business Advisors	Renton	WA	98055		
Woolley, Charles	Kingsley Group Business Services	Springfield	MO	65804	IBBA	
Waugh, Robert	Robert Waugh & Company, Inc.	Bradenton	FL	34210	IBBA	
Curtis, Stu	Murphy Brokers	Panama City	FL	32405		
O'Shields, Bill	Performance Brokers, LLC	Brentwood	TN	37027	IBBA	
Hammond, Rick	VR Inland Empire	Temecula	CA	92590	IBBA, CABB	
Ashburn, Matt	Sunbelt Business Advisors	Ankeny	IA	50021	IBBA	
Hammond, David	VR Business Brokers	Temecula	CA	92590	IBBA	
Ossin, Lee	Crowne Atlantic Properties, LLC	Orlando	FL	32819	IBBA, BBF	
Caruso, Gregory	Harvest Associates	Crownsville	MD	21032	IBBA	
Hart, Edwin	International Business Exchange Corporation	Round Rock	TX	78681	CBC, IBBA, M & A Source	CBC, FCBI
Hartman, Bud	Applied Resources of Athens	Athens	GA	30604	GABB, IBBA, IBA	CBI candidate
Heitzenroder, David A.	Rosewood Capital Partners	Pittsburgh	PA	15222	ACG, AICPA, IBBA	

Name	Company	City	State	ZIP	Certifications	
Hertenstein, Ron	Anthony Wayne Business Exchange	Fort Wayne	IN	46815		
Hicks, Henry	Georgia Business Associates, Inc.	Roswell	GA	30076	GABB, IBBA, IBA, AICPA	CBI, CPA
Hinson, Dan	Prime Business Investments	Tucker	GA	30084	GABB	
Hirsch, Suzanne	Certified Business Brokers	Houston	TX	77092		
Hoesly, Michael	Hoesly & Company, Inc.	Madison	WI	53719	IBA, IBBA	
Hoffman, Dave	Mercorp, Inc.	Burlington	ON	L7N-3M6	IBBA	
Hogan, Dennis	National Business Brokers, Inc.	Lake Forest	CA	92630-6304		
Hoskins, Tom	International Business Exchange Corporation	Austin	TX	78761	IBBA, TABB	
Hughes, Kenneth R.	Hughes Group Carolinas, Inc., The	Greenville	SC	29615	IBBA	
Humphrey, David	Beacon Capital Group	Norwood	MA	02062	AICPA, ASA, IBBA, NACVA	CPA
Hunziker, Robert	Restaurant-Brokers.com	Atlanta	GA	30328		
Hyde, Paul	Hyde Business Properties and Valuations, Inc.	Parma	ID	83660		
James, Hank	Corporate Finance Associates	Walnut Creek	CA	94598	CABB, IBBA	CBI
Janes, Tricia	Business Capital Corporation	Des Moines	IA	50309-3914	AICPA, ASA, IMAP	
Janke, Harold A.	Janke & Associates, Inc.	Carlsbad	CA	92008	CBC, IBBA	CBI
Jay, Charles A.	Jay & Associates	Macon	GA	31208-6635	GABB	

Broker	Firm Name	City	State	Zip	Association Membership	Professional Designation
Jennings, Karl	Nash & Company	Osterville	MA	02655-0012		
Jilek, James	James Jilek, Business Broker	Kalamazoo	MI	49007-5130	MBBA, IBBA	
Johnson, Ronald C.	Allen Business Investments	San Ramon	CA	94583	IBBA, CABB, NLI, GA	
Jones, Jeffery	Certified Business Brokers	Houston	TX	77092	IBBA	ASA, CBA, F
Karlson, Kris	Bowman/Hanson	San Francisco	CA	94123	IBBA	
Kentnor, Charlie	Realty Executives of Tucson, Inc.	Sonoita	AZ	85637	CBC, CCIM, IBBA	
Kerr, Brian R.	Everingham & Kerr, Inc.	Haddon Heights	NJ	08035		
Kiernan, Tom	Kiernan & Associates, Inc.	Tuscon	AZ	85712	IBBA, AABB, M&A Source	CBI
Kim, Stan	National Business Brokers, Inc.	Lake Forest	CA	92630-6304		
King, Walter C. II	Walter C. King Assoc., P.C.	Westport	CT	06880	AICPA, IBA	ASA, CPA, P
King, Lexa	Prime Business Investments	Tucker	GA	30084	GABB	
King, Lori	Business Exchange Center, Inc.	Bellevue	WA	98004	AICPA, CBC, ACG, ASA	CPA, CBC
Kitchens, William J.	Prime Business Investments	Tucker	GA	30084	GABB	
Knapp, Mark	Sunbelt Business Brokers	Kitty Hawk	NC	27949	IBBA	
Knight, Brian	Country Business, Inc.	Manchester Center	VT	05255	IBBA	FCBI

Name	Company	City	State	Zip	Certifications	
Knox, Jeanne	Sunbelt Business Brokers	Little Rock	AR	72211	IBBA	
Kogle, Jeffrey	Sunbelt Business Brokers	St. Paul	MN	55126		
Koziatek, Norb	Georgia Business Associates, Inc.	Roswell	GA	30076	GABB	
Krebs, Malcolm	Business Transitions, Inc.	Calgary	AB	T2V-5H9	IBBA, RECA	
Kroon, Jerry	Certified Business Brokers	Houston	TX	77092		
Kuchyr, Robin	Business Services of New Orleans	Metairie	LA	70002		
Larochelle, Ed	Award Business Brokers	North Palm Beach	FL	33408	FBBA, IBBA	
Lawrence, Pat	Sunbelt Business Brokers of Portland	Portland	OR	97205	IBA, IBBA	
Lefkowitz, Micheal	Benjamin Ross Group	Richboro	PA	18954	IBA, IBBA, PBBA	
Lemmerman, R. D.	Lemmerman Associates, Inc.	Rockford	MI	49341	IBA, IBBA, MBBA, CBA	CBI, MBA
Lewis, Henry G. II	Corporate Investments	Toledo	OH	43617-1009		
Limani, Randy	Arthur Berry & Company	Boise	ID	83706	ASA, IBA, IBBA, other	
Longobardo, Michael A.	Penny & Longobardo, PA	Raleigh	NC	27606		
Lowrey, Bret	Paramount Business Consultants	Grass Valley	CA	95949	IBA, IBBA	CBI
Mack, John	Crowe Thomas Group	Bettendorf	IA	52722		
Mandigo, Alfred E.	McCulloch Realty	Lake Havasu City	AZ	86406	IBBA	
Mangasarian, Greg	Fine & Mangasarian Consulting, LLP	Media	PA	19063	AICPA, NACVA	

Broker	Firm Name	City	State	Zip	Association Membership	Professional Designation
Mann, Jan	Pragma Ventures, Inc.	West Linn	OR	97068	CBC, IBA, NACVA	
McIver, Don R.	American Business Group, Inc.	Dallas	TX	75251	IBBA, BCB	FCBI
McKneely, Keeth	International Business Exchange Corporation	Austin	TX	78761		
McLanahan, Ellery	Prime Business Investments	Tucker	GA	30084	GABB	
Mecke, Mike	Sunbelt Business Brokers of Northwest Arkansas	Fayetteville	AR	72703		
Merkel, Nicholas	Falls River Group	Cleveland	OH	44124		
Merry, Jeffery E.	Business House, Inc., The	Gainesville	GA	30506-2678	GABB	
Messick, Wayne	Sunbelt Business Brokers of Tennessee	Nashville	TN	37217	IBBA	
Miles, Richard	March Group, The	Nashville	TN	37203		
Miller, Mike	International Business Exchange Corporation	Austin	TX	78761		
Miller, William	Miller & Associates	Norwood	MA	02062	IBA, IBBA	
Mitts, C. A. III	Centrillion, Inc.	Houston	TX	77057	IBBA	CBI
Moggridge, Kip	Arthur Berry & Company	Boise	ID	83706	IBBA	
Mok, Chris	Business Search Group	San Jose	CA	95126	CABB, IBBA	
Monnin, Carl R.	Corporate Investment International, Inc.	Austin	TX	78759-7455	IBBA, TABB, IBA	FCBI, CBI, B
Netanel, Nathan	Certified Business Brokers	Houston	TX	77092		

Name	Company	City	State	ZIP	Associations	
Nicholson, Nick	Nicholson & Associates, Inc.	Atlanta	GA	30305-3676	GABB, IBBA	CBI
Obieleski, Chet	CO Group Inc.	Reston	VA	20191	IBA	
O'Donohue, Brian	March Group, The	Nashville	TN	37203		
Offerdahl, Brad C.	VR Business Brokers	Charlotte	NC	28209	IBBA	
Oppenheimer, Charles K.	Amvest Financial Group, Inc.	Independence	MO	64055	ACG, IBA, IBBA, M&A Source, PIA, NAB	
Outzs, Don			GA		GABB	
Papay, Gary	CK Business Consultants, Inc.	Hughesville	PA	17737	IBBA	
Pappas, George	Corporate Investment International, Inc.	Orlando	FL	32804		
Park, Glenn	Hana Realty, Inc.	Atlanta	GA	30341	GABB	
Parque, Tiffany Y.			GA		GABB	
Patterson, Bob	Certified Business Brokers	Houston	TX	77092		
Patterson, Dirk C.	Patterson Associates, Inc.	Torrington	CT	06790-5247	CBC, IBA, IBBA, M & A Source	
Perkins, Charles M.	Boston Restaurant Group, Inc., The	Boxford	MA	01921-0327	IBBA, NRA	FCBI
Phillips, Clint	Business Venture Group	Washington	DC	20036		
Phillips, Scott	Country Business, Inc.	Manchester Center	VT	05255		
Pierfelice, Tony	ARP Services	Midland	MI	48642	MBBA	
Pitcher, Mike	Business Capital Corporation	Des Moines	IA	50309		

Broker	Firm Name	City	State	Zip	Association Membership	Professional Designation
Pollock, Stanley L.	Professional Practice Planners, Inc.	McKeesport	PA	15132-2616	CBA	DMD, CBA, C
Potts, Barbara	Catalyst Group, The	Penn Valley	CA	95946		IBBA
Powell, Vernon	Sabre Capital of Greensboro, Inc.	Greensboro	NC	27408	IBBA	
Pusch, Kathryne A.	Consultkap Associates	Conyers	GA	30094	GABB, BBN	
Ramatowski, Mike	Georgia Business Associates, Inc.	Roswell	GA	30076	GABB, IBBA	CBI
Rather, Tom	Georgia Business Associates, Inc.	Roswell	GA	30076	GABB	
Read, Richard	Corporate Investment International, Inc.	Orlando	FL	32804	CBC, CFBI, IBBA	FCBI
Redman, David	Aaron Bell International, Inc.	Aurora	CO	80014	CBC, IBBA	
Reider, Allan S.	Altus Group	Grand Rapids	MI	49546	CCIM	CBI
Renzoni, Fred	Spectrum Business Resources, Inc.	San Diego	CA	92121		
Replogle, Dan	Midwest Business Brokers, Inc.	Fort Wayne	IN	46804		
Richter, Donald	Corporate Finance Associates	Franklin	OH	45005	ACG, IBBA	
Robinson, Mike	Mercorp, Inc.	Burington	ON	L7N-3M6	IBBA	
Rogers, Jerry A.	Prime Business Investments	Tucker	GA	30084	GABB	
Rome, Mike	Mercorp, Inc.	Burington	ON	L7N-3M6	IBBA	

Name	Company	City	State	Zip	Associations	
Rose, Mike	Associated Business Brokers, Inc.	Tucker	GA	30084	GABB	
Ross, Mark A.	Ares Business Consulting, Inc.	Bettendorf	IA	52722	IBBA, AICPA	
Rubel, Michael J.	Trident Capital Partners	Seattle	WA	98101		
Ruby, Rob	Realty Associates	San Rafael	CA	94915	Realtor	
Ryan, David G.	Summa Financial Group, Inc.	Santa Rosa	CA	95401	AICPA, CBC, IBBA, NACVA CBI, CPA, C	
Sack, David	Sack Associates	Universal City	CA	91608	IBA, IBBA	
Samura, Charles E.	Amerifirst Brokerage Group, Inc.	Kennesaw	GA	30144	GABB	
Sanders, Jack R.	Corporate Growth, Inc.	Irvine	CA	92714	CBC, IBA, IBBA	CBA, CBI
Sanovich, Don	Business Search Group	San Jose	CA	95126	CABB, IBBA	
Sapci, Michael E.			GA		GABB	
Sarro, Matthew	Transworld Business Brokers	Fort Lauderdale	FL	33309		
Scarlata, Robert	March Group, The	Nashville	TN	37203	ADS, DVSG, IBA	
Schaub, Gary	HELP Appraisals & Sales, Inc.	Portland	OR	97201	IBA	
Scheel, Dennis	Dennis Scheel & Associates	Bayport	MN	55003	IBBA	
Schmerler, Loren	Bottom Line Management, Inc.	Atlanta	GA	30342	GABB	
Scribner/Kachare, Gerald	Blue Chip Financial	Los Angeles	CA	90010	IBBA	
Sears, Gerald	Country Business, Inc.	Brattleboro	VT	05302	CBI	

Broker	Firm Name	City	State	Zip	Association Membership	Professional Designation
Shappee, Mark B.	Venture Management, Inc.	Ventura	CA	93003-5450	IBBA, M&A Source, ACG	
Sheehan, John B.	Business Team	Pleasant Hill	CA	94523	IBA, IBBA	
Sink, Steve	Sunbelt Business Brokers	Peoria Heights	IL	61616	IBBA	
Sipe, Michael	Private Equities	San Jose	CA	95113	IBA, IBBA, M & A Source	
Sofet, Joseph J.	Prime Business Investments	Tucker	GA	30084	GABB	
Sommer, Ronald S.	Value Business Brokers Ltd.	Great Neck	NY	11021-5306	IBA, IBBA	
Sopchak, Thomas	Strategic Business Information Corporation	Marcellus	NY	13108		
Soublis, John	Soublis Ltd.	Dunwoody	GA	30338	GABB	
Steckler, Philip	Country Business, Inc.	Brattleboro	VT	05302	IBA, IBBA	
Steinbrueck, Larry A.	MidWest Capital Group	St. Louis	MO	63141	IBBA	
Stevens, James S.	Preferred Business Brokers, Inc.	Atlanta	GA	30342	GABB	
Stevenson, George	Stevenson & Company	Evanston	IL	60201		
Stewart, Jeff M.	Finex Company, The	Valdosta	GA	31602	GABB	
Still, David R.	Capital Endeavors, Inc.	Lawrenceville	GA	30246	GABB, IBBA	CBI
Stimets, John	Country Business, Inc.	Brattleboro	VT	05302		
Tanner, Hank S.	National Business Brokers, Inc.	Gainesville	GA	30501-3366	GABB, IBBA	
Tate, Peggy						
Taylor, Phil	Country Business, Inc.	Portland	ME	04101		

Name	Company	City	State	Zip		
Town, James A.	Prime Business Investments	Tucker	GA	30084	GABB, IBBA	CBI
Van Wiggeren, David	Monarch Advisors	Lisle	IL	60532	IBBA	
Vander Hamm, Allan	Business Value Advisory Service	Bellevue	WA	98006-3321	AICPA ABV	CPA, ABV
Veatch, Pepper	Pepper Practice Transitions	Scottsdale	AZ	85251	IBBA	
Walters, Ned	Unitech Business Group	Joplin	MO	64804	BBN	
Weiss, Michael	Anderson Weiss Group	Seattle	WA	98119		
Welch, James	Prime Business Investments	Tucker	GA	30084	GABB	
Westerheim, David	M & A Partners	Vancouver	BC	V6L2E9	IBBA	
Whipple, Thomas B.	Hoganson Venture Group, Inc.	Hindsdale	IL	60521		
Whitney, Jay	Business Development Solutions	Alpharetta	GA	30022	GABB, IBBA, M&A Source	
Whitton, Thomas	March Group, The	Nashville	TN	37203		
Williams, Blane	Prime Business Investments	Tucker	GA	30084	GABB	
Williams, Gary D.	Business Acquisitions, Ltd.	Denver	CO	80210-3945	IBBA, CABI	CBI
Williams, Mark	First Marathon Business Brokers, Inc.	Winston-Salem	NC	27114-4577	IBBA	
Wochele, Matt	Preferred Business Brokers, Inc.	Atlanta	GA	30328	GABB	
Wood, Thomas	AlphaOmega Associates	Grand Rapids	MI	49546-6742		

Broker	Firm Name	City	State	Zip	Association Membership	Professional Designation
Woodward, Roger	Business Resource Services	Ocala	FL			
Woodyard, J. S. "Woody"	Woodyard & Associates	Houston	TX	77092	CBC, IBBA, TABB, NACP	BCB, FCBI
Yoo, Jay	Certified Business Brokers	Houston	TX	77092		
Zipursky, Jim	Corporate Finance Associates, NE-LTD	Omaha	NE	68154	ACG, IBBA	
Zoglio, Michael	Tower Hill Advisors, Inc.	Doylestown	PA	18901		
Nery, Kevin A.	Nery Corporation, The	New Bedford	MA	02740	IBBA	
McDonald, Timothy	Leland Group, Inc., The	Twin Peaks	CA	92391	IBBA	
Purcell, Linda J.	Purcell Associates, LLC	Palatine	IL	60062-6639	CBC, IBA, IBBA	CBI
Larocque, Pete	Business Valuation Canada	Ottawa	ON	K1G-4Z7		
Vantarakis, Alex	Vant Group, The	Dallas	TX		IBBA	
Gould, Mark	Gould Business Group	Fair Oaks	CA	95628	IBBA	
Heimes, Don	Corporate Finance Associates, NE-LTD	Omaha	NE	68154	ACG, IBBA	
Layfield, Robert	Corporate Finance Associates, NE-LTD	Omaha	NE	68154	ACG, IBBA	
Garner, J. G. "Tex"	DFW Sunbelt Business Brokers	Fort Worth	TX	76117	IBBA	
Wilson, Brian M.	BT Brokers	Spokane	WA	99201	IBBA	

Name	Company	City	State	Zip		
Talbot, John	John Howard Group, Ltd., The	Beachwood	OH	44122	IBBA, BBN	
Klosterman, K. C.	HCS Group, LLC	Albany	OR	97321	IBBA	
Fuller, Dick	Fuller Trident Group, The	Newport Beach	CA	92660		
McConnell, Thomas H.	IBG Business Services	Denver	CO	80237		
Bungard, Brent	Arthur Berry & Company	Boise	ID	83706	ASA, IBA, IBBA, other	
Moggridge, Kip	Arthur Berry & Company	Boise	ID	83706	ASA, IBA, IBBA, other	
Grunau, William	VR\Pacific Business Brokers, Inc.	Brea	CA	92821	IBBA, CABB	
Johnson, Jeff	Corporate Finance Associates	Lafayette	CA	94549		
Gibson, William	William E. Gibson and Associates, Inc.	Pensacola	FL	32501	IBA, IBBA, NACVA	
Elias, George H.	Sausalito Business Group, The	Sausalito	CA	94965-949	IBBA	
George, Chris	George and Company	Worcester	MA	01603	IBA, IBBA	ASA
Minnig, Michael	Sunbelt Capital Group	Annapolis	MD	21403	IBBA	
Pratt, Fred	Business Team Central Coast	Santa Maria	CA	93454	IBBA, CABB	
Kurszewski, Doug	Capital Solutions	Minnetonka	MN	55305	IBA	ASA, CBA
Afinowich, Jim	Fox and Fin Financial Group	Scottsdale	AZ	85250	IBBA	
Vallee, Louis-Eric	Mallette s.e.n.c.	Quebec City		G1C-6L8		CBV
Tabar, Bill	Business Resource Center	Ogden	UT	84401	IBBA	CBI

Broker	Firm Name	City	State	Zip	Association Membership	Professional Designation
Iorio, Luke	Corporate Investment International	West Orange	NJ	07052	IBBA	
Oppeltz, Ken	VR M and A	San Diego	CA	92121	IBBA	
Smith, John	Citadel Advisory Group	Fort Collins	CO	80521	IBBA	
Braatz, Roy	Sunbelt Business Brokers	Auburn	CA	95602	IBBA	
Miner, Jack G.	Exodus Business Solutions	Freeport	MI	49325		
Kells, Greg	Business Valuation Canada	Ottawa	ON	K1G-4Z7		
Lawson, Kurt	Nash & Company	Osterville	MA	02655-0012	IBBA	
Beasley, Garry	GJB Associates	Columiba	SC	29223	ABBA, BBN	
Tobian, Gary	Alpine Business Brokers, LLC	Orem	UT	84058	IBBA	
Edwards, John	Capital Corporation, The	Spartanburg	SC	29302	IBBA	
Brean, Larry	Tannenbaum and Aalok	Cherry Hill	NJ	08002	IBBA	
Broekema, Sandra	Bostwick, LLC	Minneapolis	MN	55416	IBBA	
Mortimer, Dennis	Associated Business Brokers, Inc.	Mobile	AL	36502	IBBA	
Sandy, Beverlee	Sunbelt Business Advisors	Redwood City	CA	94063	IBBA, CABB	
Johnson, John C.	Bluestem Resources Group, Inc.	Tulsa	OK	74105	IBBA, CBC, IBA	
Snyder, David M.	D.M. Snyder, CPA, PC	Aiken	SC	29803	IBBA, AICPA	
Cushing, Todd	EBIT Associates, Ltd.	Barrington	IL	60010	IBBA, MBBI, BBN	

Name	Company	City	State	Zip	Associations
Pipes, W. B.	Breckenridge Pipes and Company	Orange Park	FL	32073	IBBA
Sweeten, David	Sweeten Business Brokerage	San Antonio	TX	78240	IBBA, TABB
Davidson, Mickey	Business Sales and Consulting, LLC	Kansas City	MO	64106	IBBA
Emerling, Tom	Corporate Acquisition and Appraisal, Inc.	Billings	MT	59101	IBBA, IBA
Kampschroer, Kyle	Calhoun Companies	St. Cloud	MN	56301	
Norris, Dave	Arthur Berry & Company	Boise	ID	83706	IBBA
Boyd, Jay	Enterprise Brokers, LLC	Denver	CO	80210	IBBA
Hauber, Mark	Bay Street Capital	Feasterville	PA	19053	IBBA
Johnson, Dairl M.	Sunbelt Business Brokers of Beverly Hills	Beverly Hills	CA	90211	IBBA, CABB
Kellenberger, David	Kellenberger and Associates	Lafayette	LA	70508	IBBA
McCaul, Ken	Joseph Associates International, Inc.	Naperville	FL	60566	IBBA, MBBI
Michail, Sobhi	Sunbelt Brokers of Pasadena	Pasadena	CA	91101	IBBA
Quilitz, Wayne	Murphy Business and Financial Services, Inc.	Dunedin	FL	34698	
Winston, Marvin	Sunbelt Business Advisors	Little Rock	AR	72211	IBBA
Travis, Stocker	Venture Opportunities, Inc.	Dallas	TX	75240	IBA, IBBA, TABB

Broker	Firm Name	City	State	Zip	Association Membership	Professional Designation
Barr, David	Venture Opportunities, Inc.	Dallas	TX	75240	CBC, IBA, IBBA, TABB	
Blackburn, Clifton	Paradigm Financial Group, Inc.	Mount Airy	NC	27030	CBC, IBBA, NCBBA	
Tveidt, C. Jay	VR Tveidt & Associates	Lynnwood	WA	98036	IBBA	
Conway, Kevin	Corporate Investment Business Brokers, Inc.	Fort Myers	FL	33912		
May, CV	Barker & May	Atlantic Beach	NC	28512	IBBA	
Hammond, Chris	IBG Business Services	Denver	CO	80237	IBBA	
Lemanski, Dan	LeMans, Inc.	Simpsonville	SC	29681		
Flowerree, Doug	First Venture Associates	Tampa	FL	33614		
Berdeque, Eduardo	NEXXO	San Antonio	TX	78209	IBBA, TABB	
Bednash, James	Ronin Capital Group, LLC	Stockton	CA	95207	IBBA	
Kinsella, Bob	Kinsella Group, Inc.	Lake Bluff	IL	60044		
Hamm, David E.	Sunbelt Business Advisors	Springfield	MO	65807	IBBA	
Cummisford, Robert	Adamy & Company, P.C.	Grand Rapids	MI	49503	AICPA, ASA, IBA	
Kogle, Jeffrey	Sunbelt Business Brokers	St. Paul	MN	55126	IBBA	
Jones, Chris	Sunbelt Business Brokers	Little Canada	MN	55126		
Ross, Franz	GAR Associates, Inc.	Amherst	NY	14228		
Gottsacker, Greg	Sunbelt Business Advisors	Minnetonka	MN	55305	IBBA	
Taylor, Blake	Synergy Business Brokers	New Rochelle	NY	10801	IBBA	

Name	Company	City	State	Zip	Affiliation
Wilhite, Phillip	Corporate Investment	Austin	TX	78759	IBBA
Blunt, Geoff	Pacific Mergers and Acquisitions	Newport Beach	CA	92660	IBBA
Kinsella, Bob	Kinsella Group, Inc.	Lake Bluff	IL	60044	IBBA
Jordan, Mark	Vercor	Dunwoody	GA	30338	
Heaney, Joe	Sea To Sand, Inc.	San Diego	CA		
Hansell, Sandy	Sandy Hansell & Associates, Inc.	Southfield	MI	48076	
Stivers, John	Professional Business Brokers, Inc.	Melbourne	FL	32940	
Schwier, Charles	Bulldog Brokers	Bozeman	MT	59718	
Smith, Raymond	Novars Group, The	Vienna	VA	22182	
Slagel, Rex	Vercor	Plainfield	IL	60544	
Thomas, Mark	MET Advisors, Inc.	Torrance	CA	90503	
Mello, Todd	Healthcare Appraisers	Delray Beach	FL	33444	NACVA
Carlson, Meg	C&H Group, LLC	Boise	ID	83702	
Ballenger, Thomas	Business Acquisition Group	Thousand Oaks	CA	91361	IBBA
O'Bey, Richard	Sunbelt Business Brokers of Coastal NC, LLC	Morehead City	NC	28557	IBBA
McCann, Tom	McCann Company, The	Lynchburg	VA	24503	IBBA, BBN
Gibson, E. Dan	ACT Consultants, Inc.	Bellevue	WA	98004	IBBA
Rasmussen, Rich	Sunbelt Business Advisors	Mesa	AZ	85201	
Gunderson, Eric	Empire Business Brokers - SE	Columbia	SC	29212	IBBA
Kiesling, Juanita	WestMark Realtors	Lubbock	TX	79423	IBBA, TABB

Broker	Firm Name	City	State	Zip	Association Membership	Professional Designation
Vescio, Lou	Sunbelt Business Brokers of Vero, Inc.	Sebastian	FL	32958	IBBA	
Lolacono, Dan	American Business Masters & Investments	Overland Park	KS	66212	IBBA	
MacLachlan, Ian	Business Team	Campbell	CA	95008	IBBA	
Hanson, Raymond	Pragma Ventures, Inc.	West Linn	OR	97068	CBC	
Cicirello, Bernie	ProForma West	Westminster	CO	80031	IBBA	
Chambliss, Paul	Front Range Business, Inc.	Boulder	CO	80303	IBBA	
McKinley, Valerie	Corporate Investment International	Boca Raton	FL	33432	BBF, IBBA	
Petersen, Don	Petersen Financial, LLC	Lake Oswego	OR	97035	ABI, NEBB, IBBA	
Allen, Erik	Boulay, Heutmaker, Zibell, & Co. PLLP	Minneapolis	MN	55344		
Adkins, Don	Adkins Business Brokerage, Inc.	Wilmington	NC	28403		
Dandridge, Wayles	Sunbelt Business Brokers	Roanoke	VA	24015	IBBA	
McKay, Andrew	Catalyst Advisors	Louisville	KY	40202		
Coffey, Guy	Coffey Owens Group, LLC	Denver	CO	80206	IBBA	
Loftin, Katrina	BTI Group/Business Team	Reno	NV	89502	IBBA	
Demske, Ken	Sunbelt Business Brokers	Brookfield	WI	53005		
Alban, Robert	GXS	Gaithersburg	MD	20878		

Index

377